WITHDRAWN

Figures of Conversion

Post-Contemporary Interventions
Series Editors:
Stanley Fish and Fredric Jameson

Figures of Conversion

"The Jewish Question" & English National Identity

MICHAEL RAGUSSIS

DUKE UNIVERSITY PRESS   *Durham and London 1995*

© 1995 Duke University Press   All rights reserved
Printed in the United States of America on acid-free paper ∞
Typeset in Plantin by Keystone Typesetting, Inc.
Library of Congress Cataloging-in-Publication Data
appear on the last printed page of this book.

Contents

Illustrations

Acknowledgments

The most congenial memories of authorship are the minutes, hours, and days spent with friends and colleagues who happily interrupted, with various kinds of support, the otherwise solitary process of writing. For supplying the quotation I couldn't find, the text I didn't know, the enthusiasm I couldn't sustain on my own, I thank James Slevin, Dennis Todd, Caren Kaplan, Eric Smoodin, Kim Hall, Jason Rosenblatt, Judith Farr, Leona Fisher, and Paul Betz. When this book was still a fledgling project, it profited from readings by Daniel Moshenberg, Eric Cheyfitz, Jill Rubenstein, and Joseph Sitterson. When half grown and more, it received unusually acute and wise attention from John Glavin and Pamela Fox. From the beginning this book has been nurtured by Evelyn Torton Beck, whose work in Jewish studies has been a powerful example to me. For that "first, fast, last friend," I turned as usual to Susan Lanser, who embraced this project with the unstinting generosity and clear-headed brilliance that are among her chief gifts.

I wish to thank the National Endowment for the Humanities and Georgetown University for granting me every writer's most precious commodity, time. I am also grateful to two journals for allowing me to reprint in altered form the following articles: "Representation, Conversion, and Literary Form: *Harrington* and the Novel of Jewish Identity," *Critical Inquiry* 16 (Autumn 1989); "The Birth of a Nation in Victorian Culture: The Spanish Inquisition, the Converted Daughter, and the 'Secret Race,'" *Critical Inquiry* 20 (Spring 1994); "Writing Nationalist History: England, the Conversion of the Jews, and *Ivanhoe*," *ELH* 60 (Spring 1993).

Introduction

I knew a Man, who having nothing but a summary Notion of Religion himself, and being wicked and profligate to the last Degree in his Life, made a thorough Reformation in himself, by labouring to convert a Jew.

A French Roman Catholic priest relates this anecdote while the English hero of *The Farther Adventures of Robinson Crusoe* (1719) listens skeptically.[1] But the ironies of history are such that, in less than a century, the kernel idea of this implausible anecdote would represent the model for a national project—not in France (where the revolutionary government was granting the Jews their civil liberties), but in England. During the Evangelical Revival, the conversion of the Jews functioned at the center of a project to reform the English nation, which had become "wicked and profligate" in the course of the eighteenth century.[2]

In the following pages I will explain the remarkable role that the idea of Jewish conversion played in Protestant England from the 1790s through the 1870s. This will allow me to record and analyze the representation of Jewish identity in Christian culture not in the conventional way—through a broad range of anti-Semitic stereotypes[3]—but through a specific discourse: the rhetoric of conversion and the figure of the Jewish convert. In my view this rhetoric of conversion is the oldest and most persistent ideological setting within which the representation of Jewish identity has functioned, originating in the textual invention of "the Jew" for the purposes of evangelization in the writings of Paul and the early Church fathers.[4] In the course of history this rhetoric has been reinvented periodically, and one of the most notable moments of such reinvention occurred during the Evangelical Revival.

I have begun with a quotation from Defoe because his two novels of the adventures of Robinson Crusoe, published within months of each other, are based entirely on the ideology of conversion and thereby anticipate the Evangelical drive to convert the nation. In the first book of his adventures Crusoe gives up what he calls the wickedness of his past life, asks repentance of God, and begins reading the Bible every day, but his own conversion seems finally realized only when he converts the "savage" Friday. This is a critical pattern in the Christian ideology of conversion: the conversion of the Other (heathen, infidel, or Jew) is the surest sign of the conversion of the self, so that the true convert proves himself by becoming a proselytizer. In *The Farther Adventures* Crusoe completes the work of conversion by returning to his island, where he converts a group of captured "savages" as well as the colony of his own countrymen and their "savage-wives." Such events are harbingers of the Evangelical crusade to reform England through a national conversion at home and the dissemination of the Gospel to "the heathen" abroad, a crusade that swept through every corner of England and every class of English society and whose effects were felt around the world, especially in India and Africa.[5] What these two novels failed to anticipate was the pivotal role that the conversion of the Jews would assume in such a cultural project and the critical function that "the Jewish question" would have in defining the national identity of England from the period of the French Revolution through the Victorian era.

But already in *The Farther Adventures* we find the kind of critique of Roman Catholic proselytism that prepared the way for Protestant England to see itself as the inheritor and the reformer of the work of conversion. In China, Crusoe meets "three Missionary *Romish* Priests" whose work, "the Conversion *as they call it,* of the *Chineses* to Christianity, is so far from the true Conversion requir'd, to bring Heathen People to the Faith of Christ, that it seems to amount to little more, than letting them know the Name of Christ, and say some Prayers to the Virgin *Mary,* and her Son, in a tongue which they understand not, and to cross themselves and the like."[6] The Evangelical project was designed at least in part to demonstrate to the world precisely how to bring the Gospel to both the heathen and the Jews, particularly in light of the Roman Catholic Church's patent failures. Defoe's novels are sprinkled with barbs aimed at these failures as part of a conventional English discourse that critiqued those nations whose religion had led them to commit the most heinous crimes. We find, for example, a consistent pattern of remarks aimed at the Inquisition in Spain and Italy—though without reference to the Jews, a telling anomaly that I will explain—and at the Spanish conquest and conversion of the native populations of the Americas.

What is being developed here is a nationalist discourse that evaluates and contrasts different nations on the basis of religious tolerance. So Defoe demonstrates the way in which national reputations are ruined— for example, "the Conduct of the *Spaniards* in all their Barbarities practis'd in *America,* where they destroy'd Millions of these People, . . . for which the very Name of a *Spaniard* is reckon'd to be frightful and terrible to all People of Humanity . . . : As if the Kingdom of *Spain* were particularly Eminent for the Product of a race of Men, who were without Principles of Tenderness, or the common Bowels of Pity to the Miserable." To understand the nationalistic function of such a discourse, we must recognize Defoe's attempt to make his hero the very model of tolerance, as if Crusoe represented the English national character par excellence. On the island that he rules as a king "we had but three Subjects, and they were of three different Religions. My man *Friday* was a Protestant, his Father was a *Pagan* and a *Cannibal,* and the *Spaniard* was a Papist: However, I allow'd Liberty of Conscience throughout my Dominions."[7]

Such a description exposes in brief the complicated double ideology of Protestant England. "My man Friday," a convert to Protestantism (and a servant to his master), is the critical sign of the way in which the ideology of conversion is located inside the English national (and nationalist) ideology of tolerance. Crusoe's treatment of Friday, including Friday's conversion, is seen as the liberal antithesis of the historical record of Catholic Spain—that is, the destruction of the natives as part of their conquest and the notorious efforts that were made to force their conversion. Thus, in Crusoe's deliverance of the "savage" Friday, first from death, and then from idolatry, we have an anticipation of an ideological paradigm that will dominate nineteenth-century English discourse, defining England as a nation that gives "pity to the miserable"—including colonizing and converting the heathen and establishing missions throughout England, Europe, and Asia to convert the Jews.

But it was precisely when the missions to convert the Jews became the subject of public scandal in the opening decades of the nineteenth century that the English national character and its reputation for tolerance were called into question. In the opening chapter of this book I will explore the public controversy that surrounded the missions to the Jews, but here I wish to locate the origins of these missions in the renewed interest in the Jews that occurred after the French Revolution. Such missions were an outgrowth of a well-known and long-standing English tradition of millenarian discourse in which the ideas of toleration and conversion were inseparable. What had been throughout most of the eighteenth century a steady (if somewhat negligible) stream of literature on the conversion of the Jews and their restoration to Palestine became nothing short of a torrent in the 1790s.[8] In the tumultuous events of the French Revolution and the Napoleonic Wars, millenarians saw the signs of the Second Coming, which, according to biblical prophecy, was to be preceded by the restoration of the Jews to Palestine and their conversion. In 1794 the subject of the poetry prize at Cambridge was "The Restoration of the Jews"; in 1794–95 Richard Brothers's declarations that, as Prince of the Hebrews, he would lead the Jews back to Palestine produced numerous pamphlets and books, large crowds in London, and a speech in the House of Commons by one of Brothers's disciples, a member of Parliament who unsuccessfully protested the government's decision to confine the prophet on the basis of criminal insanity;[9] and in 1799 Napoleon invaded Palestine, and soon thereafter issued his Egyptian Proclamation that called on the Jews to return to Palestine and thereby incited a controversial debate among English millenarians over whether England or France would lead the Jews back to their homeland. Such historical events allow us to understand the different degrees of importance assigned to the conversion of the Jews early in the eighteenth century (by Defoe in 1719, for example) and after the French Revolution.

Writing in 1841, James Huie noted this shift in his *History of the Jews,* explaining how in the period after the French Revolution the religious revival rediscovered the idea of the conversion of the Jews: "It was not expected that Christians should feel a great anxiety about the spiritual welfare of the Heathen, without, at the same time, taking a deep interest in the condition of the Jews. . . . 'They forget,' says Archbishop Leighton, 'a main point of the church's glory, that pray not daily for the Jews' conversion.' "[10] It was precisely such a view that was preached by Charles Simeon, minister of Trinity Church at Cambridge for fifty-three years and called "the finest flower of Evangelicalism."[11] Simeon took the message of the Jews throughout England and beyond, establishing "a Jews' Society" at Cambridge and traveling tirelessly in support of the London Society for Promoting Christianity amongst the Jews.[12] His influence at Cambridge was so wide and so profound—one bishop claimed that Simeon had a larger following than Newman, over a longer period of time—that his followers, the "Simeonites," "for nearly half a century went out from King's, Queens', St. John's, even Trinity, to spread the Evangelical gospel at its most characteristic over England and exert their influence on the morals of the English people."[13] His message was simple: "In our own land, an unprecedented concern begins to manifest itself in behalf of all the nations of the earth who are lying in darkness and the shadow of death. The duty of sending forth missionaries to instruct them, is now publicly acknowledged by all our governors in church and state. . . . And in this ebullition of religious zeal, can we suppose that the Jew shall be forgotten?" Soon it became commonplace to argue that the evangelization of all nonbelievers had to begin with the proselytization of the Jews: "in converting the Jews to Christ, we adopt the readiest and most certain way for the salvation of the whole world," for "the Jews in their converted state will be eminently instrumental in converting the Gentile world." So, the English people were instructed: "If you have any love to the *Gentile* world, you should bestow all possible care on the instruction of *the Jews,* since it is by the Jews chiefly that the Gentiles will be brought into the fold of Christ."[14]

From this perspective, the proselytization of the Jews took primacy over the missions to the heathen and even gained a kind of urgency, so that both strict millenarians and the larger Evangelical public began to see themselves as the benevolent guardians of the Jews. The Jews were to be preserved, "as God's ancient people," until their national conversion at the advent of the Second Coming. The conversionist societies were intended to aid in this divine plan, and with a kind of reverse logic their establishment was viewed as a sign of the proximity of the Second Coming.[15] Simeon argued that England's "Benevolence Towards God's Ancient People" was manifest in their evangelization and that the rise in missionary activity in England was a divine sign: "See what is at this moment doing amongst the more religious part of the Christian community, in the circulation of the Scriptures, and especially of the New Testament; and what efforts are making by Christian missionaries for the conversion of the Jews! And I must say, that this is a call from God to us, and that it is no less our privilege, than it is our duty, to obey it."[16] Thus, while

IS THERE NO ROOM FOR THE WANDERING JEW?
Yes: there is room in the Heart of Christ, and there ought to be in every Christian land and Church.

Figure 1. A typical piece of conversionist propaganda in which the prejudices of various nations (including England) make the Jew a homeless wanderer, while Christ offers the only refuge. From Reverend John Dunlop, *Memories of Gospel Triumphs Among the Jews During the Victorian Era* (London: S. W. Partridge, 1894), p. 449.

based on the exegesis of those biblical prophecies that revealed the role of the Jews in the Second Coming, the idea of toleration was soon put into practice in the establishment of conversionist societies and in the summons that called on the average English citizen to take every opportunity to bring the Gospel to the Jews. In either case, toleration and conversion went hand in hand, so it should not surprise us to find Lewis Way, who saved the most famous Jewish missionary society in England from financial ruin, defending the zealous efforts of the conversionists by arguing "that Christian conversion is not inconsistent with Christian toleration. . . . In the vocabulary of a Christian, conversion does not stand opposed to *toleration* but to *persecution*"[17] (figure 1).

My project begins with the claim that the novel participated in the public controversy over the missions to the Jews, and, more especially, that a particular tradition of the novel attempted to secularize this notion of tolerance toward the Jews. Emerging in the decades when millenarian discourse flourished and when the abuses of the missions to the Jews became a public scandal, this revisionist tradition of the novel attempted to reinvent the representation of Jewish identity by calling into question the ideology of conversion. Such a reinvention required disengaging the representation of Jewish identity from the sphere of biblical discourse—that is, from the narrow notion of "God's ancient people." From Maria Edgeworth and Walter Scott in the opening decades of the nineteenth century through George Eliot in the 1870s, this tradition of novelists recorded and examined English anti-Semitism in both its contemporary and historical forms, defining what such writers characterized as England's national guilt. This idea of national guilt was the bedrock of Evangelical activism. William Wilberforce consistently threatened that God would punish England for such "national crimes" as the failure to abolish the slave trade and to Christianize India, while Charles Simeon developed the same notion for England's failure to evangelize the Jews.[18] But if for the Evangelicals toleration was typically absorbed by the idea of conversion—Wilberforce went so far as to claim that the evangelization of India was more important than the abolition of the slave trade[19]—for these novelists England's liberal reputation could be recuperated only when toleration was divorced from conversion, and only after a full accounting had been rendered of England's past and present persecution of the Jews.

By restoring this novelistic tradition to the discursive and historical setting within which it operated, I hope to explain the way in which the novel functioned at the center of a crisis in national identity. This setting included the highly influential tradition of millenarian discourse, which became distinctly nationalistic when the threat of French revolutionary ideas forced on England a (re)definition of the English national character, and when war with France dragged on, almost without interruption, from 1793 to 1815, with periodic threats of a French invasion.[20] The question of which nation, Protestant England or "atheistical France," would lead the Jews back to their homeland combined religious enthusiasm with patriotic fervor and even economic self-interest, for millenarian writers did not hesitate to remind the English public of France's designs on commerce in the Near East.[21] But even more importantly, this novelistic tradition must be resituated in dialogue with the controversial literature generated by the crisis over the missions to the Jews, including a specifically conversionist literature (memoirs and novels advocating the conversion of the Jews) and a body of countertexts produced by the Anglo-Jewish community. Like the discourse of millenarianism, the memoirs and novels produced by conversionists formulated the issue of Jewish conversion in terms of national identity, defining English Protestantism for the potential Jewish convert as a superior alternative to the Roman Catholicism of Italy or Spain and the atheism of France. It is specifically in relation to these popular conversionist novels, which typically announced their ideology in their titles—*Leila Ada, The Jewish Convert* or *Julamerk; or, The Converted Jewess*—that I will define what I am calling the revisionist novel of Jewish identity, a tradition that extends from Edgeworth through Eliot. Finally, to comprehend the widest boundaries of this discursive setting, I will argue that under the influence of England's religious revival the rhetoric of conversion became so widely disseminated that it was used in a host of cultural projects, like Burke's *Reflections on the Revolution in France*, which worked to define English national identity in relation both to other European national identities and to Jewish identity. In other words, these different discourses constituted a unified—if deeply contested—field, organized around the figure of conversion.[22]

At the same time, this field of discourse was not static; in fact, it was a particularly acute register of the kinds of historical developments that occurred from the 1790s through the 1870s.[23] Specifically, I will articulate such developments by opening up "the Jewish question" to the multiple questions that often are amorphously subsumed by it—that is, by understanding how "the Jewish question" was periodically refocused in the course of the nineteenth century as a theological question (based on arguments over scriptural exegesis), a political question (based on the parliamentary debates over the civil and political disabilities of the Jews), and a racial question (based on the racial theories of the new science of ethnology). In the end, I locate the ideology of (Jewish) conversion, which stands behind all these variants of "the Jewish question," at the center of a profound crisis in nineteenth-century English national identity.

The most obvious trace of the controversy over the conversion of the Jews in the nineteenth-century novel can be found in the many satirical allusions aimed at the conversionist societies. The use of such allusions became a regular part of the comic repertoire of the novel, a kind of satirical novelistic trope. In a well-known episode from Anthony Trollope's *Barchester Towers*, for example, Bertie Stanhope writes home with the news that "he was about to start with others to Palestine on a mission for converting Jews. He did go to Judea, but being unable to convert the Jews, was converted by them."[24] In William Thackeray's *The Newcomes*, Mrs. Thomas Newcome epitomizes Evangelical enthusiasm by giving up her time "to attend to the interests of the enslaved negro; to awaken the benighted Hottentot to a sense of the truth; to convert Jews, Turks, Infidels, and Papists," while her husband, bored with his wife's enthusiasms, "yawned over the sufferings of the negroes, and wished the converted Jews at Jericho."[25] And Becky Sharp in *Vanity Fair* attempts a pious image: "She worked flannel petticoats for the Quashyboos—cotton nightcaps for the Cocoanut Indians—painted hand-screens for the conversion of the Pope and the Jews."[26] This kind of satire is especially interesting when it comes from the pen of the most famous Jewish convert of nineteenth-century England, Benjamin Disraeli, whose own conversion was the subject of suspicion and bitter satire. In *Tancred*, the third novel of his celebrated political trilogy of the 1840s, Disraeli pokes fun at the self-righteous English family that takes its relaxation in "a meeting for the conversion of the Jews," at the "journals [which] teemed with lists of proselytes and cases of conversion," and at the bogus successes that conversionist societies typically produced—"five Jews, . . . converted at twenty piastres a-week."[27]

But the participation of the novel in the public controversy over the missions to the Jews was not limited to a string of satiric allusions. Such allusions frequently functioned to trigger a critique of the ideology of conversion by influencing the entire design of a novel—that is, by exposing and undermining the conventional plot that had as its goal the conversion of the central Jewish characters. In novels such as George Eliot's *Daniel Deronda* and James Joyce's *Ulysses*, such a critique is initiated through a direct allusion to the society at the center of the controversy, the London Society for Promoting Christianity amongst the Jews. In Eliot's novel, when Daniel relates the story of Mirah Cohen, the young Jewish woman he saves from drowning, he is met with a plan for her further rescue: "Lady Mallinger was much interested in the poor girl, observing that there was a Society for the Conversion of the Jews, and that it was to be hoped Mirah would embrace Christianity."[28] But *Daniel Deronda* de-

liberately resists the conventional plot of conversion for the Jewish heroine, while transferring the plot of conversion to the Gentile heroine,
Gwendolen Harleth, who neglects the Evangelical placards calling on her
to repent and convert but who nevertheless comes under Daniel's powerful proselytizing influence. Similarly, in *Ulysses* the methods of the missionary societies, such as tempting poor Jewish children with food or
money—so brutally skewered by critics of the London Society—make
Leopold Bloom recall his father's conversion: "They say they used to give
pauper children soup to change to protestants in the time of the potato
blight. Society over the way papa went to for the conversion of poor jews.
Same bait." This direct allusion to the missions' abuses assumes a larger
function in the course of the novel, shaping the entire story of Bloom
when his own conversion is positioned inside the conversion of his father:
"in 1880 he had divulged his disbelief in the tenets of the Irish (protestant) church (to which his father Rudolf Virag (later Rudolph Bloom)
had been converted from the Israelitic faith and communion in 1865 by
the Society for promoting Christianity among the jews) subsequently
abjured by him in favour of Roman catholicism at the epoch of and with a
view to his matrimony in 1888."[29]

In her famous essay "Silly Novels by Lady Novelists," George Eliot
provides a model for understanding the way in which the plot of conversion operated in the nineteenth-century novel: " 'Adonijah' is simply
the feeblest kind of love story, supposed to be instructive, we presume,
because the hero is a Jewish captive, and the heroine a Roman vestal;
because they and their friends are converted to Christianity after the
shortest and easiest method approved by the 'Society for Promoting the
Conversion of the Jews."[30] By using Eliot's comparison between the goals
of the London Society and the conversionist novelist, we can see that the
plot of conversion was institutionalized at the same time in the missions to
the Jews and in the discourse of nineteenth-century England. My project
attempts to identify and explore the intersection of important literary and
cultural forms—that is, to locate the ideological juncture at which novelistic form and Christian culture meet. The plot of *Adonijah*, for example, is
not the construction of one "silly lady novelist" but of an entire culture;
countless conversionist novels like it were produced during the nineteenth
century. Only by recovering this long-forgotten tradition of conversionist

fiction is it possible to identify and analyze a revisionist tradition based on a critique of the ideology of Jewish conversion.

I begin this book by exploring the controversy over the conversion of the Jews, emphasizing the institutionalization of the ideology of Jewish conversion in both the conversionist societies and the conversionist novel. I then turn to the revisionist novel of Jewish identity by exploring this tradition's attempt to invent a plot that exposes and ironizes the hegemonic plot of conversion. In this way I situate a group of more or less canonical English novels within the public debate over the missions to the Jews and the larger culture of conversion. But I do not limit myself to the study of novels only, or to texts that are simply revisionist. For the revisionist novel was in continuous dialogue with other forms of discourse, and the representation of Jewish identity was the site of continuous textual conflict, where even texts that critiqued conversionism could be based not on revision but on reactionary anti-Semitism (attacking conversion because it provided the Jew with a passport into English culture).

The central narrative of my book begins with Maria Edgeworth's self-conscious initiation of a revisionist tradition in *Harrington* (1817), a novel based on a critique of the conversion plot in *The Merchant of Venice,* the ur-text of the representation of Jewish identity in England. After exploring the use of the figure of conversion in a variety of discourses, both ancient and modern, I examine the nineteenth-century novel's dialogue with a specific tradition of historical discourse that used the figure of conversion to define English national identity. The tradition of medievalist historiography extending from Sharon Turner (1768–1847) to Edward Augustus Freeman (1823–92) was no mere antiquarian enthusiasm for the distant past, but an inquiry, often patriotic in nature, into the origins of the modern English nation-state—an inquiry typically based on an ideology of conversion and assimilation. In England after the French Revolution, history became the final arbiter in discussions of national character; after all, in the face of the threatening events in France, where revolution was seen as the rejection of tradition and the abrogation of history, both a political philosopher like Edmund Burke and a historian like Sharon Turner turned to English history to establish the nature of English national identity. History, in fact, began to dictate the boundaries of English national life—hence the immense contemporary power involved in defining the origins of English national life, whether in the medieval histories of Turner and Freeman or in the medieval novels of Scott, Edward Bulwer-Lytton, and Charles Kingsley. In its apparent ability to uncover the origins of the English nation, history was used to define the limits of English national life—its religious tradition, its racial composition, its cultural heritage.

Scott's absorption of historical discourse into the novel was a way of situating the novel at the center of national life. In fact, Scott's creation of the historical novel and his writing of *Ivanhoe* in particular are the most patent signs of two parallel developments on which my book is founded: the use of history to formulate the basis of English identity, and the use of the novel to revise the representation of Jewish identity. The revisionist novel critiqued the English national character by subjecting it to a moral reevaluation on the basis of English attitudes toward the Jews. It was Scott who historicized such a project. By depicting the persecution of the Jews, including the attempt to convert them, at a critical moment in history— the founding of the English nation—*Ivanhoe* located "the Jewish question" at the heart of English national identity. Scott also located woman (in his case studies of Rebecca, Rowena, and Ulrica) at the heart of a crisis in the survival of oppressed races and cultures. Finally, the history of England (especially its treatment of the Jews) began to be used in a comparison with the histories of other European nations such as France and Spain to define different national identities. The representation of the Crusades, the Inquisition, the expulsion of the Jews from medieval England and Spain, the emancipation of the Jews in revolutionary France, all became a way of marking the different European national characters. Hence my emphasis on a kind of dialogical relationship between historical and novelistic discourses.

The last phase of this study records the emergence of a new ground on which the figure of conversion was represented and debated: Benjamin Disraeli, the most famous Jewish convert in English history. As both a popular novelist and the nation's leader, Disraeli became the new center of representations of Jewish identity in England, though scholars have neglected his profound influence on such writers as Matthew Arnold and George Eliot. I study Disraeli's attempt to establish and to enhance the place of the Jew in England and the place of Hebraism in English culture, and I go on to examine the attack on this attempt made in the name of ethnology. Locating Arnold's celebrated work on Hebraism within the context of Disraeli's project, I demonstrate the way in which Arnold appropriated and undermined it. I argue further that Disraeli, claiming as his ancestors the Jews who fled from the persecutions of the Iberian Peninsula, became the center of a particular form of anti-Semitic representation: "the secret Jew" who invades England through the passport of conversion in order to undermine English culture (whereas Disraeli argued that Hebraism was the foundation of English culture, just as Judaism was the foundation of Christianity). I focus on the moment when, during Disraeli's second prime ministry, the conversion of the Jews was attacked from two entirely different ideological positions—by Anthony Trollope, who attacked conversion because it facilitated the Jew's invasion of English culture, and by George Eliot, who attacked conversion because it annihilated the Jew's religious and cultural identity. Trollope's and Eliot's novels of the 1870s constituted a kind of public debate over the idea of "the secret Jew" and the definition of English national identity, with Disraeli as the crystallizing figure in this debate. The history of the representation of Jewish identity in England reaches a new stage, I argue, at the radical moment toward the end of Eliot's *Daniel Deronda* when the goal of defining the English national character is superseded by the goal of constructing a Jewish national identity, that is, the goal of establishing for the Jews a nation-state of their own.

I

The Culture of Conversion

In nineteenth-century England the clearest sign of the ideology of Jewish conversion was its institutionalization in such well-known societies as the London Society for Promoting Christianity amongst the Jews (founded in 1809) and the British Society for the Propagation of the Gospel among the Jews (founded in 1842).[1] Numbering among their members some of England's best-known citizens, from powerful members of Parliament to influential clergymen (including William Wilberforce, Charles Simeon, and Lord Shaftesbury), and even enjoying the royal patronage of the duke of Kent, such societies became the subject of immense public attention and intense national debate. While the ideology of the conversion of the Jews was based on the scholarly exegesis of certain key texts of the Bible, the institutionalization of such an ideology—raising money, publishing journals and books, distributing tracts, setting up Christian schools for poor Jewish children, giving financial support to prospective converts—engaged the wider public in what became a debate over the religious, social, and political status of the Jews.

This chapter explores the public debate over the conversion of the Jews in general, and, more specifically, the controversial literature that grew out of the scandal surrounding the London Society. How did what otherwise might have been a local and self-contained controversy over the misadventures of one conversionist society at the beginning of the century reach such proportions, emerging into a debate that included the entire nation and lasted for decades? I will answer this question in part by showing how the controversy over the conversion of the Jews intersected with other important nineteenth-century debates, but my emphasis will be on the various literary forms (especially the conversionist novel) that disseminated, popularized, and reinvigorated the ideology of conversion even amid growing criticism of it.

The origins, development, and ultimate impact of the nineteenth-century conversionist novel is a largely unnoticed cultural phenomenon. Especially under the influence of the Evangelical Revival, novels became for the English public a major source of information about the Jews. Robert Southey, for example, recommended to a member of Parliament that he read, in preparation for debating Jewish Emancipation, the novel *Sophia de Lissau,* the subtitle of which defined the function of such novels: *A Portraiture of the Jews of the Nineteenth Century; Being an Outline of their Religious and Domestic Habits With Explanatory Notes.*[2] The novel's preface made clear why the English public needed this information about the Jews: "how important is an intimate acquaintance with their most minute prejudices to those who would speak to them of Jesus!"[3] Novels became a tool in the work of conversion, laying the groundwork for the English public to participate in this mission and preparing (in the case of Southey's correspondent) a member of Parliament to take part in the debates over Jewish emancipation—for the ideology of conversion played an important role in the parliamentary debates on Jewish civil and political disabilities. Novels about the Jews became so popular and wielded such influence that the Society for Promoting Christian Knowledge decided to enter the field with *Sadoc and Miriam: A Jewish Tale.* This novel makes especially visible what can be found in subtler forms in the conversionist novel in general, namely, the vestigial traces of the oldest form of conversionist literature. In *Sadoc and Miriam,* narrative form is almost entirely erased in the debates between characters over the comparative values of Judaism versus Christianity, recalling those literary dialogues written by the Church fathers in which a Christian tries to convert a Jew through scriptural argument.[4] Moreover, the London Society used the popularity of novels to advertise and support its own cause, regularly quoting *Ivanhoe,* for example, and even altering a passage in a famous novel like *Daniel Deronda* to make it serve the ideology of conversion.[5]

In turning to the controversy over the Jewish conversionist societies and the way in which this controversy began to raise questions about English national identity, I explain in the first part of this chapter how the critics of such societies saw in them the sign of a kind of national insanity, "the English madness," which threatened to stain once again England's national character by being the latest development in a long history of England's abuses of the Jews. I go on to show how the literature of conversion represented England's missionary project as the sign that England was the chosen nation, the spiritual guide to all nations, initiating the salvation of the world by beckoning "the poor love of a Jew" to find refuge in "the Israel of modern times."

"The English Madness," or "This Mania of Conversion"

Writing in 1833, Isaac D'Israeli, the father of the future prime minister, offers a picture of the kind of activity that surrounded the missions to the Jews in nineteenth-century England: "The most learned Christians have composed excellent treatises; Jewish lectures have been delivered, even by converted Jews; conferences, both public and private, have been held; and societies, industrious like the 'the London,' assisted by every human means. We have arguments the most demonstrative on one side, and refutations the most complete on the other; exhortations which have drawn tears from both parties, and satires the most witty and malicious." D'Israeli, who eventually broke with the synagogue and had his children baptized—though he himself was never a convert to Christianity, as the London Society incorrectly claimed[6]—goes on to explain those practices that turned Christian proselytism into "this trade of conversion," such as "hunting after miserable proselytes in the dark purlieus of filthy quarters, parentless children, or torn from their disconsolate parents; . . . or importing young Polanders, who lose their Jewish complexion by fattening at the tables of their generous hosts."[7]

D'Israeli here is reiterating the charges that had been brought before the public on many occasions, but perhaps most directly by a series of texts, published between 1816 and 1825, that were devoted exclusively to exposing the abuses of the London Society. When Robert Southey attacked the Society in 1830, he based his remarks on one of these popular critiques: "The Society for converting Jews has *wasted* more money than any other society in this country, which is a great deal. Norris published a most complete exposure of it."[8] H. H. Norris's book, heavily indebted to two shocking exposés written by M. Sailman and B. R. Goakman, discusses the Society's notorious mismanagement of funds, its extraordinary expenditures, and its failure to win legitimate converts—as in the case of the learned rabbi from Jerusalem, the society's famous first convert, meant to convince both Christians and Jews of the success of Jewish conversion, who "went back again to the Jews" when it was discovered "that he frequently resorted to a house of ill-fame." Similar charges were leveled at no less a figure than the founder of the London Society, the Rev. Joseph Samuel Christian Frederic Frey: "his crime [was] *adultery*, not committed *once only*, but *voraciously* pursued and persisted in *in the face of detection*." Such incidents were already so well known, having been articulated in serious critiques and bitter satires, that the intention of Norris's book, it may surprise us, was not to undercut the ideology of conversion but to recuperate it.[9] Norris was attempting to preserve the goal of conversion in the face of the miserable business the London Society had made of it, arguing "that *it* is *alone* responsible for its own *total failure;* and that the conversion of the Jews remains, what the Society found it, an object of the most intense interest, left in charge to the Christian Church, as one of its most imperative obligations." Norris worried that the London Society's notorious reputation, extended across Europe with the recent establishment of foreign missions to the Jews, was giving a bad name not only to the missionary enterprise, but to England itself: "the very work itself of fetching home these out-casts to the flock of Christ, is become a bye-word and an object of scorn and ridicule amongst them, being scoffed at as '*the English madness.*' "[10]

Such critiques, while agreeing on the abuses of the London Society, were frequently based on very different ideologies. While a conversionist like Norris who saw himself as a protector of the Jews decries "all *the cruel wrongs* it [the London Society] has *itself* inflicted on that grievously oppressed people,"[11] other critics worked to another end, not to protect the Jewish community from such abuses, but to maintain the basest stereotypes of Jewish identity. This kind of critique was based on the idea that the Jews were not worth the money or the effort spent on them by the missionary societies. In *The British Critic* in 1819 a reviewer of several works dealing with the London Society used the critiques of Sailman and Goakman to reiterate the abuses of the Society—"how the half-naked and hungry Jew boy has become tempted by food and clothes"—in what was finally a conventional Christian attack on the Jews themselves: "the guilt of that blood [of Jesus Christ] still rests upon them with all its original weight." Yielding to the idea, so prevalent at the time, that "the situation of the Jews, that once highly favoured, now outcast and despised people, will ever be a subject of intense interest and awful contemplation," the reviewer claims that, even with recent advances in education, science, and morals, "their blindness has not been removed, their prejudices have not been softened, their condition not improved: they are yet a wandering, unsocial, and despised people." In short, "the Jews remain the same, in features, in habits, in customs, and in character," and their unchangeable nature becomes the basis for claiming their unconvertibility: "the real conversion of a Jew has been at all times as rare, as their whole history is wonderful."[12]

The Anglo-Jewish community suddenly found itself the object of frequent publicity and heated controversy. Quick to respond to the establishment of the London Society, the Jewish community was eager to get a hearing from the English public, for the Society attempted to forestall all debate, as Joseph Crool, an instructor of Hebrew at Cambridge, complained: "it is said that they have answered almost everything, and that a Jew has no more to say for himself." Crool's widely read work, studied by missionaries and cited by conversionist novelists,[13] took aim not at the abuses of the London Society, but at the scriptural arguments that the missionaries employed in their attempt to convince Jews that Jesus Christ was their Messiah. Crool was careful to insist that he was not "an enemy of Christianity," and to use a strategy that was a standard feature of the works written by English Jews against conversionism—the acknowledgment of a special relationship between the Jewish community and the English nation: "how much more is it our duty to pray for the nations at the present time, in particular for this country, for here we are used well, and treated better than in any other country: here we enjoy ease and security."[14]

The Anglo-Jewish community consistently appealed to the English public's generosity, its reputation for tolerance, even when attacking the London Society with a biting irony and the voice of outrage, as in a pamphlet written immediately after the Society's establishment, entitled *Letter to Mr. Frey, of the Soi-Disant Jews'-Chapel, Spitalfields; Occasioned by the Question Now in Debate at the London Forum* (1810). The author, who signed herself "A Daughter of Israel," attacked the character and actions of Frey—whom she called a "Purchaser of Babes! Corrupter of thoughtless Youth!"—condemning his "bribery system" of conversion, "the *trade* you are now employed in." Such attacks were carefully aimed at a foreign Jew, not an English Christian: "you are not a Christian, you are an Apostate Jew, alike the disgrace of the community you have entered, and that you have quitted." The author ended, first, by counseling Frey to "imitate the benign tolerant principles of the *Anglican Church*," and second, by proving the Jews' loyalty to the English nation on the basis of their loyalty to their religion: "the Jews are not to be led aside from their duty to the Almighty, nor their loyal attachment to the Government which protects them; for they are equally as firm to their God, as they are to their King."[15] In such strategic remarks we see how carefully the Anglo-Jewish community had to aim its attacks at the conversionist societies while not offending the English Protestant public in general.

In addition to attacking the scriptural arguments of the missionaries (Crool), and the character of Frey and his methods (A Daughter of Israel), Jewish critics of the London Society began to represent themselves as the protectors of England, praising the English for their generosity while warning them that they were being duped, especially as the Society's immense expenditures and the hypocrisy of its converts became better known. In *Conversion of the Jews: An Address from an Israelite to the Missionary Preachers Assembled at Liverpool to Promote Christianity amongst the Jews* (1827), M. Samuel lists the better uses to which such money could be put:

> To plead the case of distress for the poor Irish, or for the Spanish emigrants, to preach charity sermons for any particular asylum, is not sufficient for your exalted views; you aspire to a more lofty and extensive scope, to paint in a pathetic manner the blind obduracy of a chosen race, and to convince your audience, that charity cannot be better bestowed than in reclaiming the sons and daughters of Abraham from darkness to light. . . . Was there ever a more specious pretext invented to rouse the charitable spirit of the British nation!!!

Samuel leaves the English public with a startling image of the converted Jew, "his purse . . . filled with the reward of his labour," departing from England to return to his native land, "there to revel in luxurious delight over British wealth—British credulity!" Samuel addresses the members of the Society—"For twenty years you have been infected with this *mania of conversion"*—and he leaves the impression that the entire English public is in danger of becoming infected: "Now the conversion of a solitary Polish Jew in London is hailed with such triumph as to require a public announcement in all the newspapers of so glorious an accession to the strength of christianity; and . . . thousands of credulous enthusiasts flock to the sanctuary to witness this holy Patriarch undergo the first degree of apostasy."[16]

The London Society so angered and alarmed the Jewish community that even in pamphlets and books whose major focus pointed elsewhere, we find critiques of the missions to the Jews. In this way attacks on the London Society found their way into a variety of different discourses and motivated a range of different projects. For instance, in *The Inquisition and Judaism* (1845), an attempt to record a portion of the history of the Inquisition in Portugal, the strikingly contemporary and local remarks of Moses Mocatta's preface may at first seem out of place. "In many parts of the Old and New World, but more especially in Great Britain, the conversion of the Jews has become an organized system.—Here, societies and branch societies are formed, schools are established for infants and adults, and enormous sums are annually placed at the disposal of mercenary agents to further what the maudlin fanaticism of the day calls 'the good cause.'" The body of Mocatta's book presented a translation of a sermon by a Catholic archbishop and its refutation by a Jew, from another time and place, under conditions that must have seemed vastly different from those of Victorian England, but in "the history of the controversy between the 'Converters' and the disciples of the faith of Moses . . . the weapons employed have been invariably taken from the same armory." Mocatta published these translations in the hope that they would "protect them [Jewish youth] against the insidious efforts of the missionaries" in Victorian England.[17]

So, a study of the discursive practices produced by this controversy cannot be limited to those texts that took the London Society as their sole, or even their primary, subject. Moreover, a study of these practices introduces us to the various cultural issues with which the conversion of the Jews was entwined—as, in the case of Mocatta's book, the history of the Inquisition in Spain, and the nationalist contrast between intolerant Spain and tolerant England (that Mocatta's book threatens to deconstruct in its pointed if brief reference to the conversionist societies of nineteenth-century England). I now wish to turn to certain anticonversionist texts that, whether or not based primarily on a critique of the conversionist societies, show how the conversion of the Jews was linked to such pressing nineteenth-century issues as nationalism, colonialism, and race.

The debate over Jewish conversion became situated at the crossroads of a number of important social discourses and a number of national crises in England and on the Continent. Particularly with the rise of European nationalism and the spread of colonialism, "the Jewish question" began to assume central importance in the nineteenth century as different European nations sought the means to assimilate or expel "foreign" populations at home and to convert and govern "heathen" populations abroad. After the defeat of Napoleon and the expulsion of the French from the German states, for example, the Jews came under attack when German nationalists called for the expulsion of *all* foreigners—not simply the French—from Germany. While conversion was one of the suggested solutions to "the Jewish question" in Germany, one pamphleteer, who endorsed both the expulsion and the extermination of the Jews, suggested a solution linking Germany's Jews and the British empire's blacks by calling for a system of eugenics: "Let the children of Israel be sold to the English, who could employ them in their Indian plantations instead of the blacks. That they may not increase, the men should be emasculated, and their wives and daughters be lodged in houses of shame."[18] And in England, while in their critiques of the London Society the Jews argued that their loyalty to the nation was like their loyalty to their God, many of England's leading intellectuals and statesmen questioned the Jews' allegiance to a "Christian nation" and refused to grant them full civil and political liberties until they converted. Thomas Arnold's famous formulation of the Jew as a "voluntary stranger" in a Christian nation with no claim to being a citizen—unless converted—became a central obstacle to Jewish Emancipation in the debates in Parliament.[19] A more virulent version of Arnold's view of the Jew as alien occurs in William Cobbett's scalding 1830 Good Friday Sermon: "This is a *Christian nation*," Cobbett argued, and Scripture proved that the Jews "should, in no country on earth (as long as they adhered to their blasphemy), have any immunities, any privileges, any possessions in house, land or water, any civil or political rights; that they should, every where, be deemed *aliens;* and always at the *absolute disposal of the sovereign power of the state,* as completely as any inanimate substance, thrown on the land by the winds or the waves. This was the judgment passed on them by God himself."[20]

In this way, the question of Jewish conversion, which had been primarily a matter of scriptural exegesis in the decades immediately following the French Revolution, became situated from the 1830s through the 1850s at the center of the political debate over Jewish Emancipation. Conversion became the only path not merely to Christian salvation, but to English assimilation; Jewish identity and English national identity were mutually exclusive. So while the procedures of the London Society were being aggressively attacked in many critiques, the ideology of conversion was maintained, even supported, by the idea that only when once converted could the Jews become English citizens with all the civic and political privileges of their neighbors, such as sitting in Parliament or receiving degrees from Oxford and Cambridge. One could argue that "the bribery system" of the London Society, attacked by both Christians and Jews, was the same system that the English nation at large used to convert the Jews, holding out the temptation of full civil and political emancipation on the condition that they convert. A pamphlet, originally appearing in Holland and translated into English, argued this point: "will you continue to exclude the Jews from everything, in order, by these means, to compel them to the adoption of the Christian faith? Is then a forced adoption your doctrine—*forced,* in order to escape shame and contempt, an hypocritical faith—a desirable thing for you?" The English translator of this pamphlet, who is "desirous to see the Jews placed in civic situations,"[21] reveals how the ideology of conversion was institutionalized in both the conversionist societies and in a governmental system of assimilation that sought religious homogeneity as the basis of the nation-state.

Attacks on the conversionist societies consistently used the strategy of referring to England's reputation for tolerance—the pamphlet's translator addresses "the British nation, where the beneficial consequences of Liberty are so highly conspicuous"[22]—as if to embarrass the nation into recognizing the ways in which its tolerance did not extend to Jews. By such means, critiques of the conversionist societies attempted to unravel the conjunction between tolerance and conversion that had become the mainstay of Evangelical preaching. In a short satire that appeared in the *Pall Mall Gazette* in 1865, Anthony Trollope imagines a Zulu's trip to

England "to visit the great centre of the Christian religion" in what eventually becomes a test of the celebrated idea "that toleration was the grand characteristic of the English Protestant Church." The Zulu attends an Evangelical meeting "devoted to the propagation of Christianity among the Jews," with a hymn "sung by converted Jew children." At this meeting the well-known failure of the missions to the Jews is made clear when the Zulu records that the speaker's "report dealt only with tens and twenties, whereas among us our dealings are with hundreds and thousands. But the Jews are a stubborn people, and from such the evil spirit does not come out without many struggles"—the Zulu, himself a product of the missions to the heathen, having perfectly imbibed the ideology of Christian proselytism, including its origins in anti-Judaic stereotypes. Trollope's parody of the proselytizing mania reaches its highest pitch when the Zulu is told that, dressed in black coat and black gloves, he would pass unnoticed at the meeting, for everyone "would take me for a converted Jew."[23] Such a remark suggests the blind self-centeredness of Evangelical fervor, perhaps the clearest sign of "the English madness."

But such a remark also suggests the kind of racism that often surrounded the ideology of conversion in general and "the Jewish question" in particular. The conversionists' failure to recognize the difference between African and Jewish proselytes suggests a variety of racist propositions. On the one hand, the conversionists fail to recognize the cultural and religious differences between African and Jew, seeking only conformity to English Protestantism, or to mere Englishness, pictured in a kind of disguise of English gentility, "black coat and black gloves." But at the same time we can see how the anticonversionist rhetoric of Trollope's piece makes fun of both African and Jewish proselytes who try to become English, an idea to which Trollope returned in his representation of the Jewish infiltration of English culture in his novels of the 1870s.

Frequently, the anticonversionist position was fueled by a more or less blatant racism. The impossibility of the conversion of the Jew was formulated through the Jew's racial traits (and even the African's racial traits). In a satiric pamphlet, *Jewish Conversion. A Christianic Farce. Got Up With Great Effect Under the Direction of a Society For Making Bad Jews Worse Christians* (1814), the attack aimed at Frey and his company of missionaries overflows into a vicious attack against the Jews themselves. Here we have an attack on the ideology of conversion based not on philo-Semitism but anti-Semitism. The author, who characterizes the Jews as "the beggar tribe, / Who sold their God, and took the bribe!," associates "the bribery system" of conversion not so much with the conversionists, but with the Jews themselves: "Cash *buys* but cannot *keep* a jew." The conventional stereotype of the Jews as usurious traders is fitted to a system of conversion in which the Jews make themselves into a kind of high-priced commodity: "The jews advance so much in price, / And must be purchased twice or thrice." But this pamphlet's opening verses reveal the deepest way in which the issue of Jewish conversion was used to evoke a variety of contemporary racist feelings:

> The fool who scrubbed the Ethiop's back,
> Although he did not make him white
> Rubbed all the dirt from off the black,
> And left him in a tolerable plight.
> But had he painted him as angels fair,
> If fair as poets tell us angels are,
> A dirty devil he would still have been;
> For like a chimney-sweepe's back,
> Bedizened to disguise its black,
> He still had worn his hue within.
> So thus our christian makers out of Jews,
> Have this same painting system much in use. . . .[24]

The impossibility of racial transformation—the black man becoming white—becomes an analogy for the impossibility of religious conversion—the Jew becoming a Christian. Moreover, the racial slur that links and sometimes confuses black and Jew pinpoints a particular strand of English racist discourse, as in Edgeworth's Jewish Lady Rackrent, a "heretic blackamoor," or Trollope's Ferdinand Lopez, "a black Portuguese nameless Jew," or Thackeray's Miss Swartz, "the rich woolly-haired mulatto" whose father was a German Jew.[25]

By the middle of the nineteenth century the debate over conversion often shifted from religious to racial grounds, and the analogy that compared religious conversion to racial transformation began to receive the support of "science." The new science of ethnology was used to "prove," from a racial standpoint, the impossibility of converting the Jews, making the goal of the missionary societies impossible. The religious view that held the Jews to be unchanging over the centuries—outcasts wandering the earth in punishment for their great crime, the murder of Jesus Christ—now became a racial unchangeability. In his popular *The Races of Men* (1850) Robert Knox claimed "that the real Jew had never altered since the earliest recorded period; that two hundred years at least before Christ they were perambulating Italy and Europe precisely as they do now, following the same occupations—that is, no occupation at all." "Literature, science, art they possess not. It is against their nature." The Jews, Knox contended, remain "unaltered and unalterable," and, as if to put the seal on their degeneracy, he links the Jews to another "inferior" racial group: "the whole physiognomy, when swarthy, as it often is, has an African look"; "a large, massive, club-shaped, hooked nose, three or four times larger than suits the face—those are features which stamp the African character of the Jew." The science of ethnology—or what this science claimed were the laws of Nature—became the latest weapon used against the conversionist societies: "Societies are got up for their conversion! Be it so. Nothing can be said against them; but in one hundred years they will not convert one hundred Jews—not even one real Jew. . . . Nature alters not."[26]

I have been suggesting how the local controversy over the practices of the London Society found fresh combatants decade after decade and how difficult it became to locate the critiques of the conversionist societies in one community or one ideology. The attacks on these societies came from within the Jewish community and from outside it, from the friends and from the enemies of Judaism and the Jews. The battle was fought on religious, political, and racial grounds, and the controversy affected not only the Jewish community but the entire English nation.

History, Memoir, Novel: "My own darling Jew, Jesus Christ loves you"

To promulgate the ideology of conversion, its supporters created a veritable industry of sermons, tracts, stories for the young, histories of the Jews, memoirs, and novels. I will focus on two narrative forms that influenced the mainstream tradition of nineteenth-century novelistic discourse: autobiographical accounts written by recent converts from Judaism, and conversionist novels (often masquerading as autobiography) that took as their goal the narration of the conversion of a Jew. But first I wish to explore the historiography of the Jews as a form of conversionist literature in nineteenth-century England. This examination will help us see the way in which historical narratives of the collective life of the Jews functioned to frame those narratives of individual Jewish life contained in the memoir and the novel.

Histories of the Jews became popular in the nineteenth century, and the conversionist societies applauded their publication. Henry Hart Milman's *History of the Jews* (1829), according to the London Society, "undoubtedly aroused sympathy with this wonderful people and so indirectly helped on the cause."[27] The London Society even published such histories, especially when they could be easily tailored to fit the ideology of conversion. In 1818, for example, the Society was responsible for the republication of the American author Hannah Adams's *History of the Jews* (1812). By publishing such works, the Society saw itself as a kind of publicist for the Jews, keeping the issue before the public. Confessing "that a few alterations were deemed expedient, in the present edition," the Society explained its motives in publishing Adams's *History:* "the hope is warmly cherished, that when British Christians shall have been made more fully acquainted, through the medium of this publication, with the calamities which have befallen the Jews since their last dispersion, such sympathy will be excited, as to stimulate them to co-operate zealously with the above Society." Such histories were meant to support what I have defined as the double ideology of Protestant England: toleration and conversion. A comprehensive account of the Jews from ancient times through the first decade of the nineteenth century, Adams's *History* excites sympathy by means of a thorough representation of the sufferings of the Jews but periodically reminds the reader of the Christian context within which such suffering should be viewed: "while, with the most painful sensations, we read an account of calamities, which no other description of men ever experienced in any age or country, let us recollect, that the Jews had called down the divine wrath, by crucifying the Lord of glory." Adams's *History,* bearing the stamp of the new edition by the London Society, concludes with this abjuration: "the Christian reader cannot surely close this volume more suitably than with a resolution to pray frequently and fervently for their promised conversion, and with a generous desire to enrol his own name amongst those of the subscribers to the 'London Society for promoting Christianity amongst the Jews.' "[28]

Such histories began to contain accounts of, even to be preoccupied with, the recent conversionist efforts in England. The penultimate chapter of Adams's *History* contained such subheadings as "An account of several distinguished converts" and "Account of a Society formed in London for the express purpose of converting the Jews." Another historian, James Huie, had the double goal of presenting a world history of the Jews and recording the efforts made to convert them: *The History of the Jews, From the Taking of Jerusalem by Titus To the Present Time . . . With an Account of the Various Efforts Made for Their Conversion.* For Huie, the history of the Jews, even from ancient times, leads ineluctably to one end, their conversion. And his preface, with its hope to "promote the cause of Israel's conversion," makes clear that the historiography of the Jews was being designed to facilitate and hasten their conversion. Through recording centuries of Jewish persecution, such histories were meant to awaken the public's sympathies and thereby interest the public in the project of conversion. Huie's last chapter, devoted entirely to the missions to the Jews, ends:

> The race of Abraham were too long exposed to the hatred and contempt of those who bore the name of Christ. It is hoped that, among Protestants at least, none can now entertain feelings so alien to the Gospel. . . . Especially is it to be desired that Great Britain, which, on account of its spiritual and temporal privileges has been styled the Israel of modern times, may now rouse herself to active exertions in behalf of God's ancient people. Devoutly is it wished that the welfare of that remarkable race may become a subject of deep interest to all classes; and that churchmen and dissenters may strive, with a godly emulation, to forward the cause of missions to them.[29]

History becomes the record not only of the long oppression of the Jews under the Roman Catholics ("those who bore the name of Christ"), but of the beginning of a new era under the leadership of Protestant Britain, an era whose toleration of the Jews is marked most signally by the effort to convert them. Without a touch of irony, Huie sees the goal of "the Israel of modern times" in the conversion of the Israel of ancient times—the Jews who, through their own stubbornness, and through God's punishment of them, have survived into the modern world only to be converted to Christ.

One further way in which the historiography of the Jews was enmeshed in the ideology of conversion should be recorded. A prominent historian of the Jews went so far as to argue that it was only converted Jews who should write Jewish history. Moses Margoliouth, himself a convert from Judaism, claimed:

> Every well-informed scholar must maintain that neither the representatives of the Talmudical, nor those of the "Reformed" Jews, are qualified to write an unprejudiced history of the Anglo-Hebrews, or of the Hebrew nation anywhere. I would go a step farther, and maintain that the eighteen centuries of prejudice has disqualified the representatives of the residuary—I mean the Christ-rejecting Jews,—to write soberly, critically, with a "literary conscience," on any subject which appertains, directly or indirectly, to their system of theology.

This leads to Margoliouth's even more remarkable claim: "The structure of the Hebrew Christian's mind is such as to refuse to take in any theory, or statement, on trust; it must weigh everything in the justest balances,"[30] so that only the converted Jew is equipped with the objectivity necessary for the writing of Jewish history. Playing the role of objective historian himself, Margoliouth does not hesitate to take England to task for its past crimes against the Jews; he approvingly quotes Scott's *Ivanhoe* on the persecution of the Jews and in the manner of Scott shows how the history of the Jews "throws a great light upon the national character of the people of this country." But Margoliouth adds an optimistic coda: "if it be painful to Englishmen to read of massacres, extortions, and persecutions perpetrated by their ancestors, upon a defenceless people, it may, nevertheless be a subject of congratulation that they are permitted to turn their eyes upon the improved state, both of the persecuted and the persecutors." Finally, "the improved state" that Margoliouth applauds turns out to be the result of the London Society:

> Whatever over-zealous, alias mistaken friends, or open foes, may say and write against that Society, a calm and deliberate view of its operations must lead to the inevitable conclusion, that the Society effected the most important changes in the civil, political, literary, and religious conditions of the Jews in this country. . . . The Society by their publications, doctrinal and controversial, led many of the

House of Israel to examine the traditions of the Talmudic fathers, which led many of their provincial Rabbies in this country, as well as in other parts of the world, to profess the religion of Christianity.

Such exaggerated claims for the London Society—when the historical record shows that some of the Society's supporters spoke out in Parliament against the removal of Jewish disabilities—are nonetheless to be taken as objective, for the author "did not write as a politician, but as an impartial historian."[31]

As part of their focus on modern conversionist efforts, histories of the Jews began to be imbedded with the stories of converts. Huie, for example, spends a great deal of time recording the conversion of Dr. Capadose, a physician of Amsterdam. Huie calls attention to the genre of literature to which I now turn, the memoir of the Jewish convert, by acknowledging the wide influence such memoirs had: "the chief cause which has contributed to the profound impression made by his conversion on the Continent and in this country, is the very interesting account, which he has himself given, of the various circumstances that attended it. Several editions have been published of his remarkable tract, which possesses much of that interest, excited by the Confessions of Augustine."[32] While historians like Adams and Huie applauded these memoirs and summarized them in their histories, the Jewish community mocked them—at the same time attesting to their popularity—for the memoir of the Jewish convert became one of the most persuasive means of advertising the new era in Jewish-Christian relations, the era of the Protestant evangelization of the Jews. M. Samuel complained to the London Society,

> Where now are the men whom you blazoned forth as champions of conversion a few years back? have they not dropped off one after the other, some through treachery, others through repentance, leaving you nothing behind but the narrations of their wonderful conversion, monuments of their taste and industry? for as sure as you obtain a convert we are immediately favoured with the history of his life in the shape of "memoirs" as if conscious of his worthlessness, he makes this vain attempt to shield himself from the oblivion to which the world will consign him.[33]

In *Conversion of Dr. Capadose* we find many hallmarks of the genre in general, as well as the characteristics that make this particular memoir so suitable for importation into England. There is, first of all, a critique of both French Enlightenment philosophy and Roman Catholicism, between which Capadose steers the course of his journey toward faith. On the one hand, he quickly indicts the writings of Voltaire and Rousseau: "the insolidity, the infidelity, and, above all, the terrible consequences of their systems, unfolded to my eyes in the history of the French revolution, guarded me, through the grace that cometh down from on high, against their pernicious influence." On the other hand, in reading the work of a Jewish convert to Catholicism, Capadose discovers "how powerful the logic and how forcible the proof were, when contending against the opinions of a Voltaire and a Rousseau; and how weak they were when defending catholicism against the principles of the Reformation." Finally, Capadose experiences the bankruptcy of the religion of his family in a visit to the synagogue, where "those heartless ceremonies, that want of respect, those shouts, those discordant songs . . .—all this spiritless and lifeless display so disgusted me that I no longer attended regularly."[34]

In the most consistent topos of the genre, the memoirist discovers the truth of Christianity in one or more scenes of reading. Such scenes typically represent a dangerous transgression: the act of reading a Christian book in a Jewish household. Hence these are scenes of reading in secret, where a prohibited volume is hidden by the potential convert and read in snatches.[35] Such scenes are sometimes initiated by the unexpected discovery of a Christian book in a Jewish household. In the case of Capadose, he discovers in his uncle's library Justin Martyr's *Dialogue with Trypho the Jew*—one of the classic texts belonging to the Church fathers' conversionist literature—in which he found "a succinct exposition of the prophecies relating to the Messiah."[36] Huie's comment on such a scene shows the way in which the writing of Jewish history is used to validate the ideology of Christian conversion: "thus, the discussion of the ancient father, which had failed to convince his antagonist of his errors, now seventeen hundred years later, proved, in the good Providence of God, a means to direct an inquiring child of Abraham to the knowledge of the Gospel."[37] History is the unfolding of Christian time, a witness to the completion of the conversion of the Jews, an event begun in the time of the Church fathers, and to be completed in the nineteenth century under the auspices of Protestantism.

Capadose's final conversion occurs when he reads the fifty-third chapter of Isaiah,[38] the scriptural passage that becomes the central prooftext in the conversionist memoir and novel: "On reading this, it seemed impossible for a Jew to doubt that Christ was the promised Messiah."[39] In his *History of the Jews* Huie recalls that Capadose had often read this text in Isaiah, "but now he read it with spiritual discernment, for the Holy Ghost enabled him to penetrate its meaning."[40] Such a scene, in which a Jew reads anew a passage from Hebrew Scripture, is meant to suggest the immense availability and accessibility of Christianity, whose truth lies at the fingertips of the Jew, before his very eyes. Capadose underscores this idea when he explains his shock and surprise at discovering the truth of Christianity not in the Gospel but in Hebrew Scripture: filled with the proof of Christ as recorded in Isaiah, "I actually thought some other Bible had been substituted in the place of my own."[41] Another memoirist finds himself for the first time in a Protestant (as opposed to Roman Catholic) church, where the absence of images and the simplicity of the service make him "think that it was not a Christian Church, but some sort of Jewish synagogue."[42]

In such texts the radical nature of the process of conversion is minimized, for Christianity is only Judaism perfected (as we hear time and again). One convert says in his memoir: "I had not apostasized from the faith of the fathers; on the contrary, since I had embraced Jesus as my Messiah, I had become a true Israelite." The archconversionist Frey argues in his often reprinted memoir, "the Christian Religion, which I sincerely believe, and publicly preach, is contained in the Old Testament as well as in the New," and "every article of my creed may also be confirmed from the writings of our forefathers." Such a view was meant to ease the unconverted Jew into the position of Christian proselyte, reminding him that the final proof of Christianity is found in his own sacred Scripture. After all, in the words of another memoirist, "Christianity is the true Jewish religion"![43]

The scene of reading occupies a central place in the general conversionist ideology of English Protestant culture. A particularly powerful explanation of the role of reading in the culture of conversion occurs in *Robinson Crusoe* when the hero explains how easily he and even the "savage" Friday were able to gain access to God through the simple act: "the Knowledge of God, and of the Doctrine of Salvation by *Christ Jesus,* is so plainly laid down in the Word of God; so easy to be receiv'd and understood: That as the bare reading the Scripture made me capable of understanding enough of my Duty, to carry me directly on to the great Work of sincere Repentance for my Sins, . . . so the same plain Instruction serv'd to the enlightning this Savage Creature."[44] The site of conversion, apparently stripped of all social and political implications, is simply the site of reading; it contains only the individual sinner and the Bible.

The individual's direct access to truth through the Word of God, a central tenet of Protestantism, became a cornerstone of the Evangelical Revival's return to the Bible. Crusoe anticipates the argument that the Evangelicals used to distinguish Protestantism from all other religions, which rely on the intermediary of a priesthood: "there is Priestcraft, even amongst the most blinded ignorant Pagans in the World; and the Policy of making a secret Religion, in order to preserve the Veneration of the People to the Clergy, is not only to be found in the *Roman,* but perhaps among all Religions in the World, even among the most brutish and barbarous Savages."[45] One of the London Society's best-known missionaries, Joseph Wolff, explains in his *Memoir* (which describes his conversion from Judaism to Roman Catholicism to Protestantism) how a Roman Catholic priest chastised him: "You are no judge of the Holy Scriptures,—this is the great error of the Protestants: they believe that every one may understand the Scriptures! But we must hear the Popes!"[46]

The role of reading was consistently institutionalized in the culture of conversion. For example, Defoe's representation in 1719 of the ease with which Friday comprehends the Scriptures reads like an advertisement for the recently founded Society for the Propagation of the Gospel in Foreign Parts (1701). And the venture of bringing the Bible to foreign lands was revived in 1804, with the establishment of the British and Foreign Bible Society, one of the Evangelical Revival's chief instruments. Taking its cue from this highly influential group, the London Society—and the memoirs of Jewish converts—encouraged Jews to read both Hebrew Scripture and the New Testament. The London Society spent a good deal of effort and money in distributing Bibles to the Jews, and in 1817 published a translation into Hebrew of the New Testament, heralding it as a breakthrough in the evangelization of the Jews. In 1823 the Society issued the Old Testament in Hebrew—"This was most necessary, as missionaries found the Jews so ignorant of their own Scriptures that appeals to the Old Testament were useless"—and in 1825 it issued another edition of the New Testament in Hebrew, and in 1838 a revised edition. The Society's official modern historian summarized its publication record: "More than a quarter of a million copies (or portions) of the New Testament; more than 630,000 copies (or parts) of the Old Testament; and nearly five million Missionary publications have been placed in the hands of the Jews."[47]

The results of such efforts are frequently recorded in the memoirs of converted Jews. In *Conversion of Mr. and Mrs. Levi*, Abraham Joseph Levi explains that shortly after his arrival in London in 1844 a missionary "recommended me to read the Old and New Testaments, and, as I did not possess them, he presented me with a copy." And in a little parable of conversion published by the British Society for the Propagation of the Gospel among the Jews, "A Jew Converted Through a Lost Bible," some Bibles fall out of a missionary's pocket, and one is retrieved by a Jew who studies it in secret until his wife discovers him and hides the book from him; only after her death does he find the book again, and in reading it a second time his conversion is made complete. The topos of the Jew's conversion in the act of secret reading and the immense efforts made by missionaries to publish and circulate the Bible become clear when the official policy of the London Society is laid plainly before us: "The written word of God circulates, too, silently and without offence; it penetrates where the missionary could find no access, it is concealed in the bosom and read in the closet."[48] In the typical memoir, then, the conversion of the Jew depends neither on the intervention of missionaries, nor on the intervention of miracle, but on the simple act of (secret) reading.

One of the most compelling versions of this act of reading occurs in Jonas Abraham Davis's *Judaism Excelled: Or the Tale of a Conversion from Judaism to Christianity*. One day while wandering through the Gentile servants' quarters, the young Davis opens a dresser drawer: "There lay a book. I must needs open it at the first chapter of the general epistle of James. I stood before the open drawer and read the chapter through. Filled with surprise, I trembled at reading an account of my own condition, especially in a strange book." He eventually realizes that it is the New Testament he holds in his hands: "This is the 'Christian's book,' I exulted.

In a moment it came into my heart to *steal it.*" He takes the book, which now becomes fetish-like in the power it exerts on him: "I resolved upon hiding the doubtful treasure until I could find a fair chance to read it privately"; "I had a strong desire to read the forbidden book, but I did not expect to find in it truth"; "I had an irrepressible inclination to read it, if only to show up the falsity of Christianity." Trying to demystify the book's power by disputing its claims, he is defeated in a theological debate with some Christians. He returns to reading the New Testament, but this time he sets it beside Hebrew Scripture to compare the two, ultimately acknowledging that "in the person of Jesus Christ I found an exact fulfillment of the old prophecies." When he confesses his conversion to his parents, the conflict with them centers on "the forbidden book": "they filched from me any book they could find. My Testament they could not obtain." When he returns the stolen Testament to the servant, she exclaims: "it's converted my young master to Christianity since it's been gone."[49] In an interesting variation on the theme of the (Christian) child instructing the (Jewish) adult, a prominent topos in the literature of conversion, the servant becomes the instrument of the master's conversion, proving once again the accessibility of the Gospel, its discovery in the lowliest of positions, the homeliest of locations.

Once converted, the memoirist typically tells a tale of persecution that reverses the familiar history of the persecution of the Jew by the hegemonic Christian community. In the converted Jew's memoir we read of the new convert's persecution by the Jewish community. Such a tale is in some ways an anachronism, a recollection of the martyrdom of Christ and the early Christians. In an early predecessor of these memoirs we notice the prominent position of this idea of persecution in the title, *The Conversion and Persecutions of Eve Cohan* (1680), and the way in which the persecution of the Jewish convert becomes modeled on the martyrdom of Christ: "But here is a Convert that is indeed a Disciple of the Cross, and has, in all the steps she made towards her Change, been oft in danger of her Life." Like Eve Cohan, the nineteenth-century memoirists describe the persecutions they suffered from family and friends. Jonas Abraham Davis explains how his confession was received: "Threats, bribes and blows were alternately resorted to, but argument never." Another memoirist describes from personal experience "what a dreadful ordeal the Jewish convert has to pass through in encountering the persecutions and prejudices of his kindred and nation!"; "every endearing tie is torn asunder, he is spurned from the parental roof, detested, shunned, and excommunicated." One memoirist even claims that he received several letters from Jews threatening to kill him if he did not give up his new Christian faith.[50] Such accounts of persecution are meant to make plain the trials that the convert must pass through, dispelling any suspicion that the Jew converts out of simple opportunism or self-advantage.

This theme of persecution accounts for the recurring claim in conversionist literature that there are many secret Christians among the Jews— that is, Jewish believers in Christ who are afraid to confess their conversion for fear of reprisal. One memoirist claims that his brother died "a secret believer in the Lord Jesus Christ, and I believe there are many such among the Jews of the present day." And in an interesting variation on the scene of secret reading, a missionary finds a hidden book among the remains of a dead Jew: "Then under the pillows were found a few sewing materials, a small linen bag containing a few coppers, some pieces of jewellery of little value, and a New Testament, with the words written in it, 'To HANNAH, 25th December, 1876.' I believe that when we join the ransomed multitude around the throne we shall behold there many Jewish souls whom we had little or no hope of ever seeing amid the splendours of Heaven."[51] In such narratives we have a reversal not only of the Christian's persecution of the Jew, but of one of the most prominent figures in the history of the Jews, the crypto-Jew who wore the mask of the Christian to escape persecution during the Inquisition in Spain and Portugal.

As with so many other popular forms of nonfiction, the memoir of the Jewish convert was soon translated into novelistic form. Such translations often masqueraded as the original, announcing their autobiographical status in their titles: *The Converted Jewess: A Memoir of Maria* — or *Leila Ada, The Jewish Convert: An Authentic Memoir*. While both of these texts are written in the third person of novelistic discourse, they go to great lengths to legitimize their claim to the status of memoir. The author of *Leila Ada* asserts that he uses extracts from diaries and journals which the young heroine composed herself, so that the third-person narrative is interspersed with long passages from the writings of Leila Ada in the first person. In both cases the authors claim to have heard the events of the young woman's life from people who knew her intimately. The authenticity of the account becomes a typical refrain: "Finally, we again repeat that we have nowhere written one word, look, or expression which is not most exact to the truth."[52]

In these two texts a sick young woman is the focus of the conversion plot. Maria is ill at the beginning of the narrative, her illness being a vehicle for her conversion (the Lord visits her "in the seclusion of a sick room, and on the bed of suffering, to open her spiritual eye"),[53] while Leila Ada falls ill early in the novel, on arriving in Jerusalem, the land of her forefathers. The theme of illness is used for several purposes. First, it allows the writer to illustrate the fortitude and peace with which the Christian dies, a popular idea in the conversionist novel: "Voltaire laughed at Christianity. Did he ever see a Christian die?"[54] The sick chambers of these heroines function as a kind of laboratory in which the power of Christianity is proven not merely to the skeptic who has imbibed French Enlightenment philosophy, but to members of the pious Jewish family. The peaceful death of the young convert is so powerful in *Leila Ada,* for example, that it becomes the vehicle for the conversion of the Jewish father, who exclaims: "I never expected to witness a death like yours." Second, the illness of the young woman makes her sexless, without bodily wishes, entirely devoted to the realm of the spirit; Leila is "a disembodied saint of twenty years old." In both texts we are in effect let into "the chamber of a dying saint [where] the boldest blasphemer must bow in homage to the religion of Jesus."[55] As we will see, this disembodiment of the Jewish heroine places her outside the conventional novelistic marriage plot, preventing her from marrying the Christian hero, even though she has been converted.

In each of these novels the reading of Scripture thoroughly occupies the immobilized heroine. Both women, by reading Isaiah 53, are convinced of the truths of Christianity and its harmony with Hebrew Scripture. Not surprisingly, we find an almost exact reprise of the scene of reading in Davis's memoir: "she assiduously compared these prophecies with the history of Jesus in the four gospels, and borrowed her servant's New Testament, in order to have both books open before her." These two novels, nearly plotless, attempt a psychological study of the process of conversion, concentrating on the changes that occur during the heroine's act of reading: "The detail of the effects which had been produced on Maria's mind by different passages of scripture, must surely interest both Christians and Jews."[56]

The last stage of each heroine's illness turns her into a quasi-missionary. Leila Ada distributes Bibles from her deathbed to different family members and finally harvests the fruit of her death in the conversion of her father. Her final request, that her father believe in Jesus, is fulfilled when he declares his conversion while receiving the Bible that has sustained her through her illness. This book, which is typically seen as prohibited—"a fearful curse rests upon the reading of it"—now circulates freely, even excessively, throughout the household.[57] In a similar vein, Maria exemplifies the idea that the proof of one's own conversion was realized in nothing less than the desire to evangelize the globe: "Maria's interest was so much excited for the circulation of the Hebrew scriptures, and for the support of missionaries sent to her scattered and dispersed people, that she would frequently urge her friend to use every effort to increase the number of subscribers to the Jewish societies." Such a passage, based on a central idea of the culture of conversion illustrated in *Robinson Crusoe* when the hero's conversion seems sealed in his conversion of Friday, is expressed in these words in *The Converted Jewess:* "An early proof of the *reality* of conversion is given, in the persevering desire to bring those who are *near,* and afterward those afar off, to behold his salvation. Such was the missionary spirit exemplified by Maria to her last hour."[58]

Miriam; or, the Power of Truth: A Jewish Tale, though not masquerading as a memoir, bases its story on fact: an article in a magazine that records a daughter on her deathbed calling for the conversion of her Jewish father. The author shapes this article into a tale that, like *Leila Ada,* focuses on a widowed father and an only child. One critical sign of the translation of the memoir into the novel is this location of a woman at the center of the conversionist plot. This places the conversionist novel in a specific literary tradition: in *The Jew of Malta* and *The Merchant of Venice* there is a widowed Jewish father and a sole daughter, and in both texts the daughter converts to Christianity. But the location of the Jewish daughter at the center of these novelistic plots also points to a central feature of the missionary efforts to the Jews in the nineteenth century. First, it reveals the conversionists' view of the docility of the (Jewish) woman, her special vulnerability to Christian proselytism (a subject to be discussed later in this study). Second, it underlines the conversionists' claim that the Jewish woman is a particularly oppressed member of the Jewish community, in need of special liberation. This oppression is consistently recorded through a kind of shorthand by quoting a specific prayer spoken by the Jewish man. In Mills's *The British Jews* (1853), for example, in the chapter "The Jewess," we hear of the prayer the Jewish man repeats daily, "Blessed art thou, O Lord our God, King of the universe, who hast not made me a woman." This prayer, which is also cited in such revisionist novels as *Harrington* and *Daniel Deronda*, became for the conversionists the chief evidence of their claim that "Jewesses . . . were deplorably neglected by their own people. Judaism, especially rabbinism, tended to their degradation and contempt." In *Miriam* we hear a buried reference to this prayer—the Jewish woman's "sex is considered amongst the Jews a degradation, rather than a blessing"—while in *Emma de Lissau,* the sequel to *Sophia de Lissau,* the general condition of the Jewish woman is described: "The Jewish females of that day were . . . almost totally uninstructed, and sunk in mental debasement." Hence the entreaty of one of the memoirists: "Oh, that some of my dear Christian friends would but become missionaries to Jewesses."[59]

As if to rescue the "uninstructed" Jewish woman from her "mental debasement," the conversionist novel centered on her education, which is seen as nothing more than her study of Scripture. Miriam begins reading the New Testament, like Leila Ada, to acquire "proofs of the dreadful mistake which the Christians make." But soon this desire includes the additional purpose of proselytism, in another of those reversals of majority history—the Jew seems intent on converting the Christian: "I want to convince Helen that our Scriptures are divinely authorised . . . to aid her conversion." But Miriam's proselytism of Helen, one of her neighbors, in fact begins the dismantling of Miriam's own faith, because in trying to explain her religion she became "puzzled amid the intricacies and contradictions of the Talmud."[60] In the logocentric world of the conversionist novel, "the small plain bible" is pitted against the massive Talmud in a battle for the heroine's soul. In *Emma de Lissau,* where we learn that "the book is so small that you may easily conceal it," the Bible literally lies at the heart of the young convert; after accidentally finding "the small volume" in her grandfather's library, hidden behind some large books, Emma alternately conceals it in her chamber, in her mattress, and finally on her person—"she wore the precious parcel in her bosom."[61] In such scenes the humbleness of the small volume is contrasted to the magnitude of its power; the small Bible is the grand instrument of conversion, imbibed by the young proselyte, a very part of her new being.

The tale of Miriam's conversion is framed by the Romantic setting of a rural village, where she observes the happy life of the Christian cottagers who pose such a contrast to the dark and lonely life she leads with her father. The process of her conversion begins when she witnesses the succeeding illnesses of two young women, from which she brings away the moral of so many conversionist novels: "She had seen Christianity tranquilise the soul." Her movement from the error of Judaism to the truth of Christianity is then cast in the form of humbling the Jew's pride, when the ideologies of Christianity and Romanticism seem to blend: "the poorest child in Glencairn is more advanced in christian knowledge than the proud and learned daughter of Imlah—more meet to enter heaven in its infant simplicity, than I with all my unavailing talents."[62] Like the servant's Bible that teaches the Jewish master, here the uneducated cottage child teaches the learned Jew a lesson. And in *Emma de Lissau* we find another version of this idea when the young proselyte seems to defeat the learned rabbi in a religious disputation: "Emma annoyed and disconcerted this learned and proud Pharisee, who was actually more than once at a loss to reply to the plain, but searching questions of this despised, illiterate girl, who had not yet attained the twelfth year of her age!"[63] The child is father to the man; the servant to the master; the small volume to the large—these are the paradoxes that romanticize and fictionalize the conflict between Christian and Jew. In each case the vulnerable and humble voice of the Christian exposes the formidable—though essentially illegitimate—power of the proud Jew, in what amounts to a reinvention of the power dynamics of the Jew and the Christian in nineteenth-century Protestant England.

Miriam's illness becomes the catalyst for her conversion as well as her father's. The daughter dies, sacrificed, it seems, to convert her father, so that while the daughter is the center of such tales, the conversion of the intransigent Jewish father sometimes seems the final goal of the plot. The daughter's immobilization from illness, made final in her death, strikingly contrasts with the father's final empowerment in the missionary's far-reaching journey; he leaves England for Germany in an expedition to convert his former coreligionists—that is, "as a *christian missionary,* to preach and to teach the very gospel which he had once denied and reviled"[64]—and ends by bringing the word of God to such places as Syria, Palestine, and Turkey.

The novels I have discussed are all set in England, but the conversionist novel was sometimes placed in lands as exotic to the English reader as those to which Miriam's father travels, for the Evangelical Revival was determined to evangelize the globe. In *Julamerk; or, The Converted Jewess*, a novel set in Assyria, we find that a change in setting does not alter the central themes, just as the subtitle does not neglect to announce the text's central ideology. Isaac, *Julamerk*'s Christian hero, saves the life of the Jewish maiden at least three times, but to complete his role of "deliverer," "both of spirit and of condition," he seeks Zoraide's conversion. His desire for her conversion, however, is set against the other conversionist plots in the novel: the text excoriates a Roman Catholic missionary's "efforts to add nominal members to the Papal Church, by force and cruelty," while "the cruel religion of the false Prophet" is criticized when Zoraide, stolen from her father, is threatened with "forced submission to the Mahometan religion," before being saved again by her Christian champion. Only Isaac, who represents reformed Christianity, is made to acknowledge "that true conversion is not the work of man, and that the Lord is never at a loss for instruments to effect His purposes of grace."[65]

Nonetheless, while Zoraide secretly falls in love with Isaac, all he can think of is "seeing her a sincere disciple of that faith which can rob the grave of its victory, and deprive death of its sting." Such a formulation introduces the ultimate topos of the conversionist novel, a long illness and the eventual death of the young Jewish proselyte to Christianity. The heroine's debilitating illness prepares her for her bodiless function in the novel, the demonstration that death has no sting for the Christian. After fortuitously discovering a copy of the New Testament, a "forbidden book" on whose words her eyes are "riveted," Zoraide begins a careful study of the Gospel at the same time that her health worsens. The relationship between body and spirit during the conversion of these heroines is made clear: "Zoraide's increased bodily weakness, and the brightening of her spiritual hopes,"[66] develop apace.

The ultimate function of disembodying the Jewish heroine is revealed in the novel's climax. In *Julamerk*, the conversion and death of the Jewish heroine coincides with the climax of the traditional novelistic plot, the happy Christian marriages of Isaac and Zuleika, and Helena (Isaac's sister) and Paul. The wedding of the young Christians is located literally at the sickbed of Zoraide, whose death is the climax of her conversion, timed by her to coincide with the wedding of the young Christians: "I am dying, I shall not see to-morrow's sun. But I would see Zuleika become Isaac's wife, before I go hence. Forgive my importunity. . . . Could the ceremony be hastened?" The erasure and disembodiment of the Jewish woman through her death seems incorporated into the Christian marriage ceremony and its promise of Christian propagation: "Isaac and Zuleika were now husband and wife; and it seemed that Zoraide had nothing more to do in this world but to give them her parting blessing, and commend her soul into the hands of her Creator and Redeemer." In her illness, which is the path to her spiritual transformation, the "beauteous daughter of Israel"[67] is robbed of all physical beauty, all erotic allure, so that her conversion, instead of making her available for Christian marriage, simply equips her to die peacefully after fulfilling her role as spectator at the marriage she herself wanted with Isaac. While conversion historically was offered to the Jews as the alternative to banishment from such countries as England and Spain, here its deepest ideological meaning is revealed: conversion is nothing more than a masked form of banishment so radical that death is its clearest analogue (figure 2).

The converted Jewish heroine, allowed no role in the newly configured Christian community, is in effect sent into exile, banished to the Christian heaven where her disembodied spirit observes the happy Christian spouses. In the novel's last paragraph "the spirit of Zoraide" looks down on the Christian household and sees her replacement—her embodiment—represented twice. First, there is Zuleika, the wife that Zoraide had hoped to be. But in a more suggestive substitution, Zoraide is the name given to one of the children born to the couples whose weddings she blessed. By dying instead of marrying, Zoraide has been excluded from a role in propagating the Christian community. But now, through her namesake, she is given an entirely figural or symbolic role in this propagation. She is allowed to enter the Christian community only after she is reborn bodily (not just spiritually) as a Christian, in the form of the daughter of Helena and Paul, "the little Zoraide." Moreover, in an attempt to erase all traces of the Jewishness of the first Zoraide, the narrative engineers the conversion of her formerly pious Jewish parents; this is the propagation of the spirit. Having changed their faith, Zoraide's parents now seem to change

"Helena, do not weep for me. It is all dim now around me, but it is bright and clear in heaven."

Figure 2. The Jewish heroine, newly converted and about to die, and her chief proselytizer, newly married. Frontispiece, *Julamerk; or, The Converted Jewess* (London: Ward, Lock, and Tyler, n.d.).

their family, to live in an entirely symbolic order: "to Paul and Helena they were parents in kindness and affection. But the little Zoraide was the chief object of their devotion, and on her they lavished all the fondness that once was centred in their own lost child." Zoraide, then, is reinstated in the household through her namesake, in a kind of mysterious and vital nominalism, and the Jewish parents become parents to a Christian (grand)daughter. All of them now form part of "a happy and a united *Christian household.*"[68]

There were some conversionist novels whose plots centered on the conversion of a Jewish man rather than a Jewish woman. One of the most popular, *Judah's Lion,* was written by Charlotte Elizabeth, one of "the great Evangelical propagandists."[69] Reissued almost yearly in the 1840s, and intermittently between 1850 and 1880, *Judah's Lion* has as its hero an English Jew who defines himself as more English than Jewish and who sees his Jewish identity as standing in the way of his ambitions. Charlotte Elizabeth's proselytism is aimed at the modern, assimilated Jewish man without a traditional education in Judaism, grateful for the liberty he enjoys in England, but disappointed by his exclusion from full participation in English life because he is not a Christian. The Jewish hero of *Judah's Lion* explains: "I am so thoroughly the Englishman that I know of no country preferable to that in which I was born—no distinction greater than the citizenship of her great metropolis; all the privileges of which I hope one day to enjoy, when Parliament has done away with the obstacles that now encumber our path."[70]

While such a speech seems to advocate lifting the civil and political disabilities from which the English Jews of the 1840s suffered, the novel's plot suggests another alternative: conversion. And the English public was certainly well-acquainted with the power of conversion in the 1840s through the example of Benjamin Disraeli, a converted Jew who had been elected a member of Parliament for Shrewsbury two years before the publication of *Judah's Lion.* The hero's education in *Judah's Lion* seems tailored to fit him for something like Disraeli's career, which would have been impossible without his conversion, that is, "to fit him for legislative and other functions of public life, where national peculiarities would be laid aside; or rather his nationality as a Jew altogether merged in his English citizenship."[71] It is toward the English Jew with such aspirations that *Judah's Lion* is aimed.

From the beginning we learn that it was Alick's "chief glory to be an Englishman." The Jewish hero's praise of England is part of a conventional rhetoric that based the ideology of conversion on a kind of contradiction: the Jew who loves tolerant England can become more fully English only by converting. So the literature of Jewish conversion typically offers a tribute to "free, happy England," in effect prompting the Jews to pay their full debt of gratitude to England by converting to the Church of England, and making clear that the conversion of the Jews was a nationalist project. The heroine of *Emma de Lissau,* for example, completes a journey to various countries in Europe and beyond only to acknowledge herself as "a native of happy England, that favoured land of Gospel light, and generous toleration." In *The Russo-Polish Jew: A Narrative of Conversion,* the memoirist finds England a kind of haven after many years of wandering: "I am very thankful that I am in England; the English people, I think, are the best people I ever saw in my life. . . . May God bless the Queen of England, and all the English people, where I hope to remain as long as I live; for I would much rather live in England than in Russia, Germany, Poland, Austria, or anywhere else." In *Miriam; or, the Power of Truth* we hear of "England where everyone possesses an equal right of independence." In short, tolerant England becomes the site where the Jew may "freely" choose to convert. This means that England is a land free of the forced conversion that, for example, threatens the Jew in *Julamerk* as well as in *Judah's Lion,* which records in a subplot the story of "a dear young Jew . . . shut up in a strong place by some monks, to make him turn Romanist."[72]

Like so much English conversionist literature, *Judah's Lion* sets out to distinguish between the proselytism of Roman Catholicism and Protestantism, a distinction that in the end is used as evidence of the peculiar tolerance of England above all nations. A critical concern of this literature centers on the idea that "Jews do not know the difference between Papists and Scriptural Christians." Joseph Wolff, for example, who was born in a German Catholic village and grew up "Without knowing any distinction between the Protestant and Catholic denominations," converted to Roman Catholicism before later converting to Protestantism. Both in the conversionist memoir and the conversionist novel, a turning point occurs when the Jewish proselyte makes the critical discovery of the difference between Roman Catholicism and Protestantism. In fact, the Jew's view of

Roman Catholicism almost prevents any further interest in Christianity. In the words of one memoirist: "It seemed to me impossible that Christianity should be true, simply from the observation of the practice of Roman Catholics." Similarly, in *Judah's Lion,* Alick is so repulsed by the practices of Roman Catholicism that his conversion to Christianity is temporarily blocked: "this idol-worship among Christians was a continual check on his warm feelings." According to the English missions to the Jews, the proselytization of the Jews had failed historically because it had been conducted under the aegis of Roman Catholicism: "We cannot wonder that Jewish conversions have been comparatively few. . . . In Popish countries he has seen Christianity mixed up with idolatry." Moreover, England in particular becomes the nation in which the Jew can discover the distinction between true Christianity and Roman Catholicism: "We have had intercourse with Jews from all parts of Europe, and have never met with one who did not express his admiration of this land of freedom, but, on the contrary, was astonished at the vast contrast between Great Britain and all other European countries. Elsewhere the Jew has to endure the hatred and taunts of that cruel and bigoted system Roman Catholicism . . . ; but here, in happy England, for the first time he comes into contact with the genial spirit of *true Christianity.*"[73]

In many ways *Judah's Lion* functions as a kind of guidebook to the strategies by which the Jew can be painlessly converted to Protestantism. We may be surprised to find that the person who begins Alick's conversion does so by encouraging him, at least at first, to deepen his Judaism. Gordon, the gunner on the ship that is taking Alick to the land of his forefathers, hopes that "the Lord were pleased to make him [Alick] indeed a Jew." After all, as Gordon tells Alick, "Sir, I owe to your people more than my life: I owe to them this book, the writings of Moses and the prophets, who were all Jews." In short, the only true path to Christianity is through Judaism, while an immersion in Judaism leads logically to Christianity. Gordon does not make the mistake of believing that "in becoming a Christian a man must cease to be a Jew." And Gordon's strategy succeeds with Alick: "He had begun to think that Christianity—such as it appeared in Gordon—was a refined and elevated species of Judaism, and under this impression he was prepared to read the New Testament with an unprejudiced, inquiring mind." In fact, the potential Jewish convert to Christianity is invited not to apostasize but to triple his Judaic credentials:

"a Jew who embraces Christianity is three times a Jew. An Israelite according to the flesh, an Israelite according to the faith, and an Israelite according to the territorial promise." Once fully converted, Alick repeats the lesson he has learned: "Renounce Judaism? Never. Jesus never disowned it"; "Becoming a Christian, do I cease to be a Jew? God forbid."[74] Once again we see the way in which conversion is represented not as a radical leap into the new, or a turning away from the old, but as a kind of completion, or refinement, of one's religious education, a new stage in one's religious development.

At the same time, the conversion process does require the humbling of the Jew in a paradigm we have seen before; the modern, urbane Jew submits to the instruction of a young Protestant child. The fictitious portrait in *Judah's Lion* of Charley, the child who wants to be "a missionary to the poor dear Jews,"[75] is based on "a deaf and dumb" child whose unaccountable love of the Jews is described by Charlotte Elizabeth in her *Personal Recollections*. Having explained in detail her conversion of this child, she seems surprised when he tells her, " 'Jesus Christ love poor Jew; Jew soon love Jesus Christ.' When speaking of them, he would look very tender and sorrowful, moving his head slowly from side to side, and his hand as if stroking some object in a caressing way." Charlotte Elizabeth recalls that the missionary Joseph Wolff, on meeting this child, wanted to take him to Palestine to instruct "the deaf and dumb" in Christianity.[76] In *Judah's Lion,* Charley is the "little Missionary" in Palestine who chastises the steadfast Jew and proselytizes the wavering Alick (figure 3). And the author dramatizes the potency of the young child to do the work of conversion when Alick places himself entirely in the child's hands: "the youth of his teacher threw him completely off his guard: and he longed to read the Bible with him." When Alick has determined "to gather all the information his little teacher could impart," the Jewish adult and the Christian child change places: the Jewish hero, in an act of self-mortification, remarks, "now I am no better than an overgrown baby." Charley's patronization and co-optation of Alick are sounded every time the child speaks: "My own darling Jew, Jesus Christ loves you." Charley sees nothing about Alick except his Jewish identity, even referring to him as "Mr. Jew," so that the child's words of apparent affection—"you love of a Jew!"—do not simply cloy, they virtually allegorize Alick out of existence. For the conversionist, the modern Jew is nothing more than a type of "God's ancient

"He is your King for all that!"—P. 98.

Figure 3. From Charlotte Elizabeth, *Judah's Lion* (London: Seeley, Jackson, and Halliday, 1872), facing p. 98.

people." For this reason it is impossible to divide the fervent love Charley exhibits for "the darling Jew"[77] from the deliberate strategy of proselytism, especially when we realize that there was a body of conversionist literature produced specifically for young children like Charley, counseling them on the usefulness of kindness in the work of converting Jews. The Christian child was taught, "If you wish to gain a Jew, *treat him as a brother.*"[78]

Judah's Lion ends in the land of "God's ancient people," as if to return Alick ("Mr. Jew") to the world of Scripture from which the ideology of conversion refuses to release him. His conversion complete, Alick calls on his fellow English Christians to realize a central tenet of millenarian discourse, the fulfillment of the scriptural prophecy of the restoration of the Jews to Palestine. Alick's speech is given "under the proud standard of England" because this symbol has been designated to mark the shared destinies of Israel and England: "the arms of England contained only two lions, until our Richard the first added a third, after his conquest in Palestine, and that third lion he probably adopted as the well-known standard of the country where his greatest exploits were performed."[79] In effect, Alick is calling on England to embark on another crusade in Palestine, to restore the Jews to their homeland as part of the general conversion of all the nations to Christ.

In *Judah's Lion* the projects of conversionism, nationalism, and imperialism meet when the traditional millenarian doctrine of the restoration of the Jews is joined to a plan of English colonial expansion. Alick plans the spiritual and commercial resettlement of Palestine: "I have explored the country, with a view to testing its [Palestine's] present capabilities of repaying such labour and capital as might be bestowed on it. . . . I assert, that Judea . . . is even now prepared to yield a thousand-fold return to the patient cultivator. . . . [T]he path opens before us, for restoring, according to the sure word of prophecy, the dispersed of Judah to their inheritance." England's (religious and imperialist) supremacy over the other nations of the world depends finally on England's fulfillment of scriptural prophecy—that is, on the restoration and conversion of the Jews: "I love England, I desire to see her noble lion supreme among the nations; and to insure this, I would see him ever closely allied to the Lion of Judah."[80]

In short, in nineteenth-century England the proselytization of the Jews was articulated as a nationalist project. The volume celebrating the jubilee of the British Society for the Propagation of the Gospel among the Jews opens with an entreaty that the queen speak the following words: "It is my heart's desire . . . that all my Christian subjects, and all other Christians throughout the world, would begin from now to use all the means in their power to lead the Jews to CHRIST." On the same page is a portrait of the duke of Kent and the following poem:

> Our Queen's beloved sire, whose lofty views,
> Evinced compassion for the outcast Jews;
> And—not unmindful of the feeling shown,
> God sets His royal race upon earth's highest throne![81]

England's claim to be the "royal race" among all others at the close of the nineteenth century is referred back to a critical moment in the institutionalization of the conversion of the Jews at the century's start: the duke of Kent laid the foundation stone of the London Society's Episcopal chapel in 1813. In this way the extraordinary power and prestige that England achieved during the nineteenth century is explained as God's reward for England's "compassion for the outcast Jews"—that is, for England's persistent attempt at Jewish conversion.

The shadow that hovered over the project of Jewish conversion was the questionable legitimacy of the Jewish converts themselves—a shadow that, after the public attacks on the London Society, had to be acknowledged even by the conversionists. A novel like *Judah's Lion* therefore must itself acknowledge this central question: "Some people indeed doubt whether a real conversion from Judaism ever takes place." Early in the novel Alick explains that the convert was often viewed not as a Christian but as a Jew who had converted: "I should not mind turning Christian to get rid of the stigma; but then they would call me 'a converted Jew,' which is worse still."[82] In *The Converted Jewess: A Memoir of Maria* — a Jewish character argues that "it was a delusion to believe that a Jew was ever really converted to Christianity, for those who professed it did so from hypocritical motives, either to gain money, or an advantageous situation."[83]

The institution of conversion and the Jewish convert became popular subjects of mockery and critique in England. The process of conversion was shown graphically as the forcible feeding of pork to the Jew (figures 4 and 5), while the motive for the Jew's conversion was pictured as no more than his succumbing to the erotic allure of a Christian woman (figures 6 and 7). Among the most scalding critiques were those parodic revisions of the conventional memoir in which a Jew piously converts to Christianity. When Lewis Way attempted to narrate the story of Frey's conversion in saintly terms—"An obscure and unknown individual of the Jewish nation is led in a foreign land to make a profession of Christianity"—a critic was sure to come along to rewrite the account: "An obscure foreign Jew professing Christianity, who, after failing in an attempt to qualify himself as a strolling player, had served his time as a shoemaker, disgusted with manual labour, suddenly felt an inclination to become a Missionary," and so on.[84] Similarly, when the "Narrative of the Conversion of Mr. Benjamin Nehemiah Solomon, A Polish Rabbi" appeared, describing how "I was directed by the Lord . . . unto this land, which flows with spiritual milk and honey," we soon find its revision: "it was playing *at cards*, where he lost nearly two hundred ducats . . . , that caused him to leave his native land." The revisionary account proceeds with a mock-heroic story that encapsulates the critique of the Jewish convert: "he used to travel with his brother-in-law, who was here lately, and who was also converted, and after getting a new suit of clothes, a white beaver hat, and a few pounds, off he went again to Poland."[85]

Conversionist novels like *Judah's Lion* were subject to similar revision. In *The House of Bondage*, for example, when Miss Greenway, who "had a sort of craze about the Jews; not that she understood much about them," hosts a meeting of the Zion Circle, the members "read by turns 'Judah's Lion,' by the late Charlotte Elizabeth." When Miss Greenway reports on the group's accomplishments, her account of the restoration of the Jews to Palestine is markedly different from Charlotte Elizabeth's:

Miss Greenway read aloud some account of their special mission, and stated how many Jews have been converted and taken back to Palestine at the society's expense, and how it was intended by the Bradfield Branch to set up certain Jews in business in what was supposed to be the High-street of Jerusalem. Whenever the Zion Society converted a Jew, they at once took measures to restore him to his own country and to set him up in business in Jerusalem or Jericho, or in any other sacred place he chose. Half-a-dozen or more

Jews had actually set out, with merchandise and capital, for the Holy
Land, but only one was satisfactorily reported as having arrived and
opened shop in some queer street with an unpronounceable name in
the very heart of Jerusalem. The others had loitered by the way, and
there was good reason to believe that one had tarried somewhere in
Turkey and became a Mussulman.[86]

In such a passage the author demonstrates how the millenarian doctrine
of the restoration of the Jews had become merely a base commercial effort
at the center of which lies the spurious Jewish convert. The apparently
limitless convertibility of the Jew became a central topos of critiques

Figure 4. A mock-conversion of a Jew that satirically recalls the famous medieval
theological disputations between Christians and Jews, and the conversion of Jews
through the threat of bodily harm. Published in 1764 by Henry Roberts. There is
a later issue dated 1785, published by W. Hinton. Courtesy of the Library of the
Jewish Theological Seminary of America.

Figure 5. A satire on the pressure exerted on Jews to convert, recalling the trial of Rebecca in *Ivanhoe* while referring to the recent rejection of David Salomons as alderman by the Court of Aldermen. Published by C. J. Grant, 1836. Courtesy of the Library of the Jewish Theological Seminary of America.

aimed at the conversionist societies, which a Jewish writer claimed were "spending their money on persons to whom religion is nothing but a matter of pounds, shillings, and pence—who are Jews to-day, call themselves Christians to-morrow, in the prospect of certain advantages, and, for a few shillings more, would turn Mahommedans the day after!"[87]

The JEW RABBI turn'd to a CHRISTIAN

Figure 6. The Jew's purchase of the Christian courtesan. Published by W. Humphrey, 1773. There is an earlier issue dated 1772, published by F. Adams. Courtesy of the Library of the Jewish Theological Seminary of America.

A Jew turning to a Christian.

Figure 7. Another example of the popular eighteenth- and nineteenth-century subject, a Jewish man's attraction to a Christian woman staged as a kind of conversion. Anonymous. Courtesy of the Library of the Jewish Theological Seminary of America.

The Jewish convert became the center of the debate over the missions to the Jews, the object at once of the bitter cynicism of the anticonversionists and the fawning love of the conversionists. For, as the conversionists themselves had to admit: "The converted Jew is still a character but little understood—it is either a suspected or an imposing name,—excessively suspected, or unduly venerated."[88] In *Jewish Perseverance*, an autobiography entitled to signal itself as a kind of countergenre in opposition to the memoir of the Jewish convert, a Jewish memoirist steadfast to his faith calls into question the very idea of Jewish conversion, arguing that the London Society "attempts to baptize—for we cannot well call it to convert—a few straggling Jews." In this way the word "conversion" is bracketed, so that one can speak only of "so-called Jewish converts."[89] The following pages turn to this contested figure of the Jewish convert, and to the process rightly or wrongly termed conversion, in an attempt to explain how the ideology of conversion influenced a wide variety of discourses in nineteenth-century England.

2

Writing English Comedy: "Patronizing Shylock"

In 1817 Maria Edgeworth published *Harrington* as an act of personal "atonement" and "reparation." The year before she had received a letter from Rachel Mordecai, an American Jew who wrote to complain of an anti-Semitic portrait in *The Absentee* (1812).[1] In this local and personal incident between a Christian author and a Jewish reader the shape of an important tradition of English literature was radically altered. Edgeworth was not the first to give us Jewish portraits in the novel (Daniel Defoe and Samuel Richardson had already done that), nor was she the first to draw sympathetic Jewish portraits (Richard Cumberland had already done that for the drama, Tobias Smollett for the novel).[2] *Harrington* was the first work in English to inquire into the nature of the representation of Jewish identity, the first not only to record how and why the English literary tradition was especially susceptible to Jewish stereotypes, but the first to invent the forms by which such stereotypes could be inspected and perhaps overturned. With such claims I mean to challenge a critical position accepted for several decades, namely, that the tradition of Jewish portraiture in English literature is consistently naive and unselfconscious in its production of stereotypes.[3]

It was Edgeworth's deeply personal motive in writing *Harrington* that made possible the special self-reflexive quality that informs her novel. In the act of reviewing her role as a reader and a writer of anti-Semitic portraits, she was able to recognize a tradition of discourse that she had at once inherited and perpetuated. And only by recognizing such a tradition was she able both to subvert it in *Harrington* and to articulate for future writers the way to move beyond it. In short, she boldly turned her personal self-examination into a cultural critique: she diagnosed a disorder in "the imaginations of the good people of England" (148),[4] and in so doing she issued a challenge and founded a revisionary tradition. In *Harrington,* Edgeworth inquires into the trials that the English imagination must undergo if it is to exorcise the powerful figure of Shylock and thereby issues a challenge taken up in subsequent novels (including *Ivanhoe, Our Mutual Friend, Daniel Deronda,* and *Ulysses*): the revisionist novel of Jewish identity attempts to articulate, investigate, and subvert *The Merchant of Venice*'s function as the English mastertext for representing "the Jew."

But this novelistic tradition also investigates what I am claiming is the oldest and most persistent means of representing the Jew, both inside and outside England, in ancient as well as modern times: the Jew as a figure of conversion. The revisionist novel of Jewish identity explores and exposes the ideology of conversion, both as a literary strategy and as a cultural institution. Comic theory, reducing conversion to a literary trope, has tried to aestheticize the idea of conversion, to depoliticize it, to mask its history as a cultural institution. But the figure of the Jew as convert radicalizes and ironizes the trope of conversion by exposing the ideological juncture at which comic form and Christian culture meet.

Edgeworth's point of departure is to acknowledge "the indisputable authority of *printed books*" (13) and thereby to formulate the question of Jewish identity as a question of the *representation* of the Jew. In *Harrington* anti-Semitism is seen as a disease passed down from generation to generation through the medium of the printed word. Edgeworth's power to found a tradition from this formulation depends at least in part on her claim, taken up by subsequent novelists from Scott to Joyce, that *The Merchant of Venice* occupies a critical position in the English imagination and in the national character.[5] The simplest evidence for such a claim is the way in which Shakespeare's text invades the novel from *Harrington* to *Ulysses* as a sign of the play's indisputable authority; no portrait of a Jew can exist in English without reference to it, and the English imagination seems unable to free itself of Shakespeare's text. At the same time, the extraordinarily varied means by which Shakespeare's text invades the novel may suggest the capaciousness and subtlety not only of the invading, parasitic text, but of the host text; each invasion may in fact signal a deliberate introduction of the disorder in order to trap it and thereby master it. In other words, each trace of the play in the revisionist novel of

Jewish identity is an ambiguous sign of a battle of the books, part of a battle of mastery over the figure of the Jew. The history of this novelistic tradition needs to chart the strategies that succeeding novelists use in their attempt at once to recognize and to supersede Shakespeare's master text—that is, to chart the progress of the search for a cure for the disorder from which the English imagination suffers.

Edgeworth sets the scene for this kind of textual invasion by having *Harrington* take place at a special moment in history. While numerous historical markers in the novel (such as the Gordon Riots and the Jewish Naturalization Bill) illuminate the nature of "the Jewish question" in the second half of the eighteenth century, an event in *literary* history characterizes the national consciousness most powerfully for Edgeworth: Charles Macklin's brilliant revival of the role of Shylock, and his restoration of Shakespeare's text to the English stage.[6] When Harrington has difficulty locating a wealthy and accomplished Jewish gentleman he wishes to meet, Harrington's friend Lord Mowbray offers to "console me for the loss of my chance of seeing my Spanish Jew, by introducing me to the most celebrated Jew that ever appeared in England" (40). Mowbray takes Harrington to encounter Macklin's Shylock, so that the most celebrated Jew that ever appeared in England—nay, "in all Christendom, in the whole civilized world" (40)—is presented to Harrington as a substitute and replacement for the Jew Harrington sought. "[T]he real, original Jew of Venice" (40), who of course is only the figurative Jew, the Jew as representation, displaces the real Jew, Mr. Montenero: "I returned home full of the Jew of Venice" (42).

Shylock invades the text here by literally interrupting the plot, as if he walks out of the historical past, a digression whose powerful allusiveness derails the main plot line at least temporarily. Here, allusion is clothed in flesh and blood. Edgeworth's text gives us not simply a verbal cue to Shylock, but the character embodied in the actor who brings him alive on stage every night. Shylock's power to invade the plot of *Harrington* is matched by the power he seems to exert on the actor who plays him. Macklin, for example, is dissolved in the fictional character he plays, as if Shylock's power (according to the conventional anti-Semitic slur that claims the Jew is contaminating) parasitically invades the actor; Macklin becomes "Macklin, the honest Jew of Venice" (53) and "Macklin the Jew" (58). Jewish identity itself disappears, or is mysteriously relocated, as if it exists only behind a mask, only in a performance, only through a Christian mediation that confounds and absorbs it: Jewish identity exists somewhere in Macklin's performance of Shylock. The rebirth of Shylock on the stage functions as a historical marker of Edgeworth's point; Shylock perennially holds the English imagination in thrall, perennially mediates, regulates, and displaces Jewish identity for the English mind.

Harrington's use of Shylock as a fictitious master invention that preempts the "real" Jewish characters the author wants to introduce is duplicated in George Eliot's *Daniel Deronda,* when Daniel introduces Mirah to Mrs. Meyrick and her daughters. Not knowing how to introduce a Jew to these unworldly women, he can count on their having read *Ivanhoe* and consoles himself that they "would at once associate a lovely Jewess with Rebecca in 'Ivanhoe' " (*DD,* 235).[7] Mirah, then, has a secondary life, a belated existence, in relation to Scott's Rebecca, just as all Jews have a belated existence in relation to "the real, original Jew of Venice." Both in *Harrington* and *Daniel Deronda,* then, we meet examples of representation to the second power. A fictitious representation (Shylock and Rebecca) takes priority over another fictitious representation that is supposed to be real (Montenero and Mirah) in the world of the novel; and the prior fictitious representation assumes the power of the "original" and the "real." Priority in such a case signals both temporal priority (Shylock predates Montenero) and "signifying" priority (Shylock is the paradigm by which we understand and measure all other Jews). This technique of representation to the second power manages to call into question, in a particularly sophisticated way in the hands of such novelists as Edgeworth and Eliot, the very nature of representation, especially the representation of the racial Other. When Daniel Deronda reflects on "whether one oftener learns to love real objects through their representations or the representations through the real objects" (*DD,* 476), his comment functions as a gloss on Eliot's self-conscious handling of her role as a (belated) novelist of Jewish identity. In England, where the Jew is primarily a figure of the imagination and where Shylock holds the place of priority, do we learn to *hate* real Jews through their representations? And what would it mean to learn to *love* a real Jewish woman through Rebecca? With such questions this novelistic tradition explores, and ultimately seeks to control, the authority by which "printed books" construct paradigms that nurture racial hatred and perhaps even racial desire.

For this reason the central rhetorical strategy of the revisionist novel of Jewish identity is allusion. Each "new" novel that comes on the scene is imbedded with references to its predecessors, because each "new" novel inspects the representations of Jewish identity that precede it. By allusion I include the revisionist practice of recalling and reinventing the entire shape of earlier texts—the way in which in *Our Mutual Friend* and *Daniel Deronda* the education of the characters is staged as a conflict between love and money, where characters undergo their moral trials, or receive their rewards, in casket scenes that reinvent the famous casket scene in *The Merchant of Venice;* or the way in which in the final chapter of *Daniel Deronda* Eliot meticulously reworks the final chapter of *Ivanhoe,* so that Scott's love triangle (Rowena, Rebecca, Ivanhoe) is replaced by Eliot's (Mirah, Gwendolen, Daniel), while in both novels the rejected woman (the Jew in Scott's version, the Christian in Eliot's) offers a final parting memento to the married couple as the Jewish characters depart from England.

In *Harrington* allusion takes an especially complicated form because Edgeworth alludes both to her own former work and to a much larger tradition of Jewish portraiture. In this way Edgeworth is able to acknowledge that she is already a contributor to a tradition she now wishes to forswear and repudiate. In a remarkable passage Edgeworth takes responsibility for writing the kind of book that nurtures prejudice in the young child's mind. She admits this at the very moment when she is almost universally known, in England, the United States, and the Continent, not only for her tolerant pictures of the Irish, but for her immensely influential pedagogical works (coauthored with her father) and the celebrated *Moral Tales for Young People* (1801). Harrington recognizes that "in almost every work of fiction, I found them [Jews] represented as hateful beings; nay, even in modern tales of very late years, since I have come to man's estate, I have met with books by authors professing candour and toleration—books written expressly for the rising generation, called, if I mistake not, Moral Tales for Young People" (13). In *Harrington,* then, the strategy of allusion does not eschew self-allusion, even self-punishment. Late in the novel Edgeworth reveals covertly, in a dramatic scene between Harrington and his father, the proper punishment and penitence for her own earlier mistakes. Harrington forces his father to acknowledge that "your words were a libel upon Jews and Jewesses; and the most appropriate and approved punishment invented for the libeller is—to eat his own words" (200). Edgeworth conceives of *Harrington* as an act of reparation precisely insofar as she uses the novel to eat her former words.

The more typical form that allusion takes in the revisionist novel of Jewish identity suggests a similar kind of self-conscious irony, as if acknowledging the fact that writing about Jewish identity as a Christian means occupying a position outside the culture one attempts to represent. The point of departure for such a project is always the same: one must master those earlier texts that have presumed to represent Jewish identity. An ironic version of this kind of mastery is explicitly dramatized in *Harrington* when, to impress the Monteneros,

> Lord Mowbray appeared to be deeply interested and deeply read in every thing that had been written in their [the Jews'] favour. He rummaged over Tovey and Ockley; and "Priestley's Letters to the Jews," and "The Letters from certain Jews to M. de Voltaire," were books which he now continually quoted in conversation. . . . nor could he ever adequately extol Cumberland's benevolent "Jew," or Lessing's "Nathan the Wise." Quotations from one or the other were continually in readiness. . . . This I could also perceive to be an imitation of what he had seen *succeed* with me. (128)

In this passage Harrington condones his own mastery of such works but mocks Lord Mowbray's. As a reflection on Edgeworth's own project in *Harrington,* this passage is at once serious and self-mocking. Edgeworth seems to present her own credentials as a writer about Jewish identity at the same time that she is embarrassed at doing so. This is an anxiety that dominates perhaps the fullest representation of Jews by a non-Jewish writer in English literature, George Eliot's *Daniel Deronda,* and in part accounts for the massive learning that buttresses that novel. In any case, the pattern is founded here in *Harrington:* each new novel in this tradition acknowledges the earlier texts in the tradition, so that each new novel becomes a kind of storehouse of the materials necessary to write a Jewish story. By the time we get to *Daniel Deronda* and *Ulysses,* this particular practice of allusion becomes encyclopedic.

Harrington provides us with a special theoretical framework within which to explore the system of intertextual allusions by which Jewish identity is inscribed, transmitted, and recirculated. After meeting Macklin, Harrington's appetite to see the actor's celebrated Shylock is satisfied only when Mrs. Harrington promises to take her son "to patronize Shylock" (54). The phrase has the kind of resonance that I am suggesting is the hallmark of *Harrington,* managing at once to represent, literally and locally for Edgeworth's protagonist, the purchase of a theater ticket, but figuratively for the entire tradition of texts that reinvents Shylock, a specific but nonetheless suggestive intertextual transaction. To patronize Shylock—to protect, support, and favor him, whether in the act of patronage generally, or in the specific business transaction that makes us his customer—is what we do when we purchase a ticket to see him, or write a novel in which we uphold him (as Edgeworth did in *The Absentee,* where Mordicai follows in Shylock's footsteps by requiring "the bond or the body").[8] The specific economic meaning of the term "patronize" manages to place the entire history of allusions to Shylock within the context of the most patent stereotype that the novel of Jewish identity has to confront: the Jew as peddler, usurer, banker, and so on. And from one angle the idea of "patronizing Shylock" manages to maintain this stereotype; part of Shylock's power over us is made manifest by our still patronizing him, by the interest—economic and emotional—we periodically reinvest in his character. The bond from which Shylock refused to release Antonio has become the bond from which Shylock refuses to release the English imagination and the English pocketbook.

But the subversive uses to which Edgeworth puts this idea of "patronizing Shylock" reveal the Jew not as the originator and controller of such transactions but as the figure of value that Christian authors manipulate and exploit. During his first meeting with Harrington, Mr. Montenero explains how "[i]n the *true* story, from which Shakespeare took the plot of the Merchant of Venice, it was a Christian who acted the part of the Jew, and the Jew that of the Christian; it was a Christian who insisted upon having the pound of flesh from next the Jew's heart. But Shakespeare was right, as a dramatic poet, in reversing the characters" (66).[9] Instead of being the ur-text, *The Merchant of Venice* is already part of a tradition of intertexts, so that what we have inherited as the truth about Jew and Christian is exposed as merely a textual representation, and a textual "misrepresentation" (66) at that. The purely textual quality of these figures, Jew and Christian, is made apparent by Mr. Montenero's sophisticated intertextual argument that Shakespeare did not draw his characters or plot from life, but from another text, and what is more, that he drew falsely from the earlier text; it was his "business" to exploit the prejudices of his time—an exploitation that has "cost" (66) the Jews dearly: "it was his business, I acknowledge, to take advantage of the popular prejudice as a *power*" (66). In this view, Shakespeare is caught engaging in a business transaction in which the writer uses the Jew to his own advantage. In a crucial role reversal, Shakespeare becomes the extortionist Shylock—not only here, in Mr. Montenero's analysis, but in Stephen Dedalus's analysis a century later in *Ulysses:* "He [Shakespeare] drew Shylock out of his own long pocket. . . . He sued a fellowplayer for the price of a few bags of malt and exacted his pound of flesh in interest for every money lent."[10] Edgeworth and Joyce, then, imbed their novels not simply with allusions to Shakespeare's play, but with critics of that play who call into question the motives behind the representation of Jewish identity. And virtually anyone who profits from Shylock is seen as exploiting the role of the Jew (while masking his own economic motives behind the persona of Shylock), including the actor who plays the role of Shylock. Mowbray tells Harrington: "Macklin, the honest Jew of Venice, has got the pound, or whatever number of pounds he wanted to get from the manager's heart" (53).

Finally, the idea of patronizing Shylock calls to mind the history of the institution of patronage. The patron plays the role of "a defender before a court of justice," almost as if he or she is called on to play the role of Portia as the final arbiter of the conflict between Christian and Jew. But in the position of advocacy the patron is designated as a guardian of a foreign and displaced Other whose dependence on the patron is demeaning; a patron is "a citizen under whose protection a resident alien placed himself, and who transacted legal business for him and was responsible to the state for his conduct." Patronage itself is a complicated transaction; patrons give their protection "in return for certain services,"[11] and those writers who set out to authorize their own version of "the Jew" are always in danger of serving themselves, whether inadvertently or not, by patronizing Jewish identity.

The Primal Scene and the Return of the
Repressed in Harrington

Harrington at first appears to be no more than the record of a single, and singularly odd, case history—the story of a child who suffers through several stages of anti-Semitism. But Edgeworth's bold experiment uses a complicated psychological portrait of this deeply troubled child—that is, an investigation into the origins and development of a childhood neurosis—to attempt a cultural critique that questions religious and national values. Edgeworth manages this critique by implicating the national consciousness, and especially the writer's role in this consciousness, in her title character's disorder, a kind of "Jewish insanity" (43). The term "Jewish insanity" ambiguously identifies both the virulent form of the child's anti-Semitism and, after his "cure," what one might call his philo-Semitism, or what his family and friends view as his obsession with Jews, "the constancy" of his "Israelitish taste"; Harrington seems always, in the words of a longtime acquaintance, to be "intent upon a Jew" (39). The exaggerated poles of Harrington's feelings suggest that in either case the Jew functions purely as a figure of the imagination, even as a fetish, and that both of Harrington's responses, whether of dread or desire, are forms of "Jewish insanity."

In the powerful opening pages of *Harrington* the first-person narrator delineates the means by which he became, at six years of age, the "slave and . . . victim" (3) of his nursery maid. With its emphasis on the "history of the mental and corporeal ills of my childhood" (8), and specifically on the pathogenic effect of a critical scene of childhood, this opening is an early Romantic harbinger of Freud. In the narrator's declaration of the importance of the conjunction of "the science of morals and of medicine" (8), and in his apologetic and defensive encouragement that we will see "some connexion between these apparently puerile details and subjects of higher importance" (8), he justifies the mainstay of his entire project with the same tone that Freud used when he argued for the importance of early childhood impressions, their power to create a childhood neurosis, and their enduring effects later in life: "we must be content to begin at the beginning, if we would learn the history of our own mind; we must condescend to be even as little children, if we would discover or recollect those small causes which early influence the imagination, and afterwards become strong habits, prejudices, and passions" (9). What is especially remarkable in Edgeworth's enterprise is the attempt to record and to publish the origins of racial prejudice in a child, and to use this case history at once as a self-indictment and an indictment of her culture. In using the psychology of the individual to articulate the psychology of an entire nation or culture, Edgeworth anticipates the kind of study that Freud attempted first in *Totem and Taboo* (1913), when he applied the methods of psychoanalysis to a problem in *Völkerpsychologie*, and for the last time in *Moses and Monotheism* (1939), when the enterprise of *Völkerpsychologie* took as its subject the Jewish people, in a work whose initial generic description (*The man Moses, an historical novel*)[12] makes its kinship with Edgeworth's novel all the more palpable.

In Edgeworth's hands the principles of late-eighteenth-century psychology, and especially the vocabulary of associationism, become the tools by which she records the primal scene in a case history of a child's (erotic) enslavement. Not surprisingly, the event on which she chooses to construct the primal scene bears a remarkable similarity to Wordsworth's description, in book 7 of *The Prelude,* of the wonderful but shocking experience of arriving in London—only for Harrington this occurs at age six. The opening paragraph relates the arrival through the narrator's explanation, in the language Edgeworth had learned from late-eighteenth-century psychology and poetry, of how "my senses had been excited, and almost exhausted, by the vast variety of objects that were new to me" (1). As in the most memorable moment in Wordsworth's London, the poet's encounter with the blind beggar, Harrington's imagination is seized by "the face and figure of an old man" (1); but unlike the blind beggar, this old man would have had little effect on the protagonist's mind if it were not for a mediating figure, the boy's nursery maid, Fowler. The boy's fleeting initial impression of the old man suggests "a good-natured countenance." But the nursery maid, unable to get the boy to bed, issues a threat that seizes his "fancy" with "terror": " 'If you don't come quietly this minute, Master Harrington,' said she, 'I'll call to Simon the Jew there,' pointing to him, 'and he shall come up and carry you away in his great bag' " (2). Fowler's action is chilling because we recognize in it a simple pedagogical act, grotesquely distorted. By pointing to the man, and giving him a name, especially a class-name, and finally attaching this name to a rapacious act, the maid produces in the boy's imagination an association of ideas (to use the terminology of David Hartley that so influenced Edgeworth and her father) that miseducates the child, while misrepresenting the old man and Jews in general. This act of naming, of classifying and libeling, is the first of various forms of anti-Semitism that the narrative will explore. Nonetheless, the special status of this scene is clear; it is the narrative's point of departure, and the fixing moment of Harrington's early life, the primal scene with which his mature life will be burdened.

Much of the power of the novel's opening scenes depends on the fact that Harrington, in the present telling of his tale, is actually breaking a prohibition against telling, a kind of taboo that emerges from the primal scene. After successfully embroidering the image of the rapacious Jew over a period of hours and days, Fowler manages to make the boy "promise that I would never tell any body the secret she had communicated"— namely, the secret acts by which Jews "steal poor children for the purpose of killing, crucifying, and sacrificing them" (2–3). But what she really hides, by sealing the child's lips, are the secret means by which she has nurtured racial terror in him. Fowler is the force of repression; she requires the oath of silence that hides her power and allows that power to grow in the child's unconscious and unspoken mind. With the ban of silence, the neurotic terror magnifies. At the same time, the narrative that we read becomes the most patent sign of Harrington's eventual recuperation and liberation.

As an etiology of the disease of racial terror, the narrative makes clear its own power to expose the processes by which such terror is born, nurtured, and eventually cured. The single moment that precedes the boy's seeing of the old-clothes man becomes, in this sense, an allegory by which the remainder of the narrative may be read. The first sense impression that the boy records on his London trip is the inexplicable appearance of stars of light in a quick succession, not far from his balcony. The eventual discovery of the lamplighter as the cause of this wonder leads the boy to experience "as much delight as philosopher ever enjoyed in discovering the cause of a new and grand phenomenon" (1). The second wonder the child experiences, and the one that shapes his later life—the figure of the Jew (that is, Fowler's use of this figure)—is subjected to the same scrutiny of cause and effect over the course of the entire narrative. It is in this sense that the entire narrative is meant to function as a demystification of the origins of prejudice and racial terror, whose secrets will be exposed (as in the example of the lamplighter) once the human cause behind an apparently inexplicable phenomenon is seen. To discover its human cause is to put to rout one of the leading ideas about racial hatred at the time, represented by Harrington's mother—namely, that racial hatred may be no more than a *"natural* antipathy" (6) behind which lies no social or cultural cause.[13]

The boy's promise never to tell is represented in a special terminology that deepens, from the start, the Jewish theme in this novel: the promise is "extorted" (3) from the boy. In other words, the promise is not simply *about* Jews, but is secured through an act that takes the form of a conventional anti-Semitic stereotype, only here it is Fowler, the anti-Semite, who is the extortionist, the Shylock who exacts an excessive price for the bond. Moreover, Edgeworth moves the trademark of anti-Semitic literature— the scene of business transaction and exchange—to the beginning of the novel, placing the Jew outside this scene. In other words, while the initial social experience of *Harrington* is centered on a transaction—the enslavement and extortion of a child—Edgeworth shows how the Jew is used, purely as a figure, in such a transaction. In fact, the picture that Fowler gives of the Jew in order to terrorize the child—she tells him "stories of Jews who had been known to steal poor children" (2)—suggests her own enslavement and extortion of Harrington and her profound alienation of the child from his parents and the rest of the household. The "Jew," in this sense, is literally no more than an extension of her own acts and her own motives.

Once the child's terror (but not its cause) becomes known to his parents, different forms of anti-Semitism are carefully articulated within the family along the lines of gender. The child's life is shuttled between his mother's and his father's radically different "cures" for his disorder. Both parents are unable to account for their child's sudden change in temper, his sleeplessness, his fits of terror, his tantrums, all of which seize the household with the same inexplicable suddenness they exert in that paradigm of case histories, the case of the Wolf Man—only in *Harrington* no one suspects the nursery maid as the culprit. Harrington's mother, eventually getting a half-confession out of her son (only the reader of *Harrington* knows the entire story), discovers Jews (and not Fowler) as the source of her son's disorder. She and her physician take his terror of Jews as "the genuine temperament of genius" (6), and the boy, who becomes a replica of his mother—"a woman of weak health, delicate nerves, and a kind of morbid sensibility" (6)—is made to "exhibit" (6) his fears to family friends and the fashionable world of London.

The father enters the narrative suddenly in order to restore his son's manhood. Absent from the scene of enslavement and the narrative's opening chapters, the ghostly father—"My father—for all this time, though I have never mentioned him, I had a father living"—appears with the decree that the boy "should be taken out of the hands of the women" (11). Scorning what he calls "the whole *female* doctrine . . . of sympathies and antipathies," and accusing the women of "making . . . a Miss Molly of his boy" (11), the father repossesses the child at the same time that he takes charge of his gender: it is the father's job "to make a man of me" (12). This takes the form of changing the boy's (feminine) terror of Jews to his (masculine) violence against them. Edgeworth shows us two radically different forms of behavior toward Jews, but she nonetheless indicts both as forms of anti-Semitism. Now under the influence of his father, Harrington reports that "the Jews were represented to me as the lowest, meanest, vilest of mankind, and a conversion of fear into contempt was partially effected in my mind," until finally "fear and contempt" became "hatred" (14)—until the acquisition of "manly ideas" (12) was complete. Needless to say, the father succeeds not in curing his child's disorder but in advancing it to a different, even more noxious, stage.

For the fullest understanding of the relation between the different stages of Harrington's anti-Semitism and his sexual identity, we must turn to the way in which *Harrington* recalls and revises *The Merchant of Venice*. At this point it is enough to recall that Shylock's celebrated knife-whetting and his threat of the pound of flesh (both mentioned in *Harrington*) represent the Jew as a threat to Christian male identity and as an obstacle to the happy Christian nuptials in Shakespeare's play. In *Harrington*, in the primal scene of the child's abuse, the nursery maid uses the figure of the Jew to reduce the boy to a "Miss Molly" who can barely leave his bed because of the nervous disorder that is specifically marked as feminine. It remains to be seen how the question of Harrington's manhood succeeds in linking the primal scene at the beginning to the marriage plot at the end—and thereby succeeds in linking the plot of *Harrington* to the plot of *The Merchant of Venice*.

Both Shakespeare and Edgeworth employ the traditional marriage plot of comedy in which the suitor undergoes a series of trials before winning the woman's (or heiress's) hand. But *Harrington* takes the Christian love plot at the center of Shakespeare's play and gives it to the Jewish characters. Portia and her father become, in Edgeworth's revision, Berenice and Mr. Montenero. In both cases the father protects his rich daughter from fortune hunters at the same time that he finds her a husband who values her properly. But now the Jew, not the Christian, is the teacher of value, testing which suitor will choose lead over gold, will take his daughter "at all hazards" (202), in a reprise of the lead casket's message, "Who chooseth me must give and hazard all he hath."[14]

The obvious obstacle to the hero's success, both in *The Merchant of Venice* and *Harrington,* has hidden behind it other obstacles, some of which the hero can hardly understand. In both works, the obstacle to the marriage plot is overdetermined and finally suggests a subtle critique of the hero. In this way the obstacle is seen not simply as an external circumstance but as an element of the hero's character, even as another side of his character. In Shakespeare's play the money to go courting, and even the solution to the paternal riddle of the caskets, are easily found, only to make Portia realize, when the news of Antonio's impending death interrupts the young couple's marriage plans, that no marriage (or at least no consummation) with her new husband will be possible until the deep bond he has with Antonio is resolved (and sublimated); this leads to another obstacle, the ring plot, which Portia initiates to set her own trial of her husband, and which Bassanio fails miserably.

The obstacle to the hero's success in *Harrington* appears, even to Harrington's own understanding, as if it will be the difference in religion between himself and Berenice Montenero, but as we see at the end of the novel this proves not to be the case. Without knowing it, Harrington has become the victim of a plot to discredit his character. An exaggerated and damning account of his early childhood disorder is made known to the Monteneros and thereby plays on Berenice's horror of insanity, especially of marrying an insane man (as one of her friends has done). This is the unknown obstacle that stands in Harrington's way, but even behind this obstacle stands another—the anti-Semitism that Harrington thinks he has entirely conquered.

The source of the damaging account that has been lodged against

Harrington is Fowler; the nursery maid reenters the narrative twenty years later to repeat her earlier crime. The libel against Simon now becomes the libel against Harrington. Harrington is required to suffer a repetition—now in the role of the Jew—of the initiating moment of his own narrative. In numerous earlier incidents the novel has established that the primary crime the Jew suffers is libel, and Harrington knows this first hand, because he is the vindicator of the Jew in every case (except in the original case of Simon). Harrington passes his earlier trials with ease by being "the champion of the Jews" (128) and proving their innocence against false accusations (while proving his own tolerance)—more than once for Jacob, and at least once for Mr. Montenero. These trials, we now realize, have hidden behind them a deeper trial: to play the role of the Jew, and not merely to save him from a position of strength, but to suffer what he suffers. In this way the suitor's obstacle, the libel lodged against him, leads to a profound psychological trial, making Harrington suffer the role of the Jew, as if this trial were in fact his preparation for marrying a Jew. Moreover, if Harrington's anti-Semitism originated in his belief in the libel against Simon, then the compensatory justice of this tale requires that Harrington suffer from the same crime, initiated by the same woman. We should not forget that this strategy of compensation appears in a text offered as "atonement" and "reparation" for its author's own acts of libel.

Once he discovers it, Harrington portrays the libel against himself as if it constituted merely an external circumstance, but I am suggesting that it represents his most important trial, one whose psychological grounds are at the same time relevant and profound. The text makes this clear by underscoring the genuine power that Fowler still has over Harrington. Her power is not merely accidental, coincidental, but psychological; her libel represents the power she maintains over him through the primal scene. I am arguing that Fowler's return in the narrative after twenty years represents the return of the repressed; as Harrington puts it, "I was carried back so far, so forcibly" (183). While Harrington periodically declares to us that his early trauma and his early prejudice have long been outgrown, Fowler reenters the text to prove otherwise. She corroborates what Mr. Montenero half-suspects—that Harrington "had conquered what is so difficult, scarcely possible, completely to conquer—an early prepossession" (81). Harrington correctly reads this remark as a concealed fear that he might "relapse" (81).

Fowler's reappearance is only one return in a plot characterized by many. Mowbray, Jacob, and a number of other characters make dramatic reappearances after long absences. And Edgeworth's representation of Macklin's revival of *The Merchant of Venice* is a way of marking the return of "the Jew / That Shakespeare drew" (40). Moreover, the entire narrative impetus of *Harrington* can be seen as an impulse to return. Harrington, as narrator, returns to the critical scene of childhood, while Maria Edgeworth, in a reinvention of the plot of *The Merchant of Venice*, returns to the English pre-text of the novel of Jewish identity. In both cases, there is a return to the scene of a crime. Thus, in *Harrington* the return of the repressed is located in both of the ways Freud began to define it in *Moses and Monotheism:* in the individual case history and, more importantly, in the national case history. Freud's tentative approach to redefining the return of the repressed from the point of view of *Völkerpsychologie* takes this form: "What is in question is something in a people's life which is past, lost to view, superseded and which we venture to compare with what is repressed in the mental life of an individual."[15] English anti-Semitism, according to Edgeworth, assumes the same form:

> In our enlightened days, and in the present improved state of education, it may appear incredible that any nursery-maid could be so wicked as to relate, or any child of six years old so foolish as to credit, such tales; but I am speaking of what happened many years ago: nursery-maids and children, I believe, are very different now from what they were then; and in further proof of the progress of human knowledge and reason, we may recollect that many of these very stories of the Jews, which we now hold too preposterous for the infant and the nursery-maid to credit, were some centuries ago universally believed by the English nation. (3)

Within the context of this half-hearted, and at best ironic, characterization of the history of English attitudes toward the Jews, Edgeworth is bent on showing how, in Freud's words, "the psychical precipitates of the primaeval period [in a people's life] became inherited property which, in each fresh generation, called not for acquisition but only for awakening" (*MM*, 23.132), and the way in which *The Merchant of Venice* functions at once as the cause and the symptom of this national awakening, this national relapse. Harrington's trial as a suitable husband for Berenice thus may be read as the trial of England: "Do you think we have not an Englishman good enough for her?" (104), Mr. Montenero is asked, as he threatens to take Berenice back to America, where she has grown up in an environment of tolerance.

Fowler literally represents the power of repression from the moment she extorts the boy's oath of silence; at this early point she becomes the secret enemy of the entire narrative enterprise of *Harrington*. And now she reenters the tale to prevent its traditional climax, the marriage of hero and heroine. She reappears at the decisive moment of Harrington's suit of Berenice because, as the return of the repressed, she represents those symptoms that might make his marriage impossible—not simply because the Monteneros might believe the libel against him, but because he may be genuinely unfit to marry Berenice. Fowler represents the potential power to return Harrington to his childhood terror, to make him a child forever, and therefore she reenters the narrative to prevent him from proving his manhood by winning the prize of the beautiful heiress. As the unknown libeler of Harrington's character, Fowler is the power of the unconscious, making us see that the exaggerated charge against Harrington—the bald accusation that he is insane—contains a significant germ of truth, and thereby returning us to the specialized meaning such a disorder has in Lord Mowbray's mock diagnosis of Harrington's "Jewish insanity."

In *Harrington*, then, the conventional proof of the hero's manhood—his winning of the maiden's hand—is overlaid with the question of the hero's "Jewish insanity," the debilitating disorder that not only would make "a Jewess" an impossible mate for this hero, but would make the hero himself more woman than man, a "Miss Molly" unable to win a woman's hand. In this way Edgeworth radically revises *The Merchant of Venice*. The anti-Semitism of Shakespeare's play requires the Jew to function as a central obstacle to the marriage plot. Shylock holds Antonio's bond, and thereby holds Bassanio's love in stalemate, so that the Jew's knife threatens the castration of Bassanio as well as Antonio. The Jew in *The Merchant of Venice* stands in the way of the consummation of Bassanio's marriage to Portia, so that the pound of flesh the Jew requires is empowered to prevent that Christian regeneration which is the climax of Shakespeare's comedy. In *Harrington*, in contrast, anti-Semitism itself functions as a critical obstacle. Is Harrington sufficiently recovered from his "Jewish insanity" to love Berenice, to court her, to make her a successful husband,

and will he be subject to relapses—to the return of the repressed? The hero's manhood is equated with overcoming his racial terror instead of converting it to racial violence (as his father recommends). In this way the entirety of *The Merchant of Venice* is recast; not only is the Jew no longer on trial (literally in act 4 and figuratively throughout the course of Shakespeare's play), in *Harrington* the Christian is on trial vis-à-vis the Jew. The test of value that the hero must pass, for himself and for his nation, is the test of anti-Semitism.

The most profound aspect of Harrington's trial is conducted as a drama of the unconscious. For Edgeworth, as for Freud, the repressed material of the primal scene erupts through the medium of dreams. Puzzled by the mysterious obstacle that Mr. Montenero tells him stands in his way, Harrington, after presenting his suit to his intended father-in-law, has a dream: "I saw beside my bed the old figure of Simon the Jew, but he spoke to me with the voice and in the words of Mr. Montenero" (145). The dream gives Harrington the clue he seeks, but in a language he cannot understand: Simon, not the bride's father, is the obstacle to Harrington's suit. In other words, the child's primitive terror of Jews, generated through Fowler's manipulation of the figure of Simon, stands in the young lover's way twenty years later. A similar dream occurs earlier, just after Harrington meets and falls in love with Berenice: "During the whole of the night, sleeping or waking, the images of the fair Jewess [and] of Shylock . . . were continually recurring, and turning into one another" (64). Simon, the individual Jew, is canceled in the conventional sign of racial terror and prejudice, just as earlier, when the street beggars try to impersonate Simon, they mimic "the traditionary representations and vulgar notions of a malicious, revengeful, ominous looking Shylock as ever whetted his knife" (10). In this dream Shylock stands in the way of Harrington's suit by possessing the power to cancel Berenice's beauty and grace; he does so by realizing a specific side of Harrington's anti-Semitic fear, namely, that every Jew (even Berenice) eventually turns into Shylock. In Harrington's unacknowledged anti-Semitism, then, Shylock returns from *The Merchant of Venice* to prevent another marriage.

Fowler demonstrates the power of the return of the repressed when she reactivates the primal scene not simply by reinventing the scandalous tale in hints she drops in the presence of the Monteneros, but by restaging it and thereby reproducing in Harrington his childish terror. During his visit to a synagogue where he hopes to catch a glimpse of Berenice (and to demonstrate his credentials of Jewish tolerance), Harrington suffers a relapse: "Just as I had taken out my purse, I was struck by the sight of a face and figure that had terrible power over my associations—a figure exactly resembling one of the most horrible of the Jewish figures which used to haunt me when I was a child. I was so much surprised and startled by this apparition, that a nervous tremor seized me in every limb. I let the purse, which I had in my hand, fall upon the ground" (132). The dropped purse signals the failure of compensation, both economic and psychological; it signals the failure of another version of the attempt to "patronize Shylock." While his mother tried to cure his childish terror by bribing Simon (and his impersonators, dressed as Shylock), Harrington is about to reproduce the same strategy in his patronage of the Jewish community at the synagogue, but he is interrupted by the apparition from his past. I am suggesting that we see Harrington's intended contribution at the synagogue as a special form of the psychological mechanism Freud called "overcompensation": Harrington's childhood terror of Jews is "re-pudiated, and even overcompensated, but in the end establishes itself once more" (*MM*, 23.125). The power that prevents this compensation—that is, the power that comes to light in the end as the return of the repressed—is Fowler. Harrington eventually learns that it was she who returned him to his childish terror in the synagogue: "Fowler had dressed up the figure for the purpose" (202).

But *Harrington* does not refuse the idea of compensation outright. Instead, it chooses to specify the form that compensation should take. Rather than paying in coin, Harrington must pay in feeling, specifically in pain. This recalls Shylock's rejection of Bassanio and Portia's offer to pay him three times the sum Antonio owes him; Shylock chooses another form of compensation, namely, to make the Christian learn what it is to be in the Jew's power, since the Jew always experiences the opposite. Antonio and Bassanio both compensate Shylock in the pain they suffer when they are unable to meet Shylock's demands. In *Harrington* the entire trial of the hero (including his defense of himself against libel) is characterized by Mr. Montenero as just this sort of compensation; he justifies the pain it has "cost" Harrington by asking rhetorically, "do you think that the trial cost *me*, cost *us* no pain?" (204).

Mr. Montenero, as the prospective father-in-law, sets Harrington one final trial, one final cost he must pay: "it will cost you present pain" (207), he warns Harrington, as Mr. Montenero asks him to see Fowler one final time in order to forgive her. This forgiveness functions as the final step in the casting out of Fowler, that is, in conquering Harrington's phobia, in mastering the primal scene. Fowler makes a full confession of her plot to libel Harrington, and in so doing she makes public the power that until now has remained secret, repressed. But Harrington's forgiveness of her is the final step he must take to free himself from her power. Once forgiven, Fowler is given the fate that the Jews themselves typically suffer: exile. While Daniel and Mirah's exile at the end of *Daniel Deronda* is voluntary, and Rebecca and Isaac's at the end of *Ivanhoe* is more or less voluntary, Fowler's is involuntary. In *Harrington,* Fowler's exile takes the place of the exile that the Jews were about to impose on themselves. Because of the impending failure to find an English husband for Berenice, Mr. Montenero and his daughter were about to return to America, but now Fowler "sails to-morrow in the vessel which was to have taken us to America" (208).

Figurative Conversion, from the Church Fathers to Freud

The sudden departure of the Jewish characters (or Fowler in their place) is not solely, or even primarily, a solution to the formal problem of closure in these novels. These departures are important political markers; they locate the position that the Jewish minority occupies in relation to the hegemonic or Christian community. In the tradition of comedy, in which the regeneration of the community is represented through a festive wedding at the end, the departure of the Jew signals that he or she has no place in the reconstituted community. In *The Merchant of Venice,* Shylock's sudden and painfully urgent exit, while not represented as a literal exile, works perhaps even more powerfully through understatement and anticlimax. As he leaves the stage for the last time and disappears from the world of the play, he implores, "I pray you give me leave to go from hence. / I am not well" (*MV,* 4.1.395–96). Having been assigned the role of blocking the regeneration of the Christian community by blocking the act of consummation itself, the Jew in Shakespeare's comedy has no place in the festive reunion and incipient conjugals of the young couples in act 5. But in *Harrington,* where the reconstitution of the community suggests that the racial prejudices of the past (and especially of the hero's parents) are superseded in the young married couple, the exile of the anti-Semite (in place of the Jewish characters) appears to signal a radical turning point in the position of the Jew at the comic climax. Here the Jew is located within the community instead of outside it.

But when we are told at the end of *Harrington* that Berenice is no Jew, but a Christian,[16] we come upon a covert form—at once literary and cultural—by which Jewish identity is once again exiled. Berenice's suddenly disclosed Christianity is a way of converting her. I must acknowledge immediately that comedy, like the Christian community it reflects and upholds, offers the conversion of Jewish identity as an alternative to the Jew's exile. Conversion is, after all, the culturally established means by which the Jew is allowed to enter the community. Nonetheless, I will argue that the two alternatives that face the Jew, exile or conversion, are in fact the same. But first I wish to identify conversion as a critical trope in comedy and to explain how the Jew exposes the ideological structure of comedy precisely insofar as he or she functions as a figure of conversion.

The sudden unveiling of Berenice's true identity—what I am calling her conversion—is precisely the kind of event that is identified and designated as "conversion" in standard comic terminology, only without the political implications I will give it. Northrop Frye locates "conversion" at the heart of comic form: "Unlikely conversions, miraculous transformations, and providential assistance are inseparable from comedy."[17] One could read the sudden disclosure of Berenice's Christianity entirely from within the position that views comedy as a purely formal or mythic system. But such a reading is possible only because theorists of comedy understand conversion in a purely figurative sense, as a formal trope, a sudden "twist in the plot" (*AC,* 170), with no cultural or historical signification. Comic theory neglects or erases the meaning that the Jew brings to the idea of conversion because the theory of comedy itself is written from within a Christian perspective: "The action of comedy, like the action of the Christian Bible, moves from law to liberty" (*AC,* 181); even "the crudest of Plautine comedy-formulas has much the same *structure* as the central Christian myth itself" (*AC,* 185); and Dante's *Commedia,* as the title makes clear, is the central paradigm of the form (*AC,* 185).

But in a text where Jewish identity is being represented, the reduction of conversion to a purely formal or aesthetic category is no longer possible; the Jewish characters in the text will not allow it, politicizing at once the concept of conversion and the entire shape of comedy. Unable to escape the historic shadow of conversion as a cultural institution,[18] carrying with them the memory of when "our people were slaughtered wholesale if they wouldn't be baptised wholesale" (*DD*, 790), the Jewish characters require us to investigate the variety of ways in which conversion functions ideologically in comic form. It is in this light that I pose the following question: what are the consequences of recognizing that conversion is at once the master trope of a powerful genre (comedy) and the master institution of a powerful culture (Christianity)?

First, I wish to examine how the Jew as a figure of conversion functions to test the idea of comic transformation. As a potential convert, the Jew functions as a harbinger of personal transformation, even of radical change. This means that the success or failure with which the Christian community converts the Jew can be used to uphold or undermine the other personal transformations that work at the heart of comedy. In *The Merchant of Venice* we find the locus classicus of this idea when the religious conversions of Jessica (voluntary) and Shylock (involuntary) become a means of interrogating those conversions that we take for granted as the backbone of comic plotting, such as the conversion of property and identity signaled in Portia's relinquishment of herself to Bassanio: "Myself, and what is mine, to you and yours / Is now *converted*" (*MV*, 3.2.166–67; my emphasis). Does woman occupy the same position as the Jew in an institution that legitimates and facilitates the transfer of her property and her personal identity? Is marriage a kind of conversion?

With such questions we see the way in which the Jew functions to expose the conventions of comic transformation that he or she is meant to serve. In *The Merchant of Venice* the glaring absence of Shylock after he is ordered to convert tests the limits of personal transformation and of comic resolution; the new or transformed community can claim Shylock in name only. The ideology of conversion, and by extension the ideology of comic form, becomes a brutal erasure of one identity (Jew) in the name of another (Christian). What other kinds, how many other kinds, of conversion does the ideology of the "regenerate," or hegemonic, community require?

Shylock's sudden exit on receiving the order that "[h]e presently become a Christian" (*MV*, 4.1.386) exposes conversion and exile as the sole option that the Christian community offers the Jew. Shylock's failure to reappear, his manifest absence from the stage during act 5, makes of the converted Jew something between a ghost and a pure hypothesis. After conversion, the Jew has neither eyes, hands, organs, dimensions, senses; no longer can he bleed or laugh. He is the dark absence that quietly, invisibly, haunts the last act of the comedy. The community can rename him, but it cannot bring him before our eyes, cannot prove to us that he is now one of its members. Shylock's conversion remains a miracle unproved, and the audience in the theater must take his "renewed" existence on faith.

Such a reading brings to the surface the political meanings that lie repressed in Frye's purely formal or mythic account of comedy. Comedy locates the relative power of different social (including racial and religious) groups and measures the lengths to which one group is willing to go to absorb another ("the Other"). Comedy makes such measurements by articulating the transformations of identity that are required before an individual of one group may cross over into the community whose power is renewed and celebrated at the end. Conversion, the master trope of this literary form, represents the institutionalization—that is, the legitimization—of one group's mastery and absorption of another group. The triumph of one group over another is marked by a festival of incipient conjugals in which propagation and propaganda become one. The end of the struggle between the groups is made complete when the audience is persuaded that the life sources of one group have been transferred to another. In a comedy like *The Merchant of Venice* this pattern takes the form of converting both the property and the identity of the marginal group—depleting its wealth, transferring its goods "legally" to members of the hegemonic group, and finally erasing its religious and legal identity through a set of procedures that the culture regulates under the aegis of the institution known as conversion.

While I have been demonstrating the ways in which *Harrington* seeks to expose and subvert the comic formula of *The Merchant of Venice* and the conventional stereotyping of Jewish identity, I am now suggesting that Berenice's "conversion" in *Harrington* may be a sign of Edgeworth's submission to the ruling ideology. The literal banishment of the anti-Semite (the exiled Fowler) cannot entirely obscure from our view the figurative banishment of the Jew (the converted Berenice). This is especially so because, as I have claimed for this tradition generally, the Jew is always haunted by both the historic shadow of conversion (when death was often the only alternative) and the contemporary pressure to convert (fueled by the Evangelical Revival). In *Harrington* this pressure exists as a constant reminder of what the Christian community desires and requires. For this reason the disclosure of Berenice's Christianity must be seen as no less than a realization, at a figurative level, of what is expressed at a literal level numerous times in the text. Woman's conversion in this kind of case is tantamount to a rule and therefore becomes expressed as an apothegm—in the words of Voltaire, "qu'une femme est toujours de la religion de son amant" (112). The English version of this rule taunts Berenice by requiring that she in some way repeat Jessica's conversion; "your Jessica was ready, according to the custom of Jews' daughters, to jump out of a two-pair of stairs window into her lover's arms" (114). A veritable Christian chorus makes its desire known: "as to her being a Jewess—who knows what changes love might produce?" (112); perhaps Harrington can "contrive to convert her" (117); even Mr. Harrington may be able to "bring about her conversion" (177). Mr. Harrington's declaration, "I would give one of my fingers this instant, that she was not a Jewess!" (203), makes us realize that the pound of flesh is once again ready for sacrifice, but as in Shakespeare's play it will be sacrificed only in the service of *Christian* marriage—a ritual sacrifice of paternal flesh offered for the propagation of Christian flesh.

Edgeworth tries to take the sting out of conversion by making it only figurative. The author can perform the act through "a twist in the plot" and thereby preclude the institutional procedures of religious conversion. Caught between her own convictions and the ideology of her culture, Edgeworth finds a halfway position, which, while it satisfies the requirements of Christian ideology, ultimately fails the Jewish reader. Berenice's conversion is the only moment in the novel about which Rachel Mordecai complains,[19] while Sir Walter Scott confesses, "I own I breathed more freely when I found Miss Montenero was not an actual Jewess."[20] Berenice's eleventh-hour conversion certainly looks like proof that the deus ex machina of comedy is a Christian god after all.

Berenice's conversion makes possible an unusually clear glimpse of what is, by its nature, necessarily masked—the process by which cultural ideology crosses over into, and becomes obscured in, literary form. In other words, the figurative conversion of the Jew in *Harrington,* like the figure of conversion in comic form generally, has theoretical significance insofar as we can read it as a trace or symptom of a masked procedure. But Berenice's conversion seems doubly obscured; not only is the conversion process itself masked, but the history of such a process has never been recorded and hence remains unknown to us. As a literary phenomenon, figurative conversion needs to be restored to the culture and the discourse within which it originates, for the failure to record the history of an ideology facilitates the means by which it remasters succeeding generations of a culture.

The origins of figurative conversion return us to the historic moment when the Christian community was formulating and constituting Jewish identity for public consumption for the first time. This period runs from the first century through the fourth century, when the battle for hegemony between Christians and Jews ended at last through the establishment of Christianity as the religion of the state.

During this time "the Jew" becomes a figure in a literature born of the attempt of one community to displace another. This act of displacement required an unusually intricate maneuver. To prove its own legitimacy, the Church had at once to undermine the authority of the Jewish people while maintaining (in fact, appropriating) the authority of Jewish texts.[21] For this reason the battle for authority between the Church and Judaism took place within the arena of textual politics. The Church had to demonstrate that it had "inherited" (and thereby replaced) Judaism's role as the interpreter of those sacred texts that had been until then the source of Jewish authority in the pagan world. A rereading of Hebrew Scripture was then begun with two goals in mind: first, to authorize the legitimacy—even the historic primacy—of Christianity, not Judaism; second, to undermine Jewish authority through the construction of a fictitious figure, "the Jew." In this way the sacred book of the Jews was used to defame the Jews. The *adversus judaeos* literature of this period argued that Hebrew Scripture proved that the Jews had demonstrated in numerous instances their incapacity to serve as the guardians of sacred Scripture—by misreading it, mistranslating it, even mutilating it. The battle for hegemony between Christianity and Judaism became a battle over Jewish identity, or, more specifically, a battle over the representation of Jewish identity. The full transfer of power from one community to another, which in this case meant the full absorption of Judaism in Christianity, was represented in the act of naming by which the Church designated itself as the new Israel.

Figurative conversion became the central discursive strategy by which the Church rewrote Jewish identity and thereby rewrote its place in history. This became possible with the aid of a classificatory system that would redesignate the meaning of the name "Jew." In such texts as the *Preparatio Evangelica* and the *Demonstratio Evangelica,* Eusebius attempts to demonstrate the greater authority of Christianity by proving its greater antiquity. To do so, he rewrites Jewish history by a crucial redefinition of the names "Jew," "Hebrew," and "Christian." The immediate consequence of Eusebius's revisionary strategy is to make the Jews marginal in a history in which they once occupied the central position. The ultimate consequence is to alter the nature of Jewish identity not by adding or subtracting a local feature to this identity, but by thoroughly reinventing the definition of what a Jew was—by a figurative conversion of the Jews as a people in history. Eusebius does this by drawing a false distinction between "Jews" and "Hebrews"; the change of names, the conventional sign of actual conversion, becomes our best clue to the fact that a figurative conversion has occurred. The Hebrews, according to Eusebius, not only predate the Jews, but are in fact the first Christians, primordial Christians. The Jews, on the other hand, have their historic beginning only with Moses (that is, with the Mosaic Law) and play only a minor role—in fact, they function only as a digression—in (Christian) history.[22]

In this kind of discourse the actual conversion of the Jews, what the Christian community seeks, is performed figuratively behind a double veil. First, the call for conversion is masked as no more than a call to return to a former state. The Jews are counseled merely to *return* to their faith,[23] to the faith of Abraham, the Christian faith. In such a view the "Jews" are merely "apostates," so that what the Church seeks is not their conversion but their reconversion—their Hebraization or Christianization, their return to their (Christian) roots: "Judaei veteres sperando futurum Christum redemptorem, Christiani erant. . . . Igitur apostatae habeantur necesse est." [The Jews of old, through their hope of a future Christian savior, were Christians. Therefore, they should now be regarded as apostates.][24] Second, insofar as there is a call for actual conversion, it masks the fact that a figurative conversion has already taken place. The historic figures we normally take to be Jews, including Abraham and the Prophets, are rewritten as, or converted into, Christians. Renaming is not simply a practical procedure that attends the act of conversion, whereby the convert is renamed both generically (as Jew or Christian) and specifically (with a proper, or what is commonly called a Christian, name); renaming is the method by which Jews were "converted" textually, authorially, by the Church fathers.

My claim is that Abraham in Eusebius's text occupies the same position that Berenice occupies in Edgeworth's: two characters whom the reader has assumed to be Jewish are revealed, through "a trick in the plot" (whether the plot of history or the plot of the novel), as Christians. The power of such conversions lies precisely in the reader's not recognizing them as such. They are strategically buried in the unfolding of a history— whether the divine plot of sacred history or the secular plot of narrative history—and thereby seem authorized by history, once history is correctly revised; the reader is simply asked to perform the act of recognition that will confirm the revisionary history. This authorial act by which the name Jew or Christian is suddenly relocated in order to rewrite the identity of an individual or a group, and thereby to revise a history, is the most potent and persistent discursive strategy in the history of the representation of Jewish identity. It is an act that is reborn time and again, imbedded within a variety of discourses, always a sign of ideological struggle, but a sign under cover.[25]

Harrington invents a way of subverting the procedure of figurative conversion by allowing the Jew to occupy a position outside the procedure, as a reader (instead of being trapped inside, as a textual figure). When Mr. Montenero performs his deconstructive reading of *The Merchant of Venice*, the Jew is reborn as a critic in a textual battle where his Jewish identity is at stake. He is reborn to those debates, both historic and fictitious, in which the Jew was challenged to reclaim his interpretive authority over Hebrew Scripture and to disprove the anti-Judaic readings of Jewish identity that the Christian debater claimed to find in Hebrew Scripture itself.[26] Now, in Edgeworth's text, as the textual critic of *The Merchant of Venice*, the Jew is given the chance to dismantle the holy scripture of anti-Semitism.

In *Harrington*, when the Jew becomes the reader of Shakespeare's text, we get "the Jewish version of the story" (66), which Harrington himself receives when he sees the play through Jewish eyes for the first time. Mr.

Montenero's central strategy is to place the play within its textual history and thereby to demonstrate the way in which it is a revision (or misrepresentation) of an earlier text. His reading of the play allows him to return to the scene of Shylock's trial as textual critic and as judge (like Portia, in fact) in order to claim that the true solution to the trial of Jewish identity comes not in an unraveling of the text of the bond (Portia's solution), but in an unraveling of the entire text of *The Merchant of Venice* vis-à-vis an earlier text. Whereas the interpretive energies of Portia find a way to convict Shylock, those of Mr. Montenero set Shylock free, centuries after the trial: Shylock, the ur-text of Jewish identity in England, was a *Christian* in the text that Shakespeare robbed and violated.

In such a case the power of the reader depends on the power of exposing the author, of unmasking the authorial or textual conversion that occurs behind the scenes of *The Merchant of Venice*. By explaining that the prototype for Shylock was in fact a Christian, and that the demand for a pound of flesh was originally a Christian act, Mr. Montenero restores the textual *and* the racial origins of Shylock. Mr. Montenero, then, rewrites the genealogy of the Jew as a *textual genealogy* and makes us ponder the strategies by which authors (re)constitute and fabricate racial identity. His method is to restore to this classic text both its textual history (Shakespeare's manipulation of an earlier text) and its cultural history (Shakespeare's manipulation of an anti-Semitic audience). The history of the representation of Jewish identity in this way can be exposed as a system of misrepresentations based on the strategy of figurative conversion; in *The Merchant of Venice* this conversion occurs in an unusually covert form, entirely behind the scenes, even before the first act begins. The fullest significance of Mr. Montenero's reading makes us ask: what invisible textual strategies are at work in the representation of Jewish identity?

In this way the act that Edgeworth herself performs, apparently covertly, in figuratively converting Berenice is analyzed and unmasked by Mr. Montenero in his reading of Shakespeare's play. But Mr. Montenero's critical strategy, when placed within the full historical and cultural framework to which it belongs, is far more resonant. In a brilliantly ironic stroke, Mr. Montenero turns the tables on centuries of textual conversion by proving that Shylock is a Christian in Jew's clothing. While the predominant Christian textual strategy has been to convert Jewish identity, to designate Abraham and Berenice as Christians, Montenero bows to the pattern only to subvert it. He gives the Christians Shylock! And in doing so, Mr. Montenero reveals racial identity as a code whose key is based in textual history—in the procedures by which texts get manipulated, expunged, rewritten, reread, and then handed down in a system of transmission in which one community textually deauthorizes another.

It is precisely such a picture of textual manipulation as the (secret) key to racial identity that Freud gives us in *Moses and Monotheism,* when he ostensibly performs the same act for Moses that Mr. Montenero performs for Shylock. Freud presents himself as a textual restorer and thereby as a corrector of Jewish history, but in his vision the Jews themselves have manipulated the texts and figuratively converted non-Jewish identity. He argues that Moses was "an Egyptian whom the needs of a people [the Jews] sought to make into a Jew" (*MM,* 23.17). Freud's revision of Jewish history runs this way: Moses, an Egyptian, converted the Jews to his own religion of monotheism, and then the Jews figuratively converted Moses into a Jew in the writing of their history. The key to Freud's revision (which he claims is only a return to historical truth) depends on deciphering the mutilated texts of Jewish history, especially Hebrew Scripture. Freud itemizes and analyzes the many textual mutilations the Jews authorized in order to claim Moses, circumcision, and monotheism as Judaic instead of Egyptian.

While Freud represents himself as a neutral party in this project, we now can recognize the act he performs from the vantage point of a profoundly political tradition of discourse. He is the author of a text that figuratively converts Jewish identity. Like Eusebius, he performs the textual conversion of a famous Jew in history; in fact, he completes what Eusebius began, adding Moses to the list of Abraham and the Prophets. We begin to ask, where can we locate Jewish identity? We have here a tradition of texts that slowly eradicates Jewish identity by attaching to it no famous names, no native leaders. Perhaps in the startling claim, "it was this one man Moses [an Egyptian] who created the Jews" (*MM,* 23.106), Freud inadvertently reveals the truth not about the Jews but about the representation of Jewish identity. "The Jews" are a textual creation, invented and reinvented by a series of powerful individuals, authors, outsiders, each of whom is "a great foreigner" (*MM,* 23.51) like the Egyptian Moses. Freud's own position in such a history of textual reinvention is embarrassing (as he admits in the opening sentence of his study), since he performs the act of an outsider as an insider: "To deprive a people of the man whom they take pride in as the greatest of their sons is not a thing to be gladly or carelessly undertaken, least of all by someone who is himself one of them" (*MM*, 23.7).

By recognizing figurative conversion as a textual strategy whose fore-fathers are the Church fathers, and whose modern descendants include Freud, we can situate Edgeworth's novel within the literary and cultural traditions that constitute the representation of Jewish identity both inside and outside England in ancient and modern times. Only in such a setting can we recognize, for example, the full force of George Eliot's figurative conversion of Daniel Deronda—that is, his re-Judaization in the course of the novel and the final revelation of his Jewish identity. In such a strategy we see that Eliot not only reverses Edgeworth's figurative conversion of Berenice, but subverts the predominant technique by which Christian culture, from its beginnings, erases Jewish identity. In addition, Eliot makes her figurative conversion of Daniel a comment on the tradition of comedy by forcing this tradition to expand its conventional limits. When "the twist in the plot" that discloses the hero's true identity does not reveal a noble English ancestry, but in fact cancels such an ancestry in the revelation of Daniel's Jewish origins, Eliot rewrites the central plot of comedy. Eliot brilliantly manages to sustain the comic tradition within these new, expanded boundaries by fusing English comedy and Jewish history: a Jewish marriage marks at once the climax of the comedy and the regeneration of an ancient community. In sum, in *Daniel Deronda* Eliot attempts to continue the project that Edgeworth began in *Harrington:* to revise the representation of Jewish identity and to revolutionize the func-tion of comic form in England.

In exploring conversion as the literary and cultural master trope by which Jewish identity is represented and regulated, I have returned not simply to the specific English pre-text of the novel of Jewish identity, *The Merchant of Venice,* but also to the origins of figurative conversion in patristic liter-ature. My comparison between ancient and modern literatures is not meant to erase the differences between these epochs, but to challenge us to see the ways in which conversion as a literary and cultural technology is reinvented in succeeding periods—to see, for example, the ways in which the crisis over the Jew's status in nineteenth-century England took the form of a renewed attempt at conversion. So it should come as no surprise that a contemporary reader of *Harrington* links Edgeworth's novel specifically to the work of the Jewish missions. Writing in 1827, Thomas Macaulay comically warned of the power *Harrington* might have on a particular English clergyman: "I hope that Miss Edgeworth's Harrington will never fall in his way. If it should he will infallibly turn Jew, nourish his beard, and eat the Passover while his congregation is waiting for a Good Friday Sermon. Mr. Lewis Way and Wolfe [*sic*] will have to reconvert him. By bribing him with a pipe of the real Hockheimer, and taking him to see the Merchant of Venice acted he may perhaps be reclaimed."[27] According to the temper of the times, Macaulay reads *Harrington* as a conversionist text, as if it were meant to turn Christians into Jews (in direct antithesis to the popular conversionist novels). Moreover, Macaulay imagines the members of the London Society (Lewis Way and Joseph Wolff), with *The Merchant of Venice* (instead of the Gospel) in hand, turning Jews into Christians, which means that Shakespeare's play itself is defined as a Christian conversionist text in conflict with Edgeworth's Judaizing novel. Macaulay's reading of *Harrington* demonstrates the way in which the revisionist novel of Jewish identity was read within the context of the missions to the Jews and the popular literature of conversion, including *The Merchant of Venice,* whose (re)production in the nineteenth century Macaulay interprets as part of the conversionist effort.

The revisionist novel of Jewish identity can be located within a special intertextual site in which not only historic (Abraham and Moses) but also fictitious Jewish figures are re-authored and converted. I have in mind the case of Scott's Rebecca, who resurfaced in Thackeray's *Rebecca and Rowena: A Romance Upon Romance* (1850) to declare to the entire Jewish community, by way of making herself fit to be Ivanhoe's bride, that she had converted to Christianity. In a powerful restoration of English comic form and the ideology of conversion, Thackeray remade Rebecca into Jessica and reinstitutionalized the plot of *The Merchant of Venice.* Moreover, Thackeray's conversion of Scott's Rebecca placed her within the popular nineteenth-century tradition of the conversionist novel, whose central figure was the converted Jewish heroine. In this light, charting the "progress" of the novel of Jewish identity means recording an ongoing intertextual struggle against the return not simply of Shylock and Jessica, but of an ancient practice of textual reinscription and mutilation. The central figure of this practice is the convert—"the Jew" who originates in the Church fathers' revision of Hebrew Scripture and who becomes in time a palimpsest of reauthorized identities. To write the history of this literary practice of re-representation is to expose its authorization in the institution of conversion.

3

Writing English History: Nationalism and "National Guilt"

While Scott was writing his first medieval novel in the summer and fall of 1819, the revival of medievalism in the German states was taking a particularly noxious form. The rise of German nationalism, crystallized by the expulsion of the French after the defeat of Napoleon, climaxed in the famous anti-Semitic persecutions known as the "Hep! Hep!" riots. The idea of Christian medievalism became realized in these persecutions when the rioters reiterated the cry of the Crusaders who massacred the Jews in 1096.[1] The direct impact of these anti-Semitic persecutions on English politics and letters is not the subject of this chapter—neither John Cam Hobhouse's speech in 1820 to the House of Commons on the naturalization of persecuted German Jews seeking asylum in England, nor George Eliot's decision to conclude *Impressions of Theophrastus Such* with her celebrated essay "The Modern Hep! Hep! Hep!" Instead, I view these persecutions as the most palpable sign of a specific contemporary problem of international consequence to which Scott's *Ivanhoe* was a response—namely, the problem of two forms of identity in conflict: European national identity and Jewish identity.

These persecutions make clear the political consequences of what is too often seen as the primarily aesthetic nature of Romantic medievalism, as if, in the case of *Ivanhoe*, Scott had given us no more than an idle and decorative dream of the past. The persecutions can serve to explode the "innocence" of medievalism, its purely "antiquarian" nature. In this light, the apparent coincidence with which I have begun—the medieval persecutions of the Jews were being restaged in 1819 not only by Scott, for public consumption, in the form of the historical novel, but by brutal riots in Germany and Prussia—has a deeper logic. *Ivanhoe* explores the relationship between Jewish persecution and the incipient birth of English national unity in the twelfth century, and in this way replicates the crisis of national identity in Germany in 1819. In the guise of a medieval romance Scott was addressing the ways in which contemporary European nations were working out the conflict between the rise of nationalism and the claims made on behalf of Jewish Emancipation, including the idea of granting the Jews their own national identity by restoring them to Palestine. For such reasons I wish to locate *Ivanhoe* at the international crossroads of one of the most pressing political questions of the day, the relation between national identity and alien populations, between the native and the foreign.

In this chapter I will attempt to answer why Scott was drawn to the conflict between European national identity and Jewish identity. But first I wish to explain how his exploration of this conflict was shaped by the particular way in which "the Jewish question" emerged as a pressing European concern from the time of the French Revolution to the summer of 1819 when he began writing *Ivanhoe*. The status of the Jews, historically subject to the radical fluctuations of political power that occurred in the different countries in which they lived as aliens, nonetheless had never gone through such dramatic swings as in the three decades from 1789 to 1819—that is, from the emancipation of the Jews in France as a result of the French Revolution, to the plans of Napoleon and others to restore them to their homeland in Palestine (which had to wait for more than a century), to the revival of medieval atrocities in Germany, including pamphlets that called for their immediate expulsion or outright slaughter.

England was not merely a spectator of such events. The turbulence of the French Revolution and the Napoleonic Wars had the effect of reviving in England an unusually deep-rooted tradition of millenarian thought.[2] The vast political upheavals in Europe spurred the rereading of Hebrew prophecy with an eye to predicting how and when the restoration of the Jews would signal the Second Coming. Countless sermons, tracts, pamphlets, and books proclaimed the Jews the central figures of world history, and even the center of a crisis demanding the attention of every nation, as the title of James Bicheno's *The Restoration of the Jews, The Crisis of All Nations* (1800) made clear. The ongoing war between France and England became reconfigured as a contest over which of the two powers, "atheistical" France or Christian England, would lead the Jews back to their homeland, with Napoleon variously represented as the Antichrist and the Messiah (even of specifically *Jewish* birth).[3] So, when Reginald Heber read his prizewinning poem, "Palestine," to Scott in 1803, Heber was not alone in reacting to Napoleon's invasion of Palestine by criticizing the restoration of the Jews as a specifically French project: "Yet shall she rise; but not by war restored, / Nor built in murder, planted by the sword" but by "thy Father's aid."[4] Likewise, Rebecca's "medieval" beliefs in *Ivanhoe* refer the reader to the prophecies in Hebrew Scripture that were being reread and revitalized in England in the thirty-year period leading up to Scott's writing of the novel. "Rebecca, however erroneously taught to interpret the promises of Scripture to the chosen people of Heaven, did not err in supposing the present to be their hour of trial, or in trusting that the children of Zion would be one day called in with the fulness of the Gentiles" (214).[5] The restoration of the Jews, vaguely positioned as "one day" in the distant future for the medieval Jew, had become at the beginning of the nineteenth century an urgent question that mixed mystical and political interests and thereby became "the crisis of all nations." Perhaps even in the two opposing forms of delivery offered to Rebecca at her trial in *Ivanhoe,* the English champion Ivanhoe versus the reckless and atheistic Norman noble Bois-Guilbert, Scott is responding to the different English and French approaches to "the Jewish question" within the contemporary European community.

When Heber takes the restoration of the Jews out of the hands of Napoleon and places it in the hands of God, he recalls the deeply rooted tradition in England that speaks in the same breath of the Jews' restoration and their conversion. By this I mean that freedom from the "atheistical" French may in fact deliver the Jews into the bondage of the powerful English tradition of conversionism. Heber's lines in 1803 do not differ materially from Milton's lines more than a century earlier, when Christ successfully resists the temptations of Satan (Heber's Napoleon) to "restore [the Jews] / To thir inheritance" through "battles and leagues": "Yet he at length, time to himself best known, Rememb'ring Abraham, by some wond'rous call / May bring them back repentant and sincere."[6] The "call" that Scott's Rebecca expectantly awaits, and that Milton's Christ hesitantly acknowledges, is a critical touchstone of a tradition of English millenarian thought about the relation between the Jews' history and world history. Milton's lines can in fact stand for the predominant English position, at least through the beginning of the nineteenth century, when conversion was a prerequisite for restoration: "repentant and sincere," the Jews would become candidates for restoration.

In England after the French Revolution the idea of restoring the Jews to their homeland was typically linked to, and often superseded by, the project to convert the Jews. The career of Lewis Way (1772–1840), who saved the London Society for Promoting Christianity amongst the Jews from financial ruin and became one of its prime supporters, demonstrates the way in which the English conversionists entered the European arena to promote "the Jewish question" as the crisis of all nations. In the autumn before Scott began writing *Ivanhoe,* Way visited synagogues and ghettoes in Germany and Central Europe, climaxing his journey with a series of meetings with Czar Alexander of Russia, during which the two men hatched plans for the international emancipation of the Jews. Alexander finally convinced Way to speak before the most important leaders of Europe—Metternich, Castlereagh, Richelieu, Wellington—at the Congress of Aix-la-Chapelle in the fall of 1818, trying to convince the European powers to make good on the promises of emancipation for the Jews that they had made at the Congress of Vienna (1814–15). Despite his international prominence, Way could not protect the London Society from attack at home, so that, as we have seen, Way and his Society became the subjects of vigorous public attacks, for using illegitimate means to convert the Jews, for squandering funds that could better be used in more urgent social programs, and for producing too few converts, and insincere ones at that.[7]

Scandalous accounts of insincere conversions became legion in the years preceding the publication of *Ivanhoe,* so that Scott's depiction of Friar Tuck's inauthentic conversion of Isaac can be read as a mixture of medieval history and the politics of contemporary religious controversy. The genuinely tragic history of medieval Christian proselytism (Jews often faced death as the only alternative to conversion) merges with a satire on contemporary Evangelicalism when Scott depicts an incompetent cleric dragging behind him an insincere convert with a halter fastened to his neck. When Isaac finally admits that he has not understood a word the "mad" Friar spoke, and thereby "relapses," though not without the Friar reminding him of his "promise to give all thy substance to our holy order" (310–11), the Friar finally falls back on the stereotype of the recalcitrant and hard-hearted Jew: "the leopard will not change his spots, and a Jew he will continue to be" (313). The scene functions at once as a critique of the history of Christian proselytism and as a satire on what began to be characterized in early nineteenth-century Europe as a special brand of English "religious infatuation" known as *"the English madness"*[8]—English missionary zeal.

By depicting the proselytization of the Jews in this scene and elsewhere in *Ivanhoe*, and by reinscribing the persecution of the Jews as a prominent chapter in the history of medieval England, Scott enters the nineteenth-century debate on English national identity. My argument here will depend finally on demonstrating how "the Jewish question" emerged in England after the French Revolution as a way of redefining different national histories and, ultimately, different national identities. But first I will examine the way in which the rhetoric of conversion enters not only the text of *Ivanhoe*, but English historical writing in general. I will attempt to show that this rhetoric, borrowed from the religious revival, lies at the heart of the construction of English national identity from the time of Edmund Burke's *Reflections on the Revolution in France* (1790), through the tradition of medieval English historiography that runs from Sharon Turner's *History of the Anglo-Saxons* (1799–1805) to Edward Augustus Freeman's *History of the Norman Conquest* (1867–76). In fact, I will suggest that the trope of conversion becomes a crucial figure used by writers of English history to construct, regulate, maintain, and erase different racial and national identities. Scott's special position in this tradition depends on his critique of the traditional construction of English national identity—a critique made possible, at least in part, by the special position Scott occupies in *Ivanhoe* as a Scottish writer of English history. In particular, I will argue that Scott demystifies the trope of conversion by historicizing it—that is, by redefining it in the context of the history of the Jews. By rewriting English history as Anglo-Jewish history in *Ivanhoe*, Scott exposes the ways in which racial and cultural difference are regularly erased in the project of writing English nationalist history.

Apostasy, Conversion, and Genocide in Ivanhoe

Why should he then despise the first state, and the improving progress of his Saxon ancestors? This nation exhibits the conversion *of ferocious pirates, into a highly civilized, informed, and generous people—in a word, into ourselves. (emphasis added)*[9]

This passage from Sharon Turner's *The History of the Anglo-Saxons*, long acknowledged as one of the chief influences on *Ivanhoe*, allows me to introduce the way in which the figure of conversion was used in the writing of English history during the Evangelical Revival. In Turner's hands, conversion becomes the central trope of historical change: the course of history "converts" the ancient Saxon into the modern Englishman, so that conversion is defined as no more than the process of history itself—the process of "improving progress." The "conversion" described by Turner produces no more than "ourselves"; hence the term is neutralized, domesticated, in fact Anglicized. Conversion is the natural process by which Saxon ancestors became modern English gentlemen, and the historian becomes nothing more than a kind of genealogist. In such a definition "conversion" is an entirely natural process, masking the radical transformation of Jew into Christian that was the goal of Christian proselytism and the brutal coercion that the Jews experienced, both from the mob and from the state, when they were told to convert or die, to convert or go into exile, in England and in Europe generally.

Turner might be said to have articulated this view of conversion "innocently" because his *History* is not a history of the Jews. It would be more correct to say that Turner the historian does not fully historicize the concept of conversion; he mythologizes the term, mystifying it by making himself and the modern Englishman its heirs, and in so doing he empties the term of the powerful meaning it has in Anglo-Jewish history. For such a history, we have to turn to Scott. But Turner had personal knowledge of the meaning that conversion held for a contemporary Jew, for he was the godfather of Benjamin Disraeli, who explained how Turner "after much trouble" obtained Isaac D'Israeli's "half" consent to have his children baptized one day in 1817, "upon which Mr. Turner called on the day following and took us off to St. Andrew's, Holborn."[10] Perhaps the conversion of the D'Israeli children was for Turner no more than the kind of "improving progress" that history required equally of Saxon pirates and contemporary Jews to make the modern Englishman, "highly civilized, informed, and generous." Such a view, however, would fail to recognize the critical difference between the cultural institutionalization of conversion as a procedure by which the identity of the Other is suddenly transformed and the apparently natural process of social evolution by which the Saxon becomes, over centuries, the modern Englishman—the process Turner designates as "conversion."

When Scott conceives of history, and even of the evolution of English national identity, he does so (unlike Turner) by contextualizing the idea of conversion through its meaning in Jewish history, and in this way *Ivanhoe* becomes a critique of conversion. Scott undermines the definition of conversion as a form of evolutionary continuity (Turner's definition) by conceiving of it as a form of radical discontinuity; in the first definition we find no more than the *natural* history of *ourselves*, while in the second we find the *cultural* institutionalization of a division *within the self of the Other*. In the first case Scott reviewed (and critiqued) the conventional mode of English historiography, which established the perfect continuity between Saxon ancestor and modern Englishman; in the second case, in a series of scenes in which Isaac and Rebecca are proselytized, Scott explored conversion as a means of radically dividing the Jewish self from its ancestral origins.

The difference between Turner's and Scott's uses of the idea of conversion is grounded in the different relationship the two writers bear to English history. Turner occupies a critical position in the development of historiography in the early nineteenth century—that is, in the movement away from the "universalist" or "philosophic" history-writing of the Scottish Enlightenment, toward the histories of particular peoples, the history of the nation-state.[11] The new note in history-writing is sounded when Turner makes plain that his interest in the earliest periods of English history is motivated by a kind of pride in national origins, something essentially alien to Enlightenment thinking: "Why should he then despise the first state and the improving progress of his Saxon ancestors?" This new interest in Anglo-Saxon and medieval history—the periods most undervalued, sometimes even scorned, in Hume's *History of England* (1754–62)—develops out of a desire to focus on the historical epoch in which the national identity of England took shape and on the ancestors who still live in "our" present experience: "Our language, our government, and our laws, display our Gothic ancestors in every part: they live, not merely, in our annals and traditions, but in our civil institutions and perpetual discourse."[12] Turner's *History* is at least in part a product of the new English nationalism that began in reaction against the French Revolution and the subsequent Napoleonic era. His invocation to "ourselves" signals not, as it would for the philosophic historian of the Enlightenment, the triumph of a kind of universal civilization over earlier, ruder stages of human history, but the crystallization of a highly specific form of identity, English identity. And unlike the authors of the Scottish Enlightenment, who aimed at a European audience, and who felt that any national partisanship marred the writing of history, Turner's address to "ourselves" limits his audience to his English compatriots. He unashamedly writes his *History* out of "patriotic curiosity"[13] in the national forefathers, when many in England stood amazed at the extraordinary rupture in national history in France.

Scott's relationship to the *English* national character—which is, after all, the focus of *Ivanhoe,* as he confessed when he spoke of moving from the "Scottish novels" to "a subject purely English" (xi)—is much more problematic than Turner's. An almost entirely forgotten event in Scott's life, absent even from the standard biographies, can help to explain how he came to write on a "purely English" subject that incorporated the question of Jewish identity—how, in effect, the Jewish characters in *Ivanhoe* mark Scott's own personal anxiety over conversion and the idea of a "purely English" history.

When Isaac Nathan (1790–1864) was looking for a poet to write English lyrics for a collection of Hebrew melodies he wanted to publish, he asked Scott before asking Byron, who eventually brought out the *Hebrew Melodies* in 1815, only to be labeled "poet laureat to the synagogue" in a review that, equating Byron's project in verse with Lord George Gordon's conversion to Judaism, satirized the Judaization of England: "We suspect, indeed, in the great City of London, the Society for the Propagation of Judaism among Christians is rather more successful in its endeavors, though not so loud in its pretensions, as the Society for the Propagation of Christianity among the Jews."[14] Meanwhile, though he declined Nathan's offer, Scott visited Nathan's studio in 1815 to hear the composer perform the *Melodies.*[15] Nathan's choice of Scott uncannily anticipated, and perhaps even influenced, the novelist's decision to take up the Jewish past in *Ivanhoe* only a few years later.

Nathan may have chosen Scott simply because his *Minstrelsy of the Scottish Border* (1802–3) bore such a clear relationship to that relatively new literary phenomenon of the opening decades of the nineteenth century, the publication of national melodies (including Scottish, Irish, and Welsh). But I believe that Nathan recognized in Scott a voice that spoke, within Britain, for a minority population that was in danger of being entirely subsumed in the majority culture. For Scott had made plain in the introduction to the *Minstrelsy* that his collection of ballads was an attempt to contribute to "the history of my native country; the peculiar features of whose manners and character are daily melting and dissolving into those of her sister and ally. And, trivial as may appear such an offering to the manes of a kingdom, once proud and independent, I hang it upon her altar with a mixture of feelings which I shall not attempt to describe."[16] Nathan may have recognized in him a writer who experienced firsthand the dangers of assimilation. In light of the Union of 1707, in which Scotland ceased to have an independent political existence, and of the Jacobite Rebellion of 1745 (the subject of *Waverley*), Scotland could well have been characterized as a kind of "nation within a nation," the conventional phrase used to question the political status of the Jews in England, Germany, and elsewhere.[17] The typical argument against Jewish Emancipation claimed that the Jews' first allegiance would never be to England because the Jews would always represent a separate and alien nation within a modern European nation-state—unless they converted, as Thomas Arnold argued: "for the Jews I see no plea of justice whatever; they are voluntary strangers here, and have no claim to become citizens, but by conforming to our moral law, which is the Gospel."[18] Meanwhile, Byron elegized the homelessness of the Jews in his *Hebrew Melodies*— "The wild-dove hath her nest, the fox his cave, / Mankind their country— Israel but the grave!"[19]—while Scott, a few years after refusing Nathan's invitation, turned to the question of Jewish national identity in *Ivanhoe,* in which his earlier words about the former glory of Scotland, "once proud and independent," are echoed in Rebecca's paeans to ancient Israel. Scott drew the attention of the entire European community to the history of the politically disenfranchised Jews by exploring how their lack of national status was mirrored at once in the Saxons after the Norman Conquest and in the Scots after their incorporation into Great Britain.

Scott's representation of the Jews in *Ivanhoe* can in fact be seen as an extension of the project of his earlier novels—namely, the sympathetic representation of the Scottish people—and this project depended on the model of Maria Edgeworth, as Scott was happy to acknowledge on more than one occasion, both publicly in the last chapter of *Waverley* and privately when he wrote to her: "you have had a merit transcendent in my eyes, of raising your national character in the scale of public estimation; and making the rest of the British Empire acquainted with the peculiar and interesting character of a people too long neglected and too severely oppressed."[20] In this light the revisionary novel of Jewish identity owes a significant debt to the development of the regional novel. As both Edgeworth and Scott turned from their regional tales of the Irish and the Scottish, both writers developed at the beginning of the nineteenth century the additional project of representing another "people too long neglected and too severely oppressed"—that is, a novelistic tradition that explored the social and political status of the Jews in England. Edgeworth led the way once again, with the publication in 1817 of *Harrington,* a novel about the Jews in contemporary England, which Scott followed up with *Ivanhoe* in 1819, a novel about the Jews set in the period in which the nation of England was being formed—as if *Ivanhoe* were meant to function as a historical frame for understanding the "modern" anti-Semitism that Edgeworth had just anatomized in *Harrington.*

In short, when Scott came to write *Ivanhoe* he did not approach English history with simple and unambiguous "patriotic curiosity," because his own national and cultural allegiances were more complicated than Turner's. In fact, Scott deliberately ironizes the typical mode of English history-writing so well epitomized by Turner, whom Scott mentions with apparent reverence (xxii) in the Dedicatory Epistle to *Ivanhoe.* Scott's ambivalent relationship to his subject is signaled by the way in which he names himself and thereby positions himself in relation to his audience. In Turner's case, the rhetorical use of "ourselves" is part of a larger ideology which consolidates his own position and that of the English people within a unified national history: history becomes the evidence of a shared national genealogy, the record of kinship. For Scott, the use of such consolidating pronouns of national identity is an ironic fiction. In the midst of a series of insistent contrasts between English and Scottish authors (xxi), and between English and Scottish readers (xxii), Scott in the Dedicatory Epistle disguises himself as the Englishman "Laurence Templeton," the apparent author of *Ivanhoe*, and thereby erases his own Scottish identity: "I cannot but think it strange that no attempt has been made to excite an interest for the traditions and manners of Old England, similar to that which has been obtained in behalf of those of our poorer and less celebrated neighbours" (xx). Scott authenticates his claim to write on a "purely English" subject, then, by posing as an Englishman, with a characteristically English sneer at his "poorer and less celebrated neighbours" to the north. The fiction of "Laurence Templeton" is double—he is not the author of *Waverley* (he is not Scott), and he is an Englishman (he is not a Scot): "Admitting that the Author [of *Waverley*] cannot himself be supposed to have witnessed those times, he must have lived . . . among persons who had acted and suffered in them; and even within these thirty years, such an infinite change has taken place in the manners of Scotland that men look back upon the habits of society prior to their immediate ancestors as we do on those of the reign of Queen Anne, or even the period of the Revolution" (xx). Scott's use of the pronouns "our" and "we" in such passages directs us to the way in which the fiction of his English persona broaches the question of the political fiction of the modern European nation-state, in which a variety of peoples and cultures are not simply mixed but blurred and sometimes erased. Does Scott in speaking for English history speak for the future Scot, whose only traditions one day will be English? Do "we" and "our" serve as harbingers of the assimilated Scot of the future, who will have only one story to tell, the story of *English* history? The insistent recurrence of phrases such as "our forefathers," "our ancestors," and "my countrymen" (xxi–xxii), and the characterization of the entire project of *Ivanhoe* as an attempt "to illustrate the domestic antiquities of England, and particularly of our Saxon forefathers" (xix), mark the irony of Scott's position as a writer of English history and distinguish his position from Turner's simple embracing of his "Saxon ancestors."

Scott characterizes the anachronisms that mar the historical accuracy of his text as "polluting the well of history with modern inventions" (xxiii). But the purely aesthetic danger of the historical novelist is superseded by the danger of Scott the Scot reinventing himself as an Englishman—which is precisely the danger of the assimilationist politics of the Union of 1707. I am suggesting that the modern "Englishman" with an erased Scottish background is the "modern invention" that pollutes the well of history—not unlike the Christian convert with an erased Jewish past. The English persona of the Dedicatory Epistle, then, is not simply an aesthetic fiction, but a political fiction produced by recent history, and in this way Scott explores the profound anxiety of maintaining an assimilated or converted identity. *Ivanhoe* is initiated under the sign of a kind of apostasy. Scott's English credentials mark both his shame in denying his own Scottish origins and his pride in managing to "pass," to succeed at writing English history (and English prose), for in 1830 he was able to acknowledge that "he has ever since [the success of *Ivanhoe*] been permitted to exercise his powers of fictitious composition in England as well as Scotland" (xvii).

After Scott reinvents himself as a kind of convert, an Englishman who erases his identity as a Scot, he goes on to expose the modern Englishman as a kind of convert who fails to see the ways in which he denies his mixed national heritage. He attacks the conventional formulations of English history (as continuous) and English identity (as pure). For him, history is a lengthy process of racial mixture, and English history is no exception, as the plot of *Ivanhoe* will prove by delineating the mixed Saxon and Norman genealogy of the modern Englishman. In taking up English history, *Ivanhoe* attempts to dislodge the modern Englishman from a special form of complacence about the easy continuity between himself and his ancestors, for while the Scottish reader accepts a vision in which "a set of wild manners, and a state of primitive society" represent his own ancestors, the Englishman cannot believe "his own ancestors led a very different life from himself" (xxii). *Ivanhoe,* in this light, is an attack on a purely English subject, on the comfortable modern-day Englishman, "placed in his own snug parlour, and surrounded by all the comforts of an Englishman's fireside" (xxii). In short, Scott envisions history as the record of difference; and history-writing in *Ivanhoe* functions to demystify English subjectivity by reconstituting the basis of English national identity in racial and religious difference.

Given this context, we can see the full importance of the opening scene of the novel. Gurth and Wamba enter the forest glade as belated figures in a historic drama of conversion that has already been played out, in different ways, many times. For Scott's natural landscape bears not simply the marks of civilization, but the marks of conversion—those signs of religious and national change that constitute the history of civilization.

The setting of King Richard's return from the Crusades reveals the signs of a previous religious worship, "the rites of Druidical superstition"; in the midst of the glade that Scott's characters enter, "there still remained part of a circle of rough, unhewn stones, of large dimensions." While seven of these stones stand upright, "the rest had been dislodged from their places, probably by the zeal of some convert to Christianity" (4). The ground of speculation for Scott the historian is clear from the beginning. As a writer of social history, his focus is drawn to the unknown and unnamed convert who nonetheless marks the landscape with the signs of religious and national change. The convert, if not the moving force of history, is the sign of such movement, the figure within whom we read the two identities of past and present. But the convert himself often denies this double identity, so that the historian must frequently expose the work of suppression that the convert has performed. In this case, Scott must publish the almost erased drama of conversion in which the convert to Christianity attempts to "dislodge" every trace of Druidism. History-writing, then, uncovers the signs of those conversions by which one culture absorbs, erases, and succeeds another.

When "[t]he human figures which completed this landscape" (4) actually do arrive on the scene, they enter to announce the latest chapter in the history of conversion. The elaborate descriptions of Saxon dress and manners by which Scott introduces Gurth and Wamba are freighted with irony, given that the characters themselves speak of the danger of their erasure in Norman culture. Wamba recommends to Gurth the swineherd, "leave the herd to their destiny, which, whether they meet with bands of travelling soldiers, or of outlaws, or of wandering pilgrims, can be little else than to be converted into Normans before morning" (7). Wamba explains his use of the figure of conversion: while "swine" designates the live herd in "good Saxon," "the sow when she is flayed, and drawn, and quartered, and hung up by the heels . . . becomes a Norman, and is called pork, when she is carried to the castle hall to feast among the nobles" (7–8). The change in translation from one language to another signals, for Wamba, the complete absorption and erasure of one culture by another in conversion; both changes signify the difference between life and death. In the initial dialogue of the novel, then, Wamba introduces the radical definition of conversion that will frame the entire plot of *Ivanhoe:* conversion is nothing less than genocide. "Swine" is, after all, the generic name by which the Normans consistently characterize the Saxons—when, for instance, Bois-Guilbert speaks of "preparing these Saxon hogs [Cedric and Athelstane] for the slaughter-house" (231). In short, Wamba's vision of Saxon swine converted into Norman pork characterizes the Norman Conquest, the historical subject of *Ivanhoe*, as a form of racial murder. What remains to be understood are the effects, for Scott's historical novel and for English historiography, of Wamba's definition of conversion.

Ulrica's story of the Norman slaughter of her Saxon family is the novel's most potent and most condensed narrative illustration of Wamba's definition of conversion as genocide. While Scott records the slaughter of the male line of Saxons—in the case of Ulrica's family the Normans "shed the blood of infancy rather than a male of the noble house of Torquil Wolfganger should survive" (239)—he seems more interested in exploring woman's role in the annihilation or preservation of racial and national identity, in the parallel stories of Ulrica, Rowena, and Rebecca. Such an exploration helps to crystallize the idea of conversion as rape that lies just below the surface of Wamba's text; the general description of the swine "running on all fours" suddenly focuses on the gender-specific "sow" turned upside down, "the sow when she is flayed, and drawn, and quartered, and hung up." Precisely insofar as Ulrica's story demonstrates the way in which conversion functions as a sexual transgression that is at the same time a racial erasure, her story represents a narrative model that threatens to overtake the stories of the two major female characters in the novel, Rowena and Rebecca.

By exposing the double identity of the convert, Ulrica's story demonstrates the way in which the convert's case history is the model of all historical writing for Scott—the uncovering of an earlier, lost identity. By telling her story in the form of a confession to the man she designates as "Cedric called the Saxon" (238), who is at the time disguised as a priest, Ulrica declares her apostasy, with Cedric cast in the role of restoring her to her Saxon identity. Cedric is startled to meet "the murdered Ulrica" (239), for he has believed until now that she met the same fate as her father and brothers. But his description is nonetheless figuratively accurate; the murdered Ulrica is the converted Ulrica, as Wamba's definition of conversion predicts. Ulrica can be spoken of as murdered in conversion because, after the slaughter of her family, her Saxon identity disappears; she lives under the assumed name of Urfried, as "the slave" and "the paramour" (239) of her family's murderer, and she contemplates "all that she has lost by the name of Front-de-Boeuf" (284).

Living among Normans under a false name, speaking the language and assuming the customs and manners of the Normans that she secretly despises, Ulrica is like a false convert: she survives the Conquest by pretending to be Norman. With her name lost, and her face no longer clearly bearing the features of her family (240),[21] Ulrica becomes the tragic mime of the male characters in the novel who deliberately hide both name and face: Richard, Ivanhoe, Gurth, Cedric, Robin Hood. *Ivanhoe* is structured as a comedy of disguise in which the Shakespearean convention of cross-dressing crosses the border not of gender but of race and class. Typically, the Saxon men hide both name and face in order to cross over safely into the Norman world; they periodically are subject to a kind of forced conversion, when their lives depend on their assuming a Norman identity. One of the most pointed ironies of Ulrica's confession scene is that Cedric is disguised as a Norman friar, about to make his escape to freedom beyond the walls of the Norman castle, when he chastises Ulrica for her apostasy, her Norman "disguise." Gurth sounds the note of liberation and restoration for all the Saxon characters by declaring his desire to live "without hiding either my face or my name" (102); he makes this declaration when, disguised as a Norman squire-at-arms, "the translated swineherd" (163) experiences firsthand the lesson Wamba taught him about Norman translation and conversion.

The disguised male characters seek and find the moment of comic denouement when they throw off their disguises and make their names public, but such a moment comes tragically for Ulrica, as she herself predicts. She anticipates the day when Cedric will say of her, "whatever was the life of Ulrica, her death well became the daughter of the noble Torquil" (242). Ulrica's story ends in her enactment of the text's most disturbing version of racial preservation; she dies to become once again a Saxon and to support the Saxons who are currently storming the Norman castle. Only death restores her to her name—she succeeds where Front-de-Boeuf fails, to "perish as becomes my name" (284)—and in her last appearance, at the moment of committing suicide, she is described as "the Saxon Ulrica" (299). Moreover, the fire by which Ulrica kills herself allows the two heroines to escape from their Norman imprisonment at Torquilstone—an imprisonment that, in both cases, is being used to threaten them with conversion, to make Rowena a Norman (and a bride) and Rebecca a Christian (and a paramour).

The Emergence of Anglo-Jewish History

Rowena, "the Saxon heiress" (203), functions in the racial politics of medieval England as the object of two competing marriage plots, both of which subdue her personal identity to her racial identity. Prince John's plan to marry Rowena to the Norman Maurice de Bracy is an attempt at annihilating the Saxon dynasty, while Cedric's plan to marry her to Athelstane, "that last scion of Saxon royalty" (295), is an attempt at preserving it. John plans Rowena's marriage to "amend her blood, by wedding her to a Norman" (123), to "produce her not again to her kindred until she be the bride and dame of Maurice de Bracy" (144), where producing her to her kindred is a form of reproducing her—subsuming her in the name of a Norman husband, changing her lineage, eradicating her racial ancestry. Amending her blood, then, is a highly specialized version of textual correction, where the text to be amended is Rowena's Saxon genealogy. In short, forcing Rowena to marry a Norman becomes a form of forced conversion.

Rowena's marriage to Ivanhoe at the end of the novel does not represent merely the fulfillment of her own personal desire. It more importantly represents a political and historical middle ground between Cedric's plan to marry Rowena to Athelstane (thereby securing the Saxon dynasty) and John's plan to marry her to De Bracy (thereby erasing a prominent Saxon family). Once we realize that Rowena's marriage to the Normanized Ivanhoe anticipates the happy intermarriage of the races, we realize that it functions as a third alternative to the historical problem on which Scott predicates his entire novel: "Four generations had not sufficed to blend the hostile blood of the Normans and the Anglo-Saxons, or to unite, by common language and mutual interests, two hostile races" (2). The solution to the hostility of the races of the first chapter is clearly represented in the comic festival of marriage in the last chapter, when the nuptial "union" of the couple is made to signal the future political "union" of the races:

these distinguished nuptials were celebrated by the attendance of the high-born Normans, as well as Saxons, joined with the universal jubilee of the lower orders, that marked the marriage of two individuals as a pledge of the future peace and harmony betwixt two races, which, since that period, have been so completely mingled that the distinction has become wholly invisible. Cedric lived to see this union approximate toward its completion; for, as the two nations mixed in society and formed intermarriages with each other, the Normans abated their scorn, and the Saxons were refined from their rusticity. But it was not until the reign of Edward the Third that the mixed language, now termed English, was spoken at the court of London, and that the hostile distinction of Norman and Saxon seems entirely to have disappeared. (447)

As a historical novel based on "a subject purely English," *Ivanhoe*'s final public event is a marriage whose pretext is clear: to bestow on the incipient English population their proper name. The conventional announcement of progeny that frequently completes the comic marriage plot becomes freighted with historical and political significance in *Ivanhoe;* the nuptials of Rowena and Ivanhoe proleptically become a baptism of their symbolic progeny, the English people.

Rowena and Ivanhoe's marriage represents the first step toward solving the hostilities between the Normans and the Saxons insofar as it represents a kind of intermarriage. Ivanhoe, the eponymous hero, is the critical figure in Scott's plot because he represents a hero caught between two historical moments—the ancient Saxon past of his father and the new Norman ways of his king. *Ivanhoe* ends with the Normanized Ivanhoe marrying the Saxon heiress, and with an important naming ritual in which King Richard rejects the name "Richard of Anjou" to call himself "Richard of England! whose deepest interest—whose deepest wish, is to see her sons united with each other" (421), a father figure whose sons include both Saxons and Normans. In this way Scott is able to define "England" as the product of racial and cultural mixture—neither as the simple preservation of the Saxon past in the face of the Norman invasion, nor as the simple conversion of the Saxons into Normans.

The boldness of Scott's use of the Norman Conquest to authenticate the mixed racial origins of the English becomes clear when we understand the critical position the Conquest occupies in English historiography. From the seventeenth century through the end of the Victorian period and beyond, the Conquest was the key event through which ideology regularly entered and shaped the writing of English history. The Norman Conquest became the most important event in English historiography because it was the event by which the appeal to history was consistently used to establish English national identity. What became the hegemonic interpretation of the Norman Conquest in the course of the seventeenth century, and continued thereafter to be put in the service of a propagandistic brand of national self-definition, was an argument that, in maintaining both the antiquity and the continuity of English (that is, Saxon) institutions, denied that the Conquest was a conquest and managed to minimize and even erase the influence of Norman culture on English history and the English national character.[22] This took the form of deriving everything "English" from a Saxon heritage and made possible the full-blown Teutonism that eventually dominated nineteenth-century English historical and political discourse.

Scott exposes the major ideological strategy of the historiography of the Norman Conquest—namely, the attempt to read "English" tradition as purely Saxon, thereby denying the Norman contribution to the founding of the English nation—when he exposes the Anglicization of Richard throughout the novel. The Anglicized Richard—fluent in the Saxon tongue and naming himself (when disguised as the Black Knight) as "a true English knight, for so I may surely call myself" (288)—is exposed as the historian's concession to the modern Englishman's sense of historic continuity and racial purity. The lie is given to such fictionalizations in a critical footnote that explodes the ideology typically at work in the attempt to rewrite Norman identity (in this case, the Norman Richard) as "English," when "English" is no more than a code name for "Saxon." When Richard meets Friar Tuck's challenge to sing a ballad in "downright English" (159), Scott (in the person of the English antiquary Templeton) adds a footnote admitting the unlikelihood "that he [Richard] should have been able to compose or sing an English ballad; yet so much do we wish to assimilate him of the Lion Heart to the land of the warriors whom he led, that the anachronism, if there be one, may readily be forgiven" (453). This jarring note is not only a confession that a major historical figure is being fictionalized at this moment in the text, but also a suggestion that political ideology regularly enters the writing of English history, not simply in romances or historical novels, but in the hegemonic tradition of English historiography. This kind of ideological rewriting of history recalls the way in which figures such as the patriarchs of Hebrew Scripture were "assimilated" into Christian hagiology as proto-Christians instead of Jews, so that the Anglicization of Richard has its counterpart in the Christianization of, say, Abraham and Moses.

At the beginning of the twentieth century G. K. Chesterton recorded the ideological basis of English historiography: "only those will permit their patriotism to falsify history whose patriotism depends on history. A man who loves England for being English will not mind how she arose. But a man who loves England for being Anglo-Saxon may go against all facts for his fancy. He may end (like Carlyle and Freeman) maintaining that the Norman Conquest was a Saxon Conquest."[23] The Anglicization of Richard is an example of the kind of patriotic revision of the Norman Conquest that forms the cornerstone of the predominant interpretation of English history. In fact, I am arguing that Scott exposes the transformation of Richard's identity as a kind of figurative, or textual, conversion of Norman identity and thereby establishes the double, and peculiarly ironic, subject of *Ivanhoe*—while in English history the Normans conquered the Saxons, in English historiography the Saxons conquered the Normans.

Edward Augustus Freeman, to whom Chesterton refers, produced perhaps the most famous revision of the Norman Conquest as the Saxon Conquest in his celebrated *History of the Norman Conquest:* "But in a few generations we led captive our conquerors; England was England once again, and the descendants of the Norman invaders were found to be among the truest of Englishmen" (*NC*, 1.1); in short, "the Norman Conquest was a Saxon Conquest" (*NC*, 5.106).[24] While the seventeenth-century parliamentarian interpretation of the Norman Conquest focused on the continuity of constitutional rights (between ancient Saxons and modern Englishmen), for Freeman in the second half of the nineteenth century the continuity of English racial identity is more important: "The momentary effect was to make Englishmen on their own soil the subjects of foreign conquerors. The lasting effect was to change those foreign conquerors into Englishmen" (*EC*, 70). For Freeman, then, while the consequences of the Norman Conquest were political (and short-lived), the consequences of the "Saxon Conquest" were racial (and permanent)—no less than the racial conversion by which the Normans became Englishmen, and by which the category "foreign" was erased.

One could say that insofar as Freeman wanted to insure the continuity of "English" history, and Scott wanted to question it, the two were destined to meet on the question of the Norman Conquest. As a critique and revision of the "anti-English" historical practices of a work like *Ivanhoe,* Freeman's *History* can help show how English identity became a function of a battle of the books in which the name "English" became the central controversy and the history of the Norman Conquest the central weapon. A practice like Scott's naming of Cedric and Ulrica as "Saxons," for instance, is under attack in Freeman's insistence that the word "English" be used instead. Objecting to the name "Saxon," Freeman writes that "people fancy that the word English cannot be rightly applied to the nation, its language, or its institutions, till after the Norman element has been absorbed into it. . . . The refusal to call ourselves and our forefathers a thousand years back by the same name originates in a failure to realize the fact that our nation which exists now is the same nation as that which migrated from Germany to Britain in the fifth century" (*NC,* 1.363). Using a procedure of naming borrowed from Turner, Freeman erases the time that separates nineteenth-century Englishmen and their medieval forebears in the defense of a nation-state that modern historians hardly allow the Saxon confederacy at the time of the Norman Conquest, never mind as early as the fifth century. In such passages we see the project of nationalist historiography at work to make ancient, continuous, and pure the racial basis of the modern nation-state. For Freeman, the basis of English national identity is racial, so that even when examining the question of the historical origins of the English constitution, he casts the question in racial terms: "The Constitution . . . is indeed the common possession of the Teutonic race, but it is something more. We should perhaps not be wrong if we were to call it a common possession of the whole Aryan family of mankind" (*EC,* 13–14).

I wish to call "conversionist" the strategies by which Freeman maintains the continuity of English history—that is, his rewriting of "Saxon" as "English," and his rewriting of the Norman Conquest as the means by which the Normans were converted into "Englishmen." In a further conversionist gesture he reduces the impact of the Norman Conquest by reminding us that the Normans "came originally of the same stock" as the Saxons (*NC*, 1.100). He denies the otherness of the Normans by minimizing their foreignness. What elsewhere in his *History* is seen as the foreign tyranny of the Normans, the near breach in the continuous history of English tradition, now turns out to be a kind of restoration of (Teutonic) identity for the Normans; originally Danes, the Normans are in fact the kindred of Englishmen, part of the Teutonic family. In a covert use of the figure of conversion, the Normans are seen as apostates who were in need of rebaptism (through conquest): "The Norman was a Dane who, in his sojourn in Gaul, had put on a light French varnish, and who came into England to be washed clean again" (*EC*, 71); or again, "He [William the Conqueror] came, a chief of Danes and Saxons who had fallen from their first love, who had cast away the laws and the speech of their forefathers, but who now came to the Teutonic island to be won back into the Teutonic fold, to be washed clean from the traces of their sojourn in Roman lands, and to win for themselves . . . a right to an equal share in the name, the laws, the glories of Teutonic England" (*NC*, 3.270). In Freeman's vision of the Norman Conquest, the Normans wanted to be conquered, to be Anglicized, to be renamed—to be converted back to Teutonism.

Freeman's history finally devolves on a theory in which the English race masters its "foreign" counterparts through a kind of mystical absorption of the Other in the blood, or a kind of conversion of the Other through a superior proselytism. Freeman begins by trying to minimize Scott's idea that the English are a mixed race: "People talk of the 'English' as a new nation which arose, in the thirteenth century perhaps, as a mixed race of which the 'Saxons' or 'Anglo-Saxons' were only one element among several. But these elements are not coequal with the original substance of the nation. In all these cases, the foreign element was simply incorporated and assimilated . . . in the predominant English mass" (*NC*, 1.363–64). Freeman celebrates such incorporation and assimilation even when they take the most brutal form. He is "thankful for the barbarism and ferocity of our forefathers," since it was their complete eradication of the natives of Britain that assured their own purity of race, the founding of the English race:

The English wiped out everything Celtic and everything Roman. . . .
We won a country for ourselves, and we grew up, a new people in a
new land. . . . Severed from the old stock, and kept aloof from
intermixture with any other, we ceased to be Germans and we did
not become Britons or Romans. . . . [T]he Old-Saxon has lost his
national being through the subtler proselytism of the High-German;
but the Angles, Saxons, and Jutes, transplanted to the shores of
Britain, have won for themselves a new name and a new national
being, and have handed on to us the distinct and glorious inheritance
of Englishmen. (*NC,* 1.14–15)

As if in approval of the kind of conversion (as genocide) that Scott critiques, Freeman imagines the foundation of English national identity as
happily compounded of the cooperative successes of genocide and proselytism. In the first case, the "English" exterminate their colonialist predecessors, the Romans, as well as the native population of Britain. In the
second, the "English" avoid succumbing to the "proselytism" of another
race, while they themselves successfully convert Danes, Normans, and all
the other races, which, absorbed into the overmastering English blood,
mystically turn English. But another kind of proselytism is at work here.
Insofar as the Normans lose their racial and national being through the
proselytism of the English, they lose it through "the subtler proselytism"
of English historiography, as practiced by Freeman and others. *Ivanhoe*
confronts the double problem of "English" history and historiography: while Scott critiques, in English history, the conversion of Saxons
into Normans, he also critiques, in English historiography, the conversion of Normans into Saxons (as the central goal of "English" nationalist
ideology).

I have claimed that Scott's own cultural background prepared him to
critique the writing of English nationalist history—a claim I wish to support by arguing that Scott was part of a tradition of Scottish writers who
took as their project the revision of English historiography. Hume's *History of England* (1754–62) is perhaps the crucial precursor in such a
tradition insofar as it emphatically proclaimed its freedom from English
partisanship. While Hume used his new philosophic method to lay claim
to scientific objectivity, he also could have used his position as an outsider, a foreigner, for his *History* made clear his belief that the English

themselves were incapable of objectively writing their own history. Hume set out to correct the distortions that both Whigs and Tories had contributed to the tradition of English historiography from the seventeenth century onward. In so doing, he had to face the problem of the Norman Conquest, especially since his major topic, the history of the Stuarts, was so deeply enmeshed in the question of the continuity of the Saxon constitution. Hume undermined the Whig myth of ancient constitutionalism and attacked the national pride that English historians took in the Saxon form of liberty, which he characterized as no more than a form of licentiousness, an inability to submit to government. He claimed that the Norman Conquest demonstrated that the Normans were more civilized than the Saxons, and that England benefited from the contact with the foreigners. Following in the tradition of Hume, in *An Historical View of the English Government, etc.* (1787–1803) John Millar undermined the ideology of English Teutonism by claiming that "Saxon" liberty was characteristic of all primitive peoples and no more than an incapacity to submit to government (as Hume had claimed). Millar argued that those Saxon institutions that were thought to be unique actually existed in the cultures of the ancient Jews, the Highland Scots, the Irish, and so on. In short, both Hume and Millar rewrote English history within the context of the larger European community and thereby avoided—even undermined— an Anglocentric view of English history.[25] What remains to be seen is the way in which Scott, following in their footsteps, used the history of the Jews in England to critique the writing of English nationalist history.

I have read Rowena's marriage as a political allegory about English history; I now wish to read Rebecca's destiny as a political allegory about Jewish history. While the Saxon-Norman plot in *Ivanhoe* averts De Bracy's conversion of Rowena (chapter 23) through her marriage to Ivanhoe, the Jewish plot averts Bois-Guilbert's conversion of Rebecca (chapter 24), only to lead to two further attempts at converting her, and ends not with Rebecca's marriage but with her exile. And just as Rowena's three suitors represent three different solutions to a racial problem in English history, the three attempts at converting Rebecca represent three different responses to the question of Jewish identity in European history. By dramatizing the historic reality of the conversion of the Jews, these three scenes allow Scott to move beyond the use of conversion solely, or even primarily, as a rhetorical figure that represents the genocide of the Saxons. These scenes open the widest gulf between his history and the purely figurative use of conversion in English historical writing in the nineteenth century, and ultimately they suggest another way of defining English national identity.

I have hinted that Bois-Guilbert's seduction of Rebecca refers to the contemporary English debate over whether the "atheistical French" would be the nation to restore the Jews to their homeland. The atheistic Templar, who tries to woo Rebecca with visions of material advantage and military might, ends by tempting her with a vision of her queenly restoration to Palestine. The Templar's strategies of temptation stem from the question asked in so many European nations during the Enlightenment and at the beginning of the nineteenth century: would the Jews, as the price for emancipation, give up their religion for civil power? But the Templar's strategy requires not only that Rebecca "embrace our religion" (217), but that she yield to his desire, so that his demand for her conversion is inseparable from his threat of rape. Rebecca retaliates with the threat of suicide—a choice that many medieval Jews made as an alternative to forced conversion.[26]

The second attempted conversion of Rebecca functions as Scott's critique of the Catholic treatment of the Jews. The Templars' trial of Rebecca for witchcraft, reminiscent of an Inquisitorial trial, actually puts the fanaticism of priestcraft on trial in Scott's focus on the superstition and xenophobia that guide the investigation of the Jew. The particular charge of witchcraft is no more than a pretext to inspect and attack Rebecca as a Jew, for the Grand Master is willing to acquit her if she will convert: "Repent, my daughter, confess thy witchcrafts, turn thee from thine evil faith, embrace this holy emblem, and all shall yet be well with thee here and hereafter" (369). The process of forced conversion is once again exposed. At the threat of death by fire, she is asked to convert, but this Jewish "witch" (430) has already proven that, like the "Saxon witch" Ulrica (266) who willingly surrenders herself to the fires of death, Rebecca will die to preserve her racial identity. In King Richard's final dismissal of the Templars, despite the Grand Master's threat of an "appeal to Rome" (441), we find an anticipation of the Reformation and another strand of the contemporary debate over "the Jewish question"—English writers of the early nineteenth century contrasting Protestant England

and the Catholic nations of Europe (such as Spain) in their treatment of the Jews.

Scott questions this contrast by making Rowena, in her role as the harbinger of the new England, the instrument of the third and final attempt at converting Rebecca. Scott carefully positions the meeting between Rowena and Rebecca directly after the marriage celebration of Ivanhoe and Rowena, thereby displacing their marriage as the climax of the novel. In other words, the marriage that anticipates the happy union of the Norman and Saxon races is not allowed to suppress the still unresolved question of another race's future in England—that of the Jews. Rebecca's sudden and unexpected arrival in Rowena's chamber in *Ivanhoe*'s final chapter precludes the completion of the writing of English history without the inclusion of Jewish history. In the novel's climactic scene, Scott rewrites English history as Anglo-Jewish history.

The novel's final scene offsets the conventional comedic climax of marriage in a number of ways. The public festivity, in which the founding of the new English nation is anticipated, is succeeded by the private meeting between Rowena and Rebecca. Moreover, the novel's characteristic scenes of heroic battle between men give way in the end to a scene between two women. Rebecca's arrival "upon the second morning after this happy bridal" (447) functions as a kind of intrusion, as she enters Rowena's private chamber and requires all of Rowena's attendants, even her personal maid, to withdraw. Rowena is in some sense left defenseless, even to the point of Rebecca's asking her hostess to remove her veil. I read Rebecca's entrance into Rowena's private chamber as a kind of psychic intrusion, first, on the consciousness of her romantic rival, the woman now called "Lady Ivanhoe," but, more importantly, on the consciousness of England. Rebecca's sudden reentrance at the denouement represents the power of the return of the repressed. After all, she arrives from her trial by the Templars, having survived the attempt to convert her and to burn her at the stake. She is the erotic power that neither Ivanhoe nor Rowena can exorcise. But she is also the blot on the conscience of England insofar as she represents the religious and racial question that England cannot solve. She returns at the end, then, as the power of irrepressible guilt, come to expose once again the two myths that surfaced during the two earlier attempts to convert her—the myth of Christianity, which she exploded during her ironic questioning of Bois-Guilbert's Christian principles, and the myth of England, which she satirized in the masked irony of her invocation of "merry England, the hospitable, the generous, the free" (368), during her trial for witchcraft.

Having successfully acquitted herself at the trial at Templestowe, she arrives at the bride's chamber to pursue her own subtle and barely masked trial of Rowena and Christian England. The two ostensible purposes for Rebecca's visit—to have her farewell communicated to Ivanhoe, and to "pay the debt of gratitude" (447) she owes him—become vehicles for her critique of the English nation. In the first place, Rowena's solicitous questions about Rebecca's safety in England meet this response: "the people of England are a fierce race, quarrelling ever with their neighbours or among themselves, and ready to plunge the sword into the bowels of each other. Such is no safe abode for the children of my people" (448). Rebecca's visit becomes an announcement to quit Christian England for Muslim Spain; her voluntary exile anticipates the forced expulsion of the Jews from England in 1290, the earliest general expulsion of the Jews in medieval history—one that historians see as a direct consequence of the new nationalism of late medieval England and the failure of English policy to convert the Jews.[27]

The other purpose for Rebecca's visit, to requite the debt she owes to Ivanhoe for championing her at Templestowe, Rowena gracefully dismisses, acknowledging that she herself and Ivanhoe are still in Rebecca's debt: "Wilfred of Ivanhoe on that day rendered back but in slight measure your unceasing charity towards him in his wounds and misfortunes. Speak, is there aught remains in which he or I can serve thee?" (448). But Rebecca has not come to receive, to be indebted; she has come for the opposite purpose so that, after rejecting Rowena's promises of safety in England, and after saying farewell, she makes known, almost as an afterthought, her visit's further purpose: "One, the most trifling, part of my duty remains undischarged" (449). Suddenly she reveals that she means to make Lady Ivanhoe a gift of a silver-chased casket containing a diamond necklace and earrings.

At this moment Rowena's most potent trial begins, as Rebecca fires a series of rhetorical questions at her that overturn the stereotypes by which Jewish identity is traditionally distorted—especially the Shakespearean stereotypes of the Jewish father (who compares the value of his daughter and his ducats) and the Jewish daughter (who steals her father's wealth as part of her flight from him and his religion). "Think ye that I prize these sparkling fragments of stone above my liberty? or that my father values them in comparison to the honour of his only child? Accept them, lady— to me they are valueless. I will never wear jewels more" (449). Like the famous casket scene in *The Merchant of Venice,* this scene is a test of value; in Shakespeare's text the heiress's father tests the values of his daughter's prospective suitors; in Scott's, the heiress's rival tests the values of the heiress herself and, in another revision, represents the Jew, not the Christian, as the teacher of value. After all, hasn't Rebecca detected in Rowena's face, after her veil has been lifted, "a tinge of the world's pride or vanities" (449)? So the diamond necklace and earrings, housed in a casket, mark that pride and vanity, just as Rebecca's sacrifice of them marks the Jewish woman as the woman beyond the influence of worldly value. At Rebecca's surrender of the casket, Rowena patronizingly offers the solution of conversion: "You are then unhappy! . . . O, remain with us; the counsel of holy men will wean you from your erring law, and I will be a sister to you" (449). Is Christian law the law of pride and vanity, the law that would enable Rebecca to keep her jewels and enjoy them? Rebecca's answer to the invitation of conversion makes clear that her Judaism is worth more than the silver casket and more than the Christian protection that Rowena offers: "I may not change the faith of my fathers like a garment unsuited to the climate in which I seek to dwell" (449). In the end, Rebecca transfers to Lady Ivanhoe the sign of material value that stereotypically marked the Jew and that both state and Church periodically confiscated from the medieval Jew; at the same time, Rebecca refuses to wear the Christian disguise that would allow her safe settlement in England—reminding us of all the disguises in the novel, including Scott's disguise as an Englishman.

The silver casket has a meaning for the hero, too. It should be remembered that the silver casket in *The Merchant of Venice* comes as the ironic reward that challenges the value of the hero: "Who chooseth me shall get as much as he deserves." The silver casket suggests that Ivanhoe gets what he deserves in choosing Rowena over Rebecca. Moreover, every time Ivanhoe sees Rowena in these diamonds, he will recall Rebecca. Earlier in the novel Rebecca plays her role as the teacher of value when she refuses Ivanhoe's payment of his "casque full of crowns": "grant me one boon in

the stead of the silver thou dost promise me. . . . [B]elieve henceforward
that a Jew may do good service to a Christian, without desiring other
guerdon than the blessing of the Great Father who made both Jew and
Gentile" (261). Now, at the novel's end, she leaves Ivanhoe's wife the
silver casket. Ivanhoe, in having "hazarded his life" (448) for Rebecca,
has in fact earned the lead casket, or the right to her hand, according to
Shakespeare's plot: "Who chooseth me must give and hazard all he hath."
But perhaps the deepest irony of *Ivanhoe* is that, in the face of its climactic
ideology of intermarriage, it bars—primarily on the grounds of historical
accuracy, according to Scott (xvii)—the marriage of Ivanhoe and Rebecca and thereby ironically rewrites the fairy tale of the caskets. When
Thackeray in *Rebecca and Rowena: A Romance Upon Romance* (1850) has
Rebecca convert in order to marry Ivanhoe, we understand Scott's purpose in refusing the traditional literary topos of the converted Jewish
woman, exemplified in Shakespeare's Jessica.

When she takes her leave of Rowena, "as if a vision had passed before
her" (450), Rebecca leaves behind the traces of her visit not only in the
silver casket, but in the haunting, if immaterial, impression she has made:
"The fair Saxon related the singular conference to her husband, on whose
mind it made a deep impression. . . . Yet it would be inquiring too curiously to ask whether the recollection of Rebecca's beauty and magna-
nimity did not recur to his mind more frequently than the fair descendant
of Alfred might altogether have approved" (450). This "deep impression" on the mind of the eponymous hero, the prototype of the new
England, is at once the scar of unfulfilled erotic desire and the scar of
unresolved historic guilt, for in *Ivanhoe* marital union signifies the union
of the races. And I am claiming that Scott's inscription of the story of
medieval England's persecution of the Jews is his retracing of that deep
impression—his testimony, in 1819, of that lasting impression on the
mind of England.

Scott's project of rewriting English history as Anglo-Jewish history,
including his exploration of the persecution and attempted conversion of
the Jews, is a critical moment in the redefinition of English national identity at the beginning of the nineteenth century. I now wish to explain the
ways in which Scott's project overlaps with the millenarian literature that
flourished from the 1790s through the opening decades of the nineteenth
century—a literature that often attempted to develop the idea of English

national guilt in relation to England's past treatment of the Jews. One goal of this literature was to understand European history in relation to the history of the Jews—not simply the sacred history recorded in Hebrew Scripture, but the secular history of the modern Jews. In reviewing and revising different European national histories, this literature attempted the comparative (re)definition of several national identities, often in opposition to each other—French versus English, or Spanish versus English. What Bicheno means by *The Crisis of All Nations* is the European political upheaval that was a sign of divine Providence's response to "the accumulated crimes of those ancient houses of Europe," for "most of the princes of the royal houses of Europe have . . . been cruel persecutors of the Jews"[28]—an idea that Bicheno substantiates in brief historical sketches of Jewish persecution in Spain, France, Germany, Italy, and England. Millenarian discourse in England after the French Revolution became a crucial means of bringing Jewish history into the arena of modern European history and of evaluating the enterprise of the new nationalist historiography in relation to the history of the Jews. Much of this millenarian literature, like Scott's text, subjects the project of nationalist history-writing—the patriotic genealogy of the deeds of "our" English ancestors—to critical reevaluation by rewriting it as Anglo-Jewish history.

Thomas Witherby's *An Attempt to Remove Prejudices concerning the Jewish Nation. By Way of Dialogue* uses a mixture of millenarian prophecy and secular history to revise the popular account of English history on which the construction of English national identity depends. Witherby's text is a double revision insofar as it revises the oldest form of conversionist literature, originating with the early Church fathers and surviving in a work like John Clare's *The Converted Jew* (1630). In Witherby's hands the traditional dialogue in which the Jew converts in the end because he is unable to answer satisfactorily his Christian interlocutor[29] becomes a dialogue between two Christians in which English prejudices against the Jewish nation are removed. The traditional anti-Judaic dialogue becomes the means by which the anti-Semitic Christian is "converted." The first dialogue opens with "Cautious" chastising "Sudden" for using an anti-Semitic expression. Sudden justifies himself on the authority of Shakespeare's portrait of Shylock: "Did you read Shakespeare? You will there find the flinty-hearted Jew pourtrayed to the life." Cautious refutes the portrait of Shylock by arguing that "I by no means believe it to be a character copied from life."[30] Sudden responds that history will bear out what art may have exaggerated, thereby turning the argument to an examination of English history.

In this brief prologue Witherby adumbrates the procedures by which the reinvention of Jewish identity must begin in England—a program that is realized in what I have called the revisionist novel of Jewish identity. The revision of the conventions and forms of anti-Semitism in England begins with a revision of *The Merchant of Venice*, the ur-text of Jewish identity in England. The usurpation of the power that Shakespeare's play exerts on English consciousness can come only from an appeal to Anglo-Jewish history—from a historicization of the question of Jewish identity. Scott's portrait of Isaac attempts to move beyond the legendary Jew that Shakespeare drew—the threatening Jew with knife in hand, refusing all requests for mercy as he holds the Christian's life in his hands—to the Jew in history, the Jew as victim and scapegoat: "there was no race existing on the earth . . . who were the object of such an unintermitting, general, and relentless persecution as the Jews of this period" (55). And while the portrait of Isaac's trembling sycophancy is itself a stereotype, Scott nonetheless succeeds in his goal of representing the Jew as a historical construct, as the product of social circumstances rather than inherent vices; hence Scott's argument that the Jew "adopted a national character" (39) in the face of persecution. In attempting to historicize Shakespeare's portrait, Scott consistently conceives of Isaac's role as "reversing Shylock's position" (264).

Like *Ivanhoe*'s critique of the ideology of English patriotic historiography, Witherby's text makes clear that the appeal to history is a two-edged sword when Sudden justifies his anti-Semitism on historical grounds: "Let us proceed to the consideration of history, and you will find that the Jews have ever been distinguished as a knavish people" (*ARP,* 2). Cautious, in turn, makes clear that not history, but revisionist history, must remove the prejudices against the Jews: "You will grant that the historians to which we refer being Christians, and Christians who in many instances shew a degree of hatred against the Jews, some allowance is to be made in our estimates for the bias under which they wrote" (*ARP,* 4). After reviewing the slanderous legends that characterize the medieval chronicles of England (such as the numerous accounts of Jews murdering Christian children), Witherby begins the revision of Anglo-Jewish history with an intention of reevaluating the national conscience. He does so by ironically turning the tables on the traditional Christian insistence that the Jews reflect on their own history of guilt—that is, on the charge that they murdered Christ: "Well, then, if it is admitted that Christians have for these seventeen hundred years past been urging the Jews to enter into the revision of an act of their ancestors, with what face could Christians refuse to enter into the investigation of the acts of their ancestors towards the Jews . . . ?" (*ARP,* 14). This question initiates the project in which English national pride is chiseled away in a competition that the English cannot help but lose: "I will say, that if the Jews and the English were to investigate the conduct of their ancestors, and their behaviour towards each other, that the Englishman should blush at the comparison" (*ARP,* 5).

Witherby's text is not without its own nationalistic strains, for it has an anti-French element whose source lies in that kind of English reaction against the French Revolution that Edmund Burke articulated most influentially. Moreover, we cannot forget that Witherby's text is written in preparation for the restoration of the Jews: it deliberately intends to justify English, rather than French, leadership in the restoration. This means disqualifying the French for such a divine mission: "it seems beyond doubt that no atheistical democracy! no apostate faction! no revolutionary government! will ever have the honour of becoming the instruments of providence" (*ARP,* 335). Anti-French propaganda notwithstanding, Witherby's text makes clear that the mission of Protestant England must begin in a recognition of "that ponderous load of national guilt" (*ARP,* 419), which, as the Spanish incurred through their persecution of Native Americans, the English incurred through their persecution of the Jews. Such recognition can come only when England honors the traditions of Judaism, which constitute (as he argues) the foundations of Christianity, so that here in his *Dialogue,* and even more forcefully in his *Vindication of the Jews. . . . Humbly submitted to the consideration of the Missionary Society, and the London Society for promoting Christianity among the Jews* (1809), the appeal to history is an appeal to protect the modern Jew from the efforts of contemporary conversionist societies, as the subtitle of his *Vindication* suggests.

Perhaps the most famous definition of English national identity, at least in this period, is formulated through the question of Jewish identity and the rhetoric of conversion. While it is well known that Burke's *Reflections on the Revolution in France* (1790) had a profound influence in defining English identity by attacking the French revolutionary government, I wish to explore the strategy by which Burke characterizes the French not only as atheistical apostates (to use Witherby's words), but as Jewish proselytes. While Burke's text, like Witherby's, works through an appeal to English history and a comparative formulation of different European national identities, Burke takes a dramatically different position in relation to conversion and Jewish identity, explaining how to protect the modern Englishman from contemporary revolutionary or French or *Jewish* (the three terms become interchangeable) conversionist efforts.

Burke's text functions as a kind of counterdiscourse to a sermon by Richard Price that praised the French Revolution by sympathetically comparing it to the English Revolution of 1688–89. Noting that Price's sermon was delivered on the site of the old Jewish ghetto, Burke turns the simple designation of place—"the dissenting meeting house of the Old Jewry"[31]—into the infectious sign of an as yet undefined (though nonetheless threatening) principle of Jewishness, so that the place-name eventually marks the speaker, the speech, the audience, the contents of the speech, and an entire species of discourse: "the preacher of the Old Jewry" (*R*, 58), the "famous sermon of the Old Jewry" (*R*, 56), the "society of the Old Jewry" (*R*, 74), "the Old Jewry doctrine" (*R*, 17), "the sermons of the Old Jewry" (*R*, 27).

The unarticulated "logic" of this rhetoric is based on both historical and contemporary events—events that help clarify why the word "Jewry" becomes a code name for revolution in Burke's essay. First, while Burke does not openly link England's "revolutionary" events of the seventeenth century with the Jews, he nonetheless names as Price's historic "predecessor" (*R*, 10) Hugh Peter (1598–1660), a Puritan enthusiast whose Jewish sympathies had become a well-known butt of political satire, as reflected in the Restoration engraving of Peter declaring, "Let it [St. Paul's] out to ye Jews"—a reference to the allegation that the Jews had tried to purchase the cathedral with the intention of turning it into a synagogue.[32] Peter is remembered not only for having supported the readmission of the Jews into England, but for having been beheaded because of his complicity in the execution of Charles I, thereby securing Burke's association between Jewish sympathizers and revolutionaries, even regicides. Burke goes on to attach Price to the English revolution's "fifth monarchy" (*R*, 64) men, who based their radical politics in the interpretation of Hebrew prophecy, and who called for sweeping legal reform and the destruction of the national church, as well as the restoration of the Jews (as the central sign of the Second Coming, or Fifth Monarchy).[33] Second, while Burke never directly discusses the French Revolution's emancipation of the Jews, he sneers at the French by speaking of their "new Hebrew brethren" (*R*, 74). Behind both the English "Puritan Revolution" and the revolution in France, then, Burke discovers Judaizers, or at least Jewish sympathizers. In this light Price's sermon poses a genuine political threat to contemporary England; by capitalizing on the site of Price's sermon, Burke can designate Price as "the preacher of the Old Jewry" who rearticulates, in 1789, the "Old Jewry doctrine" of religious toleration, philo-Semitism, and revolution that rocked the English nation in the previous century.

Furthermore, Burke attempts to show the dangerous consequences of religious toleration, especially when realized in the separation of Church and state, by claiming that the revolutionary government in France is based on "a stock-jobbing constitution" (*R*, 46), which is code for a Jewish constitution.[34] While in England "the Jews in Change Alley have not yet dared to hint their hopes of a mortgage on the revenues belonging to the see of Canterbury" (*R*, 92), Church lands in France are in danger of being sold to "Jews and jobbers" (*R*, 47)—a reminder of the allegation that the Jews tried to buy St. Paul's. And the creators of the new government in France have behaved "like Jew brokers, contending with each other . . . with fraudulent circulation and depreciated paper" (*R*, 42); such men, "'enlightened' usurers" (*R*, 168), are like Shylock, "purchasers at the auction of their innocent fellow citizens" (*R*, 207). So, while the English aristocracy remains preserved through a government founded on the rule of inheritance rather than election, France will produce an aristocracy "bastardized and corrupted in blood" (*R*, 50): "The next generation of the nobility will resemble the artificers and clowns, and money-jobbers usurers, and Jews, who will be always their fellows, and sometimes their masters" (*R*, 43).

The demagogic basis of Burke's rhetoric functions as a warning not simply against apostasy, but against conversion, a warning against betraying one's English identity by becoming a Jew. Burke reformulates the distinction between the French and the English—the apparent subject of the

Reflections—as the distinction between Jews (French) and Christians (English). For Burke, to follow in the footsteps of the French Revolution is to become a Jew. And there is both historic and contemporary precedence for the Judaization of the English during the "Puritan Revolution" and in the contemporary case of Lord George Gordon (1751–93), the "public proselyte to Judaism" (*R*, 73).[35] While Gordon is best-known today for his role in the Gordon Riots (1780), his conversion to Judaism was a popular subject in pamphlets, chapbooks, street ballads, and engravings in the late 1780s (figures 8–9), and we have seen that a hostile reviewer linked Byron's supposed Judaization in *Hebrew Melodies* with Gordon's conversion. For Burke, Gordon is a palpable symbol of the way in which revolutionary and Jewish sympathies meet. Gordon is called "the noble libeller" (*R*, 74) of the French queen in the same breath that his unrelated conversion to Judaism is recorded. By these means, Burke boldly enlarges the equation between "revolution" and "apostasy" that writers like Witherby make. Burke defines proselytism as the cause of revolution, and the Englishman who converts to Judaism stands behind revolution, and threatens all Englishmen with the undoing of their national identity. In short, revolution is conversion writ large. After all, the entire French nation is guilty of having fallen under the powerful "proselytism" (*R*, 97) of figures like Voltaire, and England is in a similar danger, for Price is one of "the new evangelists" or "apostolic missionaries" (*R*, 12), grotesque inversions of the native English Evangelical movement. In Burke's view, these new evangelists attempt not to Christianize "the heathen" and "the infidel," but to Judaize the English. In such language we see how, in a politically charged moment of paranoia and xenophobia, the process of proselytization, usually focused safely on the identity of the Other, is imagined as threatening English national identity itself. The traditional Christian project of converting the Jews finds its corollary, in a revolutionary epoch, in the fierce protection of English national identity against all conversionist efforts, especially Jewish (or French).

English national identity, the identity Burke shares with his countrymen ("we"), depends on acknowledging a unity of faith grounded in a refusal to convert: "We are not the converts of Rousseau; we are not the disciples of Voltaire" (*R*, 75). Anticipating Turner and Freeman, Burke speaks on behalf of the present English nation as well as its forefathers, using what I have called a consolidating pronoun of national identity that

Figure 8. Lord George Gordon, former President of the Protestant Association, pictured as a Jew after his conversion in Birmingham. Published by W. Dickie, 1787. Courtesy of the Library of the Jewish Theological Seminary of America.

links the writer with all other "Englishmen" across space and time: "I assure you I do not aim at singularity. I give you opinions which have been accepted amongst us, from very early times to this moment" (*R*, 87). And again, coterminous with his national ancestors, Burke can say: "We wished at the period of the Revolution, and do now wish, to derive all we possess as *an inheritance from our forefathers*" (*R*, 27–28). Like Freeman

Figure 9. Lord George Gordon in Newgate, being fed by his new coreligionists while a Christian is about to serve him pork. Published in 1803 by S. W. Fores. There is an earlier issue dated 1788, published by T. Harmar. Courtesy of the Library of the Jewish Theological Seminary of America.

after him and a long tradition of English writers before him (Burke mentions Coke and Selden and Blackstone as prominent examples), Burke bases national identity on the (pre-Norman) antiquity of English law (*R*, 27), so that to attack the tradition of English government is to do no less than dissolve the basis of English national identity—that is, to apostasize, to become like "those children of their country who are prompt rashly to hack that aged parent in pieces" (*R*, 84), to betray the most sacred bond for "thirty pieces of silver" (*R*, 74). In Burke's emotional rhetoric it is dimly hinted that revolution is the site where parricide, regicide, and deicide—the traditional Christian charge against the Jews—become one.

I began this chapter by recalling how French influence and "the Jewish question" were linked at the center of a well-known crisis in German national identity; I have ended by showing how French influence and "the Jewish question"—and its critical sign, the figure of conversion—had a similarly powerful role in the crisis of English national identity during the period of the French Revolution. More particularly, I have shown how the German phenomenon of anti-Semitic writing during the nineteenth century's opening decades had a powerful precursor in England in Burke's *Reflections:* national identity, in England as well as in Germany, was formulated through a rejection of French influence, which merged with— and often became rewritten as—a rejection of Jewish influence. And this Jewish influence was formulated by Burke as the threat of Jewish proselytism. For Burke, conversion became a figure for revolution, and the Jewish proselyte Lord George Gordon became a symbol, and a warning, of the loss of English national identity.

Burke, however, was not alone in using "the Jewish question" to construct and contrast different European national identities at this historical moment. For, while Burke was arguing that the preservation of English national identity depended on guarding against Jewish proselytism, writers like Bicheno and Witherby were suggesting that England could maintain its traditional reputation for tolerance only by accepting "that ponderous load of national guilt" for its past persecution of the Jews and by acknowledging Jewish history and Hebrew Scripture as essential components of the destiny of England and Protestantism. But even while millenarians were reminding Europe of its past crimes against the Jews, and attempting to predict and influence which European nation (England or France) would help restore the Jews to their homeland, a writer like Witherby, while attacking the procedures of the most prominent conversionist societies, nonetheless awaited the general conversion of the Jews, if not as the work of man, then as the work of God—for the millenarian goal of restoring the Jews to their homeland included the belief in their conversion.

Finally, in Scott, we see the way in which England's guilt toward the Jews is fully secularized and historicized, no longer dependent on biblical prophecy or millenarian expectation, but based on the startling principle of history uncovered in *Ivanhoe*—namely, that historic change typically involves the absorption of one culture by another, or what Scott defines as conversion and genocide. With such a definition in mind, Scott attempts to overturn the conventional model of national identity, based on racial homogeneity, with a countermodel in which the racial intermixture between Saxons and Normans becomes the basis of cultural diversity and national identity in England. He attempts to enlist the sympathies of his English readers for the broadest basis of cultural diversity by suggesting that the project to convert the Jews (and to erase the Scots) has its parallel in the attempted genocide of the Saxons during the Norman Conquest. Thus, Scott boldly inserts the Jews into the history of the event on which English national identity traditionally depends. In critiquing the traditional concept of English identity as racially pure, Scott reminds his readers that the English nation was founded in racial exclusion as well as inclusion, and thereby he rewrites English history as Anglo-Jewish history—a history of persecution and subsequent guilt. This guilt is formulated, at least in part, in a comparison of nations that Rebecca makes when she chooses Spain over England, "for less cruel are the cruelties of the Moors unto the race of Jacob than the cruelties of the Nazarenes of England" (375). Rebecca's famous remark initiated an entire tradition of historical romances that focused on the comparative history of the persecution of the Jews in Spain and England. Following the publication of *Ivanhoe*, then, the construction of different national identities, through the representation of their treatment of the Jews, passed from millenarian discourse into the more mainstream discourse of popular fiction. So, in the period between the French Revolution and the opening decades of the nineteenth century, and especially after the publication of *Ivanhoe*, not only did the figure of conversion become the means by which writers explored the preservation, transformation, or eradication of different racial and national identities—the representation of Jewish persecution, including the history of Christian efforts at proselytizing the Jews, became a critical tool used in constructing English identity in relation to other European national identities.

4

Writing Spanish History: The Inquisition and "the Secret Race"

Writing in 1837, the American historian William Prescott remarked that "English writers have done more for the illustration of Spanish history than for that of any other, except their own."[1] In this chapter I wish to explain the ideological uses to which Spanish history was put in England, focusing on the way in which one particular moment, the period of the Inquisition, became a charged subject, especially for Victorian writers of historical romance. The forced conversion of masses of Jews, the famous edict expelling them in 1492, and the Inquisition's persecution of crypto-Jews made fifteenth-century Spain an object of fascination for nineteenth-century England, where the Evangelical drive to convert the Jews and the parliamentary debates over Jewish Emancipation had put "the Jewish question" at the center of England's national agenda. Moreover, as England attempted to define the origins of the nation-state as a way of articulating its own national identity, the history of Spain provided a dangerous model—dangerous, at least, for England's Jews, for by locating the origins of modern Spain in the conquest of the Moors at Granada and the banishment of the Jews, nineteenth-century historians and novelists alike began to use fifteenth-century Spain as a paradigm for the birth of a nation based in racial and religious homogeneity.

After the immense popular success of Scott's historical romances, the writing of history began to be taken up by the writer of romance. Prescott himself applauded the contributions that romance could make to historical study, remarking that Scott "had given new value to romance by building it on history, and new charms to history by embellishing it with the graces of romance."[2] But Victorian historical romance owed more than a general debt to Scott. The specific literary model behind Victorian romance's focus on the role of the Jews in medieval Spain was *Ivanhoe*'s depiction of Jewish persecution in medieval England. By depicting the persecution of the Jews at a critical moment in history—the founding of the English nation-state—*Ivanhoe* located "the Jewish question" at the heart of English national identity.

The historical romances I will examine, written between the 1830s and the 1860s, reveal the ways in which representations of "the Jewish question" set in fifteenth-century Spain became a means of exploring urgent issues of racial difference and national identity in Victorian England. Focused on a daughter's duty to her father and her fatherland, and the threat of her conversion, these romances define the role of women in the construction of the modern nation-state. When writers of historical romance situated the converted daughter at the founding moment of Christian Spain, she became a sign of the ideology that required Jews to convert before they could become full-fledged (English) citizens.

Each of the historical romances I examine—*Leila; or, the Siege of Granada* (1838) by Edward Bulwer-Lytton; *The Vale of Cedars; or, the Martyr* (1850) by Grace Aguilar, an English Jew; and *The Spanish Gypsy* (1868) by George Eliot—can be read as a direct response, even a sequel, to *Ivanhoe*. Rebecca's stinging critique of England at the end of *Ivanhoe*, and her explanation of her impending flight to Spain, invited Scott's successors in historical romance to take up "the Jewish question" in medieval Spain. Scott's extraordinary anachronism—Rebecca, in late-twelfth-century England, plans her protection under a king (Boabdil of Granada) who reigns in late-fifteenth-century Spain—opened the way for these sequels to undercut Scott's contrast between intolerant England and tolerant Spain, for by the late fifteenth century the relative peace and prosperity that the Jews had enjoyed under the Moors was about to end in a kind of recapitulation of Anglo-Jewish history: the expulsion of the Jews that had occurred in 1290 in England was repeated in 1492 in Spain. The persecutions of the Jews that dominated fifteenth-century Spain, including the forced conversion of masses of Spanish Jews and the eventual institution of the Inquisition, provided sufficient historical material to challenge Rebecca's choice of Spain over England.

In this light, these historical romances can be read within the field of an important form of nineteenth-century discourse in which different national identities are defined, usually through a more or less explicit contrast. Since writers had begun to use the history of Jewish persecution as a measuring rod for judging different European national identities, the horrors of the Spanish Inquisition could be used to minimize, comparatively speaking, the guilt that Scott and others had stimulated in the English consciousness when they charted the history of English anti-Semitism. And English Victorian writers of historical romance who set their tales in Spain could, if they chose, draw upon a long-standing nationalist tradition of anti-Spanish and anti-Catholic discourse.[3] Robert Southey gives us an excellent example of the way in which such a discourse became part of an elaborate contrast between Spain and England vis-à-vis "the Jewish question." Southey has an English traveler in Spain remark, "Till within the last fifty years the burning of a Jew formed the highest delight of the Portugueze"—a sentence that is frequently quoted in nineteenth-century England, especially by the conversionists[4]—while a Spanish traveler in England, shocked at England's tolerance of the Jews, declares: "England has been called the hell of horses, the purgatory of servants, and the paradise of women: it may be added that it is the heaven of the Jews,—alas, they have no other heaven to expect!"[5] In this context, the horrors of the Spanish Inquisition were used as an excuse to reinvent the Christian mission to the Jews. Claiming that an institution like the Inquisition was the reason behind Catholicism's failure to win Jewish converts, conversionists were inspired to initiate a new era of conversion under the banner of English Protestantism, making England "the heaven of the Jews."

The historical romances to be studied here are all set in Spain in the final decades of the fifteenth century, in the midst of extraordinary political upheavals out of which the modern nation-state would develop. As in *Ivanhoe,* the birth of a nation is represented as occurring in an environment of extreme racial conflict, amid the politics of religious conversion and racial annihilation. In *Ivanhoe* we saw the way in which the birth of the modern English nation was represented through the intermarriage between the Saxon and Norman races (after generations of racial conflict) and through the impending exile of the Jews (after the failure to convert them). A similar pattern emerged in Spanish history in 1492, when the Spaniards conquered the Moors at Granada, and Ferdinand and Isabella banished the Jews (after the failure of periodic attempts at converting them). In both nations, at both epochs, the Jews made up the third racial group in what was essentially a battle between two other, more powerful racial groups for control of a land on the verge of modern nationhood. In this way, late-fifteenth-century Spain replicated the conditions of late-twelfth-century England as represented in *Ivanhoe*.

But whereas Scott's history stressed the ultimate union of the conflicting Saxon and Norman races, and identified the erasure of the Jews as a blot on English history, his successors frequently used Spanish history to proclaim racial exclusivity as the basis of the nation-state. In this chapter I will show, for example, the way in which Prescott revised Scott's history to justify the Spanish conquest and even eradication of the Moors (and thereby to defend, if only indirectly, the extermination of entire Native American populations during his own nation's ongoing debate over "the Indian question"). In this way Spanish history could be used to establish the category of race as an insuperable barrier between different peoples and to define national identity on the basis of racial and religious homogeneity.

To take up the question of racial conflict in medieval Spain was simply one way for writers, whether in England or the United States, to respond to certain urgent contemporary questions at home. So, while set in medieval Spain, *Ivanhoe*'s sequels reveal the way in which "the Jewish question" began to be reformulated in England from the 1830s through the late 1860s, when public attention shifted from the grand scheme of restoring the Jews to their homeland, to the more local and practical topic that began to occupy English political life more and more, namely, the removal of Jewish civil disabilities[6]—a topic that nonetheless kept the ideology of conversion at the center of discussions about the Jew's place in England. In fact, representations of the Inquisition often became a critical weapon in the heated arguments that surrounded Catholic as well as Jewish Emancipation in a variety of publications and in important political coalitions. As we pass from *Ivanhoe* to its sequels, we move from the Crusades in twelfth-century England to the Inquisition in fifteenth-century Spain—two signal events in the history of Jewish persecution—but we nonetheless remain grounded in the continuing contemporary debates over "the Jewish question."

Before turning to the representation of the Spanish Inquisition in Victorian historical romance, I wish to explain that in England accounts of the Inquisition were traditionally produced out of patently nationalistic and religious motives; in writing the history of Spain, authors produced representations that, while specifically anti-Catholic, neglected Jewish persecution. What emerged was the representation of the martyrdom of Protestants at the hands of Spanish Catholic Inquisitors, which left a great deal of the history of the Inquisition untold. The perennial political usefulness of this kind of representation in England is especially well illustrated by John Stockdale's explanation of the origin of his influential *History of the Inquisitions* (1810),[7] one of the source texts to which Grace Aguilar alludes in *The Vale of Cedars*. At the moment when "the important question, whether the claims of the Roman Catholics to equal political rights with Protestants" was being "forced upon the parliament" (*HI*, v), Stockdale felt the urgent necessity of laying before (Protestant) England the horrors of papal power as displayed in the various inquisitions of Spain, Portugal, Venice, and so on. In other words, Stockdale writes a "history" that, while recording events of past centuries in other countries, nonetheless responds to a present and local danger to England. The precise danger that Catholic Emancipation poses to England is represented, at least at first, only in a half-veiled and ominous warning in which the rhetoric of conversion plays a critical role. Stockdale's preface ends with a warning against proselytism, reminding us of Burke's similar warning in *Reflections on the Revolution in France* twenty years earlier, only here the danger comes from Catholic rather than Jewish proselytism: "The page of history . . . clearly proves . . . that Popery, having been driven out of Rome, has taken refuge amongst us, and is, with unceasing activity, daily gaining proselytes to its cause. . . . Read the following pages with more than serious—with solemn attention, for Popery is making rapid advances against your religion: and THE EMBRYO OF THE INQUISITION (may I never find it necessary to be more explicit on this subject) IS ACTUALLY ESTABLISHED IN EVERY PART OF THE UNITED KINGDOM" (*HI*, xvi).

What actuates Stockdale's history of the Inquisition is the threat of Catholic proselytism. But, as in Burke's *Reflections,* the potential conversion of English Protestants becomes a figure for a much broader and more insidious process: the undoing of English national identity. For, according to Stockdale, it is precisely such an undoing that the Inquisition has worked on the Spanish people. He warns his fellow citizens not to make the mistake of thinking "that the character of the modern inhabitants of Spain, is the real national character"; the institution of the Inquisition has "perverted" (*HI,* 106) that "real" character. "Perversion" is a specialized term, especially prominent in the nineteenth century, for the wrong kind of conversion—a conversion to the wrong faith—as the following apothegm makes especially clear: "A Popish pervert and a Protestant convert are, indeed, two different provisionals" (*OED*).[8] In Stockdale's text the literal, religious conversion that the Inquisition attempted to enforce has its double in the figurative, national conversion that the Inquisition inadvertently effected on the entire Spanish population. According to Stockdale, the taciturn, suspicious, severe Spaniard is simply the "assumed, unnatural, fictitious" character of the Spaniard after the Inquisition. So, the Inquisition, which "persecuted to convert, and massacred through devotion" (*HI,* 110), had a further consequence: it "disfigured" and "effaced" the "most noble of features in the national character" (*HI,* 350). The ideological subtext of Stockdale's *History,* then, uses the torture and murder of the immediate victims of the Inquisition to represent what Stockdale takes to be the larger historical consequence, the perversion of Spain's national character. By neglecting the historic origins of the Inquisition in Jewish persecution, and by engaging in the popular contemporary enterprise of delineating different European national identities, Stockdale succeeds in rerouting the ostensible topic of the text; the history of the Inquisition yields to the present political crisis of Protestant England—namely, the debate over Catholic Emancipation, and the larger question of the loss of English national identity.

Stockdale's use of the terminology of conversion and perversion to represent the effacement of national identity helps to pinpoint a profound irony in the rhetoric of English conversionist discourse. At the height of English missionary activity, when the attempt to save the world by evangelizing the entire globe was in full swing, conversion was represented as a clear and present danger at home, a deadly menace about to annihilate the English national character. The figure of conversion became the central means by which events as widely different as the French Revolution and the Spanish Inquisition (according to Burke and Stockdale, respectively) were represented as key historical events that could teach England a critical lesson—to guard against the conversion of English national identity. Hence Stockdale's *History of the Inquisitions* did not merely record the historic atrocities of Catholic persecution in Spain; more importantly, it

warned the English of the subtle and extensive powers that papal influence might exert on the identity of their much-prized national character.
By prefixing his history of the Inquisition with his comments on "what
is insidiously termed Catholic Emancipation" (*HI*, xv), Stockdale makes
clear the many ideological purposes that such a history may serve. His
text can help us see how a history of the Inquisition meant to prevent Catholic Emancipation in England could also be used to foil Anglo-
Jewish interests, not simply by neglecting the persecutions that the Jews
suffered from the Inquisition. For example, English Jews took a great
interest in Catholic Emancipation, hoping that it would open the door to
removing similar disabilities from which they suffered. But Anglo-Jewry
suffered a great disappointment when Catholic Emancipation occurred
in 1829 without the immediate effects for which the Jews hoped. Catholics eventually became enlisted in the battle for Jewish Emancipation,
forming an unexpected but nonetheless important coalition, satirically
represented in the *Punch* cartoon, "Strange Bed-Fellows" (figure 10). It
was not until three decades after Catholic Emancipation that Jewish civil
and political disabilities were removed.[9]

This Jewish interest may in fact be the reason that the body of Stockdale's anti-Catholic text avoids the topic of the persecution of the Jews
and even misreads certain crucial historical events about the anti-Judaic
origins of the Inquisition in Spain. Stockdale's most powerful misrepresentation occurs when he periodically writes "Moor" when "Jew" would
be historically accurate—as in his description of Torquemada's initiation
of the Spanish Inquisition to protect Christianity from the heretical influences of the Moors. Moreover, Stockdale's accounts of persecution during the Inquisition consistently avoid showing practicing Jews as its victims. Stockdale's favorite case histories of persecuted victims are drawn
from many already famous Protestant accounts (such as William Lith-
gow's experiences, first published in 1682), but even his other case histories, when they introduce the idea of being persecuted for Judaizing, take
an unusual turn. When Judaic practices are punished in Stockdale's Inquisition, the victim is typically represented as a true Christian falsely
accused of being a Jew. In this fashion he passes over the persecution of
the Spanish and Portuguese crypto-Jews, and Judaism becomes no more
than a false slander directed at legitimate Christians. Stockdale walks a
delicate political line in his *History*, where his articulated goal—to prevent

PUNCH, OR THE LONDON CHARIVARI.—June 27, 1857.

STRANGE BED-FELLOWS!

Figure 10. Wearing the multiple hats of the old-clothes man, the Jew is helped by the Catholic in attempting to rescind the oath that required Jews to swear "upon the faith of a true Christian," words that were originally designed to stand in the way of Roman Catholics. *Punch*, June 27, 1857.

Catholic Emancipation—works hand-in-hand with an unarticulated goal: to avoid aiding Jewish Emancipation by stirring English sympathies for the Jewish martyrs of the Inquisition.

Stockdale's failure to represent the way in which the Jews were the target of the Spanish Inquisition recalls another, more popular source of information about the Inquisition that flourished from the late eighteenth century through the opening decades of the nineteenth: the Gothic novel. By the end of the eighteenth century, at least in England, the most accessible source of information about the Inquisition was the series of Gothic novels that delighted in fusing supernatural horror with the horrors of Inquisitorial persecution, blending romance with history in a Spanish or Italian setting. These depictions of Catholic atrocities became so well known that the narrator of William Godwin's *St. Leon: A Tale of the Sixteenth Century* (1799), when imprisoned by the Inquisition, can reflect belatedly on the exhaustion of this particular engine of literary horror: "It is not my intention to treat of those particulars of the holy office which are already to be found in innumerable publications."[10] But, as plentiful as Gothic depictions of the Inquisition were, they were equally devoid of scenes of Jewish persecution. For these works had the same political agenda as Stockdale's *History;* the Gothic novel functions as a critical moment in the development of English antimonastic and anti-Spanish rhetoric. In *The Monk* (1796), for example, "the superstition, which governed Madrid's Inhabitants," is a prime target of Matthew Lewis's pen: "the artifices of the Monks, and the gross absurdity of their miracles, wonders, and suppositious reliques," including "monastic cruelty,"[11] are anatomized, adding up once again to a Spanish Inquisition without Jews. In short, English discourse about the Inquisition, while consistently anti-Catholic, typically failed to be pro-Jewish.

At the same time, these Gothic novels, almost in spite of themselves, were marked by what became a characteristically Gothic Jewish figure, part of the stock horror equipment of such novels as *The Monk* and *St. Leon*—the figure of the Wandering Jew. So, it is not simply that Jewish persecution played no role in such texts, but that, as if through some half-repressed knowledge of such persecution, the Gothic novelist conjured up the Jew not as a victim of the Inquisition, not as a historical personage, but as a ghostly figure from legend, "doomed to inspire all who look on me with terror."[12] Rather than being a victim of the Inquisition, the Jew shared the stage with the Inquisition itself in exciting terror in the reader. Moreover, one can view the figure of the Wandering Jew as a mystification of the historical facts about the Jewish diaspora. He represents, in both Lewis's and Godwin's texts, a homelessness that is almost metaphysical, a weariness and alienation that is fantastic as opposed to real. This fantastic homelessness makes no reference to the historical homelessness that the Spanish Jews suffered after their banishment in 1492. So, whether in Stockdale's *History* or the Gothic novel, the Jew remained on the margins of the different discourses that represented the Inquisition, a ghostly figure of fantasy rather than a flesh-and-blood figure of history, and hence shut out from English sympathies for the victims of Catholic intolerance.

Daughter and Father(land)

In the three historical romances to be explored here, the central character is a daughter who undergoes a dramatic and painful confrontation with her father, when he pleads with her in the manner that Cedric pleads with his two symbolic daughters, Rowena and Ulrica, to uphold their racial heritage. In the politics of nineteenth-century European nationalism, woman's central trial is represented as the trial of national, religious, or racial loyalty—a paradigm originating in Scott's portraits of Rowena, Ulrica, and Rebecca in *Ivanhoe*. Filial loyalty in all these texts is simply the pretext for racial loyalty: the heroine is not simply the daughter of the father, but the daughter of the race. Unlike the heroic Rebecca, the "daughter of Israel" who decides without any counsel from her father to "tear this folly from my heart, though every fibre bleed as I rend it away,"[13] the daughters in *Ivanhoe*'s sequels must be persuaded by the father to give up a love that threatens the fatherland or the father religion ("the God of your fathers"). In all three of these romances the father enters the love plot to prohibit an intermarriage, so that at the center of each text is a battle between father and lover over the possession of the young heroine. The real object of this battle is the propagation and extinction of different, even warring, religions and races, in which the survival of a minority population is threatened through the daughter's conversion or, what amounts to the same thing, her intermarriage. The relationship in these texts between father and daughter, then, can be formulated in the following way: from *Ivanhoe* onwards, the threat of racial extinction is represented through the pairing of a widowed father, without further means of procreating his race, and his sole offspring, a daughter in danger of becoming (through conversion or intermarriage) a tool in the procreation of the enemy race. Hence the daughter's pure instrumentality in these tales; she serves the critical function of propagating the race and preserving the racial name. For this reason, these texts revise the conventional marriage plot that ends when the lover becomes the husband and changes the heroine's name to his own; in the racial plot, the father reemerges at a critical moment to reestablish the heroine's racial name and thereby to preclude the successful completion of the marriage plot.

Edward Bulwer-Lytton's *Leila* tells such a tale of Jewish father and daughter at the same time that it shows how the Inquisition could be used by English writers to maintain a long-standing tradition of anti-Catholic rhetoric without depicting the persecution of the Jews. Bulwer describes Almamen, the father of Leila: "Serpent as he was, he cared not through what mire of treachery and fraud he trailed his baleful folds, so that at last he could spring upon his prey. Nature had given him sagacity and strength. The curse of circumstance had humbled, but reconciled him to the dust. He had the crawl of the reptile,—he had also its poison and its fangs" (*L,* 27).[14] The ferocity of Almamen, a secret Jew who periodically betrays both sides in the conflict between the Spaniards and the Moors, makes impossible a tale of the victimhood of the Jew by the Catholic Inquisition. In fact, in *Leila* Jewish incendiary and Dominican monk are positioned in analogous positions, as brother fanatics, so that Protestant England, celebrated for its reason and tolerance, can look on both Jew and Catholic and be aghast. Despite their different religions, Torquemada and Almamen, the famous monk of history and Bulwer's fictitious Jew, are really parallel figures, each a fanatic in his own way: "persecution and affliction made him [Almamen] a fanatic" (*L,* 25), while Torquemada, "the stern fanatic" (*L,* 71) of countless histories and romances, is "that terrible man, THE FIRST GRAND INQUISITOR OF SPAIN" (*L,* 68). When the two men come face to face, the Jew supposedly at the mercy of the monk in an Inquisitorial tribunal, they are seen as equals, even as doubles: "it almost seemed as if those two men, each so raised above his fellows by the sternness of his nature and the energy of his passions, sought by a look alone to assert his own supremacy and crush his foe" (*L,* 75). In Bulwer's representation of the Inquisition the Jew deserves as little sympathy as the Catholic; in fact, each seems to deserve the other.

The double title of the novel, *Leila; or, the Siege of Granada,* calls attention to the parallel between the domestic plot of the daughter and the political plot of the nation, so that while we follow Almamen's complicated switching of allegiances between Christian and Moor in what eventually becomes the famous siege of Granada, we also follow the Jewish family plot—namely, the father's attempt to guard his daughter Leila's Jewish heritage. Thus, the larger historical plot involving the battle for political power among three races is paralleled in the domestic plot in which both Christian and Moor threaten the Jewish family. I will argue that these parallel plots spell the ultimate Christianization of Spain, one by battle, the other by conversion, for the conquest of Granada, in which Muslim Spain is finally put to rout, signals as well the conquest of the Jewish daughter.

Leila's plot of conversion begins when the father, while successfully secreting his daughter from her Moorish lover, inadvertently delivers her to the Christian monarchs, at whose hands Leila is subjected to the procedures of conversion by the Queen's intermediary, Donna Inez. The depiction of a Christian woman trying to convert a Jewish woman becomes a set piece in these romances, recalling the climactic moment in *Ivanhoe* when Rowena offers Rebecca the means of conversion. As in Scott's novel, the Jewish heroine in *Leila* (and in *The Vale of Cedars*) is asked to unveil herself, at which point the Christian woman in power takes pity on her and prescribes the procedures of conversion to act on "the yielding softness of our sex" (*L,* 81).

Donna Inez's specialty is "by gentle means to make the conversions which force was impotent to effect" (*L,* 87). Leila is commanded to "listen with ductile senses to her gentle ministry" (*L,* 82). But even such a gentle ministry—this proselytization of woman by woman—proceeds as a parallel to the siege of Granada that is the novel's public and masculine plot: "Donna Inez sought rather to undermine than to storm the mental fortress she hoped to man with spiritual allies" (*L,* 87). The strategies of proselytism are exposed as an arsenal of weapons that Donna Inez uses to undermine "the belief upon which she waged war" (*L,* 87). In this way, the conquest of Muslim Granada runs parallel to the conversion of the

Jewish daughter: each is part of a cooperative effort in the birth of modern Catholic Spain.

During a brief reunion with Almamen, in a striking tableau, daughter and father appear as extreme antitheses, both fantasies of the Christian ideology of conversion—the daughter the symbol of easy conversion, the father the symbol of the "stubborn race" (*L,* 110): "And so passed the hours of that night; and the father and the child—the meek convert, the revengeful fanatic—were under the same roof" (*L,* 109). This tableau, with its images of male intransigence and female docility, forecasts the reemergence of the father's authority. Stigmatizing his daughter as an "apostate" (*L,* 111), Almamen eventually succeeds in reclaiming Leila, so that the convert, converted back again, yields in the presence of patriarchal authority: "Father, wheresoever thou goest, I will wend with thee" (*L,* 113). Leila, variously named "Jewess," "Christian," and "deist" (*L,* 88–90), is the unending object of conversion, and therefore, she is most appropriately named in the address that takes away her proper name and names her by her function in the plot: "Thou, my sweet convert" (*L,* 107).

The highly symbolic function of the Jewish daughter in the clash among three races and religions in fifteenth-century Spain has its final demonstration in our last view of Leila, surrounded by all the male characters who claim her: Almamen, the Jewish (biological) father; Torquemada, the Catholic (spiritual) father; and Muza, the Muslim lover. The characters meet at the altar of a convent in which Leila is about to take her vows as a nun. While Muza hopes to revise this setting according to the conventions of the happy climax of comedy, the father turns the potential marriage altar into the altar of sacrifice, realizing the full extent of patriarchal power in the act of filicide: "thrice the blade of the Hebrew had passed through that innocent breast; thrice was it reddened with that virgin blood. Leila fell in the arms of her lover" (*L,* 160), her virgin blood spilled at the sacred altar before she can marry either the mortal, or the eternal, bridegroom. The battle over Leila ends when she is no longer able to perform her regenerative function as the "daughter of the great Hebrew race" (*L,* 20)—a function explained to her by her father earlier in the novel: "If thou perish, if thou art lost to us, thou, the last daughter of the house of Issachar, then the haughtiest family of God's great people is extinct. . . . I look to thee and thy seed for . . . regeneration" (*L,* 114).

When the father murders the daughter, he reenacts what he sees as her death through conversion, so that in *Leila* the converted Jewish daughter functions as a sign both of the birth of the Spanish nation and the extinction of the Jewish race.

Almamen's reflections on his child's procreative function are part of a larger pattern of rhetoric in *Leila* that names the child by signaling his or her function genealogically and historically—in fact, in a way that turns family genealogy into racial history. Almamen's description of his child as "the last scion of my race" (*L,* 114), for example, is anticipated when Donna Inez mourns the death of "the last scion of her house" (*L,* 86–87), while the conquest of Granada gains its historic power by being the story of "Boabdil el Chico, the last of the Moorish dynasty in Spain" (*L,* 6), "the last remnant of the Moorish name, and the last monarch of the Moorish dynasty" (*L,* 56). In short, the plot of *Leila* takes place at a historic moment in which all three races attempt to preserve their heritages in the face of the threat of extinction.

Bulwer ends his novel by pressing the analogy between the conversion of Leila (the domestic plot) and the conquest of Boabdil (the national plot) as cooperative events in the Christianization of Spain (or the extinction of Jew and Muslim): "While in this obscure and remote convent progressed the history of an individual, we are summoned back to witness the crowning fate of an expiring dynasty" (*L,* 144)—Bulwer having learned from Scott that "the history of an individual" is the history of a nation and a race. After the conquest of Granada during the final departure of the last monarch of the Moorish dynasty, Leila's conversion is recalled when Queen Isabel seeks to make the military conquest of the Moors complete by turning it into a religious conquest: "May we not hint at the blessed possibility of conversion?" (*L,* 174). But already Boabdil recognizes the ways in which this "blessed possibility" has become the accomplished fact of political power; he sees "the silver cross of Spain" float from the watchtower of the Alhambra, and he hears the chant of *Te Deum* (*L,* 172). Conquest and conversion have already become inseparable.

Finally, the climactic moments of the double plot of *Leila* are given over to parental charges of unfulfilled filial duty. While the father reproaches Leila for failing to preserve the house of Issachar, the mother reproaches Boabdil for failing to preserve the Moorish dynasty. The nature of the mother's stinging reproach makes us see in a new light the conjunction between conversion and conquest. The feminine ductility responsible for Leila's conversion also seems responsible for Boabdil's conquest, as his mother chides him, "Ay, weep like a woman over what thou couldst not defend like a man!" (*L,* 175). The converted (Jewish daughter) and the conquered (Moorish son) function under the sign of the feminine in *Leila.* Spanish history teaches us a lesson not simply in Catholic intolerance, but in the birth of the modern nation-state through the twin successes of religious conversion and racial conquest.

In its focus on the docility of "woman's heart" (*L,* 89), Bulwer's *Leila* keeps in place the conventional ideology of the convertibility of the Jewish daughter, descended from such texts as *The Jew of Malta* and *The Merchant of Venice,* and refueled in the nineteenth century by the conversionists' focus on "the Jewess." Bulwer uses the figure of the feminine to represent both the conversion of the Jews and the conquest of the Moors as decisive moments in the development of the modern nation-state of Spain. By contrast, Grace Aguilar's *The Vale of Cedars; or, the Martyr,* which was issued in numerous editions during every decade of the nineteenth century after its initial publication in 1850, depicts "the female heart" (*VC,* 173)[15] as peculiarly strong and resilient—so strong that Jewish survival depends on it. So while Bulwer, through the figure of the female convert, represents the erasure of minority cultures in the development of the racially and religiously homogenous modern nation-state, Aguilar depicts the survival of Judaic culture in fifteenth-century Spain through her heroine's unconvertibility. For Marie epitomizes Jewish steadfastness, not the stubbornness that underlies the anti-Semitic stereotype of the "stiff-necked race" (*VC,* 190), but "the martyr strength, for which she unceasingly prayed, to give up all if called upon for her God" (*VC,* 187). Marie, the martyr in Aguilar's title, recalls Scott's Rebecca, who redefines for the Templar "the heart of woman":

thou knowest not the heart of woman. . . . [N]ot in thy fiercest battles hast thou displayed more of thy vaunted courage than has been shown by woman when called upon to suffer by affection or duty. I am myself a woman, tenderly nurtured, naturally fearful of danger, and impatient of pain; yet, when we enter those fatal lists, thou to fight and I to suffer, I feel the strong assurance within me that my courage shall mount higher than thine.[16]

In these variations on the weakness and strength of "the heart of woman," nineteenth-century historical romance explores woman's role in the erasure and preservation of religious and racial identity.

The Vale of Cedars is organized around a series of trials that test Marie's capacity to withstand the attempt to rewrite her Jewish identity. The novel's plot thereby falls into three major movements: first, the proposal of marriage from Arthur Stanley, an English Catholic exile living in Spain; second, the public revelation that Marie is a Jew, and her subsequent torture under the Inquisition, during which she is threatened to yield at once her body and her faith; and finally, the attempt of Queen Isabella to convert Marie, and thereby to absorb her into Spanish Catholic society.

Aguilar uses the romance between Marie and her English lover to shape the novel for a specifically English audience. Stanley is characterized in the opening pages of the novel by those signs that Aguilar and generations of novelists learned from *Ivanhoe:* "His physiognomy told truth. Arthur Stanley was, as his name implied, an Englishman of noble family." From the first, the Englishman is set apart from "the sons of Spain" (*VC,* 4). In an extension of the physiognomic code of *Ivanhoe,* "Saxon" is distinguished from "Spaniard" (*VC,* 7). Like Marie herself, Stanley becomes a target of prejudice and intolerance in fifteenth-century Spain: Marie is a Jew, and Arthur Stanley is "the white-faced foreigner" (*VC,* 92), "the hated foreigner" (*VC,* 206). Aguilar in this way enlists her audience's sympathy for the Jewish heroine through the English hero.

At the same time Aguilar demonstrates the multiple dynamics of prejudice, decentering in a number of ways the English reader's own privileged perspective by revealing the English hero as an object of prejudice in another land at another time. By referring to Stanley as "a foreigner from the Wild Island, where they had all been busy cutting one another's throats" (*VC,* 58), the Spaniards reveal their picture of the barbaric English. The reference here is to the War of the Roses, during which Stanley's father and four brothers are killed, and after which Stanley himself eventually escapes imprisonment and flees to Spain, where he becomes a favorite with Ferdinand and Isabella. Revealed in the opening chapter, Stanley's history puts the forthcoming tale of prejudice and intolerance in Spain in the context of England's own history of persecution, complicating the conventionally nationalistic contrast between England and Spain. Beginning where *Ivanhoe* ends, *The Vale of Cedars* follows in Scott's footsteps, unraveling the conventional English critique of Spain; like Rebecca, Stanley flees England to live in peace and safety in Spain. Even when Stanley contemplates returning to England with Marie, to escape the danger of the discovery of her Judaism, he neglects the fact that the Jews have been banished from England and that Marie would be required to live as a secret Jew in England as she does in Spain. Thus, from the start, the conventional opposition between England and Spain is at least ironized, if not overturned.

Marie's first "trial" (*VC*, 9) comes when, having revealed her secret Judaism to Stanley, she sacrifices her love for him on the grounds of her religion: "There is a love, a duty stronger than that I bear to thee. I would resign all else, but not my father's God" (*VC*, 10). We already hear the paternal interdiction of this intermarriage sounded in the name of Marie's God, "my father's God." Having discovered that her father has already planned a marriage for her with her cousin Ferdinand Morales, another secret Jew, Marie announces to her father: "Oh, my father, do what thou wilt, command me as thou wilt—I am henceforth wholly thine" (*VC*, 27). This vow suggests the way in which the daughter is wed to the father, and thereby it functions in the father's plan to propagate the race through her, so that the wedding between Morales and Marie soon turns into a scene of lovemaking between father and daughter: "She threw herself upon his bosom, and covered his cheek with kisses" (*VC*, 34).

When Morales is murdered and Stanley is framed and falsely accused of the crime, Marie's trials are temporarily interrupted by his legal hearing. Asked to testify about a heated argument that she witnessed between her husband and Stanley, Marie subverts the trial in an extraordinary act of self-sacrifice which for the Jew in Christian Spain amounts to no more than an act of self-naming: "My evidence is valueless. I belong to that race whose word is never taken as witness, for or against, in a court of justice. I cannot take the oath required, for I deny the faith in which it is administered. I am a JEWESS!" (*VC*, 122). In *Ivanhoe* the Jewish heroine on trial is saved by her English champion; but in *The Vale of Cedars*, in a powerful revision of *Ivanhoe*, the English hero on trial is saved by the Jewish heroine. Moreover, this reversal occurs through a potent reminder of the contemporary English debate over requiring Jews to take the same kind of oath that Marie refuses.[17] The fullest irony of this scene, then, depends on the Victorian reader's recognition that the civil disabilities from which the

Jews suffer in contemporary Protestant England can be traced to what England typically viewed as the barbaric intolerance of fifteenth-century Catholic Spain. In short, the scene subtly unravels that contrast with Spain on which English national identity often depended.

Once the public recognition of Marie's Jewish identity occurs, the novel turns to an exploration of the institutional means by which the Spanish community attempts to convert Marie. This exploration turns first to a critique of the Inquisition. Referring to "the rack, the wheel, the screw, the cord, and fire" (*VC,* 150), the scenes of Marie's torture, reminiscent of similar scenes in the Gothic novel, become part of that common body of writing in England that critiques Catholic persecution. Such scenes, the narrator tells us, "will be found, again and again repeated, in the annals not of the Inquisition alone, but of every European state where the Romanists held sway" (*VC,* 157). The Anglo-Jewish writer calls on a (Protestant) rhetoric familiar to English readers, but she restores to it a dimension of historical accuracy that has often been missing in the past—the persecution of the Jews, and the conditions of crypto-Jewish life in general, under the Inquisition.

The man responsible for murdering Morales and for framing Stanley is now responsible for conducting Marie's trial under the auspices of the Inquisition—a trial, we learn, that is no more than a pretext for rape. Aguilar's Inquisitor pursues his lust in the form of "the mockery of a trial" that accuses Marie of "blasphemy and heresy" (*VC,* 152), so that he insists on Marie sacrificing her body to his lust and her soul to his religion. Raping Marie and converting her are part of a single desire, a single mission. Like Rebecca at the mercy of the Templar, Marie defends herself with a threat of suicide that temporarily staves off her pursuer. The bodily torture that the Inquisitor subsequently inflicts on her serves concurrently as the substitute for his passion and the instrument of his proselytism. The ideology of conversion once again merges with an ideology of the feminine: the ductility that makes woman the perfect candidate for conversion is equal to what is seen as her sexual weakness, her sexual submissiveness.

Finally rescued from the prisons of the Inquisition, Marie falls into the hands of Queen Isabella, who now begins the third and last of Marie's trials. Isabella initiates the procedure of "gentle conversion" (*VC,* 131), pointing out the error of Marie's faith but sympathizing with her sex:

"Unbeliever though she be, offspring of a race which every true Catholic must hold in abhorrence, she is yet a *woman*" (*VC*, 131). The gentle conversion that the Queen plans, like that devised by Bulwer's Isabel in *Leila*, is a specifically feminine effort bent on protecting the Jewish heroine from the severity of the fanatical monks. Nonetheless, in a reprise of Rebecca's words, Marie rejects the offer of conversion. Rebecca tells Rowena, "I may not change the faith of my fathers like a garment unsuited to the climate in which I seek to dwell,"[18] and Marie tells Isabella, "My creed . . . is no garment we may wear and cast off at pleasure" (*VC*, 196).

When all other means have failed, Isabella decides to offer "a powerful temporal temptation" (*VC*, 193) to effect Marie's conversion, and so the marriage plot enters the novel once again as a means of converting the heroine: "One word—one little word—from thee, and thou shalt be Stanley's wife!" (*VC*, 199). From the start, *The Vale of Cedars* can be said to realize, by bringing to the surface, the once suppressed erotic desire of the English hero for the Jewish heroine: what the Saxon will not allow himself in *Ivanhoe* he allows himself here—namely, to love the Jewish heroine. But the Jewish heroine is asked to pay a price for this love: to accept the Englishman's religion. Such a transaction reverberates with national and historical meanings. "'To rest this desolate heart on his? To weep upon his bosom?—feel his arm around me?—his love protect me? To be his—all his? And only on condition of speaking one little word?" (*VC*, 199). The "little word" of conversion (or, in nineteenth-century England, of the Allegiance Oath) represents the price the Jew must pay for the protecting embrace of the Englishman in an otherwise hostile world. But the Jewish heroine, who has protected the Englishman through a public confession of her Jewish identity, is not willing to deny that same identity to be protected by him.

While in both *Leila* and *The Vale of Cedars* the Jewish heroine dies, Aguilar never hints at the theme of racial extinction that so preoccupies Bulwer. Insofar as Marie is "preserved from the crime . . . [of] apostasy" (*VC*, 214), the novel records the means by which the continuity of Jewish belief was secured in fifteenth-century Spain, often at the cost of martyrdom. Moreover, Aguilar's narrative stance in the novel is a powerful way of asserting the survival of Jewish belief. I refer to those moments in the narrative when Aguilar deliberately punctures the stance of the conventional third-person narrator, anonymous and neutral, to name herself both as a woman (*VC*, 51) and as a Jew (*VC*, 144). Both acts of self-naming become narrative gestures that respond to the question of the survival of Jewish identity, addressing especially what had become the chief stereotype of apostasy, the converted Jewish woman. The narrator's identity as a Jew in nineteenth-century England becomes a special form of testimony to all those ancestors (including Aguilar's own Sephardic forebears) "whose children still survive" (*EM*, 309). In further naming herself a Jewish *woman*, the narrator realizes her authority on the nature of the Jewish woman's heart—a topic too often represented by writers at once non-Jewish and male (like Bulwer), and too often used for con-versionist ends. Aguilar sought to critique the conversionist claim that the particular iconography and ideology of Christianity were especially suited to the female heart,[19] as Bulwer's novel suggests in its picture of the pale and long-suffering Jewish heroine: "The sufferings of the Messiah, His sublime purity, His meek forgiveness, spoke to her woman's heart" (*L*, 89). Marie's steadfastness can be seen as a response to those popular nineteenth-century conversionist novels that revolved around the conver-sion of the Jewish heroine. In *The Vale of Cedars*, Marie's unconvertibility, her discovery of dignity and purpose in living as a Jew, becomes the cor-nerstone of a historical commentary on why and how the Jewish woman played a role in preserving that Judaic heritage of which the narrator herself is the latest preserver.

In such a context the narrator's own interested position of sympathy and even religious belief becomes less a sign of narrative intrusion than a testimony to the continuity of Jewish belief in nineteenth-century En-gland. After all, in Victorian England, the Christian majority doubts the power and even the existence of Jewish belief, regarding "Judaism as a sort of eccentric fossilised form" rather than "something still throbbing in human lives, still making for them the only conceivable vesture of the world" (according to the narrator of *Daniel Deronda*).[20] For this reason, the historicization of "the Jewish question" in *The Vale of Cedars* is supple-mented by the acknowledgment of the narrator's present belief. Without such an acknowledgment, the medievalism of Scott, for example, might lead the nineteenth-century reader to view the Jew as no more than an historic relic, an exotic of another time and place. George Eliot represents this danger in *Daniel Deronda* when the Meyricks view Mirah entirely in the light of Rebecca, tolerating Judaism only as a condition of medieval romance, not contemporary life: they "found the Jewish faith less reconcilable with their wishes in her [Mirah's] case than in that of Scott's Rebecca."[21] Similarly, Aguilar complains that the Jew's "modern history so little is generally known, that the word *Jew* is associated only with biblical and ancient recollections."[22] For this reason *The Vale of Cedars* represents both its heroine (of fifteenth-century Spain) and its narrator (of nineteenth-century England) as participants in the continuous development and preservation of Judaism.

The novel uses one further means to reject the theme of racial extinction. Insofar as Marie's death is succeeded by a chapter about her influence on Stanley, the novel cautiously anticipates the basis for a brighter future in Anglo-Jewish relations. Such an anticipation is signaled by the narrative's only significant change in time and place. In its final chapter *The Vale of Cedars* moves to " 'merrie England' " (*VC*, 220) to discover Stanley, now fifty-five years old, only recently returned to his native land. Aguilar reminds us that the "merrie England" to which Stanley returns has a long-standing tradition of anti-Semitism that approves of the Spanish expulsion of the Jews. "It is a good thing indeed to rid a land of such vermin" (*VC*, 222), remarks one of Stanley's countrymen. But perhaps Stanley's personal history may make some contribution toward the English toleration of the Jews, for the story that circulates about him publicizes how, even while a pious Christian, "his zeal to avert the edict [to expel the Jews] lost him, in a great measure, the confidence of Ferdinand. When he found to prevent their expulsion was impossible, he did all in his power to lessen their misfortune, if such it may be called, by relieving every unbeliever that crossed his path" (*VC*, 223).

Such a passage makes clear the way in which Stanley represents the latest stage in the evolution of the hero of the novel of Jewish identity—a heroic type initiated by Maria Edgeworth under the name "the champion of the Jews."[23] Insofar as Stanley represents an advance over Ivanhoe, Aguilar's hero pinpoints the further ways in which *The Vale of Cedars* functions as a sequel and a supplement to Scott's novel. In returning its hero to merry England the last chapter of *The Vale of Cedars,* under the auspices of an epigraph from Scott, returns to the most popular English historical novel about the Jews, in whose last chapter the Jewish heroine flees from England, leaving behind her a deep impression on the English hero, but no more—only the trace of erotic desire, and historic guilt, buried in the English psyche. *The Vale of Cedars,* in contrast, ends not with the flight from England of the Jewish heroine, but with the return home of the English hero, refashioned through his (Jewish) experiences abroad. Stanley returns to his native land bearing not only the legacy of Marie's love, but the knowledge of the persecution of the Jews during the Inquisition in Spain. In this way he represents the continued advance of historical consciousness in England; Stanley's knowledge of the conditions of crypto-Jewish life and martyrdom in fifteenth-century Spain represents the addition to English consciousness of what the dehistoricized fantasies of the Gothic novel and the anti-Catholic propagandistic histories of the Inquisition neglected.

This explains why Aguilar's many historical tales of the Inquisition so often carry with them a narrative aside that identifies their function for the English reader: "There may be some to whom the memory of such things, as common to their ancestors, may be yet familiar; but to by far the greater number of English readers, they are, in all probability, as incomprehensible as uncommon."[24] Aguilar's tales, which she chose to call " 'Records' of a people" rather than romances, direct the English reader's eye to that page of history which previously has gone unwritten or unread: "Yet who draws example from the Jew? Who lingers on the page of history when it relates to them . . . ?"[25] Moreover, in the manner of Scott, Aguilar claims that these "Records" use "fiction" only "to bring historical truth more clearly forward." Specifically, they often function to revise the kind of Jewish history that has been written from a Christian perspective. For instance, Aguilar explains that she has reinvented an episode from Stockdale's *History of the Inquisitions* by substituting a Jewish character for the non-Jewish victim represented in Stockdale.[26] In such a case (Jewish) fiction amends (Christian) history.

Aguilar's work is only one gesture in what I see as the Sephardic community's concerted effort at midcentury to record the history of the persecution of the Jews during the Inquisition. This effort included such works as Moses Mocatta's *The Inquisition and Judaism* (1845) and Elias Haim Lindo's *History of the Jews of Spain and Portugal* (1848), as well as Aguilar's many historical tales. Even when Aguilar published her "History of the Jews in England" in the popular *Chamber's Miscellany* in 1847 and thereby realized the Anglo-Jewish writer's authority in Jewish historiography—her "History" was the first study of the topic produced by a Jewish writer—she included narratives of the secret Jews of Spain and Portugal.

That a work entitled "The History of the Jews in England" included such material is a clue to the goal of all these historical works: to make clear the prehistory of England's Jewish community in the persecutions of the Jews in Spain and Portugal. For this reason, Aguilar's "History" and her historical tales are imbedded with family genealogies that record the ways by which the ancestors of an Anglo-Jewish family fled the Inquisition in Spain or Portugal and eventually settled in England, sometimes after a period of settlement in Holland. Such family genealogies represent in embryo the history of the entire resettlement of the Jews in England from the middle of the seventeenth century through the end of the eighteenth;[27] they also represent the history of Aguilar's own family,[28] and thereby they underscore the semiautobiographical nature of her historical fiction. For Aguilar, then, the writing of historical fiction about fifteenth-century Spain is a way of writing modern Anglo-Jewish history because the Inquisition's consequences are remote neither for her nor for Victorian England: "there are still families in England to trace their descendants from those who . . . were compelled to fly at an hour's warning."[29] For the English reader, historical fiction may be a way of learning about one's neighbors.

What is at stake, finally, in the full disclosure of the historical circumstances of crypto-Judaism? In the context of Victorian historical romance, I am recording the movement from a representation of the individual secret Jew in Bulwer's novel to a representation of "the secret race" (*VC*, 22) in Aguilar's writing. Aguilar's project historicizes the mystified figure of the masked Jew, whether an amoral double agent in Bulwer's novel or an amoral social climber in Trollope's novels of the 1870s, that is, the Jew who keeps his race secret to invade and to subvert the Christian world. First of all, Aguilar overturns, on historical grounds, the charge of Jewish hypocrisy, the latest libel against the Jews: "to accuse the secret Jews of Spain of hypocrisy, of departing from the pure ordinances of their religion, because *compelled* to simulate Catholicism, is taking indeed but a one-handed, short-sighted view" (*VC*, 145). Moreover, in depicting the complicated strategies of duplicity that "the secret race" developed to survive, Aguilar explores the large population of crypto-Jews of Spain and Portugal as a specific social group, living in specific historical conditions, with customs and behavior designed to meet particular—and deadly—historical exigencies.

The urgency of Aguilar's entire project depends on the fact that she writes at that historical moment when the veil that has so long masked the secret race can be lifted: "A new era is dawning for us. Persecution and intolerance have in so many lands ceased to predominate, that Israel may once more breathe in freedom; the law need no longer be preached in darkness, and obeyed in secret."[30] In short, Aguilar writes at a time when the history of "the secret race" may be written by an author who discloses her own identity as a Jew. When Aguilar depicts Marie's two weddings, or Morales's two funerals, one Catholic and public, the other Jewish and private, she removes the veil of secrecy by which the crypto-Jews preserved their beliefs and their lives. And when Aguilar, in her addresses to her reader, unveils her own identity as a Jewish woman writing for an audience uneducated in the history of the secret race, she represents for her contemporary audience what Marie herself desired: the full disclosure of Jewish identity, without reprisal; the full authenticity of the Jewish woman's word, even as evidence of the legitimacy of Jewish history and Jewish belief.

The act of unveiling in Aguilar's work becomes the central sign of a national and historical allegory about Spain and England that is meant to encourage in her native land the further development of Jewish toleration. When, in one of her historical tales, a Spanish Jew recently arrived in England is counseled to remove her veil—"it is not the custom of English ladies to wear veils"—we begin to see how Aguilar uses this figure to contrast England and Spain: "England, that blessed land, where the veil of secrecy could be removed"; or again, "The veil of secrecy was removed, they were in a land whose merciful and liberal government granted to the exile and the wanderer a home of peace and rest."[31] At the same time, Anglo-Jewish history, even when written by Aguilar, records the slow and difficult means by which the Jews who fled the Inquisition eventually won the right to safe haven in England more than 150 years later. And even Victorian England was judged only moderately enlightened in Aguilar's comparative evaluation of the different national positions on Jewish rights: "In the treatment of the Jews, Great Britain at present occupies a position between the United States of North America, France, and

Belgium, on the one hand, and Germany and Russia, with some other countries, on the other" (*EM,* 286).

The Sephardic community's attempt to record the history of the Catholic persecution of the Jews during the Inquisition had a double goal. First, this history was used as a defense against the renewed drive to convert the Jews in England, a drive reminiscent of Spanish Catholic proselytism. By translating a conversionist sermon delivered by a Catholic archbishop at an auto-da-fé in Portugal, Moses Mocatta historicized the ideology of conversion, placed it within a setting of persecution, and decried its institutionalization in contemporary Britain: "In many parts of the Old and New World, but more especially in Great Britain, the conversion of the Jews has become an organized system." Mocatta quoted Aguilar's words from *Women of Israel,* "we need a careful but perfectly simple training to supply us with reply and defence," to explain the way his own work was meant to function as a weapon against the propaganda of conversionism in Victorian England. Similarly, Lindo in his *History of the Jews in Spain and Portugal* explained the need for "an impartial history of the Jews of Spain and Portugal," especially since his predecessor in this project had "written more in the style of a conversionist than in that of an impartial historian."[32]

Second, the history of Jewish persecution in Catholic Spain was used in an attempt to remove what in Aguilar's eyes was "the last relic of religious intolerance," namely, "the disabilities under which the Jews of Great Britain labour" (*EM,* 272). English Jews said of those in Parliament who opposed Jewish Emancipation: "Their intolerance is composed of the same stuff of which the intolerance of a priest of the Inquisition was made."[33] And during the parliamentary debates on Emancipation, the denial of political power to the Jews was compared to an auto-da-fé.[34] Finally, during the debates it was not unusual for Protestants and Jews to align themselves in an anti-Catholic position: "Both Christians and Jews were apt to claim that biblical Judaism was the fount of primitive Christianity—corruption and persecution had been introduced into the Church together by the Popes, and only dispelled at the Reformation."[35] The Sephardic community's complete unveiling of Jewish persecution under the Catholic Inquisition can be seen as an indirect argument for Jewish Emancipation in a nation that had passed the Catholic Relief Act in 1828 but still failed at midcentury to grant similar relief to the Jews.

Aguilar's depiction of her Jewish heroines' *amor patriae,* even in the midst of persecution, functioned as an indirect critique of the anti-Emancipation argument that the Jews would always constitute a (foreign) nation within a nation, as opposed to loyal citizens of England. One may wonder "what secret feeling it was which thus bound them [the Spanish Jews] to a country where, acknowledged or discovered, Judaism was death." Nonetheless, Aguilar's stories record "that feeling of *amor patriae* . . . an emotion experienced in various degrees by every nation, but by the Jew in Spain with a strength and intensity equalled by none and understood but by a Jew."[36] And it is on the basis of such historical knowledge that the Jewish writer hints to the English nation that the English Jew is capable of a similar "love of fatherland" (*EM,* 260). Jewish steadfastness, traditionally seen as the obstacle to conversion, is reimagined as the hallmark of the loyal (Jewish) citizen of England.

Like Marie in *The Vale of Cedars,* Fedalma in George Eliot's *The Spanish Gypsy* is a portrait of the heroism of the female heart. The entire project of *The Spanish Gypsy* was framed from the beginning by an attempt to understand in what ways the genre of tragedy could function as a category of the feminine—that is, as a representation of a specifically female action. The project began with Eliot's meditation on a painting of the Annunciation, as she records in her "Notes on the Spanish Gypsy and Tragedy in General":

> It occurred to me that here was a great dramatic motive of the same class as those used by the Greek dramatists, yet specifically differing from them. A young maiden, believing herself to be on the eve of the chief event of her life—marriage—about to share in the ordinary lot of womanhood, full of young hope, has suddenly announced to her that she is chosen to fulfil a great destiny, entailing a terribly different experience from that of ordinary womanhood. She is chosen, not by any momentary arbitrariness, but as a result of foregoing hereditary conditions: she obeys. "Behold the handmaid of the Lord." Here, I thought, is a subject grander than that of Iphigenia, and it has never been used.[37]

Eliot's example of the Annunciation invites us to see the way in which the mortal father becomes transformed into a kind of god for whom the daughter functions as the obedient handmaid or sacrificial victim. So, while in Bulwer's and Aguilar's novels the daughter is sacrificed to what she names as the God of her fathers, in *The Spanish Gypsy* the daughter is sacrificed to the father as God. Hence Fedalma "knelt, / Clinging with piety and awed resolve / Beside this altar of her father's life" (*SG*, 4.294),[38] where she obediently sacrifices her own life while taking the pledge of worship: "He trusted me, and I will keep his trust: / My life shall be its temple. I will plant / His sacred hope within the sanctuary / And die its priestess" (*SG*, 5.310).

While Eliot defined the function of "hereditary conditions" in tragic plots in a variety of ways, more and more she came to mean *racial* conditions: "A story simply of a jealous husband is elevated into a most pathetic tragedy by the hereditary conditions of Othello's lot, which give him a subjective ground for distrust"; "a woman, say, finds herself on the earth with an inherited organization; she may be lame, she may inherit a disease, or what is tantamount to a disease; she may be a negress, or have other marks of race repulsive in the community where she is born."[39] Even in the central paradigms of Iphigenia and Mary, Eliot represents woman's tragic hereditary function as the sacrifice of the daughter either to preserve or to found a people. In the tradition of historical romance within which *The Spanish Gypsy* is written, such a function becomes concentrated in the notion of woman as the daughter of a race—Rebecca, "the daughter of Israel," or Leila, the "daughter of the great Hebrew race." Once the nineteenth-century concept of race became the medium through which Eliot would realize the tragic circumstances of her own version of the Annunciation, fifteenth-century Spain seemed the inevitable choice for the "set of historical and local conditions" that would embody her idea: "My reflections brought me nothing that would serve me except that moment in Spanish history when the struggle with the Moors was attaining its climax, and when there was the gypsy race present under such conditions as would enable me to get my heroine and the hereditary claim on her among the gypsies. I required the opposition of race to give the need for renouncing the expectation of marriage."[40]

In choosing fifteenth-century Spain, Eliot selected what had become for the nineteenth century a kind of historical laboratory in which experiments on the question of race could be performed.[41] Moreover, her growing concern over national and racial injustices climaxed in her decision to record the Gypsies' historic plight and to represent through it, at least at one level, the persecution of more than one racial minority. As early as 1856, Eliot was praising Harriet Beecher Stowe for the invention of "the Negro novel" and was comparing Stowe with Scott in the use of "that grand element—conflict of races."[42] So, in *The Spanish Gypsy,* the chief of the Gypsies encourages the other persecuted minorities of fifteenth-century Spain, "Whether of Moorish or of Hebrew blood, / Who, being galled by the hard Spaniard's yoke" (*SG,* 4.275), to become allies of the Gypsies. He addresses the Moors and the Jews as "Our kindred by the warmth of Eastern blood" (*SG,* 4.276) and thereby begins a series of oppositions that pit the "white Castilian" (*SG,* 3.228) against "the dark men" (*SG,* 4.265). When the Gypsy chief mocks the conversion of the Gypsies by taunting, "Take holy water, cross your dark skin white" (*SG,* 1.132), Eliot alludes to both the historic Spanish missions to the Americas and the contemporary English missions to Africa and India.

At the center of Eliot's text is the question of the heroine's identity, or how she is to be named. Fedalma is raised a *Christian,* rumored to be a *Jew,* dressed as a *Moor* at one point, and claimed by the chief of the Zíncali as a *Gypsy.* While Father Isidor, cast in the conventional role of the fanatical Dominican Inquisitor, contemplates Fedalma's torture and death, Zarca, the chief of the Zíncali, arrives to save her from the Inquisition. Zarca explains to Fedalma that he is her father and that she was stolen from him by a band of Spaniards when she was a young child. In requiring that she not marry Silva, her Spanish lover, the father asks his daughter to sacrifice herself in the name of the father, or the name of race, and thereby to exchange her individual identity for a corporate identity: "Fedalma dies / In leaving Silva: all that lives henceforth / Is the poor Zíncala" (*SG,* 1.138), the Spanish Gypsy of the title. This is the moment of the daughter's obedience. Zarca explains that as the sole offspring of her widowed father, she is the "Chief woman of her tribe" (*SG,* 3.239) and that after his death she will be the tribe's leader. In prohibiting the marriage with Silva, the father offers the daughter a different kind of marriage, and Fedalma accepts: "I will wed / The curse that blights my people," and "Father, now I go / To wed my people's lot" (*SG,* 1.137–38). The conventional marriage plot is reconfigured here as the means by which the daughter serves her father as the bride of his people. Intermarriage with the racial other is canceled in a figure: marriage with the entire body of one's own race.

With the death of the father, the text ends with the daughter's journey to Africa in an attempt to realize his plans to establish his people's national identity. Fedalma's journey is represented as the kind of exile we associate with Scott's Rebecca—an exile based in the sacrifice of the erotic. Moreover, Eliot makes clear the hopelessness of Fedalma's political ambitions. With the death of her father, "the tribe / That was to be the ensign of the race, . . . would still disperse / And propagate forgetfulness" (*SG*, 5.302), in a diaspora in which Fedalma's relinquishment of marriage and childbirth turns into a bitterly ironic form of propagation, the engendering not of ancestral continuity but of forgetfulness. Fedalma's procreative function is reinvented through a tragic pun: "I am but as the funeral urn that bears the ashes of a leader" (*SG*, 5.309). The daughter's body becomes no more than a kind of grave for the memorialization of the dead father.

But this kind of tragic irony does not finally displace the central ideology of the text, voiced in the father's scathing denunciation of intermarriage and conversion:

> Such love is common: I have seen it oft—
> Seen many women rend the sacred ties
> That bind them in high fellowship with men,
> Making them mothers of a people's virtue:
> Seen them so levelled to a handsome steed
> That yesterday was Moorish property,
> To-day is Christian—wears new-fashioned gear,
> Neighs to new feeders, and will prance alike
> Under all banners, so the banner be
> A master's who caresses. Such light change
> You call conversion; but we Zíncali call
> Conversion infamy. (*SG*, 3.239)

In recording the procedures by which women of a minority race or religion are absorbed by the men of the more powerful group, Zarca adds conversion to the crimes of rapine and murder by which the systematic genocide of a people proceeds. And Eliot, however she might sympathize with the tragic loss and suffering of her title character, upholds the paternal critique of conversion.

Eliot uses the specific example of the "hurry to convert the Jews" (*SG*, 1.27) in fifteenth-century Spain to ground historically what often appears to be her text's exaggerated horror of apostasy. While the main characters of *The Spanish Gypsy* are Catholics (Silva and Isidor) and Gypsies (Fedalma and Zarca), it is in her depiction of a converted Jew (Lorenzo) and a practicing Jew (Sephardo) that she attempts to provide the historical basis for her study of conversion. Even the portrait of her Gypsy heroine takes as its model the more well-known example of the converted Jewish woman; while Silva points to Fedalma's baptism, Father Isidor protests: "Ay, as a thousand Jewesses, who yet / Are brides of Satan" (*SG*, 1.69). But Eliot fails to represent the historical complexities of the issue of conversion in Spain. Instead, she is quick to make an example of the Jews to advance her argument against conversion. This results in making the converted Jew no more than the kind of opportunist Zarca warns Fedalma of becoming—the man or woman who would convert to "win / The prize of renegades" (*SG*, 1.123):

> Thus baptism seemed to him [Lorenzo] a merry game
> Not tried before, all sacraments a mode
> Of doing homage for one's property,
> And all religions a queer human whim
> Or else a vice, according to degrees. (*SG*, 1.11–12)

Because Eliot focuses on the converted Jew who easily quits his Judaism to assume a new religion for self-advantage, as in the case of the "fat-handed" (*SG*, 1.11) Lorenzo, her Jewish convert never seems to be the product of the fierce religious intolerance and racism that periodically erupted in Spain, especially in the pogroms of 1391, when masses of Jews were converted on threat of death. Instead, her portrait of the converted Jew seems to function as an indictment of Jewish hypocrisy and opportunism.

This was the prevalent picture of the Jewish *conversos* in general, and the crypto-Jews in particular, throughout the nineteenth century, as Aguilar well knew: "The fact that the most Catholic kingdom of Spain was literally peopled with secret Jews brands this unhappy people with a degree of hypocrisy, in addition to the various other evil propensities with which they have been so plentifully charged. Nay, even amongst themselves in modern times this charge has gained ascendency" (*VC*, 144). During the nineteenth century the growth of European nationalism and incipient Zionism had this effect on the historiography of the Spanish Jews: those who became martyrs for their religion and race were praised as heroes, while those who converted were vilified as cowardly opportunists and hypocrites. The Jewish historian Heinrich Graetz, an important spokesperson for Jewish rights and a major source of Eliot's knowledge of Jewish history,[43] cast Spanish Jews in the opposing roles of martyrs versus cowards, those who "remained true to their faith" versus the "weaklings." Even in the midst of acknowledging the "violent assaults" suffered by the Jews, Graetz spoke of "the weak and lukewarm among them, the comfort-loving and worldly-minded, [who] succumbed to the temptation, and saved themselves by baptism."[44]

Eliot makes her most scathing critique of the converted Jew through the words of Sephardo, the Jew who takes his entire identity, including his name, from his Jewish ancestry and belief. Sephardo argues against Silva's universal humanism:

> . . . there's no such thing
> As naked manhood. . . .
> While my heart beats, it shall wear livery—
> My people's livery, whose yellow badge
> Marks them for Christian scorn. I will not say
> Man is first man to me, then Jew or Gentile:
> That suits the rich *marranos;* but to me
> My father is first father, and then man. (*SG*, 2.162)

Like Scott's Rebecca and Aguilar's Marie before him, Sephardo declares his desire to wear the garment of his race—no disguises, and no conversion, for him. But Sephardo's representation of the Marranos as opportunists who reject their fathers and their faith—"I am a Jew, and not that infamous life / That takes on bastardy, will know no father" (*SG*, 2.174)— is historically inaccurate. In a note to Sephardo's speech, Eliot defines "Marrano" as a name for the converted Jew, but she does not designate by it the more specific meaning, the converted Jew who secretly practices Judaism—as represented, for example, in Aguilar's work, in which Marranism is shown as a way of honoring one's father—by handing down through the generations a faith that was threatened and eventually outlawed in Spain. Eliot's depiction of the converted Jew therefore is one-sided, neglecting both those *conversos* who converted out of genuine conviction, to worship devoutly and sincerely as Catholics, and those crypto-Jews who converted to Catholicism (sometimes on the threat of death) while secretly practicing Judaism.

This kind of flattening out of difference, this use of a single name to characterize a complicated and diverse population, was the means by which religious affiliation became overwritten in Spain by racial genealogy. I mean here that the creation of various *estatutos de limpieza de sangre* in the fifteenth century,[45] prohibiting *conversos* from holding various offices and titles, in effect "reconverted" *all* New Christians to Jews, despite the fact that some were sincere Catholics and others were Marranos or crypto-Jews. All New Christians were suspected of relapsing into Judaism, and thereby all were conceived as members of a special race against which legislation was enacted. This meant that, on the basis of their Jewish ancestry, the New Christians could be prevented from assimilating into Spanish Catholic life and enjoying its privileges. In short, when those Christians who had Jewish ancestors, even as far back as several generations, began to reach the highest positions of power, in the Church, the military, and the government, the doctrine of blood was used to supersede the institution of conversion and to reinstate against *Christians*—of Jewish ancestry—the old laws against the Jews. "The Old Christians" were divided from "the New Christians," so that Christianity became based on family line and race, and a Christian's authenticity depended less on the sincerity of his religious convictions and practices than on how many Jewish ancestors, how many generations ago, "polluted" his blood. Father Isidor complains about Fedalma, "That maiden's blood / Is as unchristian as the leopard's" (*SG,* 1.70)—despite her Christian education, and despite Silva's insistence that "Fedalma is a daughter of the Church— / Has been baptized and nurtured in the faith" (*SG,* 1.69).

The Spanish Gypsy does contain some version of this history, including, as part of the conventional English attack on the Catholic Inquisition, the odor of burning flesh, of "flames that, fed on heretics, still gape, / And must have heretics made to feed them still" (*SG,* 1.174–75). But Eliot fails to make clear the conditions of crypto-Judaic life in the fifteenth century, including the dangers that crypto-Jews suffered to preserve their ancestral faith and heritage when the Inquisition made returning to the faith of Judaism virtually impossible. The Inquisition initially was aimed at those converted Jews who were suspected of secretly performing Judaic rituals; from 1485 until 1500, more than 99 percent of the cases that came before the Spanish Inquisition concerned converted Jews.[46] The institution of the Inquisition crystallized the dilemma of the ideology of conversion by seeking to destroy what the missionary effort had produced. Eliot understood the historical reasons behind this system of destruction, including the economic ones, so that *The Spanish Gypsy* depicts characters callously arguing over whether a live Jew or "a well-burnt Jew" (*SG*, 1.27) would most benefit the pocket of the Church's bishops or the nation's merchants. Indeed, she even recognizes that the term "Marrano" became a slur by which all *conversos* were stigmatized as Jews, and thereby she understands how sincere converts were libeled by the slanderous epithet "Jew": "The 'old Christians' learned to use the word [Marrano] as a term of contempt for the 'new Christians,' or converted Jews and their descendants; but not too monotonously, for they often interchanged it with the fine old crusted opprobrium of the name *Jew*" (*SG*, 317). But such an apparently philo-Semitic view is part of a traditional argument that in effect did not sympathize with Jewish persecution but with sincere converts to Christianity who were stigmatized as Jews. In *The Spanish Gypsy*, then, we have a late development in the historiography of the Spanish Inquisition in England: an anti-Catholic attack that in fact includes the representation of the Jews under the Inquisition, but that understands the Jewish convert in an entirely unsympathetic light. *The Spanish Gypsy*'s horror of conversion (at least in part fueled by Eliot's knowledge of the consequences of Christian proselytism in fifteenth-century Spain) contributes to the anti-Semitic stereotype of the Jewish convert as hypocrite and opportunist, a figure reborn in the pages of Trollope's novels and in the anti-Semitic attack aimed at English converts like Disraeli.

Conquest and Conversion: Moors, Indians, Jews

I began this chapter by recalling William H. Prescott's remark on the popularity of Spanish history as a subject for English writers; I wish to close by explaining the way in which writers of Victorian historical romance owed their knowledge of fifteenth-century Spain to American writers. For example, all the poignant details of Boabdil's capitulation in Bulwer's *Leila,* from the appearance of the silver cross on the Alhambra to the mother's scalding reproach of her son's unmanliness, as well as the fully drawn portraits of Boabdil, Ferdinand, and Isabel, had already been recorded in two popular contemporary histories of early Spain, Irving's *Chronicle of the Conquest of Granada* (1829) and Prescott's *History of the Reign of Ferdinand and Isabella, the Catholic, of Spain* (1837). Even the Queen's demure offer of conversion to Boabdil in *Leila* looks like a romantic reworking of Irving's remark: "No exertions were spared by the politically pious monarch [Ferdinand] to induce him [Boabdil] to embrace the Christian religion" (*CG,* 511).[47] Not only did Irving's and Prescott's histories have a profound influence on Bulwer, Aguilar, and Eliot,[48] but the Americans in their turn owed a profound debt to Scott, for Scott was a model for them as well as for writers of historical romance.[49] Irving's and Prescott's histories in fact have some claim themselves to being considered as sequels to *Ivanhoe* and to Scott's entire historical enterprise. More specifically, these histories explored the role of conversion in racial annihilation, a topic with a special meaning for American writers whose own nation was engaged in an ongoing debate over the eradication of entire populations of Native Americans.

Designating Irving "a true son of Walter Scott," Irving's biographer speculates that, during the American writer's four-day visit with Scott in 1817, "Perhaps they chatted of Spanish themes," since the historical figure Don Roderick, an early subject of Scott's, became a subject of Irving's in 1828.[50] But scholars have neglected the more astonishing conjunction between these two writers, namely, that Scott destroyed an early composition of his own entitled *Conquest of Granada.*[51] Could the 1817 visit have planted the seed of Irving's *Conquest?* Was the "son" attempting to accomplish what the "father" had already tried and failed at? In any case, Irving constructed his *Conquest of Granada* after the model of *Ivanhoe,* in which the author's historical account of the Middle Ages is purportedly based on an ancient manuscript—a fictitious manuscript that Scott and Irving nonetheless invite their readers to inspect for themselves. Moreover, while colored by the fiction of romance, both *Ivanhoe* and *The Conquest of Granada* function as revisionary histories that attempt to call attention to those exaggerations and errors that were the result of nationalist or religious biases—in Irving's case, to those accounts "discolored by the bigotry, superstition, and fierce intolerance of the age" (*CG*, 16).[52] In both Scott's and Irving's texts the author functions as an "outsider" who subtly ironizes a historical record produced by a partisan "insider"; Scott and Irving use the accounts of their fictitious insiders, the English antiquarian Laurence Templeton and the Spanish monk Agapida, to inspect the procedures of historiography and to expose the nationalist and religious biases to which it is subject.

Irving's *Conquest of Granada* attempts to wrest early Spanish history from the hands of the monks who first recorded it. The text functions as an anti-Catholic critique that undermines the specific ideology of conquest and conversion that led to the annihilation of Muslim Spain. In his review of Irving's book, Prescott reminds us of its revisionary nature by referring to those early Spanish monk-historians who were "predisposed by education to admit as truth the grossest forgeries of fanaticism. What can their narratives be worth, distorted thus by prejudice and credulity?"[53] Agapida, the fictitious monk whose manuscripts ostensibly serve as the source of Irving's account, is "a personification of the monkish zealots who hovered about the sovereigns in their campaigns, . . . chronicling in rapturous strains every act of intolerance toward the Moors" (*CG*, 16–17). Irving, then, critiques those "united triumphs of the cross and the sword" that are euphemistically known as "holy wars" (*CG*, 13–15), and, like Scott before him, he places conversion at the center of the rhetoric and ideology of conquest: " 'Thus this pestilent nest of warfare and infidelity, the city of Ronda,' says the worthy Fray Antonio Agapida, 'was converted to the true faith by the thunder of our artillery' " (*CG*, 187). As in *Ivanhoe*, conversion and murder are indistinguishable; the machinery of conversion is no more than a mask for genocide. In Irving's account, the Moors become an example of one of those extinct races that so dominated the imagination of the nineteenth century:[54] "Nothing (says Fray Antonio Agapida) could exceed the thankfulness to God of the pious king Ferdinand for having enabled him to eradicate from Spain the empire and name of that accursed heathen race" (*CG*, 508). In Irving's text, conversion is only a pretext for the final solution, racial annihilation. In a dim echo of the history of the United States, the modern nation-state of Spain, Irving hints, is founded on the criminal eradication of a "heathen race."

Prescott's *Ferdinand and Isabella*, popularly acknowledged for many decades as the central work in English on early Spanish history, considerably broadened the focus of Irving's work and had a profound influence in Britain and America throughout the nineteenth century.[55] Under the influence of both Scott and Sharon Turner,[56] Prescott returned to the Middle Ages to discover the origins of the modern nation-state. For Prescott, the war with the Moors, climaxing in the fall of Granada, reveals racial hatred as a spur to Spanish national unity: "The war of Granada subjected all the various sects of the country to one common action, under the influence of common motives . . . while it brought them in conflict with a race, the extreme repugnance of whose institutions and character to their own served greatly to nourish the nationality of sentiment. In this way the spark of patriotism was kindled throughout the whole nation" (*FI*, 2.89). But while in Scott's England the two conflicting races eventually intermarry and merge, in Prescott's Spain one of the races, the Moors, is eradicated. The rise of the modern Spanish nation-state seems to depend on "the decay and the final extinction of a race . . . until their very name as a nation was blotted out from the map of history" (*FI*, 2.90–91). As an early-nineteenth-century American writer, Prescott was no stranger to the nationalist language of conquest and extinction, for it was often used to define and defend the founding of his own nation and the providential plan by which the native inhabitants of America were eradicated.[57] Prescott offered a patriotic paean to nature's sanctification of national unity—to "one great nation—one and indivisible, as intended by nature" (*FI*, 3.91)—even though his *History* of Spain demonstrates that such unity, or racial homogeneity, was manufactured through the arts and technologies of conquest and conversion.

As a critical moment in the development of a tradition of nineteenth-century Anglo-American historiography, Prescott's history looks back to Sharon Turner and anticipates Edward Augustus Freeman by bringing into the fold of Teutonism the entire history of the conquest and reconquest of Spain. In Prescott's opening pages we learn that for "Spaniards" we can read "Visigoths," recalling the "German origin" (*FI*, 1.7) for which the war with the Moors was fought—the reclamation of Germanic ancestral origins. The Teutonic background of the Spaniards seems to predestine the outcome of the conflict between Spaniard and Moor: "it was easy to foresee" that the "sober, hardy, and independent race" (*FI*, 1.8–9) of Visigoths, "who brought with them the same liberal principles of government which distinguished their Teutonic brethren" (*FI,* 1.4), "must ultimately prevail over a nation oppressed by despotism, and the effeminate indulgence to which it was naturally disposed by a sensual religion and a voluptuous climate" (*FI,* 1.9).

For Prescott, gender played a critical role in the racial code of history. The characterization of the Moors as "effeminate" (and "impotent") sets the scene for their conversion and conquest, as if their docility and ductility are "natural," programmed into the body of these races. Conceived as a record of progress, history becomes formulated in terms of a gendered evolutionism: the survival of the most masculine. While describing the Moors' effeminacy, Prescott insistently describes the Visigoths in opposite terms: "Whatever may have been the vices of the Spaniards, they cannot have been those of effeminate sloth" (*FI,* 1.8). And again: "These ambitious nobles did not consume their fortunes or their energies in a life of effeminate luxury" (*FI,* 1.32). And again, in a comparison with King Arthur, the Spanish Knight is said "to live abstemiously, indulging himself in none of the effeminate delights of couch or banquet" (*FI,* 1.35). So it is no surprise that the surrender of Granada and its conversion to Christianity occur under the sign of the feminine, with Boabdil's tears and his mother's accusation that he weeps like a woman for what he cannot defend like a man (*FI,* 2.85), as we saw in Bulwer's romance. In a parallel moment in Prescott's next history, *The Conquest of Mexico* (1843), Montezuma's surrender to the Spaniards is formulated through the ideology of gender: "He at once conceded all that they demanded,—his treasures, his power, even his person. For their sake, he forsook his wonted occupations, his pleasures, his most familiar habits. He might be said to forego his nature; and, as his subjects asserted, to change his sex and become a woman" (*CM,* 437–38).[58] Conquest is signaled by the moment in which the defeated leader is exposed as womanly, a moment that "naturalizes" the conquest and conversion of an entire race.

But another code complicates Prescott's history and sets the critical problem not only for *Ferdinand and Isabella,* but for *The Conquest of Mexico.* The key to this code relies on the conception of the war between the Spaniards and the Moors (like that between the Spaniards and the Aztecs) not simply as a racial conflict but as a holy war, an idea typically critiqued by historians who see themselves upholding the tradition of tolerant Anglo-American Protestantism. So, in *Ferdinand and Isabella,* for

"Spaniard" we must also read "Christian," and for "Moor" we must read "Muslim," because the Spaniard's attempt to defend his ancestral Gothic traditions soon became subsumed in what he regarded as a religious war: "His cause became the cause of Heaven. . . . He was a soldier of the Cross" (*FI*, 1.10–11). Precisely at this point Prescott's interpretation of the racial superiority of the (Visigothic) Spaniards clashes with the traditional Protestant rhetoric that critiques the fanaticism of Catholic Spain. Prescott, at this moment, divides Spain from the rest of Europe, reinstating (at least implicitly) the contrast between (Catholic) Spain and (Protestant) England on which English national identity depended: "Hence the national character became exalted by a religious fervour, which in later days, alas! settled into a fierce fanaticism. Hence that solicitude for the purity of the faith, the peculiar boast of the Spaniards, and that deep tinge of superstition for which they have ever been distinguished above the other nations of Europe" (*FI*, 1.11).

But the problem is not so easily solved, for Prescott's profound belief in history as the record of evolutionary progress does not allow him simply to criticize the conquests of the Moors or the Aztecs as examples of Catholic bigotry and fanaticism (as Irving does); in fact, he ends by upholding both conquests in the name of progress. This leads to a kind of crisis in ideology for him—and, I would argue, for nineteenth-century historians in general. This crisis is best understood in Prescott's inability to unravel the conjunction of conquest and conversion. I mean that the conquests of the Moors and the Aztecs were inseparably bound to the Catholic procedure of forced conversion, an idea that was anathema to the tradition of liberal Protestantism in which the sanctity of the individual conscience was maintained above all else. This procedure of forced conversion becomes the central blot on what Prescott otherwise takes to be the successful and necessary conquests of Granada and the New World.

In chapter 3, I showed how the idea of evolutionary history depended on keeping the idea of conversion at the level of trope, and what happened when Scott demystified this trope by exploring the actual institution of conversion in the history of the Jews. Prescott is forced to face the same historical dilemma. In recording the history of Spain, he cannot simply fall back on the use of conversion as a rhetorical trope to figure the "natural" evolution of one race or nation into another. Instead, he must record the literal and forced conversions by which Spain became first a nation and then an empire—that is, the forced conversions of Muslims and Jews in Spain itself, and of the native Indian populations in the New World. He must confront the dilemma of condoning the conquests of the Moors and the Aztecs as part of a providential plan of progress at the same time that he decries the forced conversions of these peoples. How does he attempt to resolve this dilemma?

Prescott makes clear that the link between *Ferdinand and Isabella* and *The Conquest of Mexico*, and between the histories of Spain and the Americas, is the intersection of conquest and conversion: "It would not be giving a fair view of the great objects proposed by the Spanish sovereigns in their schemes of discovery, to omit one which was paramount to all the rest, with the queen at least,—the propagation of Christianity among the heathen. The conversion and civilisation of this simple people form . . . the burden of most of her official communications from the earliest period" (*FI*, 2.442). At least at first, "conversion" and "civilization" seem interchangeable and benign processes that function to bring about the evolutionary progress of the "simple people" of the New World. *The Conquest of Mexico* records, time and again, that "the first object of Cortés was to reclaim the natives from their gross idolatry and to substitute a purer form of worship" (*CM*, 148). Nothing was allowed to stand in the way of the work of conversion: "To postpone the work of conversion was a sin" (*CM*, 194). Cortés "more than once perilled life, and fortune, and the success of his whole enterprise, by the premature and most impolitic manner in which he would have forced conversion on the natives" (*CM*, 685). The holy alliance between the two begins to look suspect when "the most impolitic manner" of the Spaniards' brand of proselytism is exposed and when the religious constancy of the Aztecs is viewed as steadfastness to "the faith of their fathers" (*CM*, 367). In such passages Prescott's ambivalence about the function of conversion as the sine qua non of conquest begins to take shape.

Although Prescott records how the conquest and the conversion of the Indians functioned as a single brutal activity, his attack on the Spaniards' procedures for converting the natives eventually turns into an endorsement. He begins by criticizing the Spaniards' use of force in converting the native population: "No doubt was entertained of the efficacy of conversion, however sudden might be the change, or however violent the means. The sword was a good argument, when the tongue failed" (*CM*, 148). He even records the way in which religious conversion is subsumed under the name of political conquest—"the conquests Cortés had achieved for Castile and Christianity" (*CM*, 160) are one and the same. Yet, as in the fall of Muslim Spain, conquest and conversion are in the end validated: "But, if the philosopher may smile at the reflection, that conversion, under these circumstances, was one of form rather than of substance, the philanthropist will console himself by considering how much the cause of humanity and good morals must have gained by the substitution of these unsullied rites for the brutal abominations of the Aztecs" (*CM*, 638).[59]

What allows Prescott to decry the use of force in conversion but in the end to uphold the conquest and conversion of the American Indians is a distinction he makes between Catholicism and Protestantism. While the forced conversion of the natives is legitimized as an advance over "the brutal abominations of the Aztecs" by the "unsullied rites" of Christianity, the means of conversion can be criticized within the framework of pointing to the next advance in the progress of civilization—that from Catholicism to Protestantism: "To the more rational spirit of the present day, enlightened by a purer Christianity, it may seem difficult to reconcile gross deviations from morals with such devotion to the cause of religion. But the religion taught in that day was one of form and elaborate ceremony, addressed too exclusively to the senses" (*CM*, 685). Prescott criticizes Catholic proselytism as addressed to "the rude child of nature," while endorsing Protestant proselytism, "which, addressed to the reason, demand[s] a degree of refinement and mental culture in the audience" (*CM*, 159). "The Protestant missionary seeks to enlighten the understanding of his convert by the pale light of reason" (*CM*, 195). Under the cover of a critique of Catholic bigotry, the conquest and conversion of the American "heathens" is legitimized in the name of progress, in anticipation of the "purer Christianity" of Protestantism.

The same legitimization occurs in *Ferdinand and Isabella* in the course of Prescott's "regret" over "the decay and final extinction of a race who had made such high advances in civilisation as the Spanish Arabs" (*FI*, 2.90). His regret does not prevent him from ultimately upholding the conquest of Muslim Spain, for the Moors' "social institutions had incapacitated them for the further production of excellence": "In this impo-

tent condition, it was wisely ordered that their territory should be occupied by a people whose religion and more liberal form of government,
however frequently misunderstood or perverted, qualified them for advancing still higher the interests of humanity" (*FI,* 2.91). With such personal glosses on the events of his history, Prescott justifies the outcome
of the holy war of the Spaniards, for in the perversion of Christianity
(known as Catholicism) he detects the embryo of its purer form.

I wish to conclude by exploring, in the context of the conversion and
extinction of the Spanish Moors and American Indians, Prescott's view
of the forced conversion of the Jews and their final expulsion from Spain.
For Prescott himself formulated the fates of these three races as a kind of
historical triptych of racial eradication in which the acts of conquest,
colonization, and banishment come together in 1492. His history of the
Catholic monarchs focuses on that moment when "they published their
memorable and most disastrous edict against the Jews; inscribing it, as it
were, with the same pen which drew up the glorious capitulation of Granada, and the treaty with Columbus" (*FI,* 2.119). How can we explain
Prescott's defense of the Jews, especially in the face of his legitimization of
the conquest and conversion of the Moors and the Indians?

Prescott's enthusiasm for Scott led him to claim that *Ivanhoe* was indis-
pensable to understanding English medieval life: "who would now imagine that he could form a satisfactory notion . . . of Richard Coeur-de-Lion
and his brave paladins, that had not read 'Ivanhoe?' "[60] It should come as
no surprise that when Prescott characterizes Jewish life in medieval Spain
in *Ferdinand and Isabella,* he refers directly to Scott. Praising Scott for "his
usual discernment" in understanding "the Jewish character," Prescott
makes clear that "the humiliating state of the Jews, however, exhibited in
this romance, affords no analogy to their social condition in Spain" (*FI,*
1.300). By establishing "the high degree of civilisation, and even political
consequence" (*FI,* 1.300) that the Jews enjoyed in Spain, he corroborates
Rebecca's critique of England and her view of the relative tolerance she
would have found in Muslim Spain. Moreover, again like Scott, and like
the other early-nineteenth-century writers who recorded England's role
in the history of anti-Semitism, Prescott explains the expulsion of the
Spanish Jews by comparing it to the English expulsion: "We need look no
further for the principle of action, in this case, than the spirit of religious
bigotry, which led to a similar expulsion of the Jews from England,

France, and other parts of Europe" (*FI*, 2.133). Finally, when he claims
that "the crusades . . . opened the way to the Inquisition" (*FI*, 1.292), we
see the way in which Scott's focus on the Crusades opened the way to
Prescott's focus on the Inquisition.

While acknowledging England's abuses of the Jews, Prescott's main
target is Catholic bigotry, with Torquemada (as we might expect) the
main target. After all, Prescott hears and evaluates the inquisitorial de-
crees with "the ear of a Protestant" (*FI*, 1.293). Torquemada, the Dominican "condemned to infamous immortality," is one of those men "who
compensate for their abstinence from sensual indulgence, by giving scope
to those deadlier vices of the heart, pride, bigotry, and intolerance" (*FI*,
1.307). The Catholic Church is seen as functioning with its "usual duplicity," where even the apparent attempt at proselytization barely covers
the base motive of "gainful traffic" (*FI*, 1.323).

It is in the context of his critique of Catholic bigotry that Prescott
formulates his unusually sympathetic view of Marranism. Some in the
nineteenth century argued that the Inquisition was a kind of justice performed in reaction to crypto-Judaism—that is, in reaction to Jewish hypocrisy. In Milman's popular *History of the Jews* (1829), which Prescott
cited, we read: "This profound and widespread hypocrisy may seem to
some almost to justify the Inquisition; but it shows also how it was baffled
in spite of all its zealous cruelty."[61] Prescott justifies crypto-Judaism by
seeing it as an understandable reaction to the threat of massacre and the
danger of the Inquisition: "In this crisis, the only remedy left to the Jews
was a real or feigned conversion to Christianity" (*FI*, 1.301). Crypto-
Judaism, then, is a political exigency that results from Catholic bigotry,
not Jewish opportunism. Moreover, Prescott supplements his sympathetic understanding of crypto-Judaism with pictures of Jewish martyrdom. After recording the harrowing facts of Jewish persecution, he remarks on the extraordinary steadfastness of Jewish faith in an argument
that reminds us of the kind that Grace Aguilar makes in *Women of Israel:*
"This extraordinary act of self-devotion for conscience' sake may be
thought, in the nineteenth century, to merit other epithets than those of
'perfidy, incredulity, and stiff-necked obstinacy' " (*FI*, 2.126).

Prescott's attitude toward the Jews, however, is not simply shaped by
his desire to expose Catholic bigotry and persecution. His general view of
providential history seems to incorporate traditional millenarian attitudes

towards the Jews. Prescott begins precisely where millenarian theories begin, with the revelation of the extraordinary historical longevity of "this remarkable people, who seem to have preserved their unity of character unbroken amid the thousand fragments into which they have been scattered" (*FI*, 1.296). By beginning with the fact of the Jews' survival, he seems to imagine a significant corollary to the view of racial extinction that he, like other nineteenth-century historians, had been developing. In the context of recording the reasons behind the extinction of such races as the Moors and the Indians, the historian must account for the extraordinary survival of the Jews. What does it mean, Prescott's *History* asks, that the Inquisition was unable to "eradicate the seed" (*FI*, 2.121)?

In Prescott's view, Spanish history teaches us a complicated double lesson: the birth of a nation through the eradication of the Moors, and the economic and moral collapse of a nation through the expulsion of the Jews. Prescott's interpretation of Spain's downfall sounds a note already popular in historiography and in millenarian prophecy. On the one hand, the most secular version of such a claim was based on an economic argument. In Milman's *History of the Jews* the Jewish expulsion was "reckoned among the most effective cause of the decline of Spanish greatness" because the Jews "carried away all the industry and the commerce of the land."[62] On the other hand, millenarians like James Bicheno asked his readers to recognize "the hand of Providence . . . in punishing and breaking to pieces the kingdoms that have been their [the Jews'] oppressors."[63] Such views became commonplace, a kind of shared belief system whose traces we still find in the twentieth century, in James Joyce's *Ulysses*, for example: "History, would you be surprised to learn, proves up to the hilt Spain decayed when the inquisition hounded the jews out."[64] This idea, that nations were punished for their cruel treatment of the Jews, was also popular with nineteenth-century Jewish writers such as Grace Aguilar and Heinrich Graetz. Graetz records perhaps the most famous Jewish version written during the period of the Inquisition: "The enemies who treated Israel so unmercifully were said to have received their punishment. The poet said of the Spaniards that Italy had become their grave; of France, that Spain has been its rod of correction; of Germany, that the Turks were its executioners . . . ; and of England, that wild and savage Scotland was a perpetual thorn in its side."[65] (It should be noted that anti-Semitic writers also used this approach. The Franciscan monk Alfonso de Espina, in his famous *Fortalitium Fidei* [1460], explained that famine and plague were a divine visitation on the English for the crimes of England's converted Jews, who continued to practice Judaism in secret. In this purely self-interested revision of English history, Espina transfers the Marrano problem of fifteenth-century Spain to thirteenth-century England and explains how the expulsion of the Jews from England—amid their general slaughter, it should be added—was the solution to England's plague.)[66]

Prescott explains the downfall of the Spanish empire by emphasizing the economic loss incurred by Spain after the expulsion. He notes the effect of "the subtraction of the mechanical skill, intelligence, and general resources of an orderly, industrious population" (*FI*, 2.131). But he goes on to flirt with the idea that both the Inquisition and the expulsion were events registered in a divine realm, eliciting a kind of divine punishment for their perpetrators. For example, the establishment of the Inquisition in Seville in 1481, with its astonishing number of executions in its first year, seems to call a divine retribution on the population: "The plague which desolated Seville this year [came] . . . as if in token of the wrath of Heaven at these enormities" (*FI*, 1.312). Elsewhere, he is less tentative in imagining the persecution of the Jews as a national crime with grave consequences:

> Providence, however, permitted that the sufferings, thus heaped on the heads of this unfortunate people, should be requited in full measure to the nation that inflicted them. The fires of the Inquisition, which were lighted exclusively for the Jews, were destined eventually to consume their oppressors. They were still more deeply avenged in the moral influence of this tribunal, which, eating like a pestilent canker into the heart of the monarchy, at the very time when it was exhibiting a most goodly promise, left it at length a base and sapless trunk. (*FI*, 1.322)

The establishment of the Inquisition seems to be the first step in the downfall of Spain conceived as a divine judgment.

The remarkable survival of the Jewish people, especially in view of the rise and fall of the great empires through the centuries, became a touchstone of nineteenth-century discourse. For the millenarian writer at least, the survival of the Jews was the surest endorsement of those sacred prophecies that foresaw the restoration of the Jews to their home-land. From this vantage point, the Jews (unlike the Spanish Moors or the American Indians) performed a special function in the modern world: the Jews' resistance to extinction was a divine sign. For a millenarian like Bicheno, this meant "the Restoration of the Jewish people, and their after-conversion,"[67] as the prelude to the Second Coming. So the survival of the Jews ultimately legitimized their eradication by another means, through conversion.

In Prescott's own work the idea that frequently grounds his historical project is the benign efficacy of conversion. Thus, the ideology of conversion lies not only at the center of the religious revival in England and its consequent missions to the Jews and the "heathens," but at the center of the historian's general view of progress. So, after criticizing the (Catholic) methods of conversion used against Muslim, Indian, and Jew, Prescott nonetheless glorifies the missionary, as if the historian seeks the impossible, to disentangle the idea of conversion from the historical realities in which it is enmeshed. Hence Prescott's sentimental tableau of "the poor and humble missionary":

> His weapons are argument and mild persuasion. It is the reason he would conquer, not the body. He wins his way by conviction, not by violence. It is a moral victory to which he aspires, more potent, and happily more permanent, than that of the blood-stained conqueror. As he thus calmly, and imperceptibly, as it were, comes to his great results, he may remind us of the slow, insensible manner in which Nature works out her great changes in the material world, that are to endure when the ravages of the hurricane are passed away and forgotten. (*CP,* 232)

Prescott attempts here to distinguish between conquest and conversion, but he inadvertently reveals conversion as a highly specialized form of conquest—the conquest of the reason. Through an extended rhetorical figure, he suddenly attempts to disguise conversion as the female power of benign Nature, when he has elsewhere represented conquest and conversion as the twin masculine powers of human progress. In such a passage we see that conversion as conquest is legitimized by being at once naturalized and moralized. In fact, in a subtle linguistic move his readers would have recognized, Prescott takes the well-known figure for conversion used during the English religious revival—"the great change"[68]—and equates it with the work of Nature. For Prescott, the work of Nature and the work of proselytism become indistinguishable.

Like Scott, Prescott sees conversion as the essential medium of all historical change. But unlike Scott, for whom conversion signals the profound and even tragic erasure of national, religious, and racial difference, summed up in his view of conversion as genocide, Prescott reinstates and naturalizes the idea of conversion in an extended rhetorical figure that makes us almost forget the literal history of forced conversion and the brutal facts of conquest—the "ravages of the hurricane" that are to be "forgotten."

It remains a final irony that Prescott performs on his mentor in historical writing the kind of conversion that so troubled Scott. I refer here to Prescott's misnaming of Scott in the midst of praising him: "Scott was a Briton, with all the peculiarities of one—at least of a North Briton."[69] In this act of cultural mastery and absorption, Prescott names Scott by that assimilated British identity that is for Prescott the seal of national unity and the sign of the kind of racial solidarity that he eagerly desired; after all, Prescott spoke often of "the Anglo-Saxon races" (*CP*, 829) who settled North America, "of our own Puritan fathers, with the true Anglo-Saxon spirit" (*CM*, 537), and he called Britain "his Father-land."[70] In his naming of Scott, the trace of cultural difference, the scar of division between Scotland and England, is named only as an afterthought, as a halfhearted and grudging correction.

Prescott's apparent carelessness in naming Scott is the sign of a new attitude toward race that, at midcentury, helps define Prescott's role in crystallizing the solidarity of Anglo-Saxonism and Teutonism in the late 1830s and early 1840s. In this context, Prescott's entire historical enterprise functions as a radical departure from Scott's, so that in the end *Ferdinand and Isabella* attempts to revise Scott's project in *Ivanhoe*. This becomes clear when we see the way in which Prescott uses the racial dynamics of *Ivanhoe* as a model to formulate the history of racial conflict between Moors and Spaniards in Spain: "The Oriental and the European for eight centuries brought into contact with one another! yet, though brought into contact, too different in blood, laws, and religion ever to coalesce. Unlike the Saxons and Normans, who sprung from a common stock, with a common faith, were gradually blended into one people;

in Spain, the conflicting elements could never mingle."[71] Prescott's history of Spain functions as a rereading of Scott's history of England, reestablishing the category of race as an insuperable barrier between different peoples, and even making the ultimate extinction of one race by the other a prerequisite for national unity. What Scott called a conflict of races, and resolved through the union of Saxons and Normans in the founding of national unity in England, Prescott disqualifies as a genuine conflict of races, placed beside the clash between "Oriental" (Moor) and "European" (Spaniard) in Spain. Such an act of rewriting is a harbinger of a new way of conceiving race—one in which, more and more, the difference between Saxon and Norman, so critical at the end of the eighteenth century and the beginning of the nineteenth, when writers focused on the various racial groups who played roles in the prehistory of Great Britain (Pict, Celt, Briton, Saxon, Norman, etc.), gave way to larger, more dangerous, and more globally divisive racial categories.

5

Israel in England: English Culture and the "Hebrew Premier"

The story of crypto-Judaism in Spain and Portugal did not remain safely bound between the covers of antique romance. It was brought to life at the center of a crisis in English public life when an especially prominent public figure not only claimed this Sephardic heritage for himself, not only imbedded stories of Jewish persecution and flight under the Inquisition in an extremely popular series of novels, but finally became himself subjected to the charge of crypto-Judaism—despite the fact that there has been till this day no evidence that his practice of Christianity was in any way suspect or lax. In fact, in his political career he was a major spokesperson for the Church of England's institutions and traditions. I am speaking of Benjamin Disraeli, who was elected to the House of Commons in 1837 on his fifth attempt, and who remained a central political force in English politics through the 1870s, when his political career reached its zenith during his years as prime minister from 1874 until 1880.

Until now I have described the idea of "the secret race" as essentially historical, of another time and another place, a subject taken up most popularly between the covers of historical romance, though not without its relevance to the question of Jewish Emancipation in England. Disraeli for two reasons became the catalyst for the popular reemergence of the idea of "the secret race" in the 1870s and its use as the center of anti-Semitic representations. First, there was the fact of Disraeli's Jewish ancestry and his conversion at a young age, a conversion that made possible his entrance into Parliament at a time when practicing Jews were barred. This conversion, if represented in any way as suspect, was capable of making Disraeli look like an English variation on the Spanish *converso* who (opportunistically, according to the stereotype) converted to Christianity but remained at heart, and often in practice, a Jew. Second, Disraeli championed Hebraic culture in his writings and in his support of Jewish Emancipation against his own party's position. What began in the 1830s as scattered anti-Semitic remarks aimed at him by the crowds in his early electioneering became in the 1870s a kind of national scrutiny of his Jewishness—a scrutiny that erupted into an anti-Semitic attack led by some of the most prominent intellectuals and politicians of the time and anchored in the charge that Disraeli was a crypto-Jew.

In 1817 Disraeli was taken by his father's friend, Sharon Turner, to be converted, an event I have already related in discussing Turner's use of the figure of conversion in the writing of English history. Turner's conversion of the young Disraeli had unexpected results, for Disraeli did not become the kind of convert who hid his Jewish ancestry or, as in the case of so many converts, who attacked the religion of Judaism. Disraeli the convert became a champion of the Jews, attempting to secure a place for Hebraic culture beside the growing Teutonism that was so profoundly monopolizing the definition of English culture by the 1840s, personified especially in the tradition of the medievalist historians of whom Turner was the forefather. In this light, Disraeli's critique of the Teutonic definition of English national identity can be viewed as a masked critique of his own conversion at the hands of the Anglo-Saxon historian.

While Disraeli the converted Jew was the most outspoken and the earliest partisan for seeing English culture as Hebraic, we typically think of Matthew Arnold as the most famous formulator of "Hebraism." Arnold used his name both to claim his authority on the subject and to demonstrate the centrality of Hebraic culture in England: "why, my very name expresses that peculiar Semitico-Saxon mixture which makes the typical Englishman."[1] Such a definition of the typical Englishman significantly alters the most common models that were being used to understand the English national character. I have shown how certain national and religious comparisons—with France and atheism, or Spain and Catholicism—were used as foils to define Protestant England; in such paradigms the figure of the Jew was used to mediate the definitions of different European national identities: France's emancipation of the Jews during the revolution and Spain's persecution of the Jews during the Inquisition

were set beside the conduct of Protestant England. But in the work of
Disraeli and Arnold, the Hebraic is moved to the center of definitions of
English national identity. Under pressure from the new science of ethnology, however, writers such as Arnold recorded the way in which the idea
of racial difference disturbed such formulations, widening the gulf between Englishman and Jew. The attempt to ground English life in Hebrew
culture was countered, then, by the racial theories of ethnology, and by
the emergence of that particular brand of anti-Semitism, centered on
Disraeli, that suspected "the secret Jew" of invading and subverting English Protestant culture.

Disraeli and Crypto-Judaism

In 1849 Disraeli published a "Memoir" of his father, Isaac D'Israeli,
prefaced to the fourteenth edition of the latter's *Curiosities of Literature,* a
work that would be issued in many more editions in the second half of the
nineteenth century. The "Memoir" proved a crucial cultural event, for in
it Disraeli claimed for himself the heritage of the persecuted Jews of the
Iberian Peninsula. In the "Memoir," therefore, the story of the Inquisition, so often popularized as historical romance, became the family history of a member of Parliament. Such events as the persecution of the
Jews by Torquemada, their expulsion from Spain, their flight to Holland
and England—all the standard repertoire of historical romance—were
framed by the following family narrative: "My grandfather, who became
an English Denizen in 1748, was an Italian descendant from one of those
Hebrew families whom the Inquisition forced to emigrate from the Spanish Peninsula at the end of the fifteenth century."[2] The family's emancipation on reaching Italian soil was signaled by a particularly symbolic name
change: "His ancestors had dropped their Gothic surname . . . , and
grateful to the God of Jacob . . . they assumed the name of DISRAELI, a
name never borne before or since by any other family, in order that their
race might be for ever recognized."[3] This critical act of naming is used to
contextualize the idea of "the secret race" within the historical conditions
of the Inquisition, when hiding one's Jewish identity was a condition of
one's survival; once free, the family chooses a name that becomes a public
badge, the most overt refusal of secrecy, the absolute seal of recognition.

Nonetheless, the bearers of the name—both the father, Isaac D'Israeli, and his son Benjamin—were accused of crypto-Judaism.

In claiming this specific heritage, Disraeli became the most prominent living example of the link between nineteenth-century England and the crypto-Judaism of fifteenth-century Spain, a link that Grace Aguilar tirelessly recorded in the 1840s and that Disraeli's own father explored. Isaac D'Israeli, in fact, was one of the first writers in England to record the experience of the Iberian crypto-Jews. In a brief entry under the title "Inquisition" in *Curiosities of Literature*, he describes the way in which Jews and Moors were "compelled to become Christians; they, at least assumed the name; but it was well known that both these nations naturally respected their own faith."[4] The topic is given fuller treatment in *The Genius of Judaism* (1833),[5] under two telling chapter titles: "History of Jewish Conversions" and "The English Jews." In the chapter on conversions, D'Israeli records the way in which Iberian Jews were "compelled to dissimulate" (*GJ*, 183) their Catholicism, and the shocking and brutal event of wholesale conversion: "At that period the saving grace of Christianity, such as Christianity then was, seems to have consisted in driving herds of them to the river side, as their driver held a crucifix in his hand. These mighty conversions, splendid in their exterior, were hollow within—and they never lasted. Violence on one side and necessity on the other, had spread a general dissimulation among this populace of converts" (*GJ*, 196–97). The failure of forced baptism in Inquisitorial Spain is compared to the unsuccessful modern attempt to convert the Jews in England, for the chapter begins with a caustic critique of the London Society for Promoting Christianity amongst the Jews, so that D'Israeli sketches in a powerful historical continuum that links (intolerant, Catholic) Spain and (tolerant, Protestant) England: "The Hebrews were no longer hunted down as wild animals, but invited, like sheep straying without a shepherd, into the fold" (*GJ*, 198). The prominence that D'Israeli gives to the "History of Jewish Conversions" allows him to record the historical reasons behind the bogus nature of these conversions and to ironize the difference between the two modes—English and Spanish—of treating the Jews: "Toleration, in a war of insult, permits but an ignominious existence; and Persecution, in a war of extermination, immolates its victims" (*GJ*, 4).[6]

In "History of Jewish Conversions" and "The English Jews," D'Israeli responds to a central problem in Jewish historiography that he raised very early in his literary career: "Not among the least of Hebrew grievances has been that of the Christians having written their history. The Jews are chiefly known by accounts drawn up by their enemies."[7] Now, in *The Genius of Judaism*, more than three decades later, in asking the question, "Who are the English Jews?," D'Israeli explains once again that the Jews "have few or no recollections of their ancestors in this country" (*GJ*, 239), and thereby he opens the way both to the kind of personal family history his son produces in the "Memoir" and the kind of history Aguilar writes in "The History of the Jews in England."

D'Israeli's meditation on the question of Anglo-Jewish identity finds its origin in the history of the persecution of the Jews in the Iberian Penin-sula, for the "Spanish and Portuguese fugitives from the infernal fires of the Autos da Fe, and the living graves of the Inquisition" "formed the first general settlement of Jews in England" (*GJ*, 244). An encapsulated his-tory of the Jews in England suggests how quickly these foreign Jews be-came English Jews: "The first and second generation of the Portuguese Jews resided in retired quarters in the city. . . . A third generation were natives. A fourth were purely English" (*GJ*, 249–50). Such a history of naturalization leads to the following conclusion: "About the time of the first George this foreign race were zealously national" (*GJ*, 250), for "The Hebrew adopts the hostilities and the alliances of the land where he was born—he calls himself by the name of his country" (*GJ*, 251–52). Pub-lished in 1833 amid the parliamentary debates on Jewish Emancipation (which raised the question of Jewish loyalty to England), *The Genius of Judaism* focused attention away from the conventional history of "the Jews in England" (typically made up of antiquarian lore and anti-Semitic legend)[8] to concentrate on "the English Jews," a new naming that asked the English public to acknowledge the members of this community as their fellow citizens.

"The English Jews" ends curiously, by leaving behind the patriotism of the English Jews and turning to the experience of their forebears, the "*Christianos Novos*" of Portugal: "They were numerous, and most of them secretly Judaised. They were known by their baptismal names, but often among themselves they had preserved their more ancient denomi-nations" (*GJ*, 253). This leads to an anecdote that concludes the chapter by arguing that "the Portuguese are almost wholly Judaic in their descent":

Under the administration of the great Pombal, the priestly party had persuaded King Joseph to renew that badge of Judaism—the yellow hat—to mark the numerous Christianos Novos among his subjects. The edict was prepared. On the following morning the minister appeared before his majesty with three yellow hats—one he offered to the King, another he brought for the Grand Inquisitor, and the third for his own head. "I obey your majesty's order," said the minister, "in providing these badges to be worn by those whose blood has been tainted by Judaism." (*GJ*, 254–55)

Such a passage was bound to be interpreted by many of D'Israeli's Christian readers as a threatening picture of the Jew's successful invasion and subversion of Christian culture. So while D'Israeli confirms the English identity of England's Jews, his insistence on the crypto-Jewish heritage of the contemporary Anglo-Jewish community could be read in two ways: a history of persecution, martyrdom, and heroic escape, or, a history of Jewish subversion in which the Jew, in the guise of a Christian, gained the most powerful positions in the land. D'Israeli the father could hardly have imagined that this latter interpretation would haunt the political career of Disraeli the son.

From the Jewish point of view, to claim certain prominent historical figures as Jewish was not simply a matter of cultural pride but an antidote to the censorship of Jewish history—a history always incomplete, always fragmentary, because of the conditions of Jewish persecution, which meant that Jewish life existed undercover. One of the legacies of the Inquisition and the crypto-Judaism that resulted from it was a falsified, or at least masked and abbreviated, record of Jewish experience. Such conditions skewed the writing of Jewish history, even the writing of Anglo-Jewish history. D'Israeli's claim that there were Jews in England in those periods "in which it is supposed there were no Jews in England—the reigns of Elizabeth, James, and Charles I" (*GJ*, 239–40) has been confirmed by modern research, so that we now understand that the expulsion of the Jews from England in 1290 did not mean the complete absence of Jews and Judaism in ensuing centuries.[9] "The English Jews" is the record of a people who, for their own survival, kept their very existence a secret.

For the anti-Semite, however, the claim that certain well-known Christians were in fact Jews inspired mockery at first, and fear, suspicion, and anger in the end. Disraeli's *Coningsby* (1844), for example, was mocked by Thackeray in *Codlingsby* (1847) for claiming certain prominent Christian figures as Jewish: "His Majesty is one of *us* . . . ; so is the Pope of Rome," Rafael Mendoza (loosely based on Disraeli's Jew, Sidonia) whispers to Lord Codlingsby. Disraeli, a rising member of Parliament and himself a convert from Judaism, is thereby viewed as the author of a fantastic dream of power, the power of crypto-Judaism. The lampooning of Disraeli has its deadly serious side, for Thackeray represents a kind of Jewish conspiracy that runs the world. When we learn that "it was Rafael Mendoza that saved the Turkish monarchy," we see that Thackeray is representing the power of Jewish money in the affairs of Europe in the nineteenth century, an idea represented in Disraeli's *Coningsby* as well. In this way the apparently fantastic dream of Jewish power (king and pope as Jews) is substantiated by the power of Mendoza, on the surface a mere old-clothes dealer, the latest disguise "the secret race" has invented. For already in *Codlingsby* we find articulated the central ideology of Jewish identity in mid-nineteenth-century England: "half the Hebrew's life is a disguise."[10] This idea reaches its apogee in Trollope's novels, where anti-Semitism takes the form of the constant suspicion of masked Jewish identity. We begin to see the way in which the history of Iberian crypto-Judaism became fraught in nineteenth-century England, when the idea of the persecution of the Jews during the Inquisition could be dissolved in the stereotype of the secret Jew—masked, subversive, and prodigiously powerful.

It is no surprise to find Isaac D'Israeli, one of the early chroniclers of crypto-Judaism, accused of hiding his Judaic origins. According to Walter Savage Landor, D'Israeli, "whether from pride or modesty, takes the greatest pains to conceal the evidence of the religion in which he was educated. In the account of his life, which he is reported to have written, no mention is made whatever of the faith which he is said to have abjured: he there descends, as the name, it is observed, announces, from an *Italian* family. He is one of the children of Israel, nevertheless, as is also announced by the name D'Israeli."[11] No record exists of D'Israeli concealing his identity in an autobiographical account, and his son's "Memoir," in any case, leaves no doubt about the family's Jewish heritage. The other side of this kind of suspicion is revealed when a guest of D'Israeli's mistakes the other guests as Jews; the suspicion of D'Israeli's concealed Jewish identity turns into the suspicion that all his friends are Jews. In 1807, Alexander Hunter observes at a party given by D'Israeli: "The whole company, except ourselves I believe, were Jews and Jewesses! . . . Our male part of the company consisted mostly of literary men—Cumberland, Turner, Disraeli, Basevi, Prince Hoare, and Mr. Cervetto."[12] This report inscribes some version of poetic justice when Sharon Turner, the man who presides over the young Benjamin's conversion, turns into a Jew.

Both Landor's and Hunter's remarks suggest the English anxiety over being able to identify a Jew, an issue that D'Israeli himself had addressed in *Vaurien* (1797) when a Jewish philosopher explodes the myth that "the Jews are distinguished by a national countenance, . . . piously conceived as a mark inflicted by the divinity, similar to that of Cain."[13] The Jew, unmarked, passes unnoticed and climbs to the highest stations in English public life. Hence the anxiety that suspects the Jew of concealing his identity (Landor) and that multiplies Jewish identity everywhere (Hunter). So the anti-Semite delights in the ultimate uncovering of Jewish identity, even to the point of imagining something like the Inquisition as a kind of ironic justice for such concealment. I have in mind Robert Southey's comment on the man who rejects the idea of the universal Jewish physiognomy: "D'Israeli . . . looks like a Portugueze who being apprehended for an assasin is convicted of being circumcised. I don't like him."[14] For Southey, circumcision, the ultimate mark that the secret Jew cannot efface, becomes the final grim joke played on the Jew who thinks he can pass.

When and how Benjamin Disraeli learned the details of Jewish persecution during the Inquisition we can only surmise. No picture has been handed down to us, as in Aguilar's case,[15] of the young child being initiated into family stories of flight and escape from the Iberian peninsula, though perhaps such stories were told, perhaps even elicited, after the son read what the father himself had written about the crypto-Jews. We do know that the young Disraeli made a memorable trip to Spain in 1830.[16] He used as one of his guides on this trip Washington Irving's *Chronicle of the Conquest of Granada,* which he recommends to his father, who was a friend of Irving's: "Look at the map and get W. I.'s Chronicle . . . ; you will find it most interesting when you remember I am wandering among the scenes. . . . Tell Irving he has left a golden name in Spain."[17] Disraeli even stayed at the boardinghouse where Irving had stayed and would have been familiar with this passage in Irving's book:

It so happened that about this time there were many families of wealth and dignity in the kingdoms of Aragon and Valencia and the principality of Catalonia whose forefathers had been Jews, but had been converted to Christianity. Notwithstanding the outward piety of these families, it was surmised, and soon came to be strongly suspected, that many of then [*sic*] had a secret hankering after Judaism, and it was even whispered that some of them practised Jewish rites in private.

The Catholic monarch (continues Agapida) had a righteous abhorrence of all kinds of heresy and a fervent zeal for the faith; he ordered, therefore, a strict investigation of the conduct of these pseudo-Christians. Inquisitors were sent into the provinces for the purpose, who proceeded with their accustomed zeal. The consequence was, that many families were convicted of apostasy from the Christian faith and of the private practice of Judaism. Some, who had grace and policy sufficient for reform in time, were again received into the Christian fold after being severely mulcted and condemned to heavy penance; others were burnt at *auto de fes* for the edification of the public, and their property was confiscated for the good of the state.[18]

In Irving's work we see a powerful representation of crypto-Judaism serving as a guide for the converted Jew through the land that, some years later, Disraeli will publicly claim as the land of his forefathers. Soon after the trip to Spain, references to Spain appear in Disraeli's writing, but it is not until *Coningsby* (1844), the first novel of his political trilogy on "the Young England," that he extensively treats the subject of the Iberian Jews.

A critical problem, both formal and thematic, that Disraeli faced in his trilogy on the "Condition-of-England Question" (*C*, 96)[19] was how to marry it to "the Jewish question." Solving this problem would mean defining himself as an English man of letters, but with an undisguised—in fact, a proudly proclaimed—Jewish heritage. Disraeli sought to write a series of novels in which he could speak authoritatively, as an Englishman, on English political life, specifically on English national institutions (such as the party system, the Church, and the monarchy). To include "the Jewish question" in such a framework, he began with the strategy used by his father in the 1830s and by Aguilar in the 1840s—to constitute and consolidate the idea of "the English Jews" by representing their pre-history in Inquisitorial Spain and Portugal. In *Coningsby* the material on the Inquisition and the crypto-Jews is largely compressed into a single chapter (book IV, chapter 10) and takes the form of the family history of the central Jewish character, Sidonia, who is defined as "An Englishman, and taught from his cradle to be proud of being an Englishman" (*C,* 237). As in the case of the "Memoir," a representation of the historical conditions that led to crypto-Judaism is located within the family history of an English citizen:

> Sidonia was descended from a very ancient and noble family of Arragon, that, in the course of ages, had given to the state many distinguished citizens. In the priesthood its members had been peculiarly eminent. Besides several prelates, they counted among their number an Archbishop of Toledo; and a Sidonia, in a season of great danger and difficulty, had exercised for a series of years the paramount office of Grand Inquisitor.
>
> Yet, strange as it may sound, it is nevertheless a fact, of which there is no lack of evidence, that this illustrious family during all this period, in common with two-thirds of the Arragonese nobility, secretly adhered to the ancient faith and ceremonies of their fathers; a belief in the unity of the God of Sinai, and the rights and observances of the laws of Moses. (*C,* 233)

The history of crypto-Judaism, here as elsewhere, is introduced on a defensive note, encouraging the incredulous English public to believe: "strange as it may sound," "there is no lack of evidence." This defensiveness is motivated by two ideas: first, that such a history has been kept a secret from the non-Jewish world, and second, that such a history shows the secret Jews having reached the most powerful positions—positions they must have used, at least in part, subversively.

The main thrust of the history of crypto-Judaism in *Coningsby* is a story of prejudice and persecution. Disraeli's history contains all the features we have come to expect: the New Christians, the conquest of the Moors, Torquemada, the auto-da-fé, the eventual arrival in England. But in Disraeli's hands this material becomes part of a larger debate on racial survival that includes, but goes beyond, the conventional claim about the fall of Spain: "Where is Spain? Its fall, its unparalleled and its irremediable fall, is mainly to be attributed to the expulsion of the large portion of its subjects, the most industrious and intelligent, who traced their origin to the Mosaic and Mohammedan Arabs" (*C*, 235). This conventional claim, typically buttressed by secular arguments about national finances or by sacred arguments about the millenium, soon turns into a remarkable claim about race: "It is a physiological fact; a simple law of nature, which has baffled Egyptian and Assyrian Kings, Roman Emperors, and Christian Inquisitors. No penal laws, no physical tortures, can effect that a superior race should be absorbed in an inferior, or be destroyed by it. The mixed persecuting races disappear; the pure persecuted race remains. And at this moment, in spite of centuries, of tens of centuries, of degradation, the Jewish mind exercises a vast influence on the affairs of Europe" (*C*, 271).

This is a critical moment in English representations of the Inquisition: a history of Jewish persecution and victimhood turns into a claim about Jewish racial superiority and world power. And, perhaps more remarkable, this claim unites the Anglo-Saxon and the Jew. For "the physiological fact" that Sidonia, the speaker here, has in mind is that "you cannot destroy a pure race of the Caucasian organisation" (*C*, 271). Central to Coningsby's education, then, is the idea of the Englishman's kinship to the Jew, which the English aristocrat learns at the knee of his symbolic father-mentor, Sidonia:

> "You must study physiology, my dear child. Pure races of Caucasus may be persecuted, but they cannot be despised except by the brutal ignorance of some mongrel breed, that brandishes fagots and howls extermination, but is itself exterminated without persecution, by that irresistible law of Nature which is fatal to curs."
>
> "But I come also from Caucasus," said Coningsby. (*C*, 273)

This role reversal, where the Jew proudly announces his superior racial makeup and his heritage as a Caucasian, and where the English nobleman almost timidly seeks his niche in the same racial category, is a richly ironic and jarring moment in the history of Anglo-Jewish relations. In the 1870 General Preface to his works, Disraeli would reflect on the radical nature of such a passage: "Familiar as we all are now with such truths, the house of Israel being now freed from the barbarism of mediaeval misconceptions, and judged, like all other races, by their contributions to the existing sum of human welfare, and the general influence of race on human action being universally recognized as the key of history, the difficulty and hazard of touching for the first time on such topics cannot now be easily appreciated."[20] If race had begun to be inscribed as the key to history in Scott's *Ivanhoe* and the historical romances that followed it, *Coningsby* was certainly the first example of a novel conceiving history as the record of Jewish racial superiority.

Sidonia's role throughout the novel is to critique the Eurocentric, and especially Teutonic, conventions of racial superiority. This will eventually lead to a brilliant maneuver—finding the most ancient basis of English life not in Teutonism but in Hebraism. For Disraeli to write as an English Jew offers no contradiction whatsoever; his project is merely to recall his English fellow citizens to those traditions more ancient than the Teutonic or Anglo-Saxon. Such a project, after Disraeli, will become sufficiently plausible to allow Matthew Arnold two decades later to conceive of Hebraism as the basis of English life.

Sidonia's critique begins at his first meeting with Coningsby. When Coningsby describes "cleanliness" as "an inheritance from our Saxon fathers" and claims that "the northern nations have a greater sense of cleanliness, of propriety, of what we call comfort," Sidonia retorts: "By no means . . . ; the East is the land of the Bath. Moses and Mahomet made cleanliness religion" (*C,* 142). This is only the beginning of a series of legacies that the European owes to the Asian, the Englishman to the Jew, in what becomes a radical reevaluation of the system of indebtedness worked out by earlier writers, including Disraeli's father, whose Jewish philosopher in *Vaurien* attempts to resolve modern Christian-Jewish relations through the following formula: "the Christian should be generous and the Jew grateful."[21] The conventional picture of the Jew's debt to England is at first embraced by Disraeli and then turned inside out. For Disraeli, while the Jew should be grateful to the Englishman—the "Memoir" ends by explaining how Isaac D'Israeli "repaid England for the protection and the hospitality which this country accorded to his father a century ago"[22]—England itself owes an even greater debt to the Jew. This debt is economic and contemporary as well as ethical and ancient. First, there is the Jewish financing of England's credit during the Napoleonic Wars.[23] In addition, there are the ancient legal and ethical traditions of the Jews, on which all of Europe but especially England depends, an idea most prominently expressed in the trilogy's third novel, *Tancred* (1847): "The life and property of England are protected by the laws of Sinai. . . . And yet they [the English] persecute the Jews, and hold up to odium the race to whom they are indebted for the sublime legislation which alleviates the inevitable lot of the labouring multitude!" (*T,* 265).[24] Disraeli reconceives the idea of the indebtedness of the Jew, and his strategy for doing so is to intertwine the very heart of English political institutions— the subject of his political trilogy—with the ancient institutions of the Jew: "Vast as the obligations of the whole human family are to the Hebrew race, there is no portion of the modern populations so much indebted to them as the British people" (*T,* 265).

Disraeli's ultimate strategy is not to conceive of two warring traditions, the European and the Asian, but to see these traditions as contiguous. Hence the paradox he raises: "why do these Saxon and Celtic societies persecute an Arabian race, from whom they have adopted laws of sublime benevolence?" (*T,* 265). To see these two traditions as potentially congenial and even integrated (instead of perpetually opposed), he imbeds *Coningsby* with all the conventional touchstones of the Teutonic identity of English national life. The novel is not simply grounded in nineteenth-century English political life; it is grounded in the conventional Teutonic prehistory of English national life. I refer to Disraeli's allusions, some relatively technical, to the character of "the northern nations" (*C,* 64), to the tradition of "popular assemblies" (*C,* 64) among such nations, to "our Saxon Wittenagemotes" (*C,* 374). Such language falls within the tradition of Anglo-Saxon historiography, from Sharon Turner through Edward Augustus Freeman; it grounds the argument that such free institutions as parliamentary government predated the Norman Conquest and were founded in Teutonic institutions. This special discourse of the "northern nations" began to gain a new hold on English consciousness from the 1840s onward, when the racial role in constituting national identity began to be emphasized more and more.[25]

In *Coningsby* this Teutonic discourse serves a double function. First, it provides evidence of Disraeli's credentials as an Englishman and an English writer of political history. No work on English political institutions, or on the "national character" (*C,* 260), could fail to include such terms. So even Sidonia, the critic of the ideology of Teutonism, must give Coningsby's race its due: "You come from the shores of the Northern Sea, land of the blue eye, and the golden hair, and the frank brow. . . . these Goths, and Saxons, and Normans were doubtless great men" (*C,* 273). Moreover, Disraeli has understood the procedure for configuring national identity in the nineteenth century, and he uses it to his own ends. Realizing that a kind of racial and cultural genealogy is the basis of constructing national identity, Disraeli simply looks beyond not only the Norman invasion but the celebrated Saxon institutions themselves to find in Hebrew culture the most profound basis of English national life. Disraeli in this way inserts himself into this Anglo-Saxon tradition, makes it his own, acknowledges his acceptance of it as an Englishman, but adds to it a more ancient tradition of values that he feels England equally depends on. In effect, he hopes to be understood as simply enlarging—not destroying—the traditional "English" argument by finding a place for Jewish traditions beside those of Teutonism. After all, he well knew the kinds of charges that one might have to face for supporting any value system thought to be " 'un-English' " (*C,* 301).

Disraeli also inserts himself into the traditional discourse on "English" institutions through a network of allusions to *Ivanhoe,* a novel that had the added advantage of prefiguring the idea of the Jew's position in England that Disraeli wants to explore. His allusions to *Ivanhoe* function as references not simply to Scott's novel, but to what had become the popular history of England—to an "ancient forest" and "Norman kings" and "Saxon outlaws" (*C,* 137). It is an irony of literary history that should not go unnoticed that Disraeli attempts to establish himself as an English writer through allusions to a work that was itself intended to authorize another outsider, Scott, in the arena of "English" literature. Perhaps for this reason, both writers depict in their novels the ultimate outsider in English life, the unconverted Jew who, even in the nineteenth century, is denied his full rights as an Englishman. The history of the Sidonia family members in Spain makes them the literary progeny of Scott's Isaac and Rebecca, completing a cycle of flight and return; the Jews who fled England for Spain have now become the Jews who fled Spain for England. Nonetheless, the Jew who returns to England still finds that he does not possess all the rights and privileges accorded to English citizens. Sidonia educates Coningsby in the ironies of English political life: "Can anything be more absurd than that a nation should apply to an individual to maintain its credit, and, with its credit, its existence as an empire, and its comfort as a people; and that individual one to whom its laws deny the proudest rights of citizenship, the privilege of sitting in its senate and of holding land?" (*C*, 270). The attack on Jewish civil disabilities no longer depends on only an embarrassing comparison between Spain and England, in which England's illiberality toward the Jew in the nineteenth century is recognized: the Englishman owes the Jew a profound debt— moral as well as financial—that should be requited in full citizenship for the Jew.

Discussions of *Coningsby*—including my own to this point—make it sound as if Jewish themes in the novel were much more prominent than they are. This is understandable, since the portrait of Sidonia is the novel's most striking feature. But the Jewish element in *Coningsby* exists almost purely on a rhetorical level, rarely entering the action. This stems in part from Sidonia's sense of himself as a disenfranchised citizen, a man denied the full possibilities of action. He speaks and acts from the sidelines, in his role as a marginal figure, an Englishman whose Jewish identity denies him the full exercise of his powers: "I am and must ever be but a dreamer of dreams. Action is not for me. I am of that faith that the Apostles professed before they followed their master" (*C*, 144). The model for George Eliot's Mordecai in *Daniel Deronda*, Sidonia is the Jewish visionary who educates the English gentleman in the aristocratic heritage of the Jew. So, while Sidonia exists in *Coningsby* as an important, even radical, strand of discourse, as a kind of countervoice to conventional English views, the novel's plot proceeds largely beyond his purview.

The plot of *Coningsby* is conceived as a kind of comedy of (political) manners, based on the Norman/Saxon racial dynamics of Scott's *Ivanhoe*. Coningsby, the aristocrat, is surrounded by a series of Norman markers, all finally devolving on his name ("Monsieur Konigby" [*C*, 46]), while Edith Millbank, his bride in the end, is said to have "a Saxon name, for she is the daughter of a Saxon" (*C*, 188). Edith's father, not unlike Sidonia, functions to critique a conventional racial stereotype, in this case the superiority of the Norman over the Saxon. Mr. Millbank decries those "noble" families who reject everyone who can "trace no mystified descent from a foreign invader" (*C*, 403). Further, he argues that England's present aristocracy is a false aristocracy—"our present peers" "adopted Norman manners while they usurped Norman titles" (*C,* 194)—at the same time that he declares there are "Saxon families . . . who can trace their pedigrees beyond the Conquest" (*C,* 193). Not unlike Scott's Cedric, another protector of a Saxon daughter, Mr. Millbank defines the novel's essential conflict in the terms of *Ivanhoe:* "Saxon industry and Norman manners never will agree; and some day, Mr. Coningsby, you will find that out" (*C,* 192). Scott's prediction of the fusion of the races in the late Middle Ages has still not occurred in the Victorian period, so, while we found Prescott minimizing the racial conflict between Saxon and Norman (declaring both as Teutonic), Mr. Millbank argues that the conflict still exists, but now largely on the basis of class warfare. The novel therefore sets itself the same goal as *Ivanhoe,* a kind of intermarriage that looks forward to a new kind of national unity, for even Sidonia argues that the "decline" of England is signaled by class struggle: "the various classes of this country are arrayed against each other" (*C,* 260). The marriage between Coningsby and Edith—the novel's climax—connects "the haughty house of Coningsby with the humble blood of the Lancashire manufacturer" (*C,* 365), so that the hero of the novel succeeds in his mission: "I would appease these hatreds" (*C,* 402).

With Sidonia's role in the novel largely rhetorical, and with the racial division between Normans and Saxons transformed into an argument about class conflict, one could argue that for Disraeli (the converted Jew) the racial plot in *Coningsby* is at once repressed and sublimated. As in *Ivanhoe,* the climactic marriage at the end of *Coningsby* deliberately excludes the Jewish character. Sidonia, while powerful, wealthy, and well-educated, seems deliberately disabled for marriage, so that he exists as no erotic threat: "He was a man without affections" (*C,* 239). When Coningsby mistakenly suspects Sidonia of loving Edith, we learn that "No earthly consideration would ever induce him to impair that purity of race on which he prides himself" (*C,* 368). Finally, when Coningsby escapes the "want of faith" (*C,* 149) that surrounds him by taking up a political career in Parliament, he becomes an echo of Disraeli's position as a converted Jew who must find his faith in English politics, in a quasi-religious devotion to English national interests that displaces the Jew's devotion to the faith of his ancestors.

In the next novel of the trilogy, *Sybil, or the Two Nations* (1845), the

Jewish element is almost entirely erased, or at least repressed, for Sidonia has temporarily disappeared. As if to balance this loss, the racial terminology of Saxon and Norman is enlarged, and the association between the Saxon and the Hebrew, when raised in the novel, is made more explicit. The narrator, for example, records the way in which the names "Sion, Bethel, Bethesda" function for the poor Saxon peasant: "names of a distant land, and the language of a persecuted and ancient race; yet such is the mysterious power of their divine quality, breathing consolation in the nineteenth century to the harrassed forms and harrowed souls of a Saxon peasantry" (*S*, 54).[26] In such a passage Disraeli demonstrates that he has learned from Scott's *Ivanhoe* the effectiveness, for the English reader, of the comparison between disenfranchised Saxons and Jews. But without the presence of a Jewish character in the novel, "the ancient race" has been reduced almost purely to a figure, remote and romantic, without contemporary significance of its own, relevant only through analogy, through its power to represent the interests of the peasantry. Without the benefit of a Jewish spokesperson like Sidonia, the Jewish element in the trilogy is inscribed as a universal figure for oppression.

The racial conflict in *Sybil*, as in *Coningsby*, is played out in a romance between a Norman aristocrat (Egremont) and a Saxon peasant (Sybil), where again the daughter's name is the proud marker of her race—"a name, I believe, that has been about our hearth as long as our race" (*S*, 174). The daughter, who defines herself as "the daughter of their blood" (*S*, 124), who "bewailed the degradation of her race" (*S*, 131), and who seeks the means by which "we may redeem our race" (*S*, 169), is a Saxon Rebecca, an only child devoted to her widowed father and to her oppressed race. In the Saxons' search for "the emancipation of their race" (*S*, 277), we find a shadowy representation of the battle for Jewish Emancipation which, even in the mid-1840s, had not yet been achieved, so that the medieval terminology of Saxon and Norman suits the oppression of both peasant and Jew. The appeasement of these "hatreds" or class conflicts takes the form of a purely figurative intermarriage; "a union between the child and brother of nobles and a daughter of the people" (*S*, 278) occurs at the end of the novel when Egremont and Sybil marry, but not without the discovery that Sybil has her own noble inheritance, a conventional plot twist in which the heroine is suddenly revealed to be well-born.

The representation of the conflict between the peasants and the aristocracy through the terminology of Saxons and Normans is based not simply on the conventions of literary allusion (that is, as a form of citation to *Ivanhoe*), but rather on a widely held belief about "the circumstances of our national history" (*S*, 31). The novel begins by reminding its readers that there is no more prominent subject in English history than "the influence of races in our early ages" (*S*, 15). If "it is the past alone that can explain the present" (*S*, 421), English national history provides Disraeli with the means of basing Victorian class conflict on the medieval racial conflict between Saxons and Normans.

Augustin Thierry functions here as the critical mediator between Scott's view of medieval English history as racial conflict and Disraeli's view of modern English history as class conflict (conceived in the terminology of racial conflict). It was Thierry's terms about his own country, formulated through his reading of Scott, that allowed Disraeli to structure *Sybil* as the story of *The Two Nations*—the Rich and the Poor: "Two nations; between whom there is no intercourse and no sympathy; who are as ignorant of each other's habits, thoughts, and feelings, as if they were dwellers in different zones, or inhabitants of different planets; who are formed by a different breeding, are fed by a different food, are ordered by different manners, and are not governed by the same laws" (*S*, 65–66). Disraeli's claim that England is really two nations descends directly from Thierry's argument about France: "We believe we are a nation, and we are two nations on one soil; two nations, inimical in their reminiscences, irreconcilable in their projects; the one formerly conquered the other" (*HE*, 89).[27] Despite Disraeli's "pilgrimage"[28] to visit the great Thierry, no one to my knowledge has noticed or examined Thierry's influence on Disraeli. Thierry's popularity among English-speaking readers depended in part on his profuse praise of Scott, not to mention that the French historian illustrated his idea of the two nations from the histories of England, Scotland, and Ireland. He sees this idea at work in Scotland, and he credits Scott with exposing "this division of Scotland between two nations" (*HE*, 59). The idea is the center of his characterization of England and Ireland as well: "the long persistence of two inimical nations on the same soil, and the variety of political, social and religious struggles, which spring, as from an inexhaustible source, out of the original hostility; the antipathy of race surviving all the revolutions of manners, laws and lan-

guage, perpetuating itself through the centuries"—all recalling the Nor-
man/Saxon conflict in Victorian England (according to Disraeli). For
this survival of the conflict between two antithetical nations and races lies
"at the bottom of the history of all European monarchies" (*HE,* xi).

Thierry credits Scott with writing the kind of history that made possible the revelation of this idea of the two nations. Before Scott, history was
written from the conqueror's perspective, so that "The consequences of
the [Norman] invasion seem to confine themselves for the conquered nation to a mere change of dynasty. The subjection of the natives of England; the confiscation of their property, and its division among the foreign invaders; all these acts of conquest, and not government, lose their
true character, and assume improperly an administrative colouring"
(*HE,* 53), until Scott writes *Ivanhoe.* Calling Scott "the greatest master of
historical divination that has ever existed" (*HE,* xi), Thierry declares:
"there is more real *history* in his novels on Scotland and England than
in the philosophically false compilations which still possess the name"
(*HE,* 55). In Thierry's monumental *Histoire de la Conquête de l'Angleterre
par les Normands* (1825), he claims that "a romance writer, a man of
genius, was the first to teach the modern English that their ancestors of
the eleventh century were not all utterly defeated and crushed in one
single day" (*HC,* 1.xxiv).[29] Following in Scott's footsteps, Thierry conceives of the historian as a kind of archaeologist recovering the "living
traces of the diversity of the races of men" that have been lost through the
conquest of one people by another, and through the modern drive toward
national unity, for "we clearly perceive the existence of several peoples in
the geographical circumscription which bears the name of one alone"
(*HC,* 1.xvii). Like Scott, he writes history in the name of the oppressed,
the forgotten, the nameless: "The obscurity in which these populations
have become involved does not arise from any unworthiness on their part
to have had historians, equally with other populations; most of them, on
the contrary, are remarkable for an originality of character which distinguishes them in the most marked manner from the great nations into
which they been absorbed" (*HC,* 1.xxii). Hence his understanding of the
creation of the modern nation-state through conquest: "The establishment of the great modern states has been mainly the work of force; the
new societies have been formed out of the wrecks of the old societies
violently destroyed, and in this labour of recomposition, large masses of

men have lost, amid heavy sufferings, their liberty, and even their names as a people, replaced by a foreign name" (*HC,* 1.xxiii).

Thierry builds his entire historical project on this idea of conquest, which figured so centrally in the work of nineteenth-century Anglo-American historians; medieval conquest became the ground on which they saw historical racial conflict realized. But in Thierry's work, medieval conquest also becomes the source of a crucial later development, the modern nation-state's division through class conflict. In this light the language of *Sybil* allows for the equivocation between the terms of race (Saxon and Norman) and class (peasantry and aristocracy), based on the medieval history of England: "we are divided between the conquerors and the conquered" is the analysis Sibyl's father makes of the present conditions in England, while his daughter reads to him from a book entitled (though nowhere identified as Thierry's) "The History of the Conquest of England by the Normans" (*S,* 171). Thierry explains the consequences of conquest: "The higher and lower classes . . . at present day . . . are in many countries the lineal representatives of the people conquering and the people conquered of an anterior epoch," for "The race of the invaders, when it ceased to be a separate nation, remained a privileged class" (*HC,* 1.xix).

Thierry's claim that the consequences of medieval conquest are found in modern class warfare undermines the ideology of national unity that we have seen dominate Anglo-Saxon historiography. Prescott, for example, who studied Thierry in preparation for writing his own histories,[30] conceives of historical progress as mandating the conquest, conversion, and eradication of minority races in the name of national unity. But for Thierry, even when the distinctions of race have apparently disappeared, they reappear in the distinctions of class, so that national unity becomes a fiction that flies in the face of the reality of "the two nations." In short, Thierry refuses the myth of national unity that is meant to hide a new form of oppression, economic and social. Thus, we can understand Disraeli's attraction to Thierry's work, which made it possible to keep alive the idea of racial oppression and to see it as the historical basis of the most contemporary political problems, even if the specific racial problem of the Jew did not play an important role in his histories.[31]

The final and perhaps most provocative way that the racial terminology of Norman and Saxon encodes "the Jewish question" in *Sybil* occurs through Disraeli's depiction of conversion as the central strategy in English class warfare. I refer to Disraeli's representation of a bogus aristocracy created by the manufacture and sale of Norman titles, a process termed conversion: "the Nabob one morning was transformed into an Irish baron," and two years before his death "the Irish baron was quietly converted into an English peer" (*S,* 78–79); "It was a great hit, in the second generation of an earldom, to convert the coronet into that of a marquis" (*S,* 208). This language functions as a subtle reflection on the nature of the converted Jew in English society. If Disraeli's conversion is in any way suspect, only an opportunist's means to success, the entire aristocracy of England is suspected of having converted its identity and thereby manufactured its privileges. In the same way, the idea of these "converted" aristocrats reflects on the problem of the crypto-Jews, so many of whom converted to save their lives, whereas the English system of aristocratic conversion is exposed as mere opportunism, based entirely on gain and greed. Disraeli represents such conversions as the work of a kind of high priest of genealogies, Baptist Hatton, who turns a profit on a new kind of conversion: "He is an heraldic antiquary; a discoverer, inventor, framer, arranger of pedigrees; profound in the mysteries of genealogies" (*S,* 237). He is the Baptist who gives new life (through old names) in the form not of spiritual conversions but of Norman pedigrees. He explains his work in this way: "besides the hush-money, my client is to defray all the expense of attempting to transform the descendant of the silkweaver of Lyons into the heir of a Norman conqueror" (*S,* 242). Through Hatton, Disraeli draws the curtain from "the grand mystification of high nobility" (*S,* 266) in England, a class that might properly be called, after the designation New Christians, "New Normans."

In *Tancred, or the New Crusade,* Disraeli boldly concludes his trilogy on the condition-of-England question by leaving England behind altogether—as if, in the discovery that the "Holy Church . . . had forgotten her sacred mission" (*S,* 54) and that the aristocracy of England was essentially bogus, a different kind of cultural pedigree must be sought. Moreover, *Tancred* is written in reaction against the rhetorical strategy of *Sybil,* where "Sion, Bethel, Bethesda" are no more than foreign names that speak of an ancient race, for *Tancred* sends its hero in search of these places and the living faith of Judaism; the merely figurative place-names become part of the plotted journey of the hero who travels to the Near East. A paean to Hebraic culture, *Tancred* seems a reaction to what I have called the repression and sublimation of the question of race, and particularly "the Jewish question," in the earlier novels of the trilogy, especially *Sybil*.

For the third time in his trilogy Disraeli puts at the center of his novel an English aristocrat who seeks a solution to "the want of faith" in England: "In nothing, whether it be religion, or government, or manners, sacred or political or social life, do I find faith" (*T,* 49). But *Tancred* denies its hero the solution of a parliamentary career, as in the earlier cases of Coningsby and Egremont. Before accepting a seat in Parliament, Tancred makes a journey to the Holy Land. But this journey, far from preparing the hero for a parliamentary career, seems to preclude it, and even to alienate him permanently from England, for after long journeying Tancred declares at the novel's end: "I shall not go back to England" (*T,* 398). In *Tancred* the English nobleman discovers true nobility not in any Norman pedigree, but in Hebraic culture, in a heritage that is older and more genuine than the Norman title that gives him his position of privilege in England.

Tancred's self-expatriation from England can be read as a continuation of Scott's critique of England. While in *Ivanhoe* the Jew must leave England behind because it is a land of persecution, inhospitable to the Jews, in *Tancred* the Christian must leave England behind to travel to the East to discover the Hebraic roots of his English Protestantism. Moreover, the attraction between the English hero and the Jewish heroine threatens to end in an interracial love plot. Interestingly, Disraeli transfers Rebecca's profound sense of guilt over such a love in *Ivanhoe*—"But I will tear this folly from my heart, though every fibre bleed as I rend it away!"[32]—to Tancred: "But I must tear up these thoughts from my heart by their roots" (*T,* 400). In Disraeli's novel it is the English hero, not the Jewish maiden, who suffers the pain of loving outside one's race and religion. Nonetheless, Disraeli's Jewish heroine, who functions as a kind of spokesperson for her people, "asserting the splendour and superiority of their race, and sighing for the restoration of their national glory" (*T,* 385), is frequently cast in the role of Scott's Rebecca. Like Scott's Jewish heroine, Eva cures the Englishman of a fatal illness, after which Disraeli's English crusader proposes marriage, so that the repressed or merely figurative interracial love plot, not only of *Ivanhoe* or *Harrington,* but of the trilogy's two earlier novels, moves one step closer to realization. The love of the English hero for the Jewish heroine is allowed by Disraeli in *Tancred.*

As the novel's subtitle makes clear, Tancred's journey to the Holy Land functions as a conscious return to *Ivanhoe* and to a critical moment in early English history. But in *Tancred, or the New Crusade* this return serves the purpose neither of concentrating the novel in the rhetoric of Norman and Saxon England nor of establishing the identity of England as a Christian nation, perhaps because so much of this novel is set outside England, thereby invoking a much larger vocabulary of culture and race than *Coningsby* and *Sybil.* Tancred defines his journey as if it were no more than a repetition of an earlier historical event: "I should wish to do that which, six centuries ago, was done by my ancestor whose name I bear" (*T,* 123). But Tancred's "new" crusade not only does not involve the massacre of Jews as part of its triumph over the infidel, but accomplishes the opposite: his journey discovers the present and eternal validity and power of Judaism. His journey to the Holy Sepulcher ends with a vision on Mount Sinai. This is in part a function of Disraeli's attempt to collapse Judaism and Christianity, erasing the traditional boundary between the two religions, making the converted Jew in many ways the best standard bearer of the roots of Christianity, the proud herald of the return to the origins of Christianity. So it is no accident that it is a Christian of Jewish ancestry, a descendant of the New Christians of fourteenth-century Spain, who suggests the itinerary that Tancred finally follows: "Sinai led to Calvary; it may be wise to trace your footsteps from Calvary to Sinai" (*T,* 225). The return to racial and national origins, so popular in the nineteenth century, now becomes extended by Disraeli to include a return to religious origins, which means the Christian's return to Judaism.

Disraeli's strategy in the trilogy's earlier novels was to suggest the essential continuity between Hebraic and English traditions, but in *Tancred* this plan begins to unravel. The expected nod in the direction of English achievement occurs, again rehearsed by Sidonia: "England flourishes. . . . it is an affair of race. A Saxon race, protected by an insular position, has stamped its diligent and methodic character on the century" (*T,* 148). But this is only a moment in a novel that systematically represents Europe and Christianity as seriously incapacitated and handicapped. Part of the revisionary impetus behind the idea of Tancred's "new" crusade stems from

Disraeli's charge that Europe has neglected the Christian principle. In recalling the earlier Tancred's journey to the Holy Sepulchre, the narrator claims that "Christendom cares nothing for that tomb now, has indeed forgotten its own name, and calls itself enlightened Europe. But enlightened Europe is not happy" (*T,* 224). Such an argument functions, at least in part, as a traditionally English charge against the French Enlightenment, and more specifically against the French Revolution: "Half a century ago, Europe made a violent and apparently successful effort to disembarrass itself of its Asian faith" (*T,* 170). Such a reference to the French Revolution is surely meant to exclude England from Disraeli's critique, but to speak in favor of Christianity by calling it an "Asian faith" is to use a discourse that most of his fellow citizens hardly recognized as English.

In *Tancred,* then, the revelation of the continuity between Hebraic and English traditions often takes the form of minimizing certain boundaries that the English use to define their own national character: the boundary between European and Asian, or between Christian and Jew. Disraeli seeks to reestablish at least the historic validity of Judaism, if only as a critical and integral epoch leading to Christianity, an epoch that no longer can simply be evaded, erased. He attempts "to do justice to the race which had founded Christianity,"[33] and on a more personal note, he confesses: "I look upon the Church as the only Jewish institution that remains, and . . . must ever cling to it as the visible means which embalms the memory of my race."[34] Publicly, as a member of Parliament, he took the same position, despite the unwelcome reception such ideas were destined to receive. In his speech to the House of Commons in 1847, the year *Tancred* was published, he spoke in support of removing Jewish disabilities by reminding his audience that " 'All the early Christians were Jews,' " and he was met with "cries of 'Oh! oh!' at intervals, and many other signs of general impatience": " 'Yes, it is as a Christian that I will not take upon me the awful responsibility of excluding from the legislation those who are of the religion in the bosom of which my Lord and Saviour was born.' "[35]

As an attempt at reinscribing into (Christian) history the immense contributions of Judaism, *Tancred* attacks the practical means of erasing Jewish identity through conversion. There are, for example, a series of gibes aimed at the business of conversion—at the pious English family that takes its relaxation in "a meeting for the conversion of the Jews" (*T,* 13); at the bogus successes that conversionist societies typically produced—"five Jews, . . . converted at twenty piastres a-week" (*T,* 181); at the "journals [which] teemed with lists of proselytes and cases of conversion" (*T,* 69); at those believers in "the millenium, [who] were persuaded that the conversion of the Roman Catholic population of Ireland to the true faith, which was their own, was at hand" (*T,* 69)—the same millenarian expectation that predicted the conversion of the Jews and that was articulated so popularly in Charlotte Elizabeth's *Judah's Lion,* to which Disraeli's *Tancred* is certainly a response. For, if in *Judah's Lion* an English Jew sets out to the East, only to discover the value of Christianity, in *Tancred* an English Christian sets out to the East, only to discover the value of Judaism. *Tancred,* published four years after *Judah's Lion,* radically reverses Charlotte Elizabeth's conventional plot of conversion in which the Jew becomes a Christian. In Disraeli's novel the journey to the Holy Land functions essentially to Judaize the English Protestant hero, a plot George Eliot later borrowed for *Daniel Deronda.*

The most protracted critique of conversionism in *Tancred* occurs when the hero meets in Syria a Hebrew family whose daughters have recently spent the year in Marseilles. The Mesdemoiselles Laurealls "were ashamed of their race, and not fanatically devoted to their religion, which might be true, but certainly was not fashionable." One of these daughters felt "that all they [the Jews] had to do was to imitate as closely as possible the habits and customs of the nation among whom they chanced to live; and she really did believe that eventually, such was the progressive spirit of the age, a difference in religion would cease to be regarded, and that a respectable Hebrew, particularly if well dressed and well mannered, might be able to pass through society without being discovered, or at least noticed" (*T,* 383). Here is the idea of "the secret race" scaled down to meet the exigencies of "the progressive spirit of the age," a portrait of Jews attempting to pass for Christians that will occur time and again in Trollope's novels.

As an antidote to those Jews who seek to pass as Christians, Tancred is characterized as an Englishman who seems to rewrite his ancestry as if he were a Jew, or desired to be a Jew. What begins as an attempt to put Judaism back into Christianity—as "the faith of Moses and of Christ" (*T,* 122)—soon becomes Tancred's bold assertion: "Christianity is Judaism for the multitude, but still it is Judaism" (*T,* 427). And soon we have the

Englishman who so profoundly acknowledges his debt to ancient Hebrew culture that he is ashamed of his more recent ancestors: "Alas! I am . . . sprung from a horde of Baltic pirates, who never were heard of during the greater annals of the world, a descent which I have been educated to believe was the greatest of honours. What we should have become, had not the Syro-Arabian creeds formed our minds, I dare not contemplate" (*T*, 427). Contemporary England is left behind—"I have appealed to the holy influence in vain in England" (*T*, 123)—for "God has never spoken to a European" (*T*, 261). Worried that "he was deficient in that qualification of race which was necessary for the high communion to which he aspired" (*T*, 263), Tancred must declare with some disappointment: "I am an Arab only in religion" (*T*, 260). This Christian Englishman declares in Arabia: "I come to the land whose laws I obey, whose religion I profess" (*T*, 266). Finally, he prays atop Mount Sinai: "O Lord God of Israel, creator of the Universe, ineffable Jehovah! a child of Christendom, I come to thine ancient Arabian altars to pour forth the heart of tortured Europe" (*T*, 289).

To most of Disraeli's reading public, Tancred must have looked suspiciously like Disraeli himself, renouncing—in the safe world of fiction—his more recent heritage as a Christian Englishman for his Sephardic Jewish ancestry. In sum, depending on how strictly one divides Asian from European, or Jew from Christian, Tancred's new crusade can look like either the discovery of an ancient genealogy or the renunciation and betrayal of European and Christian values. Betrayal is the interpretation that Disraeli's political opponents proposed later in the century in a rather extraordinary circumstance, a prime minister's novels being used as evidence against his governmental policies.

From the beginning, Disraeli's trilogy met with anti-Semitic responses. *Punch* was tireless in its mockery: "It has been remarked by the surpassing author of the brilliant *Coningsby*, that the world, although it dreams not of the glory, is at the present time governed by the Hebrew mind! PUNCH can bear testimony to the fact. Once PUNCH wanted money. Who lent it to him at sixty percent.?—a Jew! Who sued him on the bill?—a Jew! Who arrested him?—a Jew! Who sold him up?—a Jew!" ("Prize Preface," 1844). And after the publication of *Tancred*, *Punch* remarked in a piece entitled "The Jewish Champion": "After reading his last work of *Tancred*, we took quite a fresh view of all the itinerant sons of Abraham we met in the streets of the Great Metropolis. 'Look at that old clothes-man,' said we to ourselves; 'who would think that the unmixed blood of Caucasus runs through the veins of that individual . . . ?' It is evident that Mr. Disraeli has determined in his own mind, that until there is a Mosaic Parliament, sitting in Rag Fair, the object of his great mission will be unaccomplished" (April 10, 1847).

But I wish to explore the way in which the trilogy, published in the 1840s, was used to attack his ministry in the mid-1870s during the Eastern crisis. "The Eastern question," quiet for a number of years after the Crimean War, erupted again in English politics in the summer of 1875, when rebellion against Turkish rule spread in the Balkans. Historically, England had backed Turkish rule in an attempt to prevent the spread of Russia's influence southward, and, more particularly, the interference of Russia in India. Turkish rule, known for its corruption and even cruelty, became more difficult to uphold in 1876, when England rang with the cry of Turkish atrocities committed against the Bulgarians—reports in the *Daily News* spoke of slaughter, torture, sodomy, and rape. English popular sentiment began to swing away from Turkey and toward Russia, especially when the problem of Turkey-in-Europe began to be viewed as the victimization of Christian subjects by an "Oriental" people.[36]

This situation eventually triggered an outbreak of English anti-Semitism. The Anglo-Jewish community was pro-Turkish for several reasons, but most importantly because Turkish rule of the East had by tradition been comparatively tolerant to Jews; the Jewish community in England was unable to ignore, for example, the persecution of Jews by Orthodox Christianity in Russia, Romania, and Serbia. The importance of the re-emergence of the Eastern question for the international Jewish community is reflected in an 1876 conference in Paris, to which more than forty Jewish organizations from Europe and America sent representatives to discuss improving the condition of Eastern Jews. In England, Jewish support of the Turkish policy led to an outbreak of anti-Semitism (figure 11) that was exacerbated by, and especially aimed at, what the *Church Times* called the "Jew Premier," with his pro-Turkish sympathies (figure 12).[37]

To understand the strategies of the anti-Semitic attack against Disraeli and the role his novels played in such an attack, I wish to look first at T. P. O'Connor's *Lord Beaconsfield* (1877).[38] While O'Connor calls his book "A Biography," he readily admits: "This book was written in the midst

PROFESSIONAL VIEW OF THE SITUATION.

"Awful dem Rooshian Atrohshities—Shtrippin' de poor Creeturs naked Von ting—Ole Clo's 'll be sheap!"

Figure 11. Two Jewish old-clothes men callously calculate what they stand to gain by the Bulgarian atrocities. *Punch,* August 4, 1877.

NEUTRALITY UNDER DIFFICULTIES.

Dizzy. "BULGARIAN ATROCITIES! I CAN'T FIND THEM IN THE 'OFFICIAL REPORTS'!!!"

Figure 12. Disraeli's policy of neutrality is represented as coldhearted indifference to the sufferings of the Bulgarians at the hands of the Turks. *Punch*, August 5, 1876.

of a great and exciting political struggle" (*LB*, xxii)—that is, under the urgency of the Eastern crisis. In the Introduction, written some years after the first edition, O'Connor formulates the un-English identity of Disraeli by comparing him to Lord Derby, who possessed "a character essentially English" (*LB*, xvii): "The somewhat commonplace English-man, with notions of duty to his country, a horror of bloodshed, the fears of an avenging conscience, had no chance in times of perilous and fateful resolves against the brilliant, callous, self-adoring Oriental" (*LB*, xviii). "[T]he descendant of a long line of wealthy peers" is contrasted to "the son of a Hebrew *litterateur*" (*LB*, xvii). So, a physiological contrast is in order: "the robust and massive frame of the Englishman" is pitted against "the thin, light, though lithe, frame of the Oriental" (*LB*, xviii).

I am interested in tracing not the general outline of the anti-Semitic attack against Disraeli, but a particular trope used to characterize him: Disraeli as an actor. In his Introduction, O'Connor calls Disraeli "an actor that never took off his wig or rouge or robes" (*LB*, xxi), an "Eastern showman" (*LB*, xvii). In the body of the biography, Disraeli is called a "charlatan" (*LB*, 314), a "mountebank" (*LB*, 314), and an "impostor" (*LB*, 675): "the great ideal he bodies forth in all his earlier and sincerer utterances, was that of triumphant imposture" (*LB*, 612). O'Connor por-trays Disraeli as a highly skilled actor deceiving the English public: "He had only his part to play of a clever foreigner trifling with the interests and playing upon the passions of the people to whose race he was proud not to belong, and in whose creed he scorned to believe" (*LB*, 591). This figure of Disraeli the actor is fueled by the anti-Semitic stereotype of the crypto-Jew who hid behind the mask of Christianity to subvert the culture of Christian Spain and Portugal.

The figure of Disraeli as an actor dogged him throughout his political career. *Punch* was fond of portraying him as a kind of trickster or illusion-ist; he appeared as "the Political Chameleon"; a "will-o'-the-wisp"; a professional puppeteer who worked the dummy Lord Derby; an acrobat thrilling (and fooling) the crowd; a professional magician; a performer of "The Great 'Trick Act' " at the circus (figure 13). He was shown "Dress-ing for a Masquerade," and "Dressing for an Oxford Bal Masque," and as the actor "Bendizzy," the star of *Hamlet*, mesmerized by his own image in the mirror.[39] Similar characterizations seem especially gratuitous in George Henry Lewes's 1849 review of the fifth edition of *Coningsby*. The

PUNCH, OR THE LONDON CHARIVARI.—JULY 4, 1874.

THE GREAT "TRICK ACT."

RING-MASTER (MR. CROSS). " NOW, THEN, MR. WITTLER, STAND OUT O' THE WAY ! "
CLOWN (LITTLE WITTLER). " OH AH, OF CORSE ! OF CORSE I GAVE 'ER A LEG-UP, AND CHALK'D 'ER SHOES OF CORSE, AND OF CORSE I'M TO GET NOTHING FOR IT ! THAT'S WHAT I CALL WITTLER'S ALLOWANCE ! "
[*Exit, disgusted.*

Figure 13. Disraeli's government (with Richard Cross as Home Secretary) was seen as betraying its supporters by legislatively neglecting their interests in 1874. *Punch,* July 4, 1874.

opening judgment on *Coningsby*, with its "oriental gorgeousness," con-
signs it "no place in our literature." Disraeli is once again characterized as
a "charlatan," "an acrobat in literature," a "showman." "His writings
abound with similar instances of tawdry falsehood. They are thrown in
probably out of that love of ornament, which is characteristic of his race;
they are the mosaic chains and rings with which the young 'gentlemen of
the Hebrew persuasion' adorn their persons, to give a *faux air de gen-
tilhomme* to that which no adornment can disguise."[40] Typically, then,
Disraeli is shown as an actor, showman, or magician who is caught in the
act, a variation on the theme of the secret Jew whose mask is finally
penetrated by the Inquisition. Sir John Skelton, a Scottish man of letters,
met Disraeli in 1867 and wrote: "The face is more like a mask than ever,"
and "They say, and say truly enough, What an actor the man is!"[41]

Such accounts usually turn on the ability to provoke suspicion about
Disraeli's religious sincerity and often use the story of his conversion as
the hidden center of their attack. O'Connor accounts for Disraeli's childhood conversion on the basis of mere whim, incorrectly attributing it not
to Sharon Turner but to a man whose reputation is suspect: "Fancy the
champion-in-chief of our Established Church owing his Christianity to
the whim of a man unconnected with him in blood—and the whim of
such a man!" (*LB*, 7). Skelton appears to refuse the entire idea of Disraeli's Christianity on physiological terms: "And the potent wizard himself, with his olive complexion and coal-black eyes, and the mighty dome
of his forehead (no Christian temple, be sure), is unlike any living creature one has met."[42] And Lewes hints at the bogusness of Disraeli's conversion by referring to a figurative conversion, Disraeli's dramatic change
of political affiliation early in his career, which has often been seen as the
chief sign of his falsehood—his "sudden conversion from radicalism to
toryism." But Lewes adds an unusual twist to this idea; he claims that
Disraeli was never a radical in the first place, but only "allowed the false
appearance,"[43] just as he allows other false appearances. In short, Disraeli's "conversion" is fake; he is no different, after his (political) conversion, from the way he was before it, a suggestive reflection on Disraeli as
a converted Jew. In all of these accounts the process of conversion seems
no more than the Jew's attempt to mask himself in order to infiltrate English culture.

But it was Disraeli's Eastern policy that was seen as ultimately unmasking him. Skelton's idea, in 1867, that "England is the Israel of his imagination,"[44] had a special power for Disraeli's critics during the Eastern crisis. O'Connor's entire project revolved around discovering "the secret" (*LB*, xxi) behind Disraeli's Eastern policy, and both O'Connor and *Punch* pictured the secretive prime minister with "a face set in sphinx-like impassiveness" (*LB*, xxi) (figure 14). The secret O'Connor discovers is that Disraeli's Eastern policy represents "the triumph, not of England, not of an English policy, not of an Englishman," but "the triumph of Judaea, a Jewish policy, a Jew" (*LB*, 672). For "as a Jew he is a kinsman of the Turk, and . . . , as a Jew, he feels bound to make common cause with the Turk against the Christian" (*LB*, 610). O'Connor bemoans the way in which his fellow citizens have fallen "under the spell of our Oriental dictator" (*LB*, 663); "the Hebrew Premier had indeed reduced the Gentiles to an abyssmal depth of degradation" (*LB*, 660). O'Connor imagines that a vengeful vendetta for the wrongs committed against Jews spurs on Disraeli's fantasy of Jewish power. "Would not the shame of Israel be blotted out . . . if in . . . this nineteenth century of Jewish persecution, Jewish degradation, Jewish humiliation by Christians, a single Jew could mould the whole policy of Christendom to Jewish aims,—could make it friendly to the friends and hostile to the foes of Judaea!" (*LB*, 611–12). And if Disraeli's Eastern policy finally unmasked him as the foreigner he was—even his friend Derby, after thirty years of cooperation with Disraeli, declared during the Eastern crisis that Disraeli's mind was that of a foreigner[45]—it was his novels (especially *Coningsby* and *Tancred*), quoted profusely by O'Connor, that finally sealed this interpretation: "Those passages alone, I think, would suffice to show the truth of my argument, that the Eastern policy of Lord Beaconsfield was Hebrew—or, to use what he himself considers the proper name for the two peoples, different in creeds but alike in race—was an Arab policy. People who will persist in thinking that it was an English policy can only be those who have not read Lord Beaconsfield's works, or who, having read, have not intelligence to interpret them" (*LB*, 611). Disraeli's critics could even point to what looked like *Tancred*'s extraordinary prediction, in 1847, of its author's own political success in the 1870s, that moment in which Tancred is amazed to discover who heads the Egyptian government—"A Hebrew for prime minister!" (*T*, 396).

Like O'Connor, Edward Augustus Freeman published a book, *The*

THE SPHINX IS SILENT.

Figure 14. Frequently picturing Disraeli as the Sphinx, *Punch* fueled the growing perception that as a Jew Disraeli was an unreadable (Oriental) enigma to the common English citizen. *Punch,* July 15, 1876.

Ottoman Power in Europe (1877), which argued: "We cannot have England or Europe governed by a Hebrew policy."[46] With his credentials as the celebrated historian of the Norman Conquest and defender of Anglo-Saxon values, Freeman saw it as his duty to protect England from Disraeli's policy. His Preface, like O'Connor's Introduction, sought to differentiate between Lord Derby and Lord Beaconsfield once again on the grounds of race. While no advocate for Derby, Freeman nonetheless entirely disqualifies Disraeli from leading England during the crisis: "While Lord Derby simply wishes to do nothing one way or another, Lord Beaconsfield is the active friend of the Turk. The alliance runs through all Europe. Throughout the East, the Turk and the Jew are leagued against the Christian" (*OP,* xix). And again: "It may be assumed everywhere, with the smallest class of exceptions, that the Jew is the friend of the Turk and the enemy of the Christian" (*OP,* xx). Referring to a phrase that Disraeli had used in *Tancred* and that had become something of a popular catchword for Disraeli's eccentric Hebrew sympathies, Freeman insists that "we cannot sacrifice our people, the people of Aryan and Christian Europe, to the most genuine belief in an Asian mystery" (*OP,* xix), while *Punch,* two decades earlier, had run a cartoon picturing a dark-skinned Disraeli concocting a strange brew for Parliament under the caption "The Asiatic Mystery" (figure 15).

The remainder of *The Ottoman Power in Europe* does not focus on Disraeli; Freeman's scurrilous anti-Semitic remarks about Disraeli were reserved for elsewhere.[47] Freeman's book does, however, go on to demonstrate, from a racialist point of view, the impossibility of supporting the alien Turk's intrusion on Aryan and Christian Europe. Freeman remarks on the unity of "the nations of civilized Europe," on "how they stand together as members of one body, bound together by many ties, how they are kinsfolk whose points of unlikeness are after all trifling compared with their points of likeness" (*OP,* 3–4)—this, suddenly, from the master singer of Teutonic superiority! And after distinguishing "European man from Asiatic or African man" (*OP,* 2) on the basis of race—"all the nations of Europe belong to the one common Aryan stock" (*OP,* 4)—Freeman, yielding the ground Disraeli had won in the trilogy and elsewhere about the Judaic origins of Christianity, nonetheless asserts: "In its origin Semitic and Asiatic, Christianity became in its history preeminently European and Aryan" (*OP,* 7). It is in such terms that the "Hebrew policy" of

PUNCH, OR THE LONDON CHARIVARI.—August 8, 1857.

THE ASIATIC MYSTERY.

As Prepared by Sepoy D'Israeli.

Figure 15. In disagreement with the policy of westernizing India (including the missionary project of conversion), Disraeli spoke in support of Indian culture after the mutiny among Indian troops in 1857. *Punch,* August 8, 1857.

the prime minister must be seen as anti-European, anti-Aryan, and anti-Christian.

The Eastern crisis of 1876 not only crystallized the anti-Semitism that had shadowed Disraeli's career from the beginning; it threatened his attempt, in his writings, to reveal Hebrew culture as the basis of English life, and in his public career, to prove that a person of Jewish ancestry could successfully govern England. So, while Skelton in 1867 posed the problem of Disraeli's Jewishness—"What's England to him, or he to England?"[48]—such a question seemed asked by all of Disraeli's political opponents in 1876 and became the basis of numerous public attacks. It was a question that reduced Disraeli to a foreigner, an alien, a Jew in England, rather than one of those English Jews of whom his father had written, and of whom Disraeli had hoped to be an illustrious example.

Furthermore, the Eastern crisis created the political climate in which Disraeli's opponents could finally make the charge of crypto-Judaism. When Disraeli's old political opponent Gladstone came out of semiretirement to crusade against the "savage" Turks, he characterized Disraeli as "not quite such a Turk as I had thought. What he hates is Christian liberty and reconstruction."[49] Having entered the fray, Gladstone went off to read *Tancred* to bolster his charges against Disraeli.[50] Gladstone and the duke of Argyll, like Freeman and O'Connor, agreed that Disraeli's policy was Jewish rather than English, although Disraeli's modern biographers have agreed that his pro-Turkish, anti-Russian position had been the traditional English policy on the Eastern question for many years.[51] The duke of Argyll believed that "Disraeli . . . may be willing to risk his government for his Judaic feeling." Gladstone told the duke, "I have a strong suspicion . . . that Dizzy's crypto-judaism has had to do with his policy."[52] In short, the Eastern crisis proved, according to his detractors, that Disraeli was an example of the way in which "the secret Jew" could infiltrate the culture of Victorian England. Jewish conversion was only a mask. As English culture began to use the terms of Inquisitorial Spain to read both Isaac D'Israeli and Benjamin Disraeli as crypto-Jews, certain continuities between fifteenth-century Spain and nineteenth-century England emerged. When, for example, Richard Burton remarked about Disraeli's conversion, "even the waters of baptism cannot wash away blood," and about the English in general, "there is scarcely a titled house in England that is not leavened with Jewish blood,"[53] he replicated the kind of paranoia that characterized Inquisitorial Spain, where every converted Jew was suspected of lapsing, where Christian affiliation finally was not allowed to supersede Jewish filiation, and where the famous pamphlet *Tizón de la nobleza española* claimed that all the great families of Spain had intermarried with Jews.

Arnold's Hebraism and the "Science of Origins"

Disraeli's location of English Protestant culture within the context of the cultural history of the Jews should not be seen as a personal eccentricity, outside the mainstream of nineteenth-century English discourse. First, Disraeli's trilogy was a direct response to a kind of discourse about race and culture already in place by the early 1840s; and second, the trilogy was to have a profound influence on one of the most famous representations of English culture later in the century, Matthew Arnold's celebrated formulation of the Hebraic foundation of English national life.

The rhetoric of Saxon, Norman, and Jew in Disraeli's trilogy is best understood as a reaction against a kind of revolution in English racial and cultural discourse that was occurring in the early Victorian period. Under the influence of the developing ideologies of nationalism, imperialism, and colonialism, the discourse about the Anglo-Saxons underwent two critical changes between the late eighteenth century and the early 1840s. First, as scholars have noted, this discourse more and more became based not simply on cultural institutions, but on race.[54] Second, it is my claim that this discourse became diffused in a much broader kind of terminology, focusing no longer simply on the composition of the British people (that is, on the relative merits of Britons, Picts, Celts, Normans, Saxons, etc.), but on the position of the Anglo-Saxons in such larger racial "families" as the Caucasian and the Aryan. By the time Disraeli came to write his trilogy, the flowering of Anglo-Saxon historiography, the development of comparative philology, but most of all, the birth of the new discipline of ethnology—what Arnold called the "science of origins"[55]— had already begun to crystallize the idea of the superiority of the Anglo-Saxon race and its place in the Caucasian or Aryan racial family.

In an influential work, *The Races of Men* (1850), Robert Knox referred directly to Disraeli's novels, arguing "that the real Jew has no ear for music as a race, no love of science or literature; that he invents nothing, pursues no inquiry; that the theory of 'Coningsby' is not merely a fable as applied to the real and undoubted Jew, but is absolutely refuted by all history." Knox's work was not unlike many of the other racialist works that passed for science in the mid-nineteenth century. Knox found it easy to use the name of science to invalidate the mere novels that Disraeli produced: "A respect for scientific truth forbids me refuting the romances of Disraeli; it is sufficient merely to observe that, in the long list of names of distinguished persons whom Mr. Disraeli has described as of Jewish descent, I have not met with a single Jewish trait in their countenance, in so far as I can discover; *and, therefore, they are not Jews,* nor of Jewish origin."[56] So much for the penetrating empiricism of the "science" of origins, a science that writers such as Arnold were too willing to believe without question.

Criticizing Disraeli as the great popularizer of the word "Caucasian," the ethnologist offers no scientific argument, only anti-Semitic stereotypes. Using the "cast-off" speculations of Blumenbach's racial categories, Disraeli, "true to *his race,* . . . picks up the worn-out, threadbare rag, and *declares* it to be a sound and excellent garment—'as good as new.' " Here, "the bold and chivalrous author of 'Tancred' and 'Coningsby' "[57] is revealed as no more than an old-clothes man, the same anti-Semitic stereotype that Thackeray used in *Codlingsby* to mock Disraeli's Sidonia and that the crowds used to mock Disraeli during his early election campaigns.[58] The detection of Jewish identity in nineteenth-century England seems always to require the same unveiling: in the socially mobile world of the time, the Jew's racial origins, masked behind the powers and achievements he has won, can be exposed by revealing him to be no more than a dealer in rags—and for Knox, "Caucasian" is no more than an invention, in Disraeli's hands, used to whitewash that reality.

What we call the prejudice of stereotyping, Knox called the science of ethnology: the Jew is always reducible to a certain set of marked characteristics (figure 16). It is no accident that Knox at the same time refuses to believe in the power of conversion, for the unconvertibility of the Jew is a boon to the racial doctrine that attempts to fix—permanently—each person in his or her racial category. Hence Knox's apparently gratuitous reflections on the conversion of the Jews: "Societies are got up for their conversion! Be it so. Nothing can be said against them; but in one hundred years they will not convert one hundred Jews—not even one real Jew. . . . Nature alters not."[59] Knox calls into question the work of the

[*The Jew.*]

Figure 16. From Robert Knox, M.D., *The Races of Men: A Philosophical Enquiry into the Influence of Race over the Destinies of Nations,* 2nd ed. (London: Henry Renshaw, 1862), p. 193.

conversionist societies, not because of the questionable ethics of their procedures, but because of the Jew's unchangeable racial nature. In so doing, Knox comes dangerously close to the ideology of fifteenth-century Spain, where religious affiliation became a matter of biological filiation, a matter of race. In establishing the power of race, the new science of ethnology enters the debate over the conversion of the Jews by placing the barrier of "Nature" in the way.

It was such an idea that Arnold encountered when, in a series of works written during the 1860s and 1870s, he followed Disraeli in defining the basis of English culture as Hebraic. While it has been a critical commonplace to claim that Arnold borrowed the ideas of "Hellenism" and "Hebraism" from Heine, I wish to argue that Arnold's use of these terms more urgently reflects his response to Disraeli's view of the Hebraic foundation of English culture.[60] But first I would claim that Arnold's cultural criticism is descended not only from Disraeli, but from Scott. At a pivotal point in *On the Study of Celtic Literature* (1866) Arnold attempts to dislodge the English from a conception of themselves as a unicultural and uniracial nation. Like Scott, who insisted on the mutuality of the Norman and Saxon contributions to the English nation, and like Disraeli, who insisted on the Hebraic contribution to English life, Arnold sets out to prove the value of the Celtic genius and its place in "English" culture. He rejects the myth of national unity, of England's cultural and racial "purity," but unlike Scott and Disraeli, he is able to do so from the inside, as an Englishman whose heritage is unquestioned: "But true Anglo-Saxons, simply and sincerely rooted in the German nature, we are not and cannot be" (*CP*, 3.383), Arnold argued, despite his father's claim in 1841, "Our English race is the German race."[61] Like Scott and Disraeli, Arnold refuses the equation between England and Anglo-Saxon Teutonism, an idea that had continued to grow in the decades that led up to the period of his cultural criticism.

Arnold uses a concept very much like Scott's idea of conversion as racial annihilation to frame the ongoing Victorian debate over the value of Celtic culture. With sharp mockery, he poses the rhetorical question: "Might not these divine English gifts, and the English language in which they are preached, have a better chance of making their way among the poor Celtic heathen, if the English apostle delivered his message a little more agreeably?" (*CP*, 3.392)—a suggestion that had been traditionally made, from the time of the Reformation, about the Christian proselytization of the Jews. Arnold uses this figure of conversion to expose England's goal as the utter erasure of Celtic culture. In this text on the survival of the Welsh language and culture, he criticizes the characteristic English claim that the successful colonization of the world by the language and culture of England was proof of Anglo-Saxon superiority. This was the view that his father propounded when he characterized England as "this great English nation, whose race and language are now overrunning the earth from one end of it to the other"—the same view that, later in the century, Freeman, like so many other Victorian intellectuals, continued to propound.[62] But according to Arnold, the English are in danger of committing the crime of racial extermination—no crime, of course, within the perspective of the hegemonic ideology of conquest and conversion: "we [Saxons] have plenty of strength for swallowing up and absorbing as much as we choose; there is nothing to hinder us from effacing the last poor material remains of that Celtic power which once was everywhere, but has long since, in the race of civilisation, fallen out of sight. We may threaten them with extinction if we will" (*CP,* 3.298). The conversion of the Celts into the English, the extermination of the inferior race in the ever-forward-moving "race of civilisation," is part of that ideology which Scott, and after him Thierry, anatomized.

Like Scott and Thierry, Arnold philosophically accepts the inevitability of the assimilation of races as part of modern civilization: "The fusion of all the inhabitants of these islands into one homogeneous, English-speaking whole, the breaking down of barriers between us, the swallowing up of separate provincial nationalities, is a consummation to which the natural course of things irresistibly tends" (*CP,* 3.296–97). Almost no nineteenth-century writer withstands this idea of the exigencies of "modern civilisation" (*CP,* 3.297), but like Scott and Thierry, Arnold argues for the preservation of cultural diversity. Such a position, in all three writers, sometimes seems like no more than a cultural archaeology in which a politically disenfranchised people is preserved simply through its artifacts in a kind of museum of cultural diversity. Nonetheless, it is important to recognize that even such a view was a minority position increasingly difficult to maintain as the century progressed and as the ideology of cultural and national homogeneity, based on the notion of the superiority of some races, became more and more popular. Arnold's writings, we must remember, have been criticized as "anti-patriotic" from the time of their appearance through the beginning of the twentieth century, with the claim that Arnold was in fact "a stranger," an alien, failing to understand the English character.[63]

Moreover, the concrete political contexts and consequences of such arguments about cultural diversity should not be minimized, for even an argument about the value of medieval Celtic literature could be used in contemporary political debate. In the manner of Thierry's idea of the two nations, Arnold explodes the myth of the one nation: "in England the Englishman proper is in union of spirit with no one except other Englishmen proper like himself. His Welsh and Irish fellow-citizens are hardly more amalgamated with him now than they were when Wales and Ireland were first conquered, and the true unity of even these small islands has yet to be achieved" (*CP,* 3.393). Arnold shows that the ideology of conquest and racial absorption does not lead to national unity (as historians like Prescott and Freeman claimed) but to a nation that remains divided on the basis of race. In such a light, *On the Study of Celtic Literature* becomes no mere literary project; behind it stands the entire parliamentary debate on Home Rule for Ireland, since the argument about the racial inferiority of the Celts (which Arnold claims to have learned at his father's knee) was an argument about the way in which the Irish (Celts), unlike the English (Saxons), have no gift for self-government[64]—an argument that the president of the Anthropological Society of London supported by using the racial theories of Robert Knox.[65] Similarly, Disraeli's argument about the Hebraic basis of English culture was an argument for enfranchising the Jews as English citizens. So, such topics as ancient Hebrew culture and medieval Celtic literature had in Victorian England a shared political goal in helping to determine what role to assign the modern representatives of such races in English government and culture.

A critical moment in *On the Study of Celtic Literature* occurs when a specifically racial argument emerges. Both here and in succeeding texts, Arnold highlights the moment in the history of English cultural discourse when ethnology becomes accepted as a science empowered to revise not only the place of the Celts but that of the Hebrews. This crucial moment is given special power by being at once a turning point in English cultural discourse and in Arnold's personal life.

Arnold recollects his youth by recalling the way in which the English were raised with an antipathy to the Celts and an affinity to the Hebrews. He begins with a picture of his father's influence on him in the matter of race: "I remember, when I was young, I was taught to think of Celt as separated by an impassable gulf from Teuton; my father, in particular, was never weary of contrasting them; he insisted much oftener on the separation between us and them than on the separation between us and any other race in the world; in the same way Lord Lyndhurst, in words long famous, called the Irish, 'aliens in speech, in religion, in blood' " (*CP,* 3.299–300). Arnold goes on to use the Jew as a figure to measure varying degrees of foreignness, but in Arnold's example the Jew is conceived as the cultural brother of the Teuton! "Certainly the Jew,—the Jew of ancient times, at least,—then seemed a thousand degrees nearer than the Celt to us," he explains. "Puritanism has so assimilated Bible ideas and phraseology; names like Ebenezer, and notions like that of hewing Agag in pieces, came so natural to us, that the sense of affinity between the Teutonic and the Hebrew nature was quite strong" (*CP,* 3.300). In such a passage we see the beginning of Arnold's more famous and elaborate articulation of the Hebraic foundation of English life a few years later in *Culture and Anarchy* (1869). But we also notice what I might term the negative historicization of the Jews, by means of which they are fictionalized and figuralized as no more than an ancient race, divorced from the living Jews of contemporary England—a process of historical distancing that writers such as Grace Aguilar and George Eliot critiqued.

But Arnold's depiction of the English affinity for the Jew over the Celt suddenly turns into a way of recording a radical revolution in such cultural representations. This revolution is caused by the institutionalization of the science of ethnology from the 1840s to the 1860s in England: "But meanwhile, the pregnant and striking ideas of the ethnologists about the true natural grouping of the human race, the doctrine of a great Indo-European unity, comprising Hindoos, Persians, Greeks, Latins, Celts, Teutons, Slavonians, on the one hand, and, on the other hand, of a Semitic unity and of a Mongolian unity, separated by profound distinguishing marks from the Indo-European unity and from one another, was slowly acquiring consistency and popularising itself" (*CP,* 3.300–301). While ethnology made the Celts "our brothers in the great Indo-European family" (*CP,* 3.302)—an idea that Arnold eagerly embraces, in support of his claims for the Celtic genius—ethnology at the same time, on the basis of race, upset a profound cultural affinity between the English and the Hebrews.

Arnold accepts the argument about race as a profound chasm in the continuity of English and Hebrew cultural traditions. He echoes Knox's remarks about the barrier of Nature: "we are none the better for trying to make ourselves Semitic, when Nature has made us Indo-European" (*CP,* 3.369). He accepts the modern tendency "to establish a sense of native diversity between our European bent and the Semitic bent, and to eliminate, even in our religion, certain elements as purely and excessively Semitic, and therefore, in right, not combinable with our European nature, not assimilable by it" (*CP,* 3.301). Such passages certainly seem to close the door on Disraeli's Hebraic project, and, in what shortly will be articulated as a call for the Hellenic over the Hebraic in *Culture and Anarchy,* Disraeli's project is seen as increasingly suspect. In the following pages I suggest, first, that Arnold's famous formulation of Hellenism and Hebraism in the 1860s and early 1870s is a complicated double movement in relationship to Disraeli—an endorsement and elaboration of Disraeli's formulation of the historical basis of Hebraic England, and a critique and revision of the powerful role of Hebraism in present-day England—and, second, that the new racialism of ethnology becomes an especially powerful tool in this revisionary process.

Because Arnold refused to give up the more broadly based notion of the importance of cultural traditions (as opposed to racial categories), he does not restrict himself in *Culture and Anarchy* to reiterating the racial differences between the Semite and the Indo-European. He characterizes Hebraism in ways that Disraeli would have approved—in ways, in fact, that copy Disraeli's formulations in *Coningsby, Tancred,* and elsewhere. When Arnold sent a copy of *Culture and Anarchy* to Disraeli, perhaps he had in mind not simply influencing a member of Parliament on certain political issues of the day, but also acknowledging this text as a sequel to, and revision of, Disraeli's attempt to Hebraize England. Disraeli certainly would have approved of many of Arnold's remarks, especially those in which Christianity and Hebraism seem interchangeable terms: "Christianity changed nothing in this essential bent of Hebraism to set doing above knowing" (*CP,* 5.165); "the great movement of Christianity was a triumph of Hebraism" (*CP,* 5.172). When Arnold calls Christianity "the later, the more spiritual, the more attractive development of Hebraism," and speaks of Christianity's "deeper effectiveness" and "wider influence" (*CP,* 5.169–70), he sounds like Tancred claiming that "Christianity is Judaism for the multitude, but still it is Judaism"—or even like the elder D'Israeli, who claimed in *Vaurien* that "Christianity is nothing but improved Judaism"; or, in *Genius of Judaism,* that "in Judaism we trace our Christianity, and in Christianity we are reminded of our Judaism."[66]

In such passages in *Culture and Anarchy* Arnold attempts to use Hebraism in the same way that he used the Celtic genius in *On the Study of Celtic Literature.* We have a striking explanation of this goal in a letter he wrote to Louisa de Rothschild, an intimate Jewish friend in whom he often confided about his work. While acknowledging the idea of racial difference, he explains at least one critical function that Hebraic culture holds for his English audience: "It is curious that, though Indo-European, the English people is so constituted and trained that there is a thousand times more chance of bringing it to a more philosophical conception of religion than its present conception of Christianity as something utterly unique, isolated, and self-subsistent, through Judaism and its phenomena, than through Hellenism and its phenomena."[67] As usual, what Arnold regularly called the Philistinism of the English is their failure to recognize the cultural diversity that stands behind their most prized institutions, so that, just as the proper valuation of the Celtic genius can show the English the varied origins of their national culture and history, an understanding of Judaism can expand their narrow view of Christianity as unique, isolated, and self-subsistent.

Only one month later, in a letter written to another woman who exerted an even more powerful influence on Arnold's life, especially insofar as she was the guardian of Thomas Arnold's memory, Arnold writes to his mother about not the Hebraic but the Hellenic origins of Christianity—with the added notion of devaluing the Hebraic contribution to Christianity:

I have been reading this year in connexion with the New Testament a good deal of Aristotle and Plato, and this has brought papa very much to my mind. Bunsen used to say that our great business was to get rid of all that was purely Semitic in Christianity, and to make it Indo-Germanic, and Schleiermacher that in the Christianity of us Western nations there was really much more of Plato and Socrates than of Joshua and David; and, on the whole, papa worked in the direction of these ideas of Bunsen and Schleiermacher, and was perhaps the only powerful Englishman of his day who did so.[68]

So, while in his letter to Lady de Rothschild, Arnold thinks that the English need to comprehend the Judaic origins of their Christianity, in his letter to his mother, his classical reading—especially as a reminder of his dead father—seems to function as a vehicle to reinstate the connection of the English to the Hellenic by means of the racial category of the Indo-Germanic, recalling both the classical learning and the long-prized Teutonism of his father. Suddenly, what seems called for is "to get rid of all that was purely Semitic in Christianity"—as if, while Arnold's theoretical project might be to establish the historical origins of Christianity in Judaism, his practical goal was to purge, for the contemporary Englishman, the Semitic element in Christianity.

In trying to specify the nature and extent of the Jewish influence on *Culture and Anarchy,* we must understand Lady de Rothschild's role both in her direct relationship with Arnold and in her function as the mediator of Arnold's relationship with Disraeli, setting up meetings, carrying messages between them, sending Arnold's work to Disraeli, and so on. It is more than fitting that she is the recipient of the letter in which Arnold (like Disraeli) seems to take as his goal the attempt to demonstrate to the English the Judaic roots of Christianity. For Arnold began to use Lady de Rothschild as a sounding board for such an idea in the time leading up to the writing of *Culture and Anarchy,* just as he used her as a go-between in his relationship with Disraeli. Arnold's biographer even suggests her influence on his book on Celtic literature: "Cultivated, learned, realistic, she had a sense of impermanence and change, of the suffering of her race, of the pathos of the historic past," that contributed to Arnold's sympathy for the downtrodden Celts.[69] Finding the power of Jewish women captivating, Arnold seems to bring alive that long line of fictional English heroes (including Harrington, Ivanhoe, Arthur Stanley, and Tancred) who find their Anglo-Saxon sympathies broadened in the encounter with Jewish women. Arnold wrote to his mother: "What women these Jewesses are! with a *force* which seems triple that of the women of our Western and Northern races."[70] Perhaps Arnold even imagined himself a kind of heroic champion of the Jews—certainly his flirtation with Lady de Rothschild, and their long and intimate relationship, leads one to believe that she was not without her influence in the formulation of the idea of the Hebraic roots of Christianity. Her influence on *Culture and Anarchy* was perhaps most fully acknowledged when Arnold, having completed the book, assigned her the role of messenger: "I hope a copy of my book has to-day gone to you; and I have also sent a copy of it to Mr. Disraeli, as I told you I should. It will be very kind of you if you will tell him that it needs no acknowledgment."[71] Not only is she the recipient of the book—she is the recipient of a message for Disraeli. And as their go-between, she carries a curiously suggestive message from Arnold, the new purveyor of the Hebraic, to Disraeli, the man who decades earlier had been a kind of prophet for the idea of Hebraism: "no acknowledgment" is necessary— on Disraeli's part, or on Arnold's?

Disraeli would have approved of the view of Christianity as an extension of Judaism in *Culture and Anarchy*. And he did, on more than one occasion, find himself in a position to approve of Arnold's work, just as Arnold flattered Disraeli on the score of his literary accomplishments. Arnold told Disraeli of mentioning "to Gladstone some of the epigrammatic things in *Endymion*," Disraeli's last novel—an anecdote that must have delighted Disraeli, especially since the old political rivals had been cast as well in the role of literary rivals. Disraeli in turn responded with a compliment that Arnold was happy to record in a letter to his sister: "He went on to say that he read me with delight, that I was doing very great good, and ended by declaring that I was the only living Englishman who had become a classic in his own lifetime." Arnold realized that "what I have done in establishing a number of current phrases—such as Philistinism, sweetness and light, and all that—is just the sort of thing to strike him."[72] This similarity between the two writers did not go unnoticed by the public when, as early as 1869, a reviewer of *Culture and Anarchy* made a telling comparison between them: "Mr. Arnold's phrases are themselves a possession. He has all Mr. Disraeli's knack *plus* a sincerity which Mr. Disraeli has not, and grafted on a poetic and intellectual temperament of a transcendently higher stamp."[73]

When Arnold and Disraeli shared the podium in 1875 at the Royal Academy, Arnold used his speech to refer directly to Disraeli, who, as prime minister, was one of the honored guests and scheduled speakers. Arnold told a fascinating anecdote about a colony of Greeks settled in

Italy, "who retained for an extraordinary length of time their Greek language and civilization" (*CP,* 8.374)—a figure, in Arnold's speech, for the way in which the artist (as statesman) strives to keep alive the Greek ideal of art, even amid the demands of state. Disraeli was the central example. After all, Arnold continued, "the brilliant statesman at the Head of Her Majesty's Government, to whom we shall listen with so much admiration by-and-by, may even boast that he was born in Arcadia" (*CP,* 8.374). The remark is a subtle attempt to convert by flattery the man whom Arnold had called, only two years earlier, a Hebrew who disparaged the Greek genius (*CP,* 6.164). Now, at the Royal Academy, he suggests that if Disraeli, sitting among the artists present, wished to be a member of the community, he would have to see himself as a Greek, a remarkable realization of Arnold's desire to Hellenize Hebraic England by calling on the Hebrew prime minister to convert. Arnold seems not to recognize that his story of the Greek colony could be read as a figure of Disraeli's fondness not for his figurative past as an artist (or Greek), but for his literal ancestry, for the glory of his Hebrew past. Arnold concludes by calling on everyone present (including Disraeli) "to confess that we were once Greeks" (*CP,* 8.375), a subtle pressure on the man who was for Arnold the leading exponent of Hebraism as opposed to Hellenism.

Arnold's apparently playful attempt to acknowledge Disraeli as an artist while attempting to de-Hebraize him and his value system is, I would argue, the key to the uneasy relationship that existed below the surface of their public encounters. It is of course Arnold's literary relationship to Disraeli that lies at the center of this uneasiness. The literary anxiety Arnold felt in relation to Disraeli is most openly expressed in the essay "Equality" (1878) when Arnold explains his motive in writing: "About four years ago Lord Beaconsfield held it [equality] up to reprobation in a speech to the students at Glasgow;—a speech so interesting, that being asked soon afterwards to hold a discussion at Glasgow, I said that if one spoke there at all at that time it would be impossible to speak on any other subject but equality. . . . I never yet have been able to go and speak there. But the testimonies against equality have been steadily accumulating from the date of Lord Beaconsfield's Glasgow speech" (*CP,* 8.278). Arnold's analysis of his intentions here represents, on a broader level, the literary relationship he shared with Disraeli. First, Arnold characterizes Disraeli as setting the literary agenda—as Disraeli did in the case of Hebraism, placing it at the center of discussions of English national identity. Next, Arnold characterizes his own belated text, "Equality" (or, I would argue, *Culture and Anarchy*), as a corrective, at once borrowing Disraeli's subject and revising the terms of that subject—only in *Culture and Anarchy* Arnold was far less open in his acknowledgment of Disraeli's influence. Even when Arnold came to announce writing a series of religious works immediately after *Culture and Anarchy*, taking up once again the idea of Hebraism, he seems to mock Disraeli as a potential model: "And this we propose to do in three or four attempts, attempts which, perhaps, if they were novels and we were Mr. Disraeli, we should call a trilogy or tetralogy; but which, they and we being what we are, we shall call simply three or four essays" (*CP,* 6.537–38). On the one hand, these words are excised from the fuller book-length version of *Literature and Dogma* because they were no longer true of the form that Arnold's work took. On the other hand, the deleted words remain a clue to the way in which Disraeli's trilogy exists as a kind of erased, or sublimated, or parodied precursor of Arnold's cultural criticism.

In *Culture and Anarchy* Arnold borrows not only Disraeli's formulations of the Hebraic basis of Christianity, but his central idea that the English owe a debt to the Hebrews. In an elaborate reformulation of that debt, Arnold sets out to show its limits:

And, immense as is our debt to the Hebrew race and its genius, incomparable as is its authority on certain profoundly important sides of our human nature, worthy as it is to be described as having uttered, for those sides, the voice of the deepest necessities of our nature, the statutes of the divine and eternal order of things, the law of God—who, that is not manacled and hoodwinked by his Hebraism, can believe that, as to love and marriage, our reason and the necessities of our humanity have their true, sufficient, and divine law expressed for them by the voice of any Oriental and polygamous nation like the Hebrews? (*CP,* 5.208)

In this passage Arnold is demonstrating the political urgency of the otherwise apparently neutral and transhistorical terminology of Hebraism and Hellenism by speaking against a bill that, on the authority of Hebrew Scripture, would allow a man to marry the sister of his deceased wife. By calling the Jews an "Oriental" nation, he falls back on that series of references to race that seals his argument for Hellenism and against Hebraism; he asks if an "Indo-European race, the race which invented the Muses, and chivalry, and the Madonna, is to find its last word on this question in the institutions of a Semitic people, whose wisest king had seven hundred wives and three hundred concubines?" (*CP,* 5.208). In the end, Arnold uses the authority of ethnology to frame his argument that in England the corrective influence of Hellenism (against Hebraism) is needed: "Science has now made visible to everybody the great and pregnant elements of difference which lie in race, and in how signal a manner they make the genius and history of an Indo-European people vary from those of a Semitic people. Hellenism is of Indo-European growth, Hebraism is of Semitic growth; and we English, a nation of Indo-European stock, seem to belong naturally to the movement of Hellenism" (*CP,* 5.173). By using what I earlier called a consolidating pronoun of national identity ("we English"), Arnold reconstructs the English nation as the "natural" home of one "race" (Indo-European) and not another (Semitic). In short, he uses race as the final arbiter in a debate about cultural diversity and national identity. In a profound act of renaming, Arnold now seems to renounce the name that demonstrated "that peculiar Semitico-Saxon mixture which makes the typical Englishman" in favor of a name that excludes the Semitic from the national community consolidated in "we English"— excluding, in some sense, the Jews even from the readership of *Culture and Anarchy.* Finally, while I have been arguing that Arnold performs an act of authorial appropriation on Disraeli's work, here Arnold seems to perform an act of cultural appropriation. He absorbs Hebraic culture in English culture (like the absorption of Judaism in Christianity, or Hebrew Scripture in the Christian Bible), authorizing himself to limit and even to eradicate the elements of difference by which Hebraism undermines his definition of what is English—here, a racially pure definition of the English nation.

In attempting to convert Disraeli the Hebrew to Hellenism, and to absorb Hebrew culture in English culture by performing the same kind of conversion, Arnold returns to what he announced as the controlling metaphor for his work early in his career. In the early 1860s he styled himself as a kind of cosmopolitan apostle to the Philistines, "with the risk always before me, if I cannot charm the wild beast of Philistinism while I am trying to convert him, of being torn in pieces by him; and, even if I succeed to the utmost and convert him, of dying in a ditch or a workhouse at the end of it all."[74] Nor should we forget that he framed *Culture and Anarchy*, in his Preface, with the figure of conversion: "For our part, we rejoice to see our dear old friends, the Hebraising Philistines, gathered in force in the Valley of Jehoshaphat previous to their final conversion, which will certainly come" (*CP,* 5.254). Arnold's contemporary critics were quick to chastise him for his proselytizing tone in *Culture and Anarchy*, for his tendency "to preach the gospel of urbanity."[75] Moreover, we cannot neglect to notice that his attempt to convert the Philistines uses the Jew as the model of the convert. He attempts to bring the gospel of culture to "born Hebraisers" (*CP,* 5.199), to "rigid Hebraisers" (*CP,* 5.208), to those who follow "the stiff and stark notions of Hebraism" (*CP,* 5.208). Finally, the Preface to *Culture and Anarchy* endorses an ideology of assimilation that bears directly on Jewish identity: "it would still have been better for a man, during the last eighteen hundred years, to have been a Christian and a member of one of the great Christian communities, than to have been a Jew or a Socinian; because the being in contact with the main stream of human life is of more moment for a man's total spiritual growth" (*CP,* 5.251).

If *Culture and Anarchy* can be seen as an attempt to absorb, revise, and even undermine the Hebraism of Disraeli's project, it should come as no surprise that, with the publication of his first novel since *Tancred*, after a twenty-three-year hiatus, Disraeli entered the latest battle in the race wars of Victorian England by acknowledging the presence of a new participant. Disraeli's *Lothair*, published in 1870 immediately after *Culture and Anarchy*, makes direct reference to Arnold's famous formulation of Hellenism and Hebraism, and even tentatively endorses it, though not without producing a striking critique of the extremes of Hellenism, since what Arnold had done was to critique the extremes of Hebraism. And Disraeli's critique of Arnold's formulation of Hellenism did not go unnoticed by the younger author, for it was to *Lothair* that Arnold referred in *Literature and Dogma* (1873) when he spoke of Disraeli as "Lord Beaconsfield, treating Hellenic things with the scornful negligence natural to a Hebrew" (*CP,* 6.164). But, while Arnold here is referring to a passage in *Lothair*, Disraeli had already worked the ground of Hebraism and Hellenism as early as 1852, long before Arnold: "The Greek nevertheless appears exhausted. The creative genius of Israel, on the contrary, never shone so bright."[76] In *Lothair*, Disraeli's critique of Hellenism is aimed at the extreme Aryanist, Mr. Phoebus, an artist who represents pure Hellenism, or the kind of "worship of the beautiful"[77] for which Arnold was publicly taken to task in his formulation of Hellenism in *Culture and Anarchy*.[78] Mr. Phoebus attempts to (mis)educate Lothair:

> so strong and perfect a type as the original Aryan must be yet abundant among the millions, and may be developed. But for this you want great changes in your laws. It is the first duty of a state to attend to the frame and health of the subject. The Spartans understood this. They permitted no marriage the probable consequences of which might be a feeble progeny; they even took measures to secure a vigorous one. The Romans doomed the deformed to immediate destruction. The union of the races concerns the welfare of the commonwealth much too nearly to be entrusted to individual arrangement. The fate of a nation will ultimately depend upon the strength and health of the population. . . . Laws should be passed to secure all this, and some day they will be. But nothing can be done until the Aryan races are extricated from Semitism.[79]

Disraeli shrewdly exposes the ideology of Hellenism as based on a racial critique of the Jews, chillingly anticipating the consequences of such an ideology in the Nazism of the Third Reich.

Elsewhere in *Lothair*, however, Disraeli was willing to give some ground to Arnold's celebrated formulation of Hebraism and Hellenism. Modeled on the earlier mentorship between Sidonia and Tancred, the Syrian Paraclete instructs Lothair, a young English nobleman who is on a pilgrimage to the Holy Land:

> "In My Father's house are many mansions," and by the various families of nations the designs of the Creator are accomplished. God works by races, and one was appointed in due season and after many developments to reveal and expound in this land the spiritual nature of man. The Aryan and the Semite are of the same blood and origin, but when they quitted their central land they were ordained to follow opposite courses. Each division of the great race has developed one portion of the double nature of humanity, till after all their wanderings they met again, and, represented by their two choicest families,

the Hellenes and the Hebrews, brought together the treasures of their accumulated wisdom and secured the civilisation of man (emphasis added).[80]

This speech, while not neglecting the Semitic genius for spirituality, focuses on the racial kinship of Aryan and Semite, an idea that Arnold had disputed not only in *Culture and Anarchy* but also in *On the Study of Celtic Literature* on the basis of the recent claims of ethnology. Disraeli gives Arnold his due by citing his famous formulation, but refuses to submit to the racial argument to which Arnold yields: "Hellenes" and "Hebrews" are related "families" that descend from the same "great race," and hence they are conceived as collaborators in the great work of civilization.

Just as Disraeli seemed willing to yield some ground to Hellenism, Arnold followed *Culture and Anarchy* (and Disraeli's *Lothair,* I would add) with the publication of *Literature and Dogma,* in which he defines the limits of his acceptance of racial theories for his interpretation of Hebraism. He responds to the work of Emile Burnouf, who argues that "the oracles of God were not committed to a Semitic race at all, but to the Aryan; that the true God is not Israel's God at all, but is 'the idea of the absolute' which Israel could never properly master" (*CP,* 6.239). Arnold's reaction to Burnouf's claim is an ironic remark that baits the Philistine self-congratulation that he so often associates with the largest part of his fellow countrymen: "So that we Christians, who are Aryas, may have the satisfaction of thinking that 'the religion of Christ has not come to us from the Semites'" (*CP,* 6.239). Burnouf argues that what we traditionally have taken to be Israel's original position in relation to God is historically untrue; in fact, Israel represents only a kind of bastardization of the original divine message, based on the inferiority of the Semitic races. Arnold quotes Burnouf: "'in passing from the Aryan race to the inferior races, religion underwent a deterioration due to the physical and moral constitution of these races'" (*CP,* 6.239–40). Again, Arnold's double-edged barb is aimed at once at Burnouf and those Englishmen who will gladly rejoice in another sign of Indo-European superiority: "As Aryas or Aryans, then, we ought to be pleased at having vindicated the greatness of our race" (*CP,* 6.240). In such remarks the seeds of a full-fledged critique of the science of racialism appear, but Arnold never develops them, though he does mock the extremes of racial discourse: "Israel, therefore, instead of being a light of the Gentiles and a salvation to the ends of the earth, falls to a place in the world's religious history behind the Arya. He is dismissed as ranking anthropologically between the Aryas and the yellow men; as having frizzled hair, thick lips, small calves, flat feet, and belonging, above all, to those 'occipital races' whose brain cannot grow above the age of sixteen; whereas the brain of a theological Arya, such as one of our bishops, may go on growing all his life" (*CP,* 6.240).

This documentation of Burnouf's theories is another pivotal moment in Arnold's own personal history and the history of cultural discourse in England and Europe generally. Burnouf's *La Science des Religions,* published serially between 1864 and 1869 and in book form in 1872, marks the point when the science of race becomes empowered not simply to claim the inferiority of the Jews (as in Knox's ethnology), but to displace them from what Burnouf calls the "foremost" position in the history of religion and morals often accorded them. This is the critical moment when the ideology of race becomes empowered to disauthorize religious affiliations and to rewrite the history of religions, arguing, for example, that the Semites as a race are incapable of producing the religion of Christianity. The science of race has become, as the title of Burnouf's book proclaims, the basis for a science of religion. Burnouf's kind of racial theory found numerous proponents at the turn of the century, when, for example, Houston Stewart Chamberlain argued that the Teutons, not the Jews, were the great religious race, and that Christ, a member of the Galilean people (who had Aryan blood in them), was not a Jew.[81] Chamberlain's view develops from Burnouf's taking to its racial extreme Ernest Renan's division between Galilee and Jerusalem. We have seen how racial conflict became in nineteenth-century historiography the central historical background to the foundation of the modern nation-state. Now Burnouf imagines a kind of race war at the foundation of the religion of Christianity: "The more or less modified Mosaic doctrines of Israel only suited people of mixed races whose capital was Jerusalem; it had not the universality which characterizes a common religion, nor the transcendent metaphysics demanded by the Aryan genius. This is why, when the new religion was first preached, its earliest enemies were the Semites of Judaea; they killed Jesus."[82] The nineteenth century's racial rereadings of medieval history—produced by such writers as Scott,

Thierry, Prescott, and Freeman—function as the ideological context for a racial rereading of biblical history. The Jews are reinvented as the murderers of Christ in a kind of modern-day race war that pits Semites against the Aryan Christ.

Such ideas reinvent in the late nineteenth century the kind of argument made by the Church fathers in their formulation of early Christianity. Eusebius argued that Abraham and other famous Jews were not Jews at all, but Hebrews, a code word for proto-Christians. Eusebius even argued that Christianity in its primordial form predated the religion of the Jews. In the nineteenth century such arguments are fueled by the science of race. Burnouf argues that Aryan religious doctrines predate the religion of the Semites, which is no more than a corruption of the purer, earlier religion. His explanation makes racial history the frame for understanding the history of religions: "every religion which is conveyed into the midst of an inferior race must there undergo decay."[83] Such an idea widens the gulf that we saw Disraeli closing. What he had argued was the historical continuity between two creeds, one developing out of the other, now has become a kind of racial impossibility, opening ever more widely the avenue for anti-Semitism by disinheriting the Jews, on the basis of race, from their position as the ancestors of Christianity.

Disquieted at the rising stakes in such racial arguments, Arnold retreats by taking up his position in support of Hebrew Scripture and the legitimacy of the claim that makes the Jews our first and foremost teachers in the sphere of conduct: "But we, who think that the Old Testament leads surely up to the New, who believe that, indeed, 'salvation is of the Jews,' and that, for what concerns conduct or righteousness (that is, for what concerns three-fourths of human life), they and their documents can no more be neglected by whoever would make proficiency in it, than Greece can be neglected by anyone who would make proficiency in art . . .—*we* are naturally not satisfied with this treatment of Israel and the Bible" (*CP,* 6.240–41). But such a judgment on the side of Israel, the Bible, and Hebraism comes not without its own anxieties, sounded in the elaborate statement that, as a kind of safety net, allows Arnold to speak in favor of Israel only when speaking in the same breath in favor of Greece.

Such anxieties are expressed most tellingly in Arnold's dissociation of himself from Disraeli at the beginning of *Literature and Dogma,* a fascinating maneuver in the text that is perhaps Arnold's most Hebraic. It is in the opening sentence of the Introduction that Arnold characterizes Disraeli as "Lord Beaconsfield, treating Hellenic things with the scornful negligence natural to a Hebrew" (*CP,* 6.164). But I am suggesting that we read this criticism of the Hebraic Disraeli as a sign of Arnold's own anxiety over what may be seen as an equivocation on his part, as if, renegade-like, he has suddenly turned his back on his great Hellenic, Indo-European heritage, failing to follow the advice he himself set forth in *Culture and Anarchy* by uncritically embracing Hebraism. Arnold publicly discloses this anxiety when he confesses in his Conclusion to *Literature and Dogma:* "But now, after all we have been saying of the pre-eminency of righteousness, we remember what we have said formerly in praise of culture and of Hellenism, and against too much Hebraism. . . . And we cannot wonder whether we shall not be reproached with inconsistency" (*CP,* 6.407). The text ends in a gesture of reconciliation that does not refuse the terms of race and that even takes a tentative step toward Burnouf's theories: "And so far let us venture to poach on M. Emile Burnouf's manor, and to talk about the Aryan genius, as to say, that the love of art and science, and the energy and honesty in the pursuit of art and science, in the best of the Aryan races, do seem to correspond in a remarkable way to the love of conduct, and the energy and honesty in the pursuit of conduct, in the best of the Semitic" (*CP,* 6.410). *Literature and Dogma,* then, begins by setting up Disraeli as the Hebrew who undermines the Hellenic genius—lest Arnold himself, in this newly Hebraic work that mocks Aryan pride, be so accused—and it ends by anticipating that the charge of Hebraism may now be leveled against Arnold himself and by seeking to reestablish the difficult balance between Hebraism and Hellenism.

While he tried to dissociate himself from Disraeli's project, Arnold found himself in the 1870s defending Hebraism against the specific kinds of attacks that Disraeli himself had described earlier in the century. Disraeli had recorded a series of historical events and cultural developments that attempted to undermine the significance of Semitic culture: the French Enlightenment and the French Revolution, or more recently, the German school of biblical criticism, or more recently still, the science of ethnology. Disraeli located such developments within a highly ordered series of historical alternations that anticipate Arnold's conception of the alternation between Hebraism and Hellenism, but Disraeli named them differently—"a continual struggle between Asia and the North" (*T,* 217). Disraeli placed side by side, for example, the German school of biblical criticism and the French Enlightenment as parallel, but ultimately doomed, critiques of Semitic power: "But there is no reason to believe that the Teutonic rebellion of this century against the Divine truths entrusted to the Semites will ultimately meet with more success than the Celtic insurrection of the preceding age."[84] Disraeli understood these "rebellions" as part of a cyclical pattern that was perpetually fated to fail: "I believe the state of affairs is only one of the periodical revolts of the Northern races against Semitic truth, influenced mainly by mortified vanity in never having been the medium of direct communication with the Almighty."[85] He recorded periodic disruptions, from the North, of the bedrock of Semitic truth, a view that Arnold, to his own surprise, inched towards in the 1870s.

In Disraeli's General Preface to his works, published in 1870, we find an extraordinarily accurate history of the religious doubts and attacks on the Church of England against which Arnold found himself fighting more and more after *Culture and Anarchy.* In fact, Disraeli's 1870 picture in many ways could serve as an introduction to *Literature and Dogma,* which started appearing serially in 1871. Disraeli begins with a characterization of the origins of the Church of England—"Resting on the Church of Jerusalem, modified by the divine school of Galilee, it would have found that rock of truth which Providence, by the instrumentality of the Semitic race, had promised to St. Peter"—and proceeds to characterize the enemies of religion that Arnold will come to face: "This disturbance in the mind of nations has been occasioned by two causes; first, by the powerful assault on the divinity of the Semitic literature by the Germans, and secondly, by recent discoveries of science, which are hastily supposed to be inconsistent with our long-received convictions as to the relations between the creator and the created." In the midst of this description of the causes of doubt in Victorian England, Disraeli subtly criticizes Arnold's recent stance in *Culture and Anarchy,* a stance Arnold himself goes on to critique in *Literature and Dogma* because of his renewed faith in Hebraism: "To those who believe that an atheistical society, though it may be polished and amiable, involves the seeds of anarchy, the prospect is full of gloom."[86] In such a statement Disraeli ironically inverts Arnold's famous formulation: "anarchy" proceeds from a society that has turned its back on Hebraism, a Hellenic society that is "polished and amiable" but morally empty.

Such a view is the basis of the kind of prognosis that Arnold began to make from 1870 on, with the fall of France:

> her fall is mainly due to that want of a serious conception of righteousness and the need of it, the consequences of which so often show themselves in the world's history, and in regard to the Graeco-Latin nations more particularly. The fall of Greece, the fall of Rome, the fall of the brilliant Italy of the fifteenth century, and now the fall of France, are all examples. Nothing gives more freshness and depth to one's reading of the Bible than the sense that this is so, and that this testimony is perpetually being borne to the book of righteousness, though the nation out of which it came was itself a political failure so utter and miserable.[87]

Disraeli had already made this point, using the conventional distinction between (godless) France and (Christian) England, while representing England as the land of Hebraism: "Since the great revolt of the Celts against the first and second testament, at the close of the last century, France has been alternately in a state of collapse or convulsion. Throughout the awful trials of the last sixty years, England, notwithstanding her deficient and meagre theology, has always remembered Sion."[88] The same idea, without the compliment to England, was to work its way into Arnold's rereading of the Bible in *Literature and Dogma:* "Down they come, one after another; Assyria falls, Babylon, Greece, Rome; they all fall for want of *conduct,* righteousness" (*CP,* 6.387). Disraeli made the point in this way, some two decades earlier: establishing that "The Jews represent the Semitic principle; all that is spiritual in our nature," he claims, "It may be observed that the decline and disasters of modern communities have generally been relative to their degree of sedition against the Semitic principle."[89]

Time and again cast in the role of the defender of Israel in the 1870s, Arnold sounds more and more like Disraeli. Both men produced encapsulated world histories in which the degeneration and fall of nations and empires depended on a failure in morals, that is, on a failure in upholding the Semitic principle of moral conduct. I locate such histories within the context of an emerging debate on Teutonism, articulated (for instance) by Thomas Arnold when he defined the Teutonic race as "the regenerating element in modern Europe,"[90] a view Disraeli's *Tancred* answered: "It is Arabia alone that can regenerate the world" (*T,* 465). In such a vein Arnold responded to one of his critics in a book entitled *God and the Bible* (1875): "And although we may willingly allow ... that the mind and life of our Aryan race has deeply modified the religion of Semitic Israel already, and will yet modify it much more, still that cannot prevent the root of the matter for us, in this immense concern of religion, being in the Israel of the Bible, and he is our spiritual progenitor—*A Syrian ready to perish was thy father*" (*CP,* 7.395). Arnold's quotation, taken from Deuteronomy 26:5, is worthy of Disraeli's *Tancred,* with its Syrian settings and its melancholy protest against the failure of Europe to remember the Asian beginnings of its faith. Conceived in this way, Disraeli and Arnold here can be seen as revising the work of the patriotic nineteenth-century historiographers of the Middle Ages, who ask the modern Englishman to recall his early Teutonic ancestors, or the work of Arnold's own father, who spoke of "our Saxon and Teutonic forefathers."[91] Both Disraeli and Arnold became enlisted in the same battle to save the dying Syrian father in a genealogy of morals that sought the origins of modern Christian England in Israel, "our spiritual progenitor." In his religious studies of the 1870s, then, Arnold shared with Disraeli the strategy of asking his readers to see the way in which the moral genealogy of the English people was as important as their racial genealogy.

6

Moses in Egypt: The Secret Jew in England

During the pinnacle of Benjamin Disraeli's political career in the 1870s, Anthony Trollope produced a series of novels whose anti-Semitism is unparalleled in the nineteenth century, while George Eliot wrote the novel that has justly claimed its place as the most celebrated philo-Semitic novel written in England. This extreme antithesis in the representation of Jewish identity indicates the pitch that "the Jewish question" reached during Disraeli's public prominence, especially during his prime ministry (1874–80), when "the attention of Britain and, for much of the time, Europe, too, was centred upon Disraeli."[1]

In *Barchester Towers* (1857) Trollope included a brief parody of the most famous character that Disraeli the novelist ever produced, the Jew Sidonia. This parody, however pointed, hardly prepares us for the way in which Trollope, with Disraeli as his most prominent model, represented the Jewish infiltration of English culture in such novels as *The Eustace Diamonds* (1873) and *Phineas Redux* (1874), climaxing in *The Way We Live Now* (1875) and *The Prime Minister* (1876). *The Way We Live Now* began appearing in monthly installments in 1874 during the same month that Disraeli became prime minister. The novel contained some pointed references to Disraeli as the leader of the Conservative party, as well as a fictional plot in which the career of the vulgar but immensely successful financier Melmotte, thought to be a Jew, is capped by his election to Parliament as a Conservative member. Eliot and George Henry Lewes were reading these installments in the summer of 1874 while she was completing the opening chapters of *Daniel Deronda*.[2] For this reason it is possible to see Eliot's novel as a response not simply to Disraeli, but to the way in which her friend Trollope was recording his own version of Jewish identity, especially as he imagined it enacted in the prime minister's daily activities. In the fall of the following year Trollope sent Eliot the first part of *The Prime Minister* while she was engaged in writing the middle books of *Daniel Deronda*, but she claimed not to read it: "When I am writing, or only thinking of writing fiction of my own, I cannot risk the reading of other English fiction. I was obliged to tell Anthony Trollope so when he sent the first part of his Prime Minister, though this must seem sadly ungracious to those who don't share my susceptibilities" (*GEL*, 6.199). What Lewes may have told her about *The Prime Minister*, we can only speculate; Lewes recorded reading Trollope's latest Jewish novel and remarking to Eliot's publisher about its handsome wide margins as a possible model for *Daniel Deronda* (*GEL*, 6.194n., 6.197). This chain of interlocking political and literary events reached a climax in 1876, when Disraeli was named earl of Beaconsfield by the queen and when *Daniel Deronda* and *The Prime Minister* were published in book form, Trollope's title making patent his growing obsession with the real prime minister.

Disraeli's influence on Trollope's and Eliot's fiction actually began as a literary influence—that is, as the influence of Disraeli the novelist, the celebrated author of the political trilogy of the 1840s. Both Trollope and Eliot made no secret that they saw Disraeli as their precursor in Jewish portraiture. In his *Autobiography* (1883) Trollope grudgingly included "the present Prime Minister of England" among "the best known English novelists of my own time," only to produce a scathing denunciation of Disraeli's fiction.[3] Reading this attack, we cannot forget that Disraeli was Trollope's precursor not simply in Jewish portraiture, but, even more importantly in Trollope's eyes, in the creation and development of an entire genre, the political novel. Trollope and Disraeli were pitted against each other as rival practitioners in this genre from the time that Trollope's Palliser novels began to appear, with Disraeli often winning the competition in a debate that continues today.[4] The clearest signs of Eliot's anxiety of influence occurred when, during one of her most painful bouts of self-doubt over the Jewish sections of *Daniel Deronda*, she wondered if the readers of her new novel would simply dismiss Mordecai in favor of his celebrated precursor: "Doubtless the wider public of novel readers must feel more interest in Sidonia than in Mordecai. But then, I was not born to paint Sidonia" (*GEL*, 6.223). It was not surprising for her to look to

Disraeli as the supreme judge of *Daniel Deronda*. John Blackwood, Eliot's longtime publisher, after remarking to her that "the praise of the Chief Rabbi is truly gratifying," added, "I could not hear whether Disraeli gave any utterances on the subject" (*GEL*, 6.218). But Disraeli failed to pass sentence: " 'When I want to read a novel, I write one,' he is supposed to have said to someone who asked him whether he had read *Daniel Deronda*."⁵

I have already shown the way in which the idea of the Jew as an imposter, epitomized in the view of Disraeli as an accomplished actor, became a popular way of "up-dating" in Victorian England the historical idea of the Iberian crypto-Jew. The ideas of imposture and theatricality, and their function in representing Jewish identity, reached their fullest articulation in the fiction of Trollope and Eliot. More specifically, the idea of "the secret Jew," crystallized at the same time in Disraeli's fiction and in his political career, became the focus of Trollope's novels of the 1870s as well as *Daniel Deronda*.

The story of Moses in Egypt was used in Victorian England, especially in the 1870s, to underscore the idea of the secret Jew who subverts and eventually destroys the dominant culture in which he lives. *Punch* periodically used the story to satirize Disraeli, whether making fun of Disraeli the novelist or Disraeli the politician. One *Punch* cartoon debunked England's modern-day Moses as no more than a sly opportunist, with the tribe of Israel mocked as "the tribe of Old Clo!" and the wisdom of the prophet reduced to "the cunning of MOSES" (figure 17). Some years later in *Punch*, Disraeli was depicted in the following terms: "To get out of Egyptian bonds, as we know, / Moses led to the Red Sea his clients Judaic: / Now, into the same bonds Britannia must go, / To reach the same sea, with a guide as Mosaic" (December 11, 1875). Here, *Punch* was referring to Disraeli's engineering of a sudden, behind-the-scenes purchase of a huge number of shares in the Suez Canal Company, with the aid of a large loan from the Rothschilds. *Punch* ominously suggests the way in which the Jewish premier leads his adopted people into (rather than out of) captivity, while also hinting that Disraeli has trapped England in a Shylock-like bond. And in a *Punch* cartoon entitled "D'israel-i in Triumph; The Modern Sphynx," Disraeli is pictured as a Jewish Sphinx drawn by parliamentary "slaves" (figure 18). Such versions of Moses in Egypt begin to suggest the way in which Disraeli could be seen as the wily

CARTOON FOR THE MERCHANT TAILORS.

MOSES AND SON ATTIRING YOUNG ENGLAND.

THE novel of Coningsby clearly discloses
The pride of the world are the children of MOSES.
Mosaic, the bankers—the soldiers, the sailors,
The statesmen—and so, by-the-by, are the tailors.
Mosaic, the gold—that is worthless and hollow ;
Mosaic, the people—the bailiffs that follow.
The new generation—the party that claim
To take to themselves of Young England the name ;
In spite of their waistcoats much whiter than snow,
It seems after all are the tribe of Old Clo !
Then where in the world can Young England repair
To purchase the garments it wishes to wear—
Unless to that mart whose success but discloses
The folly of man, and the cunning of MOSES ?

Figure 17. Young England is preposterously overdressed by a Jewish tailor who is no other than Disraeli. *Punch,* June 15, 1844.

D'ISRAEL-I IN TRIUMPH; THE MODERN SPHYNX.
(Suggested by Mr. POYNTER's admirable Picture of " Israel in Egypt."

Figure 18. The mysteriously powerful Disraeli passes the Reform Bill with only a minority government, while Gladstone, whose efforts at reform failed the previous year, looks back in bitterness and suspicion. *Punch*, June 15, 1867.

and triumphant Jew, raised by another people as one of their own, only to become their enslaver, their fiercest enemy, the vehicle of the deadly plagues that destroy them. Finally, in 1876, the British public was presented with three versions of the Moses story. *Punch* represented Disraeli as the Egyptian Sphinx, "the voice of the great Asian Mystery," recalling "our great forefather Moses, who first taught Jews the spoiling of Egyptians" (January 8, 1876). And along such lines Trollope invented his own Mosaic despoiler of the English people in *The Prime Minister*, while in profound revision of this idea Eliot created *Daniel Deronda*.

Despoiling the Egyptians: Trollope's Jewish Criminals

In a novel as full of parodic invention and literary mischief as *Barchester Towers*, it is easy to overlook Trollope's parody of *Coningsby*. But the brief satiric attack is a harbinger of things to come. Trollope's parody is indebted not simply to the original work, but to an earlier parody of it by Thackeray, Trollope's comic master.[6] Following in Thackeray's footsteps, Trollope alludes to Disraeli's novel satirically in the story of Ethelbert Stanhope's encounter with a member of the Sidonia family in Palestine: "This Sidonia, however, did not take so strong a fancy to him as another of that family once did to a young English nobleman." Unmasking the Jew who is seen as the educator and savior of a young Englishman, Trollope reveals nothing more than the stereotype of the shrewd Jewish moneylender. Trollope's revision of Disraeli's text ends with Bertie in debt and Sidonia reduced to Shylock. In this way Disraeli's Sidonia begins to emerge as a new site of textual conflict in the history of Jewish portraiture. While Trollope (following Thackeray) reduces Sidonia to "a dirty little old man," Eliot attempts to resurrect "the wonderful prophet" (*BT*, 1.79)[7] in the person of Mordecai in *Daniel Deronda*.

Trollope ironizes Sidonia's influence on the young Englishman by introducing a plot of conversion in which Bertie unwittingly becomes a proselyte to Judaism:

> he soon wrote home for money, saying that he had been converted to the Mother Church, that he was already an acolyte of the Jesuits, and that he was about to start with others to Palestine on a mission for converting Jews. He did go to Judea, but being unable to convert the Jews, was converted by them. He again wrote home, to say that Moses was the only giver of perfect laws to the world, that the coming of the true Messiah was at hand, that great things were doing in Palestine, and that he had met one of the family of Sidonia, a most remarkable man. (*BT*, 1.79)

In depicting the power of "the wonderful prophet," Trollope depicts what many took to be a kind of subtle proselytism in Disraeli's trilogy and his politics, as if Disraeli's real goal were to make Jews out of his fellow citizens. And the English public was always willing to respond to this danger. In a comic revival of the famous charge that Cromwell was going to sell St. Paul's to the Jews, *Punch* satirized those who feared "the subversion of Christianity, for the triumph of Judaism," by joking that "Disraeli . . . has been heard to prophesy that, in eighteen months, the Chief Rabbi of the Jews will preach in St. Paul's Church" (October 20, 1849). Trollope himself was willing to play on such fears and prejudices. When campaigning for a seat in Parliament, he warned his audience that Disraeli was capable of producing a bill that would not simply disestablish the Irish Church but would abolish Protestantism generally.[8]

"The Judaised Ethelbert" (*BT*, 1.79), then, can be read as a sign, at once comic and serious, of the Englishman on the brink of losing his traditional identity in Disraeli's England. Historically, the "Judaized" Englishman represented revolutionary politics, whether in the late eighteenth century in the cases of Lord George Gordon and Richard Brothers, or in the seventeenth century in the well-known case of John Traske, who was imprisoned and sentenced to have the letter "J" burned on his forehead for his Jewish beliefs. Termed "a Maran" (after the Marranos of Spain) by Lancelot Andrewes, Traske caused a major scandal in London when he and his followers mixed Jewish and Christian practices.[9] While the foolish Bertie Stanhope seems a far cry from the politics of revolution, by the middle of the nineteenth century there had appeared on the scene a new model of the Judaized Englishman in the title hero of *Tancred,* or, for that matter, in Disraeli himself. And the most famous Judaized Englishman in the history of the novel, George Eliot's Daniel Deronda, was on the horizon. In this light, Trollope's portrait of the Judaized Englishman can be seen as a warning of the danger that lurked in Disraeli's program of a Hebraized England (figure 19).

In novel after novel in the 1870s we find Trollope representing the threat of a Judaized England. This threat makes serious the idea of the foreign invasion of English culture that seemed no more than a comic subtext in *Barchester Towers* when, in a parody of *Ivanhoe,* Miss Thorne holds fast to Saxon traditions and complains of the effects of the Norman Conquest. "The base invading Norman" (*BT*, 1.216) of *Barchester Towers,* no more than the ancient and impalpable figure of an old woman's eccentric daydreams, is replaced by another kind of invader in Trollope's novels of 1870s, a class of social climbers who attempt to suppress or erase their Jewish origins, two of whom (like Disraeli) aim at careers in Parliament. Such invaders, while apparently assimilated as Englishmen, in fact carry with them the threat of Judaizing England, not through religious proselytism, but through the corruption of the traditional system of values defined as English.

The Jew in *Barchester Towers,* intended as the object of our laughter, inhabits an essentially literary world, for his name declares that he is a

THE HOUSE OF COMMONS ACCORDING TO MR. DISRAELI'S VIEWS.

Figure 19. *Punch*'s satirical view of a Judaized Parliament. *Punch,* April 10, 1847.

fiction, a descendant of a purely literary figure, a satiric revision of the famous Sidonia that Disraeli created in the previous decade. But while Sidonia is safely encased in the world of metafiction, the Jews in Trollope's later novels, even those who appear as minor characters, become central players in the action, if only because their criminal acts make them important agents of the novels' plots. And while they may have literary antecedents, they occupy their ground in these novels with a grim substantiality all their own.

These Jewish characters appear in the form of the assimilated Jew, the converted Jew, the Jew with pretensions to being first an Englishman, then a gentleman, and finally a member of Parliament. Trollope's attack on such figures demonstrates the ultimate dilemma of the conversionist plot in Christian culture. The conventional attack on the stereotypical "stiff-necked Jew" whose hard heart cannot be penetrated by Christianity soon turns into an attack on the Jew who converts and thereby gains access to the highest echelons of Christian society. In this way Victorian England faced its own version of the *converso* problem in Spain and Portugal—how to cut short the Jews' success in entering the hegemonic culture once they had converted and assimilated.

The most marked characteristic of Trollope's representation of Jewish identity is its genealogical uncertainty. Jewish identity is represented as a suspicion or rumor that haunts certain characters. In *Phineas Finn*, Madame Max Goesler's "enemies say that her father was a German Jew" (*PF*, 2.31); in *The Eustace Diamonds*, Mr. Emilius is introduced as "the Rev. Joseph Emilius, of whom it was said that he was born a Jew in Hungary" (*ED*, 1.327); in *Phineas Redux*, Mr. Emilius "was supposed, a Bohemian Jew" (*PR*, 2.38); in *The Way We Live Now*, Mr. Alf "was supposed to have been born a German Jew" (*WWLN*, 1.8), and "it was suspected by many, and was now being whispered to the world at large, that Melmotte had been born a Jew" (*WWLN*, 2.52); and in *The Prime Minister*, Ferdinand Lopez is "a probable Jew" (*PM*, 1.31).[10] It is "said," "supposed," and "suspected" of persons that they are Jewish, for in this world there is no Jewish badge, and Jewish origins are hidden, suppressed; Jewish identity is a secret identity, in need of ferreting out. For this reason, Jewish identity often seems without substance, the product of whispers and rumors, sometimes no more than mere fabrication, so that the most meaningless detail of one's life can lead to the erroneous charge of Jewish identity: "[Mr. Squercum] seldom or never came to his office on a Saturday, and many among his enemies said that he was a Jew" (*WWLN*, 2.71). In this way the signifier "Jew" circulates freely, in the possession of any person to bestow on any other person of questionable (especially foreign) origins. Even the characters whose Jewish identity does not seem in doubt do not entirely fit within the conventional stereotype, and so they require the observer's shrewdest powers of detection: Madame Melmotte is "fat and fair,—unlike in colour to our traditional Jewesses; but she had the Jewish nose and the Jewish contraction in the eyes" (*WWLN*, 1.31). Jewish identity is grasped from the outside; it is guessed at, pieced together, measured by certain (not altogether reliable) rules of physiognomy or behavior. But such measures are finally recognized as unreliable, and the Jewish diaspora becomes reimagined as the process of Jewish infiltration and subversion, as in Lady Pomona Longestaffe's version of biblical history: "An accursed race . . . expelled from Paradise. . . . Scattered about all over the world, so that nobody knows who anybody is" (*WWLN*, 2.263).

While Trollope shows the way in which Jewish identity is constructed from the outside, manufactured through suspicion, rumor, innuendo, and prejudice, he suggests that such constructions are the consequence of a world in which Jews reinvent their own identities in order to hide their Jewish origins, returning us to Thackeray's remark that "half the Hebrew's life is a disguise." The suspicion and paranoia of the hegemonic community, then, seems to originate in Jewish deceit, and Trollope's novels are determined to expose the means of disguise that Jews employ, along the lines of the theatrical self-reinvention of which Disraeli was accused. In this way Trollope's novels become an inquisitorial investigation of "the secret race" that was known to exert its subversive power in the Iberian Peninsula while wearing the mask of Christianity. Finally, the masked Jew, typically the product of his own attempt to infiltrate English culture, is sometimes seen as the product of English culture itself, for Trollope eventually reveals the way in which Christians collude in hiding Jewish origins. Georgiana Longestaffe, in considering marrying Ezekial Brehgert, plans on hiding his Jewish identity: "As to her husband, though she did not suppose that she could ever get him to church,—nor perhaps would it be desirable,—she thought that she might induce him to go nowhere, so that she might be able to pass him off as a Christian. She knew that such was the Christianity of young Goldsheiner, of which the Starts were now boasting" (*WWLN*, 2.93). In such a case the secret Jew in Victorian England is the product of the collusion between the Jew who wants to enter English society and the Christian who, for selfish reasons (usually monetary), wants the Jew to pass as a Christian.

Mr. Emilius in *The Eustace Diamonds* is a portrait of the Jew who makes himself over to infiltrate English society. Trollope places Mr. Emilius in a plot that functions as a recapitulation of *The Merchant of Venice*. For example, Shakespeare's three caskets and their respective suitors are replaced by one very important iron case (containing the Eustace diamonds) and three suitors (Lord Fawn, Frank Greystock, and Mr. Emilius). In both texts the three suitors court a rich heiress, but in Trollope's novel the heiress, Lizzie Eustace, lives a life that runs counter to the advice enclosed in Shakespeare's gold casket: "All is not gold that glistens, Lady Eustace" (*ED*, 2.137). In Trollope's revision of Shakespeare's text for Victorian England, the Jew is no longer the moneylender on the sidelines of the marriage plot; instead, he is disguised as an English clergyman who becomes one of the suitors for the heiress's hand. Such a revision "updates" the anti-Semitism of the original text, making the Jewish threat to Christian culture all the more potent, for the Jew not only successfully enters English culture—in the end he wins the hand of the heiress. The irony of Trollope's revision can be stated in the following way: the conversion of Shylock, the goal of the Jewish plot in *The Merchant of Venice,* has come back to haunt English culture, for Mr. Emilius's successes, as a preacher and as a suitor of Lizzie, show us the consequences of admitting the converted Jew into English culture.

With Trollope's converted Jews, conversion often becomes no more than the most successful of Jewish disguises, and the following remark from *Is He Popenjoy?* (1878) about another converted Jewish clergyman colors all of Trollope's portraits of Jewish converts: "I'm not quite sure . . . whether any good is ever done by converting a Jew."[11] Trollope's depiction of the converted Jewish clergyman in *The Eustace Diamonds* recalls the kind of portrait that became popular during the controversy over the London Society for Promoting Christianity amongst the Jews: the Jew from another country who converts in order to make a comfortable living in England as a clergyman. Mr. Emilius is introduced in *The Eustace Diamonds* as "among the most eloquent of London preachers" (*ED,* 1.327), but from the beginning he carries the hint of the parvenu: he is "the fashionable preacher" (*ED,* 1.334) who "had come up quite suddenly within the last season" (*ED,* 1.327). Like another well-known converted Jew who went on to become prime minister, Mr. Emilius's self-proclaimed eloquence seems tinged with willful, even opportunistic, manipulation of his audience: "I can move the masses" (*ED,* 2.314). By the end of the novel his suspected Jewish lineage consistently threatens to overtake his credentials as a clergyman and a Christian—"Mr. Emilius, the fashionable foreign ci-devant Jew preacher" (*ED,* 2.237)—until his status as a *former* Jew seems overridden by those facts of physiognomy and behavior that indict him as a Jew: "The man was a nasty, greasy, lying, squinting Jew preacher" (*ED,* 2.314). What is a Jew preacher? Mr. Emilius's entire identity collapses in such a counterphrase. And in the end his conversion seems only a sign of the betrayal of his ancestral faith, for he is termed "a renegade Jew" (*ED,* 2.241), another sign of the dilemma of Christian proselytism, whose successes produce renegade Jews (apostates who use their Christianity as a passport into Christian society) and whose failures give further evidence of "the stiff-necked race." In such a world there seems no such thing as a legitimate convert. Mr. Emilius—"a greasy, fawning, pawing, creeping, black-browed rascal" (*ED*, 2.241–2)—is "A Bohemian Jew . . . an impostor who has come over here to make a fortune" (*ED*, 2.373).

While Trollope is sometimes seen as exposing the virulence of Victorian anti-Semitism, his novels at the same time endorse this anti-Semitism by finally indicting the Jewish characters, often literally indicting them when their criminality is discovered. In *The Eustace Diamonds* the anti-Semitic slurs aimed at Mr. Emilius—for example, that he will be discovered to be a pickpocket—turn out to be based on fact when Trollope subtly merges the identities of Mr. Emilius and the jewelers who engineer the robbery of Lizzie's diamonds. While these jewelers are introduced more than once in the early sections of the novel as Messrs. Harter and Benjamin, after the jewels are stolen the text records, for the first time, that the jewelers are Jews, an idea repeated in the following satiric wordplay: "the Jew jewellers" (*ED*, 2.134). While "Benjamin, the Jew" (*ED*, 2.374) is tried and found guilty, the stolen jewels are never recovered, so that Trollope's heiress (unlike Shakespeare's) suffers defeat at the hands of Jewish wiliness. In Trollope's novels the Jews, even when their criminal activity is discovered, usually manage to elude some aspect of the law. But more importantly, the heiress in *The Eustace Diamonds* seems outsmarted not by one but by two Jewish adventurers, for Mr. Emilius's marriage to Lizzie the heiress is seen as simply a more subtle means of (Jewish) robbery. So, while the trial finds Benjamin guilty of absconding with the heiress's property, Trollope's plot finds Emilius guilty of absconding with the heiress herself. In Victorian England the comic resolution of *The Merchant of Venice* founders, first, when "the Jew jeweller" succeeds in robbing the heiress, and second, when "the Jew preacher" succeeds in marrying her.

In *Phineas Redux*, published immediately after *The Eustace Diamonds*, Mr. Emilius is finally proven to be an impostor. Trollope manages to make the discovery of Emilius's criminal activity, his bigamy, merge with the proof of his Jewish identity, as if these two were one and the same. In the course of the novel the ferreting out of his crime often seems no more than an attempt to document his Jewish origins: "He a foreigner and a Jew, by name Yosef Mealyus,—as every one was very careful to call him,— had come to England, had got himself to be ordained as a clergyman, had called himself Emilius, and had married a rich wife with a title, although he had a former wife still living in his own country" (*PR*, 2.287). But of the further crime in *Phineas Redux*, the murder of Mr. Bonteen (who exposes Emilius as a bigamist), Mr. Emilius is not convicted, even though the reader is led to believe him guilty. In the end, the murder of Mr. Bonteen, like the whereabouts of the stolen Eustace diamonds, remains a mystery, the accomplishment of Jewish cunning. Behind such mysteries there seems to be one certainty: "Of course the Jew did it" (*PR*, 2.73), "It was that Jew who did it" (*PR*, 2.139).

The double life, the false names, the hidden crimes, the masked Jewish origins are the earmarks of the secret Jew in Victorian England, as Trollope's fiction exposes him. Like Emilius, Melmotte in *The Way We Live Now* commits a crime that signals the entire bogusness of his identity: forgery. The secret Jew, the bigamist or forger, is the man who pretends to be what he is not. Hence, like Emilius, Melmotte seems to have led several lives and to have changed his identity periodically to suit his surroundings. His career in England seems to commence with the Anglicization of his name, for in England "The world had received the man as Augustus Melmotte, Esq." "It was thus that the gentleman chose to have himself designated, though within the last two years he had arrived in London from Paris, and had at first been known as M. Melmotte. But he had declared of himself that he had been born in England, and that he was an Englishman" (*WWLN*, 1.30–31). Trollope keeps the history of Melmotte and his family a mystery, tantalizing the reader with clues that are scattered throughout the novel but refusing to present an integrated, authoritative family history. Melmotte's daughter becomes a victim of her father's identity changes, vaguely recalling being taken as a very young child to Frankfurt, where her father had married her present mother, "her pseudo-mother": "she was told that from henceforth she was to be a Jewess. But there had soon come another change. They went from Frankfort to Paris, and there they were all Christians" (*WWLN*, 1.106). Unlike Emilius, Melmotte is never disclosed with certainty to be a Jew by birth. But then, in this group of novels, unknown ancestry and Jewish ancestry are almost synonymous.

In the story of Melmotte and his daughter, Trollope ironically collapses the two different father-daughter plots of *The Merchant of Venice*. As the father of one of the richest heiresses in the world, Melmotte is like Portia's father, in charge of protecting his heiress daughter against adventurers; but Melmotte thinks "his daughter was valuable to him because she might make him the father-in-law of a Marquis or an Earl" (*WWLN*, 1.233), reminding us of the Jewish father who seems to measure the worth of his daughter at the value of so many ducats. Moreover, when Marie "cooly proposed to rob [her father]" (*WWLN*, 1.274), we see the ways in which Trollope has revived the anti-Semitic myth of the Jewish family of *The Merchant of Venice:* the father who values money and power over his daughter, and the daughter who steals her father's money while running off with a Christian lover. If Melmotte's actual genealogy is in question, Trollope in this way makes Melmotte's literary ancestry clear: he is the Jewish father, with an only child, a daughter, who betrays him.

This group of novels time and again offers a sometimes mocking, sometimes pathetic picture of the Jew trying to solve the puzzle of English culture. While "it was the proudest boast of his life to be an Englishman" (*WWLN*, 2.121), Melmotte is consistently shown as an inept student of English culture, and when money cannot buy his way into the mysteries of English life, he remains on the outside. "It was everything to Melmotte that he should understand the ways of the country which he had adopted; and when he did not understand, he was clever at hiding his ignorance" (*WWLN*, 1.221). The intricacies of English culture, when not mastered, are faked. Entering Parliament and being made a baronet are the two goals by which Melmotte attempts to crown his career as an Englishman. When worried that "they should say that I'm not an Englishman," Melmotte is reassured: "Lord Alfred had explained that it was not necessary that he should have been born in England, or even that he should have an English name" (*WWLN*, 1.233). Trollope does not hesitate to allude to Disraeli, a Jew with an un-English name who in fact entered Parliament, as a model for Melmotte: "Melmotte was not the first vulgar man whom the Conservatives had taken by the hand, and patted on the back, and told that he was a god" (*WWLN*, 2.37); and "Melmotte might become as it were a Conservative tribune of the people,— . . . he might be the realization of that hitherto hazy mixture of Radicalism and old-fogeyism, of which we have lately heard from a political master" (*WWLN*, 2.171). Such pointed references to Disraeli, like the entire plot in which the vulgar Melmotte secures his parliamentary seat, must have been motivated by the frustration of what Trollope called his own "almost insane desire"[12] to sit in Parliament, a desire he failed to realize in 1868: "Worst of all was the publicity of his resounding defeat by the party of Disraeli in a year in which, ironically, the Gladstonian landslide brought the Liberal party emphatically back to power."[13]

The success of Melmotte's assimilation, or what Trollope sees as his infiltration, into English culture depends on the culture's willingness to be duped by the secret Jew—that is, on its willingness to be seduced by the millionaire's money and power. Trollope excoriates the men and women of England for seeking to use Melmotte's name, to borrow his money, to marry their sons to his daughter, to elect him to Parliament, to win him a title, and, finally, to convert him, to make him part of their religious institutions. The idea of conversion, the most ironic version of the attempted induction of Melmotte into English Victorian culture, is introduced through Father John Barham, a Roman Catholic priest who "took his degree at Oxford, and then became what we call a pervert, and what I suppose they call a convert" (*WWLN*, 1.134). Barham is a new type of comic character, the man whose single and overpowering humor is his desire to convert others: "he had but one duty before him,—to do his part towards bringing over the world to his faith. It might be that with the toil of his whole life he should convert but one; that he should but half convert one; that he should do no more than disturb the thoughts of one so that future conversion might be possible. But even that would be work done" (*WWLN*, 1.150–51). Father Barham proudly announces to Roger Carbury that "Mr. Melmotte is a convert to our faith" (*WWLN*, 2.48) on the evidence that he has made a contribution to a new Catholic church, while Carbury explains that Melmotte has just made a contribution to a Protestant cause as well. The Jew and the Catholic are the double object of Trollope's satire here—the campaigning Jew who unscrupulously attempts to catch both the Protestant and Roman Catholic vote, and "the fervent Romanists" who "have a desire for the conversion of men which is honest in an exactly inverse ratio to the dishonesty of the means which they employ to produce it" (*WWLN*, 2.52). Such conventional anti-Catholic rhetoric neglects the historical fact that Protestant groups such as the London Society had come under attack in nineteenth-century England for the means they used to convert English Jews and for the entirely bogus converts they produced. Trollope tries to ignore that the mania for conversion was a phenomenon of the Evangelical Revival—that is, a native product of English Protestant culture. Similarly, in *Barchester Towers* Bertie Stanhope is first converted by the Roman Catholics and then by the Jews, as if English Protestant culture were in danger of being erased by both of these religious minorities.

Unable to explain why Melmotte virtually throws him out of his house as a lunatic, Father Barham attempts to maintain Melmotte as a genuine Catholic convert: "That a man should be at heart a Catholic, and live in the world professing the Protestant religion, was not to Father Barham either improbable or distressing. Kings who had done so were to him objects of veneration. By such subterfuges and falsehood of life had they been best able to keep alive the spark of heavenly fire" (*WWLN*, 2.53). Trollope's ironic undercutting of Father Barham's picture of the millionaire Melmotte as a martyred secret Catholic reflects on the more well-known history of the crypto-Jews who hid their faith to keep it alive amid persecution; Father Barham's secret Catholic martyr is no more than a secret Jewish adventurer. Trollope's irony seems directed once again at both Catholics and Jews. While the Roman Catholic priest constructs his vision of the convert Melmotte to win his money, the Jewish millionaire hides his religious and racial origins for purely opportunistic reasons.

Trollope's representation of the foreign Jew masked as an Englishman reaches its climax in *The Prime Minister*. Once again, this idea begins with the depiction of a suspected Jew whose family background is unknown. In *The Eustace Diamonds* we hear of Mr. Emilius, "Of grandfather or grandmother belonging to himself he had probably never heard" (*ED*, 2.314), and in *Phineas Redux*, Lady Laura asks about Madame Max Goesler, "who was her father or who was her mother?" (*PR*, 2.225). This idea reaches exaggerated proportions in *The Prime Minister* when we learn about Ferdinand Lopez: "He had no father or mother, no uncle, aunt, brother or sister, no cousin even whom he could mention in a cursory way to his dearest friend" (*PM*, 1.2). From the standpoint of genealogy, such characters are mere ciphers. We have seen that in Trollope's novels the Jew is almost by definition the person whose genealogy is uncertain, unknowable. I now wish to explore how such an idea plays a crucial role in the revision of a familiar topos of the English novel: the orphan whose mysterious origins are discovered in the denouement of the novel. Lopez names himself through an exaggerated version of this character-type: "I was an orphan before I understood what it was to have a parent" (*PM*, 1.27).

In merging the traditional comic plot of the orphan with the story of the Jewish adventurer (in an interesting confusion of the roles of Oliver and Fagin in *Oliver Twist*), Trollope critiques the idea of the self-made man who is seen as the product of Jewish opportunism and Victorian social mobility. For Trollope, the self-made man is a kind of monstrous prodigy not unlike the scientifically made man of Mary Shelley's *Frankenstein*. Both Melmotte and Lopez are given unusual, even unnatural, births that anticipate their monstrous fates. Melmotte is "Brought into the world in a gutter, without father or mother" (*WWLN*, 2.134), while Lopez's origins are represented in a kind of fantasy: "He had been as though he had been created self-sufficient, independent of mother's milk or father's money" (*PM*, 1.13). Because "none of them knew whence he had come, or what was his family" (*PM*, 1.3), the solitary Jewish stranger, like Shelley's outcast, attempts to make for himself a place in society, as opposed to being given a place from birth. Moreover, neither Melmotte nor Lopez is granted the prize that comes at the end of the traditional comic plot of the orphan, final integration into English society through the revelation of his family origins. Like Shelley's "monster," both Jewish strangers, seen as unfit to take up their place in the community, commit suicide. The self-made man becomes the self-destroyed man.

The Prime Minister opens not with narrative but with social commentary, so that the story of Lopez seems no more than a novelistic pretext for Trollope's study of the monstrosity of the self-made man:

> It is certainly of service to a man to know who were his grandfathers and who were his grandmothers if he entertain an ambition to move in the upper circles of society. . . . No doubt we all entertain great respect for those who by their own energies have raised themselves in the world; and when we hear that the son of a washerwoman has become Lord Chancellor or Archbishop of Canterbury we do, theoretically and abstractedly, feel a higher reverence for such self-made magnate than for one who has been as it were born into forensic or ecclesiastical purple. (*PM*, 1.1)

Trollope fleshes out—and undercuts—our theoretical choice of the self-made man over the well-born man in the story of the Jewish adventurer who hides the few details he knows about his origins: "He did not know very much himself, but what little he did know he kept altogether to himself" (*PM*, 1.2). Instead of the traditional orphan who is the victim of his own ignorance about his origins, Lopez is the orphan who victimizes others by withholding his family origins; in short, he is the Jew who hides his origins to climb the Victorian social ladder.

The Prime Minister examines the self-made man's success at representing himself as a gentleman and thereby winning access to an old English family by marrying one of its daughters. Here, Trollope uses the story of Lopez, the masked Jew, to revise once again the traditional marriage plot of English comedy. As in *The Eustace Diamonds*, a suspected Jew not only woos but wins the hand of an Englishwoman who is supposed to bring with her a rich inheritance. Such marriages have, after all, become the signs of the times: "peers' daughters were bestowing themselves on Jews and shopkeepers" (*PM*, 1.77). When Lopez becomes a suitor for Emily Wharton's hand, a string of questions about his family origins and social status is voiced by Emily's father: "I don't know who your father was,—whether he was an Englishman, whether he was a Christian, whether he was a Protestant,—not even whether he was a gentleman." When Lopez admits that his father was "a Portuguese" and his mother "an English lady," and claims that he himself is an English Protestant, Mr. Wharton feels that at least "the foreign blood was proved," and what is more, that "he detected Jewish signs" (*PM*, 1.27–28).

These signs explode in a series of racist slurs and epithets, anchored in Shakespeare's two most famous plays about racial prejudice. First, Trollope reimagines *Othello*, with Lopez the dark-skinned interloper who uses magic to steal the daughter from her father and her fellow countrymen:

[Mr. Wharton] thought as did Brabantio, that it could not be that without magic his daughter who had—
    "The wealthy curled darlings of our nation,
    Would ever have, to incur a general mock,
    Run from her guardage to the sooty bosom
    Of such a thing as"—
this distasteful Portuguese. (*PM*, 1.117)

This allusion allows a double racial slur to tag Lopez throughout the novel: he is "a black Portuguese nameless Jew" (*PM*, 1.146), "a greasy, black foreigner" (*PM*, 1.152). After Lopez's suicide, the narrator remarks that "a self-inflicted death caused by remorse will, in the minds of many, wash a blackamoor almost white" (*PM*, 2.205). And even after his death, Lopez's blackness has the power to defile Emily, for blackness, like Jewishness, is a contaminant; Emily describes herself as "foul and blackened" (*PM*, 2.330), as "black and defiled" (*PM*, 2.341).

Lopez is made to confess his identity with another Shakespearean outsider, as if attesting to the Jewish identity of which he is suspected. In the habit of alluding to *The Merchant of Venice*, Lopez first describes himself to Mr. Wharton as a kind of merchant prince: "As with the merchants whom Shakespeare and the other dramatists described,—so it is with me. My caravels are out at sea, and will not always come home in time" (*PM*, 2.51). This Bassanio, an adventurer who seeks his financial security in a rich wife, describes himself as Antonio, only later to confess: "I'm like Shylock, you know" (*PM*, 2.58). When Lopez declares that he likes "to know that my money is fructifying" (*PM*, 2.58), he not only recapitulates Shylock's ideas on the breeding of money but discloses the motivation of the Jewish adventurer cast in the role of the Jewish lover: he is the man who merges financial negotiation and sexual propagation. This is the suitor for whom "the love of money" (*PM*, 2.275) takes precedence over other kinds of love. By turning the man who enters the marriage plot not for love but for money (Shakespeare's Bassanio) into a Jew, even into a type of Shylock, Trollope supplements and completes the anti-Semitism of Shakespeare's text.

Critics have noted that Lopez is named after the historical figure who is often seen as the catalyst for Shakespeare's writing of *The Merchant of Venice*.[14] Dr. Roderigo Lopez, a Portuguese New Christian who was deeply involved in the Marrano community of London, became medical attendant to Elizabeth in 1586 and was arrested in 1593 and executed in 1594 for plotting to poison the queen[15]—a case history that could be read as a kind of parable of the life and death of the secret Jew who subversively turns on the society he has infiltrated and exploited. Both in Elizabethan and Victorian England, then, the Jewish threat to English culture is personified in the secret Jew whose lineage can be traced to the Iberian Peninsula—a pertinent reminder of the origins of the man who was serving as actual prime minister when *The Prime Minister* appeared.

The secret Jew's invasion of English culture is represented by Lopez's intrusion into the traditional (Christian) marriage plot. Marking Lopez, like Emilius before him, with a grotesque erotic appeal, Trollope mocks the Christian woman who, in a kind of perversion, finds him appealing. Lizzie is sexually excited by those qualities that mark Emilius as a Jew: "She found his hooky nose to be handsome" (*ED*, 2.363); "She certainly liked the grease and nastiness" (*ED*, 2.314). In *The Prime Minister* the erotic appeal of the Jewish man is a sign of the degeneration of the times: "Girls . . . like dark, greasy men with slippery voices, who are up to dodges and full of secrets" (*PM*, 1.139). Lopez the interloper, the foreign Jew, is represented as stealing the English heroine from her Christian lover, Arthur Fletcher, whose unrequited love is represented as "crucify-ing him": "he was so maimed and mutilated as to be only half a man" (*PM*, 1.141–42). The crucified Christian bridegroom, "this paragon" who "looked like one of those happy sons of the gods" (*PM*, 1.135), becomes the latest casualty in the Jewish subversion of Christian mar-riage. Shylock's castrating knife (which intrudes on Bassanio and Portia's nuptials) has been exchanged for a subtler means of preventing Christian marriages, in Lopez's tempting looks and manners; "a bright eye, and a hook nose, and a glib tongue" (*PM*, 1.146), "soft words and a false demeanour" (*PM*, 2.290) win Emily from Arthur Fletcher.

In a particularly noxious engraving on this theme of intermarriage, the predatory and bestial Jewish suitor, looking as if he is about to feed on the Christian woman's body, woos and converts in one gesture (figure 20). The Jewish suitor who courts, consumes, and converts the Christian woman threatens the annihilation of Christianity and the Judaization of England. In Trollope's novels the Jewish lover is portrayed as a magician who wins the heroine through deceit and then becomes in marriage a nightmarish monstrosity, a "terrible incubus" (*PM*, 2.126), a "dreadful incubus" (*PM*, 2.175)—like Mr. Emilius, who is described as "the in-cubus which afflicted [Lizzie]" (*PR*, 2.290). Even Emily, once married to Lopez, seems to confirm her father's worst fears about Lopez's powers over her: "It seemed to her that she had given herself over body and soul and mind to some evil genius, and that there was no escape" (*PM*, 2.62). This figure of the incubus suggests that these husbands, Emilius and Lopez, are illegal sexual invaders, robbers who steal, and then control and exhaust, their wives' bodies as well as their wealth.

In Trollope's work the Jew is consistently viewed as a foreigner, and the picture of Emilius and Lopez as performers of an illegal sexual act repre-sents the Jew as making a false claim on Englishwomen, even though

Figure 20. Engraved from a drawing by Frederick George Byron. Published by William Holland, 1801. Courtesy of the Library of the Jewish Theological Seminary of America.

Lopez is born and bred in England, and both Emilius and Lopez are legally married to the women on whom they are said to prey as foreign invaders. The protection of the daughter functions as a kind of metonymy for the protection of the nation, so while the actual foreign invasion of England is discredited—"No one really thought that the Prussians and French combined would invade our shores and devastate our fields, and plunder London, and carry our daughters away into captivity" (*PM*, 2.148)—Trollope represents another kind of invasion, the Jewish invasion of the English nation. From the beginning, Mr. Wharton views Lopez's pursuit of his daughter as a kind of invasion; Lopez's schemes are an attempt "to assault and invade the very kernel of another man's heart, to share with him, and indeed to take from him, the very dearest of his possessions, to become part and parcel with him" (*PM*, 1.29). So, what Trollope satirized in *Barchester Towers*, the protection of the old Saxon ways from foreign invasion, becomes realized in *The Prime Minister* with Mr. Wharton cast in the role of guarding "a name so grandly Saxon as Wharton" (*PM*, 1.197). Mr. Wharton protects this Saxon name from a Jewish invasion, for he knows: "The world as it was now didn't care whether its sons-in-law were Christian or Jewish;—whether they had the fair skin and bold eyes and uncertain words of an English gentleman, or the swarthy colour and false grimace and glib tongue of some inferior Latin race" (*PM*, 1.132). Cast in the role of foreign invader, Lopez does in fact threaten to "carry our daughters away into captivity" when, in pursuit of a money-making scheme in Guatemala, he attempts to force Emily into expatriation. Thus, the historical record in England is revised: the banishment of the Jews from England is rewritten as the Jew's "threatened banishment" (*PM*, 2.113) of the Saxon daughter.

Like Disraeli, Lopez seems to succeed because he is a superb actor. He is the Jew who largely masters the outward appearance of an English gentleman. The analytical powers of the narrator are frequently required to expose Lopez's attempt to reinvent himself as a gentleman: "In a sense he was what is called a gentleman. He knew how to speak, and how to look, how to use a knife and fork, how to dress himself, and how to walk. But he had not the faintest notion of the feelings of a gentleman" (*PM*, 2.168). Similarly, the narrator disqualifies Lopez's claims to being English: "Though this man had lived nearly all his life in England, he had not quite acquired that knowledge of the way in which things are done which is so general among men of a certain class" (*PM*, 2.24). This narrative voice positions the narrator and his readers in the same camp; it becomes the Englishman's responsibility to recognize the false article, the Jew pretending to be an English gentleman. By such a device, Trollope legitimizes Mr. Wharton's prejudices, which position Lopez and Fletcher in antithetical roles—"With such an English gentleman as Arthur Fletcher on one side, and with this Portuguese Jew on the other" (*PM*, 1.124). While the novel opens by tentatively accepting the world's opinion of Lopez—"It was admitted on all sides that Ferdinand Lopez was a 'gentleman'"—it ends by exposing the artifice of the fatherless and motherless self-made man, as if to reinstate the traditional definition of gentleman that Trollope quotes from Dr. Johnson, "a man of ancestry" (*PM*, 1.2).

The novel reestablishes the traditional connection between gentleman and Christian by recalling the kind of wordplay on "gentle / Gentile" that Shakespeare was fond of using. While Emily tries to overcome her father's prejudice for "this gift of gentle blood and of gentle nurture" (*PM*, 1.189), eventually she seems to accept her father's proverb, even with its racial overtones: "you could not make a silk purse out of a sow's ear" (*PM*, 1.289). In the end she seems to give the kind of racially based reading of her two lovers that her father initially gave, when she contrasts (the Saxon) Fletcher, "fair-haired, open-eyed," with (the Jew) Lopez: "She had learned the false meaning of every glance of his eyes, the subtlety of his mouth, the counterfeit manoeuvres of his body,—the deceit even of his dress. He had been all a lie from head to foot" (*PM*, 2.289–90). Such representations recall the kind of debate pursued in the popular press over whether or not a Jew could be a gentleman. In an article entitled "Gentlemen Jews," *Punch* questions the *Morning Post*'s calling a Jew "a gentleman," and then goes on to quote from Sir Thomas Browne the old claim that "those odoriferous people, the Jews" were "aromatised by their conversion" (February 17, 1844)—as if conversion were an elixir empowered to make a Jew a gentleman.

Lopez's decision to flee England is the beginning of the end of what might be termed his English masquerade. Ultimately, his plan to flee is represented as an attempt to escape a Christian nation whose stringent moral standards he cannot keep, to escape "from the miserable thraldom of this country bound in swaddling cloths" (*PM*, 2.139). The modern-day Jew, not exiled by the state's proclamation of expulsion, decides to leave because he discovers that he has no place in Christian England, that he can no longer support his disguise as a Christian English gentleman. He decides to leave in recognition of his own foreignness. After all, England seems unable finally to support him and his schemes: "He had failed in everything as far as England was concerned" (*PM*, 2.171).

The Prime Minister ends like those racial father-and-daughter plots examined in chapter 4, where the values of fatherhood and fatherland are reinstated over the claims of the interloping, or racially other, young lover. The father's (racial) objections to the lover win out in the end, and the father and daughter are realigned against the lover-husband. Lopez recognizes his failure as interloper when he confesses about Emily, "she clung to her father instead of clinging to her husband" (*PM*, 2.170). But while in the texts I have examined it was a minority race (Jew or Gypsy) that was threatened in the racial plot, in *The Prime Minister* it is the daughter of the hegemonic community who stands in need of protection and who is required to uphold her father's religion and race. Arthur woos Emily again, and Emily is "taken back into the flock" (*PM*, 2.368), re-establishing the Christian structure of comedy and undermining the Jew's attempt to threaten this structure. In a fundamentally Christian act, Emily recognizes Arthur as "the very pearl" (*PM*, 1.134) that he is, like the "pearl of great price" in the Christian parable (Matt. 13:46). The "crucified" Christian bridegroom, once mutilated, is now resurrected, and instead of threatening the father's domain, the young lover comes to reinstate it, to make heaven on earth; the Christian bridegroom does not steal the bride from the father but shows her the way back into the fold, functioning as an agent of the father's reminder to the wayward daughter: "You are one of us" (*PM*, 2.377). The Saxon heiress is reeducated, reminded of the insuperable differences between Englishmen and foreigners, Christians and Jews.

All of this is made possible only after the Jew has been eradicated from the plot. Conversion, a kind of deus ex machina in *The Merchant of Venice*, is no longer a suitable means of effecting the comic denouement; in fact, conversion is viewed as part of the social problem the text attempts to expose, for conversion is the Jew's passport into Christian society. Therefore, a more desperate means of erasing the Jew is imagined in the cases of both Melmotte (who poisons himself) and Lopez (who jumps under the wheels of a train). Suicide is a kind of murder about which the Christian community can feel guiltless, because the murderer and the victim are one. Just as Lopez decides to flee on his own instead of being forcibly expelled, so he decides to take his own life instead of being murdered; no Christian hand is raised against this Jew. Lopez's suicide amounts to a kind of Christian fantasy. The false Christian mask that the Jew wears finally leads the Jew to complete (self-)annihilation as the result of being unable to sustain the masquerade. The self-made man "logically" becomes the self-destroyed man. No marks exist to identify the dead man because his identity, from head to foot, has been nothing but a lie: "It seemed as though the man had been careful to carry with him no record of identity, the nature of which would permit it to outlive the crash of the train. No card was found, no scrap of paper with his name; and it was discovered at last that when he left the house on the fatal morning he had been careful to dress himself in shirt and socks, with handkerchief and collar that had been newly purchased for his proposed journey and which bore no mark. The fragments of his body set identity at defiance, and even his watch had been crumpled into ashes" (*PM*, 2.195). The life of the fatherless and motherless orphan ends in the kind of indistinguishable nothingness out of which he seems to have come.

The Christian fantasy of *The Prime Minister* keeps the Jew outside the social order in both the private and the public domains: he is ejected from the domestic plot by failing as a husband, and he is ejected from the national plot by failing as a candidate for Parliament. It is this second plot that comes closest to Trollope's own private fantasy—that is, to the way in which Disraeli "afflicted Trollope with the fascination of horror."[16] In producing *The Prime Minister* during Disraeli's prime ministry, Trollope yielded to a kind of social and political fantasy: Lopez, the man who runs but fails to win a seat in Parliament, is the epitome of the opportunism and moral bankruptcy of "the secret Jew," while Trollope makes his fictitious prime minister, Plantagenet Palliser, a paragon of virtue and "the truest nobleman in all England" (*PM*, 1.168). Trollope rewrites contemporary British politics, unseating Disraeli the Jew and replacing him with the perfect English gentleman. Such an act must remind us that novel-writing for Trollope was a consciously political act that had by the 1870s come to take the place of the parliamentary career he lamented not having; so it is no surprise that he describes his novel-writing as an analogous activity to Disraeli's political career, remarking "how frequently I have used them (the Pallisers) for the expression of my political and social convictions. They have been as real to me as free trade was to Mr. Cobden, or the dominion of a party to Mr. Disraeli; and as I have not been able to speak from the benches of the House of Commons, or to thunder from platforms, or to be efficacious as a lecturer, they have served me as safety-valves by which to deliver my soul."[17] In *The Prime Minister*, Trollope delivers his soul in a blast of revenge at the Jew who not only accomplished the political goal that Trollope himself failed to achieve, but who achieved the position of prime minister.

In the end Trollope's Jew becomes a sign of the historical continuity of Jewish infiltration and subversion, especially insofar as he becomes a kind of reference point not only for the present Jewish prime minister, or for the historical Lopez who was convicted of attempting to poison the queen, but for the biblical Moses who brought the ten plagues on Egypt. In the story of Moses, the Jew who brought down the people among whom he had been raised, Trollope saw a lesson for his own time and his own people. Lopez's reinvention of his ancient ancestor's divinely ordered object, the spoliation of Egypt (Ex. 3:22), is meant to expose the Victorian Jew's vitriol against the English nation within which he and his people live as aliens in bondage. Lopez tells Emily: "You know that the Israelites despoiled the Egyptians, and it was taken as a merit on their part. Your father is an Egyptian to me, and I will despoil him" (*PM*, 2.122–23).

In his contemporary biography of Disraeli, T. P. O'Connor presents the prime minister as the model of this kind of Jewish revenge and subversion. Disraeli is the Jewish outsider who, having won access to the innermost circles of English culture, feels nothing but contempt for the English:

Lord Beaconsfield knows the English people: it is a knowledge of which he often boasts; and the boast is made in the tone of the foreigner who is eyeing with tolerant contempt from the easy height of his own superior blood the vagaries of an eccentric, vulgar, if not barbarous race. And that is the view of every genuine Jew for the Christian people among whom he lives. He bows down within the recesses of his heart before his own people, as still, if not the chosen of God, yet as immeasurably supreme among men; and other nations are but the mushroom races, whose fathers were barbarians when Judaea was the land of civilization.[18]

Disraeli becomes a paradigm by which we can read Jewish identity: every Jew is a crypto-Jew, performing the rite of secret worship, if not to the Jewish God, then to the Jewish race; and every Jew is motivated in the same way, by secret contempt for the people among whom he lives. It is these hidden recesses of the secret Jew's heart that must be revealed to the English nation—especially when such a Jew heads the government—lest England be despoiled like Egypt.

"An accomplished Egyptian": Eliot's English Gentleman

In 1847–48, almost three decades before publishing *Daniel Deronda,* Eliot recorded her reactions to Disraeli's popular trilogy, first by chastising Sara Hennell "for being in the least pleased with 'Tancred'" (*GEL,* 1.241), and then by excoriating Disraeli for his "theory of races" in a letter to John Sibree, Jr.:

> The fellowship of race, to which D'Israeli exultingly refers the munifence of Sidonia, is so evidently an inferior impulse which must ultimately be superseded that I wonder even he, Jew as he is, dares to boast of it. My Gentile nature kicks most resolutely against any assumption of superiority in the Jews, and is almost ready to echo Voltaire's vituperation. I bow to the supremacy of Hebrew poetry, but much of their early mythology and almost all their history is utterly revolting. Their stock has produced a Moses and a Jesus, but Moses was impregnated with Egyptian philosophy and Jesus is venerated and adored by us only for that wherein he transcended or resisted Judaism. . . . Everything *specifically* Jewish is of a low grade.

This response, in which Eliot seems about to choose the notorious anti-Semitism of Voltaire against Disraeli's Hebrasim, will be revised in *Daniel Deronda.* Nonetheless, Eliot's response is significant on several counts. It shows how widely diffused and accepted theories of race had become by the 1840s, for while Eliot objects to the notion of the Jews as superior, she accepts the notion of superior and inferior races: "Extermination up to a certain point seems to be the law for the inferior races—for the rest, fusion both for physical and moral ends" (*GEL,* 1.246–47). The extermination of "inferior races," we have already seen, was central to the conception of the origins of the nation-state that was being worked out in the first half of the nineteenth century.

Eliot's early response to Disraeli's novels also suggests how strong a hold the ideological division between Judaism and Christianity had on English thought in the 1840s. This division, which she would later repudiate, was especially popular in the Liberal Anglican view of history in which racial typology and religious dogma often met.[19] Eliot would have seen the insistent way in which the division between Judaism and Christianity was maintained when she read Henry Hart Milman's warning in his *History of the Jews:*

> The Jews were in fact more or less barbarians, . . . up to the "fulness of time," when Christianity, the religion of civilized and enlightened man, was to reveal in all its perfection the nature of the beneficent Creator. . . . [T]he Deity did not yet think it time to correct the savage, I will add, unchristian spirit, inseparable from that period of the social state. In fact, in our reverence for "the Bible," we are apt to throw back the full light of Christianity on the Older Volume, but we should ever remember that the best and wisest Jews were not Christians.[20]

Precisely such a view was being critiqued by Disraeli when he argued for the historical continuity between Judaism and Christianity—indeed, for Christianity's immense debt to Judaism—but in Eliot's reaction to Disraeli's novels we see the way in which he may have produced the opposite effect on his readers. Eliot's Gentile nature kicks against Disraeli's Hebraism, and her understanding of Christianity in 1848 naively divides Jesus from the religion and the culture in which he was bred and nurtured.

By the time Eliot came to write *Daniel Deronda,* however, she represented the belief in the radical division between Judaism and Christianity as the central mark of English Philistinism. After all, both Emanuel Deutsch, in his celebrated article on the Talmud that appeared in the *British Quarterly* in 1867, and Matthew Arnold, in *Culture and Anarchy* (1869) and *Literature and Dogma* (1873), had already taken steps to repair the rift between Judaism and Christianity. Eliot met Deutsch in 1866 and remained close friends with him until his death in 1873; she read his article on the Talmud in proof and enthusiastically recommended it to her friends (*GEL,* 4.385, 390). Arnold recorded the popular reception of Deutsch's article in a letter to Lady de Rothschild: "The English religious world is reading the article with extraordinary avidity and interest. What most interests them [is] the abundance of Christian doctrine and dispositions present in Judaism towards the time of the Christian era." In the same letter he recognized how useful Judaism could be in attempting to dislodge the English from their "present conception of Christianity as something utterly unique, isolated, and self-subsistent"[21]—that is, as entirely independent of Judaism, out of which Christianity developed. In other words, Deutsch's Talmud article seemed to confirm what Arnold was just about to claim in *Culture and Anarchy,* namely, the historical connections between Judaism and Christianity.

But Deutsch's article goes well beyond what Arnold would allow in *Culture and Anarchy,* which after all recommended Hellenism over Hebraism (while demonstrating the continuity between Judaism and Christianity in the most general cultural terms). Deutsch opens his article by providing a succinct history of the Talmud, including the attempts made by Christians and Jewish converts to Christianity at "the wholesale murder of a book 'written by Christ's nearest relations.' "[22] In chapter 1, I explained how the conversionists consistently picked out the Talmud for attack, going so far as to claim that "neither the Romans nor the Greeks, neither Spanish Inquisition nor Damascus fiends, have ever caused to the Jews such a lasting loss as that which the Talmud has caused to them."[23] It should come as no surprise that Moses Margoliouth, the converted Jew who became a historian of the Jews and an advocate of the London Society, called Deutsch's article (without ever actually naming it) "the notoriously highly-coloured and romantic article, which appeared a couple of years ago in the 'Quarterly Review,' under the title *Talmud.* . . . I venture to say that no bantam has ever had the assurance to make such a jubilant noise, over so unsavoury a heap . . . as some Jews have made over the Talmud since that article was published. The marvel is, that many sceptical Gentile 'Christians' should take the writer's *ipse dixit* for sober truth."[24] Margoliouth was right about one thing, the immense sympathy that writers like Arnold and Eliot felt for Deutsch's attempt to dismantle the Christian myths that put up an impassable gulf between Judaism and Christianity, between the Talmud and the New Testament:

> Were not the whole of our general views on the difference between Judaism and Christianity greatly confused, people would certainly not be so very much surprised at the striking parallels of dogma and parable, of allegory and proverb, exhibited by the Gospel and the Talmudical writings . . . for such terms as "Redemption," "Baptism," "Grace," "Faith," "Salvation," "Regeneration," "Son of Man," "Son of God," "Kingdom of Heaven," were not, as we are apt to think, invented by Christianity, but were household words of Talmudical Judaism.[25]

In a powerful textual analysis of the Talmud, Deutsch exposes Christianity's co-optation of the central terms of Hebrew Scripture as Christian. In *Daniel Deronda*, Mordecai makes the same point, characterizing the Christian's response to the Jew, "What is yours is ours, and no longer yours" (*DD*, 591), while Deronda (sounding like Disraeli) argues, "Our religion is chiefly a Hebrew religion" (*DD*, 424).[26] Deutsch concludes by making the point that had been made in the 1830s and 1840s by Isaac D'Israeli (even while attacking rabbinical learning and the Talmud) and then by Benjamin Disraeli—namely, that Christianity historically became the great popularizer of Judaic values: "It is the glory of Christianity to have carried those golden germs, hidden in the schools and among the 'silent community' of the learned, into the market of Humanity. It has communicated that 'Kingdom of Heaven,' of which the Talmud is full from the first page to the last, to the herd, even to the lepers."[27]

Like Arnold in the late 1860s and early 1870s, Eliot took as her goal in *Daniel Deronda*, and later in "The Modern Hep! Hep! Hep!" chapter of *Impressions of Theophrastus Such* (1879), the reeducation of the English nation in its shared heritage with the Jews, even in what she called "affinities of disposition between our own race and the Jewish."[28] Reminiscent of Arnold's letter explaining the usefulness of Judaism to critique the English view of Christianity as unique and self-sufficient, Eliot wrote to Harriet Beecher Stowe in 1876, explaining the motives behind *Daniel Deronda* by attacking the Philistinism of the English—that is, their failure to recognize the origins of Christianity in Judaism: "There is nothing I should care more to do, if it were possible, than to rouse the imagination of men and women to a vision of human claims in those races of their fellow-men who most differ from them in customs and beliefs. But towards the Hebrews we western people who have been reared in Christianity, have a peculiar debt and, whether we acknowledge it or not, a peculiar thoroughness of fellowship in religious and moral sentiment" (*GEL*, 6.301–2). Here we see Eliot characterizing the relationship between Judaism and Christianity in terms of the "debt" that Disraeli worked so hard to encourage the English nation to acknowledge, while elsewhere, in a bold gesture, Eliot underscores her own understanding of the historical link between Judaism and Christianity by echoing the kind of formulation for which Disraeli was notorious: "The Christ of Matthew had the heart of a Jew" (*ITS*, 264). Eliot, who patronizingly mocked Sidonia in 1848, now echoes him, as if she suddenly inherits his task, the (re)education of the English gentleman.

In "The Modern Hep! Hep! Hep!" Eliot attempts to explain how and why her countrymen at the present time fail to recognize Christianity's debt to Judaism. In so doing, she records the decline in the millenarian tradition that I have explored as a powerful influence on English thought from the time of the French Revolution through the 1840s: "Formerly, evangelical orthodoxy was prone to dwell on the fulfilment of prophecy in the 'restoration of the Jews.' Such interpretation of the prophets is less in vogue now. The dominant mode is to insist on a Christianity that disowns its origins, that is not a substantial growth having a genealogy, but is a vaporous reflex of modern notions" (*ITS*, 264). She goes on to speculate about a specific contemporary cause behind the revival of anti-Semitism in the 1870s—the public prominence of Disraeli: "The value of the Hebrew race has been measured by the unfavourable opinion of a prime minister who is a Jew by lineage" (*ITS*, 261); she finds in the fact that "the head of the Conservative ministry in England is a Jew . . . the ground for the obvious jealousy which is now stimulating the revived expression of old antipathies" (*ITS*, 255). I will argue that *Daniel Deronda* functions both to revive the millenarian notion of the restoration of the Jews by secularizing it (that is, by endorsing the establishment of a national state for the Jews) and to overturn the anti-Semitism that is specifically based in a kind of racial jealousy surrounding Disraeli.

In her letter to Stowe, Eliot characterizes the consequences of the failed historical consciousness of the modern Englishman:

Can anything be more disgusting than to hear people called "educated" making small jokes about eating ham, and showing themselves empty of any real knowledge as to the relation of their own social and religious life to the history of the people they think themselves witty in insulting? They hardly know that Christ was a Jew. And I find men educated at Rugby supposing that Christ spoke Greek. To my feeling, this deadness to the history which has prepared half our world for us, this inability to find interest in any form of life that is not clad in the same coat-tails and flounces as our own lies very close to the worst kind of irreligion. The best that can be said of it is, that it is a sign of the intellectual narrowness—in plain English, the stupidity, which is still the average mark of our culture. (*GEL*, 6.302)

While in reacting against Disraeli in 1848 Eliot dissociated Moses and Jesus from their Jewish origins, here she argues the opposite, recalling the kind of argument that Disraeli made in Parliament, "All the early Christians were Jews"[29]—though, as I have shown, Milman worked to undermine such a view, warning his fellow Christians "that we should ever remember that the best and wisest Jews were not Christians." Eliot's attack on English stupidity echoes Arnold—she and Lewes read Arnold's essays on religion and culture with approval (*GEL*, 6.87)—but her remark about Rugby looks like a barb aimed at Thomas Arnold's (and perhaps even Matthew Arnold's) Hellenism. In any case, the educated Rugby man, uneducated in the Judaic origins of Christianity, is the sign of the miseducation of the English gentleman, one of *Daniel Deronda*'s central themes.

Not accidentally, Eliot directs her explanation of the "national disgrace" of England to Harriet Beecher Stowe. Stowe is a crucial mediating figure between Eliot's rejection in 1848 of the Jewish themes of Disraeli's trilogy and her attempt almost three decades later in *Daniel Deronda* to expose English anti-Semitism and to celebrate Judaic culture. It was in reading Stowe's antislavery novels that Eliot began to see the dignity of "the fellowship of race," at which she had sneered when responding to Disraeli's trilogy in 1848. In a review of Stowe's *Dred* that Eliot wrote for the *Westminster Review* in 1856, we begin to see her change of mind on the question of race in fiction. In fact, it is under the tutelage of Stowe, and through the additional influence of Scott and Thierry, that Eliot first comes to contemplate racial and national subjects for her own work, bearing fruit in the 1860s and 1870s in such texts as *Romola, The Spanish Gypsy,* and finally *Daniel Deronda* and *Theophrastus Such.* In her review Eliot makes the following claims for Stowe: "Mrs. Stowe has *invented* the Negro novel, and it is a novel not only fresh in its scenery and its manners, but possessing that *conflict of races* which Augustin Thierry has pointed out as the great source of romantic interest—witness 'Ivanhoe.' "[30] Eliot is engaged here in the delineation of a literary tradition to which she will shortly add herself, beginning with *Romola,* a tradition focused on social history, racial conflicts, and national interests. Late in her career, with the publication of *Daniel Deronda,* she was proud to reflect on her influence in this tradition: "A statesman who shall be nameless has said that I first opened to him a vision of Italian life, then of Spanish, and now I have kindled in him a quite new understanding of the Jewish people. This is what I wanted to do—to widen the English vision a little" (*GEL,* 6.304).

Eliot makes even greater claims for Stowe: "But Mrs. Stowe's novels have not only that grand element—conflict of races; they have another element equally grand, which she also shares with Scott, and in which she has, in some respects, surpassed him. This is the exhibition of a people to whom what we may call Hebraic Christianity is still a reality, still an animating belief, and by whom the theocratic conceptions of the Old Testament are literally applied to their daily life."[31] In recognizing in Scott's Covenanters (in *Old Mortality*) and Stowe's Negroes (in *Uncle Tom's Cabin* and *Dred*) a people who believe in "what we may call Hebraic Christianity," Eliot finds practical examples of what she will later define as the profound connection between Judaism and Christianity. Based on the figure of the persecuted Israel, the depictions of religious persecution in Scott and racial persecution in Stowe were stepping-stones to Eliot's own depiction of religious and racial persecution in *Daniel Deronda.* But in Eliot's novel the persecuted Israel signals not merely a well-known Christian figure, as in Scott and Stowe, but the contemporary phenomenon of anti-Semitism.

Stowe's influence on Eliot seems to me to have been even more specific. Isn't the ending of *Uncle Tom's Cabin* a blueprint for the ending of *Daniel Deronda?* Stowe's novel ends with George Harris, the African American who can pass as a white man, deciding to leave the United States to dedicate himself to the work of his oppressed race, especially in the cause of bestowing on them a national identity: "It is with the oppressed, enslaved African race that I cast in my lot. . . . The desire and yearning of my soul is for an African *nationality*."[32] *Daniel Deronda* ends with Eliot's Jewish hero, who can pass as a Christian, leaving England to dedicate himself to the work of his oppressed race, especially in the cause of establishing its national identity. In "The Modern Hep! Hep! Hep!" Eliot makes explicit her comparison between these two oppressed races: "As the slaveholders in the United States counted the curse on Ham a justification of negro slavery, so the curse on the Jews was counted a justification for hindering them from pursuing agriculture and handicrafts; for marking them out as execrable figures by a peculiar dress . . . ; for putting it to them whether they would be baptized or burned" (*ITS*, 247). Finally, in claiming that " 'Uncle Tom' and 'Dred' will assure [Stowe] a place in that highest rank of novelists who can give us a national life in all its phases,"[33] Eliot was preparing for her own depiction of national life and national disgrace. In *Daniel Deronda,* Eliot transforms Stowe's depiction of the American disgrace of slavery into the English disgrace of anti-Semitism. Eliot wrote to Stowe in 1876, "not only towards the Jews, but towards all oriental peoples with whom we English come in contact, a spirit of arrogance and contemptuous dictatorialness is observable which has become a national disgrace to us" (*GEL*, 6.301).

Predictably, the plot of conversion in *Daniel Deronda* is initially directed at Mirah Cohen, the Jewish heroine, through a direct reference to the London Society. On hearing about Mirah, Lady Mallinger remarks "that there was a Society for the Conversion of the Jews, and that it was to be hoped Mirah would embrace Christianity" (*DD*, 267). Even the Meyrick family seems obsessively concerned about Mirah's Judaism and her potential conversion: "Amy and Mab, who had accompanied Mirah to the synagogue, found the Jewish faith less reconcilable with their wishes in her case than in that of Scott's Rebecca," and Mab self-deprecatingly asks, "How can an ugly Christian, who is always dropping her work, convert a beautiful Jewess, who has not a fault?" (*DD*, 410). And Amy's naive, Christian-centered universe seems to her the inevitable end for Mirah: "Perhaps it [Judaism] would gradually melt away from her, and she would pass into Christianity like the rest of the world" (*DD*, 410).

Hans, hoping to marry Mirah, falls back on the male-empowered marriage plot as the conventional means of Mirah's conversion: "who ever heard in tale or history that a woman's love went in the track of her race and religion? Moslem and Jewish damsels were always attracted towards Christians" (*DD*, 798). In such a view, Hans attempts to define Mirah not as Rebecca but as Jessica. And Mrs. Meyrick constructs a happy utopia based on the ideology of assimilation and conversion: "But if Jews and Jewesses went on changing their religion, and making no difference between themselves and Christians, there would come a time when there would be no Jews to be seen" (*DD*, 425). In other words, Mrs. Meyrick openly contemplates conversion as the process of Jewish annihilation.

But in the course of *Daniel Deronda*, Gwendolen becomes the novel's central object of conversion as part of Eliot's profound revision of the traditional plot of conversion in the English novel. Only two pages after it is suggested that Mirah seek salvation through the London Society, Gwendolen notices in the railway station "the texts in large letters calling on her to repent and be converted" (*DD*, 269). Gwendolen essentially ignores the Evangelical texts that indiscriminately make this exhortation to all passers-by. At this point in the novel, Gwendolen thinks of such texts as merely "part of the dreary prospect opened by her family troubles" (*DD*, 269). In fact, in the early sections of the novel Gwendolen periodically trivializes the idea of conversion. She uses the term playfully, to represent her own power to enthrall and transform the men around her—conversion here is no more than a kind of feminine charm. After failing to impress Klesmer the music master, she thinks of opportunities "for converting him to a more admiring state of mind" (*DD*, 82); and after displaying her talents at archery, she hopes to win Grandcourt's admiration for the sport, and of course, for herself—"Are you converted today?" (*DD*, 146), she asks him.

In constructing a novel around a heroine in the "Jewish" plot who is steadfast in her faith, refusing the pressures of conversion, and a heroine in the "English" plot who undergoes the powerful process of conversion (not to Judaism but to the religious life in general), Eliot subverts the plot of conversion so popular in the nineteenth-century English novel. She had pointed out this kind of plot in a critique of those novels that convert the Jewish characters "after the shortest and easiest method approved by the 'Society for Promoting the Conversion of the Jews.' "[34] In displacing the plot of conversion from Mirah to Gwendolen, *Daniel Deronda* functions as a radical critique of such novels as *Leila Ada, The Jewish Convert, Julamerk; or, The Converted Jewess,* and *The Converted Jewess: A Memoir of Maria* —.

The plot of Gwendolen's conversion functions at the center of the larger plot of her (re)education, making us see the way in which the education plot in the bildungsroman often functions as a covert plot of conversion. Gwendolen's earlier education is everywhere anatomized in the novel: "Gwendolen's uncontrolled reading . . . had somehow not prepared her for this encounter with reality" (*DD*, 193); her "less expensive" education is compared with that of her male contemporaries (*DD*, 320–21); "her French reading had given her some girlish notions" (*DD*, 484). Deronda, on deciding that she is "ill-educated" (*DD*, 466), seems ready to cast himself in the role of her teacher, and she wonders "what books he would tell her to take up" (*DD*, 607). While Deronda's education of Gwendolen goes well beyond recommending good reading, the library becomes the place in which she seeks him out (in chapters 35 and 36) and the place in which she comes under both his pedagogical sway and his proselytizing power.

When the library begins to function "like a private chapel" (*DD*, 505), we see Deronda the teacher become confused with Deronda the priest: "Without the aid of sacred ceremony or costume, her feelings had turned this man, only a few years older than herself, into a priest" (*DD*, 485). At this moment the theme of education becomes confused with the theme of conversion, so that Gwendolen's reeducation does not simply include an occasional confession, but becomes nothing short of Gwendolen's "transforming process—all the old nature shaken to its depths" (*DD*, 477): "It is one of the secrets in that change of mental poise which has been fitly named conversion, that to many among us neither heaven nor earth has any revelation till some personality touches theirs with a peculiar influence, subduing them into receptiveness" (*DD*, 484–85).

Half-teacher and half-priest, Deronda educates and converts Gwendolen by offering her "the higher, the religious life" (*DD*, 507), what Arnold's religious essays of the early 1870s offered the English public. Deronda functions as Gwendolen's primary teacher in conduct, conceived along the lines that Arnold repeatedly outlined in his religious and social essays. Gwendolen is the perfect example of English Philistinism, for "her favourite key of life . . . [was] doing as she liked" (*DD*, 173)—the phrase is borrowed from the title of the second chapter of *Culture and Anarchy*, "Doing as One Likes." In confessing that in the past she has been in the habit of "doing as I liked" (*DD*, 501), Gwendolen now places her conduct entirely in Deronda's hands: "You must tell me what to think and what to do" (*DD*, 501).

By formulating Gwendolen's reeducation as a kind of conversion, Eliot explores the ways in which both processes involve power and force, even submission and coercion, for in *Daniel Deronda* both education and conversion are modes of mastery. The effect of Deronda's conversion of Gwendolen, for example, is represented in the following way: "Young reverence for one who is also young is the most coercive of all" (*DD*, 485). And when Gwendolen turns herself over to Deronda entirely, asking him to tell her what to think and do, she repeats the scene in which she turns herself over to her husband's brutal reign of terror. Dressed for dinner at Brackenshaw Castle, Gwendolen asks Grandcourt, "Am I altogether as you like?" (*DD*, 480), and when he answers "No," she asks, "How am I to alter myself?" (*DD*, 481), offering the same submission she offers to Deronda. Grandcourt forces Gwendolen to conform to her new role of "Mrs. Grandcourt," reminding us of what we have seen as the association between marriage and conversion, patriarchal processes in which changes of name and allegiance go hand in hand. So, Gwendolen's early, playful "conversion" of Grandcourt at the archery tournament has turned into his stifling conversion of her into "Mrs. Grandcourt." This scene of Gwendolen's submission to Grandcourt's desires occurs in the same chapter as Gwendolen's "conversion" (*DD*, 484) at the hands of Deronda, so that she becomes positioned between two masters who attempt to reinvent her, two powerful proselytizers, one attempting to master her soul, the other attempting to master her body.

These remakings of Gwendolen are paralleled by the same kind of coercive conversion to which both Deronda and Hans Meyrick attempt to submit Mirah, the ostensible object of conversion in the novel. In their preparations for launching Mirah's career in London, the men argue over the name she is to bear (chapter 37) and the dress she is to wear (chapter 39), recalling the scene in chapter 35 in which Grandcourt remakes Gwendolen as "Mrs. Grandcourt." Mirah wants to keep her real name, but Deronda protests: " 'I assure you, you must not be called Cohen. The name is inadmissable for a singer. This is one of the trifles in which we must conform to vulgar prejudice. We could choose some other name, however—such as singers ordinarily choose—an Italian or Spanish name, which would suit your *physique*.' To Deronda just now the name Cohen was equivalent to the ugliest of yellow badges" (*DD*, 524–25). While Deronda is angry at Hans for "the idea of appropriating her" (*DD*, 525), Deronda's attempt at suppressing Mirah's Jewish identity is tantamount to converting her. The English hero's conversion of Gwendolen is ironically mirrored in his conversion of the Jewish heroine—as if he succumbs, unwittingly, to the conventional plot of Jewish conversion, whereby his initial rescue of the Jewish heroine from death turns into his rescue of her from Judaism. The motive behind Deronda's rejection of the name Cohen is subtly mirrored, and thereby underscored, in Hans's rejection of the dress Mirah wants to wear: " 'It looks a little too theatrical. We must not make you a *role* of the poor Jewess—or of being a Jewess at all.' Hans had a secret desire to neutralize the Jewess in private life, which he was in danger of not keeping secret" (*DD*, 545–46). Deronda's complicity in the erasure of Mirah's Jewish identity plays a critical role in identifying the kind of reeducation he himself must undergo, even though he is so often cast in the role of "mentor" (*DD*, 520), for Gwendolen, for Mirah, and for Hans. Eliot in this way begins to question the kind of exaggerated power Deronda—in his role as guide, guardian, teacher, and priest—exerts over the lives of those around him.

All these scenes of the remaking of Gwendolen and Mirah occur under the title "Mordecai" because Mordecai is the novel's tutelary figure of education and conversion. He is the man who immediately strikes one as "a fervid student of some kind" (*DD*, 528), the man who is distinguished by his love of study, by the life-transforming education he had, and by the life-transforming education he offers. Mordecai is the man Daniel first meets in a bookstore, the man entrusted with the "guardianship of the old book-shop" (*DD*, 536). The encounters between Mordecai and Daniel in the old bookshop (chapters 33 and 40) recall the meetings between Gwendolen and Daniel in the library, and they mark a change in Daniel's role from mentor to pupil. Mordecai's entire story revolves around his student days—"my true life was nourished in Holland, at the feet of my mother's brother, a Rabbi skilled in special learning" (*DD*, 555)—and his days as a teacher in the present and future, for he is now in charge of educating Jacob Cohen and will soon become Deronda's mentor. Mordecai's education of the young Jacob looks like a system of indoctrination, especially since the boy so resists the learning Mordecai offers: "with the boy tethered, he [Mordecai] would begin to repeat a Hebrew poem of his own"; Mordecai is "satisfied if the young organs of speech would submit themselves" to the Hebrew words; "the boy will get them engraved within him . . . ; it is a way of printing"; "My words may rule him some day" (*DD*, 533). "His printing of Hebrew on little Jacob's mind" (*DD*, 537) is an attempt at guarding against conversion, or apostasy, or the kind of assimilation that so easily erases the Jew's particular identity and heritage in Protestant England. After all, what Mordecai finds articulated so often in England, most threateningly among Jews themselves, is an attitude of assimilation against which he hopes to guard Jacob: "There's no reason now why we shouldn't melt gradually into the populations we live among. That's the order of the day in point of progress. I would as soon my children married Christians as Jews" (*DD*, 586), remarks Gideon, one of Mordecai's fellow Jews at the Philosophers Club. In contemplating the way in which Mordecai's words fall on deaf ears, Deronda sympathizes with him more than with "a missionary tomahawked without any considerate rejection of his doctrines" (*DD*, 586), for the proselytizing Mordecai suffers the "slow martyrdom" (*DD*, 586) of having his ideas consistently mocked and resisted without the satisfaction of having anyone "converted to your doctrine" (*DD*, 595). In short, Mordecai is the ultimate example of the educator as proselytizer.

The most obvious model for the relationship between Mordecai and Daniel is that between Sidonia and Coningsby, but Eliot hints at an even earlier influence in Balfour of Burley (*GEL*, 6.223). Like Deronda, Henry Morton in *Old Mortality* is paralyzed by "a diffidence and reserve," even "an air of indecision and of indifference," despite his natural "detestation of oppression," and Balfour becomes the central agent in Morton's moral revolution: "The more artful Balfour then dismissed the impatient preacher, and returned to his proselyte," finally effecting "the conversion of young Morton to his cause."[35] Conversion, then, is the central figure for the change in the hero who has been paralyzed by indecision in both *Old Mortality* and *Daniel Deronda*.

Cast in the roles of pupil and disciple, Deronda experiences the immense and sometimes overwhelming power of Mordecai. In the final chapter of "Mordecai" Deronda experiences a kind of coercive conversion when Mordecai unaccountably asks him to accept a heritage he believes not to be his own: "you will take the sacred inheritance of the Jew" (*DD*, 558). Deronda feels "half dominated" (*DD*, 567) by Mordecai's ideas, by his "demand of discipleship" (*DD*, 570). So, while Deronda is engaged, consciously or unconsciously, in the education and conversion of Gwendolen, he begins to be educated and converted by Mordecai. And while Gwendolen asks Deronda to tell her what to think and do, Mordecai expects to see Deronda "believing my belief—being moved by my reasons—hoping my hope" (*DD*, 557), so that Gwendolen seems headed to lose herself in Deronda, Deronda in Mordecai.

To understand Eliot's focus on Deronda's education over the course of the novel, we must look first at the famous scene in which he is studying with his tutor as a boy of thirteen, the age at which he would be participating in the ceremony that would make him an adult member of the Jewish community. Instead, Daniel is pictured undergoing a kind of trauma that calls into doubt his origins and fails to find a place for him in any community. In this scene the young boy is studying a history book in the presence of his tutor. His "passion for history" (*DD*, 203) will soon disclose the lack of knowledge he has about his own history and, eventually, about the history of his people, the Jews. During the lesson, in discovering that the popes' and cardinals' "nephews" are in fact their illegitimate children, Daniel decides that he is Sir Hugo's illegitimate son. Eliot's irony makes us see the way in which the formal scene of education, with text and tutor in place, pales in significance beside the underground workings of Daniel's imagination—workings that shape his entire character, as "a premature reserve" (*DD*, 207) takes hold of the boy: "It is in such experiences of boy or girlhood, while elders are debating whether most education lies in science or literature, that the main lines of character are often laid down" (*DD*, 210). Moreover, the formal scene of education crystallizes what the novel will ultimately reveal as the boy's miseducation, really a double miseducation; not only does this scene of study lead to Daniel's incorrect reconstruction of his history, but it displaces the education that he should have as a Jew, a point that will be forcefully made later in the novel.

This primal scene of study shapes Deronda's desire for a particular kind of education; believing he is a bastard, he wants an education that will make him an English gentleman. But through his years at Cambridge he realizes the limits of such an education, so that he decides "to quit the university and go to study abroad" (*DD*, 224). When Sir Hugo questions him—"So you don't want to be an Englishman to the backbone after all?"—Daniel answers: "I want to be an Englishman, but I want to understand other points of view. And I want to get rid of a merely English attitude in studies" (*DD*, 224). Sir Hugo accepts his attempt at "doffing some of our national prejudices" (*DD*, 224), and Daniel completes his education abroad, but without having succeeded in doffing all the national prejudices, as becomes evident when certain events bring to the surface the tolerant English gentleman's anti-Semitism.

It is only when Deronda has completed his formal education in England and abroad that his reeducation—in Jewish history and culture—begins. The chapter in which Deronda meets Mirah opens: "It was already a year or more since he had come back to England, with the understanding that his education was finished, and that he was somehow to take his place in English society" (*DD*, 225). With this prelude we see once more the way in which Eliot critiques the institutions of formal education in order to chart the reeducation of her characters, for Daniel's education is far from being "finished." While rowing on the Thames, contemplating his own "roots of indecision" and "whether it were worth while to take part in the battle of the world" (*DD*, 225), Daniel discovers Mirah and rescues her from her attempt at suicide. At first this rescue may be read as a familiar scene in the tradition of heroic romance, with Daniel cast in the role of a latter-day Ivanhoe, the champion of the Jews who rescues the Jewish maiden from death, especially since Daniel and the Meyricks explicitly think of Mirah as Rebecca. But we come to see the way in which Daniel's rescue of Mirah functions as a kind of self-rescue, precisely insofar as this scene begins his reeducation.

The scene of rescue becomes the catalyst for Daniel's reeducation. He becomes enlisted in Mirah's quest to find her lost mother and brother, her lost Jewish origins, a quest that he discovers he is hardly prepared to undertake. "With all his masculine instruction"—as opposed to "the irregular foraging to which clever girls have usually been reduced"—Deronda is "roused . . . to the consciousness of knowing hardly anything about modern Judaism or the inner Jewish history" (*DD*, 411). For "his interest had never been practically drawn towards existing Jews, and the facts he knew about them, whether they walked conspicuous in fine apparel or lurked in by-streets, were chiefly of the sort most repugnant to him" (*DD*, 246). Hence the discovery of Mirah has as its immediate consequence the surfacing of Deronda's anti-Semitism, as he imagines his quest for Mirah's mother and brother: "he saw himself guided by some official scout into a dingy street; he entered through a dim doorway, and saw a hawk-eyed woman, rough-headed, and unwashed, cheapening a hungry girl's last bit of finery; or in some quarter . . . , he found himself under the breath of a young Jew talkative and familiar" (*DD*, 247). Like his fellow citizens, Deronda "regarded Judaism as a sort of eccentric fossilized form, which an accomplished man might dispense with study-ing," but Mirah "flashed on him the hitherto neglected reality that Juda-ism was something still throbbing in human lives." So "he began to look for the outsides of synagogues, and the titles of books about the Jews" (*DD*, 411). "He went often rambling in those parts of London which are most inhabited by common Jews: he walked to the synagogues at times of service, he looked into shops, he observed faces" (*DD*, 430). The meeting with Mirah initiates for Deronda nothing short of a course of study, a kind of ethnographic investigation of otherness, "very much as if, Mirah being related to Welsh miners, he had gone to look more closely at the ways of those people, not without wishing at the same time to get a little light of detail on the history of Strikes" (*DD*, 432). After all, the Meyricks think of her "as if she were a native from a new country" (*DD*, 409), while there are "minds to which the idea of live Jews, out of a book, suggested a difference deep enough to be almost zoological, as of a strange race in Pliny's Natural History that might sleep under the shade of its own ears" (*DD*, 775). In such passages the complete otherness of Jewish identity is made clear, even though Mirah explains to Deronda at their first meeting that she is English, an English Jew.

The investigation into Jewish culture that Deronda makes—as in the case of Maria Edgeworth's hero, Harrington—uncovers in the hero the conventional English prejudices against the Jews, even though the hero's quest often looks as if it were simply the product of a newly found philo-Semitism. For example, in both Edgeworth's and Eliot's novels the hero's anti-Semitism is exposed during his visit to a synagogue. In *Harrington* the hero's visit to the synagogue, where he is attempting to display his philo-Semitism, is cut short by an anti-Semitic recollection, a ghost of his former prejudice, that causes him to fall ill. In *Daniel Deronda* the hero's anti-Semitism is already on display before his arrival at the synagogue, when he notes the "Jew dialect" and the "chosen nose" (*DD*, 415) that mark the Jews in Frankfurt: "In his anxiety about Mirah's relatives, he had lately been thinking of vulgar Jews with a sort of personal alarm" (*DD*, 415). Deronda, "becoming more conscious that he was falling into unfairness and ridiculous exaggeration" (*DD*, 415), heads toward the synagogue, whose service he finds inspiring as an "expression of a binding history, tragic and yet glorious" (*DD*, 417). But as he notices the "many indifferent faces and vulgar figures," he has the supercilious thought that "he had probably been alone in this feeling, and perhaps the only person in the congregation for whom the service was more than a dull routine" (*DD*, 417). At this moment he stands in a particularly ironic position, as the Christian who understands Judaism, Hebrew Scripture, and Jewish history better than the Jew himself—that is, in the historical position of the Christian who co-opts Judaism for his own purposes.

The scene in the synagogue takes an unexpected turn when a Jew seems to claim Daniel for Judaism, reversing Daniel's absorption of Judaism into his own (universal and sentimental) system of values. As Deronda is about to leave, the man who had pushed an open prayer book before him during the service—a gesture in which the educator is once again a kind of proselytizer—makes a "claim" on Deronda, putting his hand on Deronda's arm: "Excuse me, young gentleman—allow me—what is your parentage—your mother's family—her maiden name?" Deronda responds abruptly and uncommunicatively: "I am an Englishman" (*DD*, 417). Daniel's (mis)construction of his origins has suddenly become useful; while he may be a bastard, at least he is an Englishman and not a Jew. Deronda's announcement of his Englishness is his defense against further inquiry about his origins and the sign of his growing paranoia about those origins, not to mention a protection of the privileges he enjoys as an English gentleman. In this scene Daniel in fact defers discovering his origins, for the stranger who "claims" him is Joseph Kalonymos, the close friend of Daniel's grandfather. And so it is that the visit to the synagogue, an investigation of the otherness of Judaic culture, sets in motion a series of events by which Deronda's own Jewish origins will be discovered to him.

Deronda precludes and postpones the solution to the mystery of both his own and Mirah's origins. He actually considers hiding from Mirah the mother and brother she seeks, contriving "to conceal the fact of close kindred" (*DD*, 435): "in both cases he felt that there might be an unfulfilled duty to a parent, but in both cases there was an overpowering repugnance to the possible truth" (*DD*, 429). This repugnance involves Deronda, otherwise so guileless, in a series of embarrassing deferrals and deceptions. First, he must admit that he is not seeking Mirah's family in the most direct or expeditious manner: "Why did he not address himself to an influential Rabbi or other member of a Jewish community, to consult on the chances of finding a mother named Cohen, with a son named Ezra, and a lost daughter named Mirah?" (*DD*, 430). Then, when he discovers a shop with the name "Ezra Cohen" over it, he does not immediately enter to make the necessary inquiry. Finally, some days later, when he returns to the shop, this time to enter, he constructs an elaborate scheme, a kind of disguise, that will allow him to control the effects of the information he seeks. He hopes to find out if the Cohens are Mirah's relatives, without letting them or Mirah herself know, so that he alone can be in charge of the power of disclosure. This means he must lie to the Cohen family and "ingratiate himself" (*DD*, 440) with the boy Jacob and with the entire family, scheming to discover the information he desires. These actions are perhaps the clearest external signs of the kind of crisis in class and race prejudice that Deronda undergoes. The mark of inauthentic behavior in the novel—Gwendolen's persistent acting, her manipulation of others through a kind of performance—now characterizes Deronda. The man who refuses the career of singer and who seems to have a kind of instinctive horror of all theatrics and all deception now undertakes "a plan which was certainly more like acting than anything he had been aware of in his own conduct before" (*DD*, 442). Even the particular act Deronda performs reminds us of Gwendolen. Deronda leaves his diamond ring with a Jewish pawnbroker, just as Gwendolen once sold her necklace to one of "these Jew dealers [who] were so unscrupulous in taking advantage of Christians" (*DD*, 48). In any case, Deronda, the student of Judaic culture, has become a kind of spy, entering under false pretenses the Cohen shop and even "the private hearth" (*DD*, 446) at the moment of the celebration of the Sabbath. Moreover, in assuming a kind of disguise, in appearing what he is not, he underscores what we will learn about him later—that his entire life has been a kind of disguise or performance.

Eliot represents Deronda as an example of the tolerant Victorian gentleman who so romanticizes and idealizes the facts of Jewish history that he measures every modern Jew as falling short of the heroic Jews of the past:

> Lying dreamily in a boat, imagining one's self in quest of a beautiful maiden's relatives in Cordova elbowed by Jews in the time of Ibn-Gebirol, all the physical incidents can be borne without shock. Or if the scenery of St Mary Axe and Whitechapel were imaginatively transported to the borders of the Rhine at the end of the eleventh century, when in the ears listening for the signals of the Messiah, the Hep! Hep! Hep! of the Crusaders came like the bay of bloodhounds; and in the presence of those devilish missionaries with sword and firebrand the crouching figure of the reviled Jew turned round erect, heroic, flashing with sublime constancy in the face of torture and death—what would the dingy shops and unbeautiful faces signify to the thrill of contemplative emotion? (*DD*, 431)

For Deronda there is a radical division between the ancient (or heroic) and the modern (or vulgar) Jew. Deronda is simply a product of his culture, for the "philo-Semitic" representation of Jewish history in nineteenth-century England in large part depended on locating the Jew in the past—in historical romances (in characters like Rebecca in Scott's *Ivanhoe*), or in the Bible (in the affinity that Arnold found between Englishmen and "the Jews of ancient times").[36] Eliot invents Mordecai to close the gap between the ancient and modern Jew, for in Mordecai we find a modern Jew inspired with all the vision and enthusiasm of the ancient Jewish hero. In Mordecai, Deronda recognizes "such a physiognomy as that might possibly have been seen in a prophet of the Exile, or in some New Hebrew poet of the medieval time" (*DD*, 436). But while Mordecai represents the modern Jew inspired by the ancient Judaic vision, he does not prevent Deronda from keeping intact his prejudice against the modern shopkeeping Jew. In an attempt to distinguish her prophet from Disraeli's, Eliot has cut off Mordecai entirely from all wealth, unlike the fabulously wealthy Sidonia. In so doing, Eliot has unwittingly perpetuated an opposition that rests on certain well-known stereotypes about the Jews, for example, the opposition between "scholar and merchant" (*DD*, 556) that Disraeli undoes in inventing Sidonia. So, while Mordecai brings alive the ancient physiognomy and vision of the Hebrew prophets, Ezra Cohen is consistently measured against certain romantic notions of what Jewish identity should be—that is, against what the liberal, tolerant Christian requires—and is hardly ever allowed his own reality, his own integrity. We find Deronda "rashly pronouncing this Ezra Cohen to be the most unpoetic Jew he had ever met with in books or life: his phraseology was as little as possible like that of the Old Testament; and no shadow of a Suffering Race distinguished his vulgarity of soul" (*DD*, 442–43); "Ezra Cohen was not clad in the sublime pathos of the martyr" (*DD*, 575). And Mordecai is the ultimate measuring rod beside which Ezra is consistently, even obsessively, placed: Mordecai is "as different probably as a Jew could well be from Ezra Cohen . . . whose flourishing face glistening on the way to fatness was hanging over the counter in negotiation" (*DD*, 438). "It was an unaccountable conjunction—the presence among these common, prosperous, shop-keeping types, of a man who, in an emaciated threadbare condition, impressed a certain awe on Deronda" (*DD*, 451– 52). The discovery that Mordecai and not the shopkeeping Ezra is Mirah's brother brings Deronda a personal relief that is ironically underscored by being represented as a kind of "deliverance" (*DD*, 604). The deliverer of the Jewish maiden, Daniel is himself delivered from the toonear touch of these vulgar Jews. After all, the narrator has "confessed" Deronda's prejudice from the beginning of his quest for Mirah's family: "I confess, he particularly desired that Ezra Cohen should not keep a shop" (*DD*, 432).

Rejecting the shopkeeping Ezra, the man who confesses, "I've had something else to do than to get book-learning" (*DD*, 451), Deronda chooses to be educated by the scholar Ezra Mordecai, the man with the face of a prophet. Both Mirah and Daniel deliver themselves into the hands of the master pedagogue for their education in Judaic culture. Mirah declares to Mordecai, "you will teach me to be a good Jewess" (*DD*, 643), and Daniel addresses him, "You shall have books about you. I shall want to learn of you" (*DD*, 633). What at first may appear to be the difference between Mirah and Daniel's past education—between the Jewish heroine and the Christian hero—turns out to be remarkably similar; both are Jews who have been denied the traditional Judaic education by their parents—by a father in Mirah's case, by a mother in Daniel's.

I now turn to Daniel's meeting with his mother in Genoa, for his re-

education in Judaic culture has as its endpoint his discovery of his own
family history, including the conditions under which his own Jewish origins were erased. Moreover, when Daniel accepts his Jewish ancestry
during his meeting with his mother, we see the ultimate consequence of
his reeducation, for as he confesses to Mordecai: "It is quite true that you
and Mirah have been my teachers. If this revelation had been made to me
before I had known you both, I think my mind would have rebelled
against it" (*DD*, 819).

Eliot stages the revelation of Deronda's Jewish ancestry against the
backdrop of a famous historical tableau from the time of the Spanish
Inquisition. Deronda's mother summons him to a meeting in Genoa,
where he meditates on the specific Jewish history of this setting even
before he finds out the news that he is a Jew:

> [A]mong the thoughts that most filled his mind while his boat was
> pushing about within view of the grand harbour was that of the
> multitudinous Spanish Jews centuries ago driven destitute from their
> Spanish homes, suffered to land from the crowded ships only for
> brief rest on this grand quay of Genoa, overspreading it with a pall
> of famine and plague—dying mothers with dying children at their
> breasts—fathers and sons agaze at each other's haggardness, like
> groups from a hundred Hunger-towers turned out beneath the mid-
> day sun. (*DD*, 682)

In the opening pages of "The Mother and the Son," Deronda reflects on
the history of the Spanish Jews, as if he has read the famous histories of
Henry Hart Milman or William H. Prescott or Heinrich Graetz in the
course of his reeducation (as Eliot had).[37] Indeed, Deronda reflects as if
a page from one of these well-known histories were running through
his mind:

> No one . . . could behold the sufferings of the Jewish exiles unmoved.
> A great many perished of hunger, especially those of tender years.
> Mothers, with scarcely strength to support themselves, carried their
> famished infants in their arms, and died with them. Many fell victims
> to the cold, others to intense thirst, while the unaccustomed dis-
> tresses incident to a sea voyage aggravated their maladies. . . . One
> might have taken them for spectres, so emaciated were they, so ca-

daverous in their aspect, and with eyes so sunken; they differed in nothing from the dead, except in the power of motion, which indeed they scarcely retained.[38]

This well-known historical tableau of Jewish persecution and martyrdom was used by Eliot not only in *Daniel Deronda;* she had reinscribed this famous historical scene in 1862 in *Romola,* in what I take to be a striking anticipation of *Daniel Deronda.* So in two prominent novels by Eliot, we encounter another example of how the story of the Inquisition, and the subsequent banishment and diaspora of the Iberian Jews, reenters the literature of England. Even the man who serves as Deronda's mentor, as a kind of symbolic father, is represented through the story of the Jewish martyrs of the Inquisition when Deronda finds Mordecai, impoverished and sickly, with no outlet for his vision, as "in some past prison of the Inquisition" (*DD,* 437), as if the story of Inquisitorial oppression continues, in its own way, in Victorian England.

The prelude to Daniel's acceptance of his inheritance as a Jew, then, comes with a return to what I have contended is for Victorian England the critical moment of Jewish history. My argument has been based in part on an understanding of the work of Sephardic Jews in the 1840s in restoring to the nineteenth-century Anglo-Jewish community its historical origins in the Iberian diaspora. Moreover, a critical moment in Victorian England's consciousness of Jewish identity occurred with the publication of Disraeli's "Memoir," in which he claimed the martyred and heroic history of the Inquisition and expulsion as his own family history. And here, in *Daniel Deronda,* Eliot maps onto the story of her hero the genealogy of the current prime minister. We discover in the course of the mother's tale that Deronda has the same family lineage as Disraeli; both are descended not only from English and Italian Jews but from those Iberian Jews persecuted and banished in the late fifteenth century. And like Disraeli, Deronda is fond of emphasizing one particular strand of this lineage: "And it is not only that I am a Jew . . . but I come of a strain that has ardently maintained the fellowship of our race—a line of Spanish Jews that has borne many students and men of practical power" (*DD,* 817). I think it no accident that one can hear the echo of "Disraeli" in "Deronda."

Eliot had already told a version of the life stories of Disraeli and Deronda in a highly compressed and symbolic form in *Romola* during that strange interlude when the heroine flees from her home in Florence and floats suicidally in a boat on the sea until she awakens the next morning to hear the piercing cry of an infant from the nearby shore. In searching for the child, Romola experiences firsthand what Deronda at the beginning of "The Mother and the Son" imaginatively reconstructs from his reading. When Romola discovers a group of dead bodies surrounding the crying infant, she meets the victims of the Iberian Inquisition and banishment, once again represented in the manner of such writers as Milman and Prescott: "The strongly marked type of race in their features, and their peculiar garb, made her conjecture that they were Spanish or Portuguese Jews, who had perhaps been put ashore and abandoned there by rapacious sailors, to whom their property remained as a prey. Such things were happening continually to Jews compelled to abandon their homes by the Inquisition. . . ."[39] Eliot uses this historical tableau as the scene of rebirth for Romola. Aimless, exhausted by her past life, in search of death, Romola finds a new life in the deliverance of this Jewish child. The rescue of the Jewish child from death, then, functions as a kind of revival of consciousness, even as a catalyst for action, for the title characters in both novels. Romola is a female version of a figure we have met time and again, even in Deronda as the rescuer of Mirah—the champion of the Jews. Eliot's work represents the latest and most explicit stage in the development of this topos: the regeneration of (English) consciousness through the deliverance of the persecuted Jew. This topos descends from that popular form of millenarian discourse which placed the deliverance and the restoration of Israel at the center of English moral regeneration.

Romola's discovery and rescue of the orphaned Jewish child is rewritten in *Daniel Deronda* in a way that marks the development of Eliot's consciousness of Jewish identity. At first, the scene in *Romola* seems merely to be copied in *Daniel Deronda*. Deronda, after a dreamy boat ride like Romola's, rescues Mirah, and finds new purpose in his life because of this rescue. But whereas Deronda's deliverance of Mirah also becomes, as the plot unfolds, the rescue of her Jewish family and heritage (and Deronda's as well), the rescue of the Jewish child in *Romola* ends in conversion: "the Hebrew baby was a tottering tumbling Christian, Benedetto by name, having been baptised." Conversion is the means by which the Christian community assimilates "the queer little black Benedetto,"[40] the quintessential outsider who seems to bear a kind of double racial marking (like

Trollope's Ferdinand Lopez). In the story of Deronda, Eliot returns to the Hebrew baby raised as a Christian with no knowledge of his Jewish origins, but in her retelling of the story she returns this child to the Jewish heritage that was lost when he was absorbed by the Christian community. Moreover, it is critical to remember that *Daniel Deronda* is a return not simply to the story of the converted Hebrew baby in *Romola*, but to a highly specific historical tableau that both novels share—the tableau that pictures the consequences of the Iberian Inquisition and expulsion. Eliot poses the following historical question: can the child whose Jewish identity was erased in the age of the Inquisition be re-Judaized in the more tolerant nineteenth century? In answering such a question, we must consider the way in which the story of the baptized Hebrew baby may encode the story not only of Deronda but also of Disraeli, who recalled the setting of the Inquisition to tell his own family history. For the Christianized Benedetto in some sense recalls the Christianized Benjamin Disraeli: the Jewish child baptized in order to be assimilated and, finally, to enjoy all the rights and privileges of the hegemonic Christian community. Perhaps Queen Victoria half-sensed this meaning when she presented Disraeli with a copy of the 1880 edition of *Romola*.[41] The queen must have viewed the conversion of the Hebrew baby with enthusiastic approval; after all, a similar event had delivered to her her beloved prime minister, the leader of Protestant England. But it is precisely from this perspective that the story of the hero in *Daniel Deronda* flows athwart the mainstream of history—the history of both Inquisitorial Spain and Victorian England— for instead of simply recording the Christianization of the Jew, it sets about to re-Judaize the Christian, to return him to the Jewish origins that the events of history have so often required that he abandon. *Daniel Deronda* thus makes a critique not only of the scene of conversion associated with the period of the Inquisition, but of the social and political conditions in Victorian England that required the current prime minister's conversion.

But Eliot also aims her critique at the Jew who yields to such social pressures and converts out of self-advantage. For however much Eliot sympathizes with the suffering that Deronda's mother describes as her Jewish experience, she nonetheless makes the story of Leonora a critique of the Jew who converts out of ambition and opportunism. Eliot attempts to win our approval of this critique by making the story of Leonora's apostasy and eventual conversion the story of Leonora's abandonment of her child. Eliot encourages our condemnation of Leonora by setting her story against the historical backdrop of the heroic Jewish mother in the time of the Inquisition. Deronda, in his recollection of the banished Jews from Spain, recalls "dying mothers with dying children at their breasts" (*DD*, 682), but the story he is about to hear from his own mother is very different. Deronda's mother is the Jewish mother who abandoned her son, even the mother who is seen as squelching his life, in some sense murdering him. Leonora told Kalonymos that Daniel was dead, for "I meant you to be dead to all the world of my childhood" (*DD*, 700). Daniel is the dead Jewish baby of the historical tableau, with a difference: he is killed not by persecution and famine but by a form of symbolic infanticide. He is the Jewish child symbolically murdered by Leonora when she puts out the report that he is dead and when she gives him away to be remade as an English Christian. He is the child his mother "willed to annihilate" (*DD*, 727). Here, we see the peculiar pathos of Eliot's use of the historical backdrop of the banished Iberian Jews as a prelude to recording Deronda's family history. Deronda was banished by no national edict, but by maternal interdiction. In his meeting with his mother, Deronda accuses her: "You renounced me—you still banish me—as a son" (*DD*, 727).

The modern conditions of Jewish self-hatred become the center of Eliot's representation of the mother's conversion and the abandonment of her son. But this self-hatred is often masked by another modern phenomenon, descended from Enlightenment thinking—the progressive critique of Judaism made on intellectual grounds. In Disraeli's family, this critique took the form of Isaac D'Israeli's famous diatribes against rabbinical "superstitions" in such works as *Curiosities of Literature* and *The Genius of Judaism*. In *Daniel Deronda* it is aimed not simply at the "superstitions" of Judaism, but also at a kind of coercive system of education, like that pictured in Mordecai's instruction of Jacob, but far worse for the female child. Leonora explains the kind of education her father gave her:

> He never comprehended me, or if he did, he only thought of fettering me into obedience. I was to be what he called "the Jewish woman" under pain of his curse. I was to feel everything I did not feel, and believe everything I did not believe. I was to feel awe for the bit of

parchment in the *mezuza* over the door; to dread lest a bit of butter should touch a bit of meat; to think it beautiful that men should bind the *tephillin* on them, and women not,—to adore the wisdom of such laws, however silly they might seem to me. I was to love the long prayers in the ugly synagogue, and the howling, and the gabbling, and the dreadful fasts, and the tiresome feasts, and my father's endless discoursing about Our People, which was a thunder without meaning in my ears. . . . Teaching, teaching for everlasting—"this you must be," "that you must not be"—pressed on me like a frame that got tighter and tighter as I grew. (*DD*, 691–92)

We are most sympathetic to Leonora when her attack on Judaism is conceived in feminist terms. But we should beware of the way in which her argument overlaps with a highly conventional argument often used in the nineteenth-century as one of the main props of the ideology of conversion. For Eliot's critique of patriarchal Judaism is not original. Leonora uses the kind of argument against Judaism that was often aimed at Jewish women by Christian proselytizers—that Judaism degraded the Jewish woman. I have recorded the conversionists' wide dissemination of this idea and Grace Aguilar's response at midcentury. The evidence for this critique of patriarchal Judaism typically took the form of quoting this prayer: "A man is bound to thank God, as we do every Sabbath, that he was not made a woman" (*DD*, 636).

Leonora's argument against Judaism hardly disguises her profound Jewish self-hatred, which leads her to convert: "I rid myself of the Jewish tatters and gibberish that make people nudge each other at sight of us, as if we were tatooed under our clothes, though our faces are as whole as theirs" (*DD*, 698); "Before I married the second time I was baptised; I made myself like the people I lived among" (*DD*, 698). It is a story that Eliot could have learned from Disraeli's "Memoir," where Jewish self-hatred was subtly analyzed in terms that anticipate Leonora's story. Disraeli describes his beautiful and vain grandmother, who "imbibed that dislike for her race which the vain are too apt to adopt when they find that they are born to public contempt": "The indignant feeling that should be reserved for the persecutor, in the mortification of their disturbed sensibility, is too often visited on the victim; and the cause of annoyance is recognized not in the ignorant malevolence of the powerful, but in the conscientious conviction of the innocent sufferer."[42] Jewish self-hatred and its corollary, the impetus to assimilate and convert,[43] provides the modern context for understanding the family stories of both Disraeli and Deronda (including the conversion they underwent as children), even though these sons, one real and one fictitious, are quick to emphasize the more heroic history of persecution and martyrdom that stands behind them.

For we must read Deronda's story as a conversion story. Leonora's critique of traditional Jewish education is balanced by Eliot's critique of Daniel's education as an English gentleman, which is nothing short of a kind of underground, or implicit, conversion: a Jewish child, unaware of his own origins, has been raised as a Christian. It is in this sense that we can view Mordecai's reeducation of Daniel, which at first looks so much like an attempt to convert him, as a form of repairing Daniel's involuntary apostasy. And it is in this sense that Kalonymos rejoices that Deronda is "no longer perverted from the fellowship of your people" (*DD*, 788), reminding us of that specialized but popular Victorian use of the term "perversion" for a kind of conversion in the wrong direction. Kalonymos particularly notices the work of Daniel's education in this perversion. Recalling Daniel's grandfather, Kalonymos tells the grandson: "You would perhaps have been such a man as he if your education had not hindered" (*DD*, 790). So, the education the mother secures for the son is tantamount to his conversion, as she knows; it is exactly the antithesis of the education she had. In her eyes, the education she gives him is the ultimate justification of her motherhood: "You are an English gentleman. I secured you that" (*DD*, 690). Leonora asks him: "What better could the most loving mother have done? I relieved you from the bondage of having been born a Jew" (*DD*, 689). "I delivered you from the pelting contempt that pursues Jewish separateness" (*DD*, 698).

In this regard, Mirah's story duplicates Daniel's. Both stories involve parents who praise themselves for the education they have given their children, and children who realize that they have been deprived of the education they want and need. Like Leonora, Lapidoth justifies himself as a parent by praising the education he has given Mirah, an education to prepare her for a career on the stage: "I had given up everything for the sake of getting you an education which was to be a fortune to you" (*DD*, 805–6). Also like Leonora, Lapidoth provides the novel with a case history in Jewish self-hatred; Mirah recalls not simply the Judaic education he refused her, but the way in which "he would even ridicule our own people; . . . imitating their movements and their tones in prayer, only to make others laugh" (*DD*, 256). When Mirah recollects her father's neglect in this regard, she emphasizes her own attempt to (re)educate herself by relying on her Jewish landlady: "I read in her prayer-book and Bible, and when I had money enough I asked her to buy me books. . . . In this way I have come to know a little of our religion, and the history of our people, besides piecing together what I read in plays and other books about Jews and Jewesses" (*DD*, 254). Such a piecemeal and secretive education in Judaism recalls the kind of attenuated and unorthodox Judaism practiced by the Marranos because they were denied access to Jewish books and a Jewish community[44]—only it is Mirah's father, not the state or the Church, who stands in the way of her education in Judaism.

Both Daniel's and Mirah's stories represent the robbery of the Jewish child. We have seen Eliot exploring the theme of the stolen child in *The Spanish Gypsy:* the Spaniards rob the Gypsy child Fedalma, and then educate, convert, and assimilate her. But in *Daniel Deronda* Eliot radically revises this traditional theme of "the stolen offspring" (*DD*, 819). The robbery of the Jewish child occurs within the Jewish community; it is a crime committed by Jews against Jews. This picture of Jewish crime comes very close to the conventional stereotype of the Jewish father who monetarily values, and even sells, his child. Leonora is accused of "robbery of my own child" (*DD*, 701), while Mordecai accuses Lapidoth of having "robbed" (*DD*, 847) Mirah from her mother, and finally of attempting "to sell my sister" (*DD*, 847). Such ideas have the effect of focusing the novel less on the persecution that Jews suffer at the hands of Christians, and more on the persecution Jews suffer from Jews. One could argue that the Jewish criminal is reimagined in *Daniel Deronda* in the following way: while in Trollope's novels the Jewish criminal preys on the Christian community, in *Daniel Deronda* the Jewish criminal, once again in order to infiltrate Christian society, commits the crime of stealing the Jewish child from the Jewish community. As in *The Spanish Gypsy*, Eliot's critique of the ideology of assimilation and conversion, when realized in a representation of Jewish opportunism, is in danger of producing only a variation on certain conventional anti-Semitic stereotypes.

While attacking the politics of assimilation, Eliot nonetheless acknowl-

edges a certain legitimate empowerment that occurs through the process—that is, when the assimilated Jew, eschewing self-advantage, works
to empower his poorer and less privileged fellow Jews. Eliot, or rather
Mordecai, makes this point through the story of Moses. Here is Mordecai's initial vision of the man who will take over his quest: "he must be a
Jew, intellectually cultured, morally fervid . . . but his face and frame must
be beautiful and strong, he must have been used to all the refinements of
social life, his voice must flow with a full and easy current, his circumstances be free from sordid need" (*DD*, 529). Mordecai recognizes in the
assimilated Deronda the kind of power he himself lacks: "it is a precious
thought to me that he has a preparation which I lacked, and is an accomplished Egyptian" (*DD*, 721). Later in the novel, Mordecai returns to this
idea: "the erring and unloving wills of men have helped to prepare you, as
Moses was prepared, to serve your people the better" (*DD*, 818). Even
Deronda, in disapproval of his mother's scheme to hide his lineage, confesses: "I will admit that there may come some benefit from the education
you chose for me" (*DD*, 725).

While *Daniel Deronda* critiques those Jewish parents who require the assimilation and conversion of their children, it at the same time acknowledges the practical power of the assimilated Jew. The novel could not
ignore what the English public well knew, namely, that as an unconverted
Jew, Disraeli would not have been able to enter Parliament or become
prime minister. With the conventional plot of the converted Jewish daughter (Leonora) occupying only a subsidiary position, the plot of the converted Jewish son becomes the focus of *Daniel Deronda* (as well as Trollope's novels) because it was precisely such a plot that was enacted on the
stage of English public life in Disraeli's career. The ending of *Daniel
Deronda* is a kind of fantasy that rewrites this career. During the period
that Disraeli, a converted Jew, was the leader of Protestant England—that
is, of his adopted people—Eliot produced a novel in which her hero, also
a converted Jew, decides to leave England to become the leader of his
ancestral people. Deronda explains to Mordecai: "Since I began to read
and know, I have always longed for some ideal task, in which I might
feel myself the heart and brain of a multitude—some social captainship,
which would come to me as a duty, and not be striven for as a personal
prize. You have raised the image of such a task for me—to bind our race

together" (*DD*, 819–20). While Trollope's *The Prime Minister* rewrites Disraeli's life story by imagining an Englishman descended from Iberian Jews losing his bid for Parliament and eventually committing suicide, Eliot's novel imagines something much different. Deronda, an Englishman descended from Iberian Jews, chooses to throw in his lot with his disenfranchised and oppressed people, rather than to climb to the highest rung of the ladder of English Protestant society. Deronda is a Moses who does in fact turn his back on the people who have adopted him, not to despoil them but to direct his attention to liberating his oppressed fellow Jews. As a fantasy based on the life of England's prime minister in 1876, such a plot functions symbolically to liberate Disraeli to do what his critics accused him of doing, under cover of being the leader of Protestant England—to represent his own ancestral people, to seek their best interest.

Such a plot depends on Eliot's refocusing of the history of crypto-Judaism in a way that ultimately undercuts the paranoiac view of "the secret race." Unlike the secret Jew in Trollope's novels, who manipulates the secret of his origins to infiltrate and ultimately subvert English society, the secret Jew in *Daniel Deronda* is shown to be victimized by, even held hostage to, the secrecy of his Jewish origins. So it is fitting that Deronda's most liberated moment comes with his open acknowledgment of his Jewish identity—that is, with his refusal of the secrecy of his Jewish identity. Moreover, the history of those martyred crypto-Jews who ultimately confess their Jewish identity becomes the model for Deronda's own story as well as a kind of paradigm by which he understands and admires Mirah: "she seemed to Deronda a personification of that spirit which impelled men after a long inheritance of professed Catholicism to leave wealth and high place, and risk their lives in flight, that they might join their own people and say, 'I am a Jew' " (*DD*, 426).

The idea of the Jew (whether Disraeli or Deronda) working toward the liberation of his oppressed people is legitimated in *Daniel Deronda* by the complete endorsement of the claims of Jewish identity, that is, by the endorsement of the need for a Jewish state. Unlike "the secret Jew" that Disraeli's critics paranoiacally constructed—the Hebrew premier who worked secretly to support Jewish interests (and thereby to undermine the English nation)—Deronda works openly for the establishment of a Jewish state. Hence his decision at the end of the novel to travel to Palestine. Eliot here shifts the setting of the popular story of the nation-state's origins from medieval England and Spain to modern Palestine, a new center of nationalist activity at the end of *Daniel Deronda*.

With Deronda's departure for the East, we again have an example of the Jew leaving England at the end of the text. But unlike the journey of the suffering Jew, seeking asylum in another land at the mercy of another ruler—as in the case of Scott's Isaac and Rebecca—Deronda's journey is meant to preclude, once and for all, the Jews' homeless wandering, their dependence on a nation not their own. With Deronda's quest to restore the Jews to Palestine, we arrive at the redefinition of a centuries-old tradition in England, popular in the seventeenth century and revitalized during the Evangelical Revival. Daniel's view of the restoration is not conceived as the sign of Christian power—the conversion of the Jews—as it is in traditional millenarian discourse, in a novel like Charlotte Elizabeth's *Judah's Lion*, in which an English Jew travels to the East, converts to Christianity, and then calls for the restoration of the Jews. Nor does Deronda's trip to the East function as a purely figurative Judaization of the Englishman, as it does in Disraeli's *Tancred*, in which the English hero's Judaization and his desire for the Jewish heroine are left unresolved, incomplete. *Daniel Deronda* ends with its English gentleman hero fully Judaized, marrying the Jewish heroine "according to the Jewish rite" (*DD*, 880), and preparing to journey to the East in order to work toward providing the Jews with a national identity of their own, like England's. Deronda embarks to fulfill Mordecai's wish, "to found a new Jewish polity" (*DD*, 594). In Mordecai's words, "Then our race shall have an organic centre, a heart and brain to watch and guide and execute; the outraged Jew shall have a defence in the court of nations, as the outraged Englishman or American" (*DD*, 595). At the end of *Daniel Deronda*, Daniel and Mirah step outside the predominant configuration of Jewish identity in English discourse. Not only do their stories function to critique the predominant ideology of Jewish conversion; at the end of the novel the Jewish characters no longer serve the purpose of helping to define the English national character, but instead work toward the construction of their own national identity.

Epilogue

*Miss Edgeworth['s] Irish characters have gone so far to make the English familiar with
the character of their gay and kind-hearted neighbours of Ireland, that she may be truly
said to have done more towards completing the Union, than perhaps all the legislative
enactments by which it has been followed up.—Sir Walter Scott*

*George Eliot has laid open before a larger audience than had ever before been summoned
for a similar purpose, the aims and scope and innermost thoughts of Judaism, and she
has accomplished more for the cause of toleration and enlightenment, than could have
been achieved by any amount of legislation.—James Picciotto*

This book has charted the development of a novelistic tradition whose
powers in the work of national reform were said to exceed the legislative
powers of government. I began by arguing that Edgeworth's and Scott's
depictions of Irish and Scottish minorities in Great Britain prepared
the way for their depiction of anti-Semitism in *Harrington* and *Ivanhoe*.
Working in a similar vein, Eliot used allusions to slavery in the United
States, and to anti-Irish and anti-Scottish feeling in England, to explore
the nature of anti-Semitism, as in the following example: "All of which is
mirrored in an analogy, namely, that of the Irish, also a servile race, who
have rejected Protestantism, though it has been repeatedly urged on them
by fire and sword and penal laws, and whose place in the moral scale may
be judged by our advertisements, where the clause, 'No Irish need apply,'
parallels the sentence which for many polite persons sums up the question of Judaism—'I never *did* like the Jews.' "[1] Recognizing the immensely
influential power of the novelist, the reading public actually called on
novelists to do the work of national reform. *Harrington* was initiated by a
Jewish reader offended by anti-Semitic portraits in Edgeworth's earlier
work, while a reader of *Daniel Deronda* pressed on Eliot the similarities
between the Celts and the Hebrews to persuade her to help in "further[ing] that appreciation of the Celts which is now interesting many
highly instructed writers."[2] From Edgeworth and Scott at the beginning

of the century to Eliot in the 1870s, the novelist became a kind of arbiter of the wrongs of those "people[s] too long neglected and too severely oppressed."[3]

Often the novelist and the legislator went about their critiques in similar ways. Both Edgeworth and Eliot exposed anti-Semitism not solely, or even primarily, in the palpable and bluntly stupid bigotry of characters like Mrs. Harrington or Lady Mallinger, but in the subtle prejudices of an English gentleman known for his liberal sympathies. In this way, both writers explored the kind of unconscious anti-Semitism that Disraeli made the center of the parliamentary debate on Jewish disabilities in 1847 when he brilliantly diagnosed the half-repressed fears and prejudices of those members of Parliament who opposed Jewish Emancipation: "you are influenced by the darkest superstitions of the darkest ages that ever existed in this country. It is this feeling that has been kept out of this debate; indeed, that has been kept secret in yourselves—enlightened as you are—and that is unknowingly influencing you as it is influencing others abroad."[4] Disraeli replaces the central construction of nineteenth-century anti-Semitism, the secret Jew, with the secret anti-Semite, the enlightened and liberal Englishman—like Edgeworth's Harrington and Eliot's Deronda—who keeps his own prejudices secret, even to himself. A Jewish reviewer of *Daniel Deronda* explained the difficulty of legislating against such secret prejudices: "fifteen centuries of hatred are not to be wiped out by any legislative enactment. . . . There yet remains a deep unconscious undercurrent of prejudice against the Jew which conscientious Englishmen have often to fight against as part of that lower nature, a survival of the less perfect development of our ancestors."[5] This deep unconscious prejudice, so difficult to legislate against, became the target of the revisionary novelist.

James Picciotto's review of *Daniel Deronda*, in which he claims that Eliot's novel accomplished more than "any amount of legislation," does more than make plain the political consequences of the tradition that links Eliot's project in the 1870s with Edgeworth's at the beginning of the century. Picciotto's review, which appeared in *Gentleman's Magazine* (1876), as well as David Kaufmann's *George Eliot and Judaism* (1877) and Heinrich Graetz's *Correspondence of an English Lady on Judaism and Semitism* (1883) are powerful signs of the new level to which Eliot's novel brought the dialogue between the Jewish and Gentile communities, both in England and on the Continent. These texts demonstrate how directly the revisionary novelist was engaged with her reading public, and how directly that reading public responded to the novelist who took on herself the goal of national reform.

Picciotto's review of Eliot's novel pinpoints the novelist's rare, even unprecedented, accomplishment: "A great novelist of non-Jewish extraction . . . has acquired an extended and profound knowledge of the rites, aspirations, hopes, fears, and desires of the Israelites of the day. She has read their books, inquired into their modes of thought, searched their traditions, accompanied them to the synagogue; nay, she has taken their very words from their lips, and . . . has unroofed their houses."[6] By representing Jewish life in such detail and with such accuracy, *Daniel Deronda* bore witness to the fact that the Jewish experience could be understood by a non-Jew. George Henry Lewes remarked, "we have both been much gratified at the fervent admiration of the Chief Rabbi and other learned Jews, and their astonishment that a Christian should know so much about them and enter so completely into their feelings and aspirations" (*GEL,* 6.294). At the same time, the very depth and completeness of the representation of Jewish life in Eliot's novel meant that only a Jew could properly judge it, praise its accuracy while identifying its few and minor errors—"To say that some slight errors have crept into *Daniel Deronda* is to say that no human work is perfect; and these inaccuracies are singularly few and unimportant."[7] In fact, as the Jewish community both at home and abroad rushed to praise the novel,[8] Eliot imagined who the best readers of the novel were and what it would have meant if she could have chosen its audience. She wrote to David Kaufmann: "Certainly, if I had been asked to choose *what* should be written about my book and *who* should write it, I should have sketched—well, not anything so good as what you have written, but an article which must be written by a Jew who showed not merely sympathy with the best aspirations of his race, but a remarkable insight into the nature of art and the processes of the artistic mind" (*GEL,* 6.378). Kaufmann had already written that " 'Daniel Deronda' is a Jewish book not only in the sense that it treats of Jews, but also in the sense that it is pre-eminently fitted for being understood and appreciated by Jews; indeed, they only are qualified to embrace and enjoy its full significance."[9] In an extraordinary reconfiguration of the conventional roles of writer and reader, *Daniel Deronda* is "a Jewish book," written by a non-Jew, that authorizes the Jewish reader as its best reader, its only judge. The empowerment of the Jewish reader, pictured within the fictional world of *Harrington* when Mr. Montenero rereads *The Merchant of Venice* by giving "the Jewish version of the story,"[10] enters the real world when Jewish readers claim that they are best qualified to read *Daniel Deronda* and when the author corroborates such claims.

It was precisely as an English Jew that Picciotto was in a special position not only to judge the Jewish aspects of the novel but also to correct the reviewing process at large, noting for example: "Curiously enough the Jewish episodes in *Daniel Deronda* have been barely adverted to by the reviewers."[11] It became the job of the Jewish reader to restore the proper subject of Eliot's novel. The title of Picciotto's review left no doubt about his own focus. "Deronda the Jew" depicted Eliot's text as a revisionary novel that corrects the extremes, on the one hand, of Disraeli's Sidonia, "a transcendent genius," and on the other hand, of the common Jewish stereotypes found in novels ("a coiner, a buyer of stolen goods, a trainer of young thieves, a pettifogging attorney, a sheriff's officer, a money-lender, a swindling financier").[12] Moreover, Picciotto recognized the specifically subversive structure of the novel in the context of the ideology of conversion. Like the readings I have produced in this book, Picciotto interpreted *Daniel Deronda* through the idea of the conversion plot: "Mirah Cohen, with a San Benito over her lovely head, standing in the midst of roaring flames lighted by fierce fanaticism, would sing a hymn to the Lord of Israel; whilst in all human probability Gwendolen Harleth would readily embrace any faith that offered her wealth and a well-appointed establishment."[13] In a powerful revisionary act directed against the kind of secret Jew popularized by a writer like Trollope, Picciotto's Mirah is the Spanish Jew who martyrs herself to avoid apostasy, while the Christian Gwendolen becomes the type of the hypocritical Jewish *converso* who will "embrace any faith" that furthers her material well-being. Moreover, despite her eastern European ancestry, Mirah is placed in the context of the Iberian persecution of the Jews, recalling the central importance of the discourse of the Inquisition in the construction of Jewish identity in nineteenth-century England.

Picciotto's review marks a special moment in nineteenth-century England when a kind of shared historical consciousness about Christian-

Jewish relations is reached by a Gentile writer and a Jewish reader. This shared consciousness reverses the moment with which I began this study, a Jewish reader's chastisement of a Christian author's work, the event that brought *Harrington* into the world. But Picciotto was not simply the recipient of Eliot's Hebraic vision, the critical reviewer who praised her achievement; he was in his own right one of the prime architects of this new shared consciousness. His *Sketches of Anglo-Jewish History* began appearing in the *Jewish Chronicle* in 1872 and were published in book form in 1875, the year before *Daniel Deronda* began appearing; Eliot recorded a passage from the *Sketches* in her working notebooks.[14] Picciotto's *Sketches* proudly announced: "the author claims to be the first Israelite who has given a full and connected account of the vicissitudes passed through by the Jews of Great Britain."[15] While I take *Daniel Deronda* to be a culmination of a novelistic tradition initiated by Edgeworth and Scott that focused on the representation of the Jews in England, Picciotto's *Sketches* brings to fruition the earlier historical efforts of such writers as Isaac D'Israeli (in the historical chapters of *The Genius of Judaism*) and Grace Aguilar (in her article-length "History of the Jews in England"). At the same time, Picciotto's claim to be the first Jew to provide such a history sharply distinguishes his work from that of a converted Jew like Moses Margoliouth, who upheld the ideology of conversion in his *History of the Jews in Great Britain* and who claimed that only converted Jews were capable of writing accurate histories of the Jews. Even the *Times* reviewer noted the significance of Picciotto's book by recalling that histories of the Jews had been previously produced by "clergymen belonging to the Established Church or . . . Christian converts." The *Times* reviewer went on to explain why such a history had finally to be written by a Jew: "the rulers of the Synagogues . . . permitted him to scrutinize and to study for several months the documents which had been denied to his predecessors."[16] But while Picciotto's status as a Jew makes his text both unique and authoritative, his history is deliberately aimed at a double audience: "But though they were written by a Jew for Jews, the author trusts that Christians, whose faith was founded by members of the Jewish race, will find in these chapters . . . much that may be of interest also to them. He hopes that as Christians learn to know better, they will also learn to like and appreciate better, Englishmen of the Jewish faith."[17] Picciotto's *Sketches,* like *Daniel Deronda,* gave the reading public what was seen in the mid-1870s as an unprecedented look at Jewish life in England. Moreover, these texts attempted to define and create a reading public of "Englishmen" that included Jews and Christians, side by side, as members of one nation.

In this light Picciotto's *Sketches* functioned as an attack on the conversionist ideology that required a Jew to become Christian in order to become English. The idea of Jewish conversion appears time and again in the book's chapter headings, culminating in chapter 37, "Rise of the London Society." In the manner of the earlier critics of the conversionist societies, Picciotto records how "These organizations . . . have their field of operations principally among the uneducated children of the indigent and among destitute foreigners. Their salaried agents do not disdain the use of bribery and misrepresentations." He explains how, in the last decades of the eighteenth century and the opening decades of the nineteenth, baptism functioned as "a tempting bait" to the Jew, "for Parliament was to him a dreamland altogether beyond his reach; the magistracy would not be contaminated by his presence; all political, civil, and municipal offices were strictly closed against him, and even society looked at him askance." Sympathetically but nonetheless frankly analyzing the "temporal" reasons behind these apparent spiritual transformations, Picciotto sums up the question of Jewish conversion by arguing that "in the great majority of cases, these conversions were not the result of researches after religious truths, nor were they likely to shake the belief of those who have followed faithfully the dispensation of Moses." Hence Picciotto calls into question the very term conversion—"these changes of creed, or at all events of outward forms of worship."[18]

The subject of conversion constitutes the initiating moment of Graetz's *The Correspondence of an English Lady on Judaism and Semitism,* a text that openly and continuously marks itself in dialogue with *Daniel Deronda.* The problem that Graetz's text poses from the beginning is the temptation, among intelligent and well-to-do Jews, to convert out of self-protection and self-advantage. The English lady of the title, Edith, overhears the following remarks from another Jewish woman, and challenges her correspondent, Caspi, to respond: "First of all, we baptize our children. Should we expose them to the ridicule of their classmates and to the spiteful allusions of teachers who fancy themselves comic with their Jewish intonation?" The unnamed Jewish woman, who goes on to list the numerous indignities suffered by Jews and to explain that she will herself convert at the time she converts her children, sounds remarkably like Eliot's converted Leonora Halm-Eberstein, the mother of Deronda, who hides her child's Jewish origins to protect him from Christian abuse and to secure his future social position. In fact, Graetz's text begins to function as a kind of supplement to Eliot's by demonstrating how to bring the modern, skeptical Jewish woman—in this case, the doubting Edith—back into the fold. In the end, Graetz rewrites Leonora's conversion to Christianity in Edith's eventual embracing of Judaism. Positioned ideologically somewhere between the steadfast Mirah and the apostate Leonora, Edith early on makes a direct allusion to *Daniel Deronda* to explain that she has not fallen under the spell of its central prophet and that she still needs to be convinced of the value of Judaism. When Caspi lectures Edith on the miraculous indestructibility of the Jewish race, she remarks to him, "our George Eliot in her equally superb literary and philosophic novel *Daniel Deronda* has the half-prophetic, half-deluded, restless Mordecai propound something similar."[19] But while Caspi may at times sound like Eliot's Mordecai, Mordecai himself echoes a number of historical personages Eliot read about in Graetz's celebrated *History of the Jews* (1853–76) in what was a continually evolving interdependence between these two writers. In fact, one of the Jewish reviewers of *Daniel Deronda* suggested that critics had difficulty in understanding the novel because they had not read Graetz's *History*.[20] So, like Picciotto, Graetz was not simply a respondent to Eliot's work but a powerful influence on it, as part of that extraordinary dialogue that took place between Eliot and the Jewish community.

Caspi returns the question of Jewish conversion to what had become the central historical puzzle of Jewish history: the survival of the Jews despite the unending war to exterminate them. In this context, refusing conversion becomes part of a great historical dictum: to keep the tradition through which generations of Jews have handed down the great wisdom of their ethical teachings and for which generations of Jews have martyred themselves. When Caspi finally convinces Edith (along the lines of Mordecai's thinking in Eliot's novel) that the survival of the Jews has a moral significance, Edith is quick to distinguish this idea from that made famous by another prominent Victorian novelist whose ancestry is the same as her own: "The miracle of the continued existence of the Jewish race despite the war of extermination against it can in any case be accounted for physiologically in terms of race. That is the hobbyhorse of our Disraeli who even as Prime Minister was proud of his Jewish descent and in several of his novels intoned the vigor of the Jews. But this is a dangerous precipice." Turning away from the "dangerous precipice" of the theory of race, Graetz explains the continued existence of the Jews in the modern world not in physiological but in spiritual and ethical terms—"to become the teacher of the nations in matters of justice and truth."[21]

In his *Correspondence* Graetz has cleverly reinvented the ancient Christian literary form of the anti-Judaic dialogue that set Jew and Christian against each other as disputants and that often ended in the Jew's conversion. In Graetz's revision, doubting Jew and steadfast Jew are the interlocutors, with the conversion of Edith to a strong adherent of the faith at the end: "I realize now that every Jew must take care that the link which binds him to a chain of ancestors spreading over several thousand years must not be broken." A telling sign of her conversion is her final allusion to *Daniel Deronda*, when she no longer questions the vision of Mordecai and adopts the position of Deronda, embracing his vocation in the last sentence of the *Correspondence:* "Daniel Deronda, who set out on a wedding trip to Palestine with his wife, will find not a few followers."[22]

The ending of every history, like the beginning of every fiction (as Eliot remarks in *Daniel Deronda*), is at least in some ways makeshift. This history of the novel's role in the culture of conversion has concluded by focusing on the remarkable and unprecedented dialogue that took place between a Gentile writer and the Jewish community in the 1870s and 1880s. But I must add that even the Jewish community did not react uniformly with praise for Eliot. One of the English Jews in Amy Levy's *Reuben Sachs* (1888) pokes fun at a recent convert to Judaism: "I think . . . that he was shocked at finding us so little like the people in *Daniel Deronda*,"[23] as if Eliot herself had constructed a simple conversionist novel designed to turn naive Christians into Jews. Similarly, while Eliot's project marks the culmination of the revisionary tradition whose history has been charted in this study, I have viewed *Daniel Deronda* not as a terminus but as a junction, a kind of crossroads at which various other popular contemporary fictional projects meet, from didactic conversionist novels like *Adonijah* to the kind of anti-Semitic fiction that Trollope was producing in the early and mid-1870s. Moreover, Eliot's anticonversionist novel did not mark the end of the ideology of conversion in England, for in the 1870s renewed efforts were made to convert the Jews, with the establishment of several new societies (although none of these achieved the prominence of the London Society), such as the Parochial Missions to the Jews at Home and Abroad (1875), the Mildmay Mission to the Jews (1876), the East London Mission to the Jews (1877), and the Barbican Mission to the Jews (1879). Finally, I have located Eliot's novel in the midst of the growing anti-Semitism of the 1870s that she diagnosed as a reaction to Disraeli's public prominence. In Eliot's recognition of the "revived expression of old antipathies,"[24] we have perhaps the best expression of the contour of the history of anti-Judaism and anti-Semitism: whatever their origins, the world has been witness to their perpetual reinvention.

In this light, it is important to recall that the ideology of Jewish conversion, whose institutionalization in the textual and cultural life of nineteenth-century England I have explored, has been viewed by historians of the Holocaust as a critical stage in the development of "the final solution of the Jewish question." In such a view the failure of the project to convert the Jews made necessary the invention of more violent solutions, such as expulsion and finally genocide. The interrelationship of these three "solutions," which I have suggested throughout this study, is marked by one historian of the Holocaust when she records the solution to "the Jewish question" devised by the chief adviser to Czar Alexander III in 1881: one-third of the Jews would convert, one-third would emigrate, and one-third would die of hunger.[25] Another historian of the Holocaust explains the historical continuity in this way: "The process began with the attempt to drive the Jews into Christianity. The development was continued in order to force the victims into exile. It was finished when the Jews were driven to their deaths."[26] Of course, modern historians have accurately distinguished between Germany's and England's treatment of the Jews. Nonetheless, as I have showed, as part of the debate over the missions to the Jews, England was forced to acknowledge that even its own celebrated reputation for tolerance was stained by a national history that included massacres of the Jews and the famous edict of expulsion. While such events were not part of England's modern history, we have seen how their recollection—in what became a collective, national act—played a critical role in the battle over how to represent Jewish (and English) identity in the nineteenth century. And I have explained how the revisionary novelist educated the public in England's past crimes while demonstrating that the powerful ideology of conversion was in fact the latest tyranny from which the Jewish people needed to be set free.

Notes

Introduction

1 Daniel Defoe, *The Farther Adventures of Robinson Crusoe,* in *The Novels and Selected Writings of Daniel Defoe,* Shakespeare Head ed., 14 vols. (New York and Boston: Basil Blackwell, Oxford University Press, and Houghton Mifflin, 1927–28), 9.37.

2 For an example of the Evangelical reaction to the eighteenth century, see Edward Cooper, *The Crisis; or, An Attempt to Shew from Prophecy; Illustrated by the Signs of the Times, The Prospects and the Duties of the Church of Christ at the Present Period* (London, 1826): "Such appears to have been the awfully declining state of the country, as to religion and morals, during the greatest part of the eighteenth century" (p. 215). For an excellent analysis of the Evangelical critique of the eighteenth century, see Ford K. Brown, *Fathers of the Victorians: The Age of Wilberforce* (Cambridge: Cambridge University Press, 1961), esp. the foreword and chap. 1.

3 See, for example, Bernard Glassman, *Anti-Semitic Stereotypes Without Jews: Images of the Jews in England 1290–1700* (Detroit: Wayne State University Press, 1975). On the analysis of such stereotypes in English literature, see what remains the finest study after more than thirty years, Edgar Rosenberg, *From Shylock to Svengali: Jewish Stereotypes in English Fiction* (Stanford, Calif.: Stanford University Press, 1960). For a subsequent study along the same lines, see Anne Aresty Naman, *The Jew in the Victorian Novel: Some Relationships Between Prejudice and Art* (New York: AMS Press, 1980).

4 On the representation of "the Jew" during the early centuries of Christianity, see James Parkes, *The Conflict of the Church and the Synagogue: A Study in the Origins of Antisemitism* (London: Soncino Press, 1934); John G. Gager, *The Origins of Anti-Semitism: Attitudes Toward Judaism in Pagan and Christian Antiquity* (New York and Oxford: Oxford University Press, 1983); Marcel Simon, *Verus Israel: A Study of the Relations Between Christians and Jews in the Roman Empire (135–425),* trans. H. McKeating (New York: Oxford University Press, 1986); and chap. 2 below.

5 For an excellent discussion of the way in which the "doctrine of conversion stood at the heart of Evangelical theology" (p. 21), see Ian Bradley, *The Call to Seriousness: The*

Evangelical Impact on the Victorians (New York: Macmillan, 1976), esp. chaps. "Converting the Nation" and "A Mission to the Heathen."

6 Defoe, *The Farther Adventures,* in *Novels and Selected Writings,* 9.144.

7 Defoe, *Adventures of Robinson Crusoe,* in *Novels and Selected Writings,* 7.198–99, 8.30–31.

8 On the widespread popularity of the millenarian tradition in English culture and the use of current events to demonstrate the fulfillment of biblical prophecy, see Clarke Garrett, *Respectable Folly: Millenarians and the French Revolution in France and England* (Baltimore: Johns Hopkins University Press, 1975), esp. the introduction and chaps. 6 and 7. On the restoration and conversion of the Jews in millenarian thinking during this period, see N. I. Matar, "The Controversy over the Restoration of the Jews in English Protestant Thought: 1701–1753," *Durham University Journal* 49 (June 1988): 241–56, and Mayir Vrete, "The Restoration of the Jews in English Protestant Thought 1790–1840," *Middle Eastern Studies* 8 (1972): 3–50. On the role of the restoration of the Jews in seventeenth-century millenarian thinking, see David S. Katz, *Philo-Semitism and the Readmission of the Jews to England, 1603–1655* (Oxford: Oxford University Press, 1982), chap. 3.

9 On the popular impact of Brothers, see Vrete, "The Restoration of the Jews in English Protestant Thought 1790–1840": "Immediately his prophecies began to be published, he attracted a large group of followers and devotees. His and some of his followers' works appeared in many editions and were sold in the thousands. From many parts of the country people came flocking to behold the new Messiah, and in London the population became so affected that the government deemed it necessary to apprehend him" (p. 9). Also see Cecil Roth, *The Nephew of the Almighty: An Experimental Account of the Life and Aftermath of Richard Brothers, R.N.* (London: Edward Goldston, 1933): "Many persons throughout England began to make preparations for the immediate removal to the Holy Land. . . . 'Testimonies' of the Prophet's many adherents poured out in profusion from the press, and in some cases ran through one impression after another in the course of a few days" (pp. 64–65). On the disciples of Brothers, see Garrett, *Respectable Folly,* pp. 191–95, who shows that Brothers and his writings "represented traditions long present in English popular religion" (p. 189).

10 James Huie, *The History of the Jews, From the Taking of Jerusalem by Titus to The Present Time; Containing a Narrative of their Wanderings, Persecutions, Commercial Enterprises, and Literary Exertions; With an Account of the Various Efforts Made for Their Conversion,* 2nd ed., rev. and enlarged (Edinburgh, 1841), pp. 261–62.

11 Brown, *Fathers of the Victorians,* p. 292.

12 See *Memoirs of the Life of the Rev. Charles Simeon,* ed. Rev. William Carus, American ed. (New York, 1847), esp. pp. 322–30.

13 Brown, *Fathers of the Victorians,* p. 295.

14 Charles Simeon, *Discourses in Behalf of the Jews* (London, 1839), pp. 319, 54, 165, and 333. This idea was the bulwark of Simeon's sermons: "It is the commencement, and not the completion, of the ingathering of the Gentiles, that marks the season for the conversion of the Jews: and therefore the stir which there is at this moment amongst the

Gentile world, is amongst other signs of the times, a proof that the time for the conversion of the Jews is near at hand" (p. 320). For a similar view, announced in the title of his sermon, see George Stanley Faber, *The Conversion of the Jews to the Faith of Christ, The True Medium of the Conversion of the Gentile World* (London, 1822).

15   See, for example, Perseverans, *A Letter to the English Israelite, in Answer to his Observations on the Mission of C. F. Frey for the Conversion of the Jews* (London, 1809): "You will observe, Sir, that so as a Jew be converted to Christianity, it is (in our judgement) equally a symptom of the near approach of the great event, which must happen if God is faithful, whether he be converted through our instrumentality, or that of any other Society" (p. 39).

16   Simeon, *Discourses in Behalf of the Jews*, p. 320.

17   Lewis Way, *Jewish Repository* 1 (London, 1813): 279–80.

18   See Robert Isaac Wilberforce and Samuel Wilberforce, *The Life of William Wilberforce*, 5 vols. (Freeport, N.Y.: Books for Libraries Press, 1972): "It is often rather in the way of a gradual decline . . . than of violent and sudden shocks, that national crimes are punished" (3.290). Wilberforce called the failure to evangelize India "the greatest by far, now that the Slave Trade has ceased, of all the national crimes by which we are provoking the vengeance and suffering the chastisement of heaven" (3.352). "This is clear, that in the Scriptures no national crime is condemned so frequently, and few so strongly, as oppression and cruelty, and the not using our best endeavours to deliver our fellow-creatures from them" (4.375). See Simeon, *Discourses in Behalf of the Jews:* "the command has never been repealed, 'Preach my gospel, *to the Jews first,* and also to the Gentiles.' Indeed, my brethren, great guilt attaches to us on this account" (p. 273). Also see Cooper, *The Crisis,* on "our national sins and iniquities" (p. 245), and on the signs of the "revival in religion" that took place after the French Revolution—namely, the establishment of "Institutions for the universal dissemination of the Scriptures, and for their translation into all languages; for conveying the blessings of Christianity into heathen lands; for the conversion of the Jews" (p. 225).

19   See *The Life of William Wilberforce*, where Wilberforce calls the evangelization of India "that greatest of all causes, for I really place it before the Abolition" (4.126).

20   The government even used millenarian discourse to prepare the English public for war with France in 1792: "One form that this preparation seems to have taken was the utilization of England's tradition of biblical exegesis for the interpretation of prophecy for patriotic purposes. Under the government's covert sponsorship, prophecies were disseminated in newspapers and pamphlets that cast the French Republic in the role of the Beast of Revelation." Garrett, *Respectable Folly,* p. 167. Similarly, Richard Brothers was arrested in 1795 when the *Times* reported that he had declared, in the best millenarian tradition, that France had been the nation chosen to fulfill God's plan. Garrett, *Respectable Folly,* p. 197.

21   See James Bicheno, *The Restoration of the Jews, The Crisis of All Nations; To Which is Now Prefixed, A Brief History of the Jews, From Their First Dispersion to the Calling of Their Grand Sanhedrim at Paris, October 6th, 1806. And An Address on the Present State of Affairs, In Europe in general, and in This Country in Particular,* 2nd ed. (London,

1807): "He who should have sufficient power, or interest, to re-establish the Jewish commonwealth, would be amply rewarded by such an alliance and treaty of commerce. . . . And should the policy of the French government be directed to this object . . . our ruin in the East would not be far distant" (pp. 207–8). On the profound influence and popularity of millenarian discourse and the way in which it functioned as a form of political and social discourse, see W. H. Oliver, *Prophets and Millennialists: The Uses of Biblical Prophecy in England from the 1790s to the 1840s* (Oxford: Oxford University Press, 1978). For a useful overview of the various modern interpretations of millenarian thinking as a social and political phenomenon, see Garrett, *Respectable Folly,* "Introduction: Historians and the Millennium."

22 In recent years Todd M. Endelman has produced fine historical accounts of the crisis over acculturation and assimilation in the Anglo-Jewish community in *The Jews of Georgian England 1714–1830: Tradition and Change in a Liberal Society* (Philadelphia: Jewish Publication Society of America, 1979) and *Radical Assimilation in English Jewish History, 1656–1945* (Bloomington: Indiana University Press, 1990). Sander L. Gilman has written an excellent analysis of "The Drive for Conversion" (esp. in Germany) in *Jewish Self-Hatred: Anti-Semitism and the Hidden Language of the Jews* (Baltimore: Johns Hopkins University Press, 1986). Linda Gertlin Zatlin in a brief chapter, "The Challenge from Without: Appeals to Convert," initiated the study of the Anglo-Jewish novel as a response to the pressure to convert, in *The Nineteenth-Century Anglo-Jewish Novel* (Boston: Twayne Publishers, 1981), pp. 55–69. But there has been no thorough analysis of the discursive practices produced by the crisis over conversion in nineteenth-century England.

23 Discussions of Jewish stereotypes in English literature have tended to eschew historical analysis so that in *From Shylock to Svengali,* for example, Edgar Rosenberg justifies "the glaring omission" of Benjamin Disraeli on the basis that "I can find no place for him in a study that deals with fixed and recurrent caricatures and their antipodes" (p. 8). Rosenberg's study of stereotyping, which functions without reference to "a particular climate of opinion" (p. 13), claims that "the topicality of the material" (p. 8) in Disraeli's work makes it unfit for typological analysis.

24 Anthony Trollope, *Barchester Towers* (Oxford: Oxford University Press, 1991), p. 79.

25 William Makepeace Thackeray, *The Newcomes: Memoirs of A Most Respectable Family, The Works of William Makepeace Thackeray,* 13 vols. (London: Smith, Elder, 1898), 8.16–17.

26 William Makepeace Thackeray, *Vanity Fair: A Novel Without a Hero* (New York and Oxford: Oxford University Press, 1991), p. 818.

27 Benjamin Disraeli, *Tancred; or the New Crusade* (St. Clair Shores, Mich.: Scholarly Press, 1970), pp. 13, 69, and 181.

28 George Eliot, *Daniel Deronda* (Harmondsworth, Eng.: Penguin, 1986), p. 267.

29 James Joyce, *Ulysses,* ed. Hans Walter Gabler (New York: Random House, 1986), pp. 148 and 588.

30 George Eliot, "Silly Novels by Lady Novelists," in *Essays of George Eliot,* ed. Thomas Pinney (London: Routledge and Kegan Paul, 1963), p. 321.

1. The Culture of Conversion

1 For a history of the London Society, one may consult the official historians of the Society itself, such as Thomas D. Halsted, *Our Missions: Being a History of the Principal Missionary Transactions of the London Society for Promoting Christianity amongst the Jews, from its Foundation in 1809, to the Present Year* (London, 1866), and W. T. Gidney, *The History of the London Society for Promoting Christianity Amongst the Jews, from 1809 to 1908* (London, 1908). For a more objective account, see chap. 6 in Mel Scult, *Millennial Expectations and Jewish Liberties: A Study of the Efforts to Convert the Jews in Britain, Up to the Mid Nineteenth Century* (Leiden: E. J. Brill, 1978), and Robert Michael Smith, "The London Jews' Society and Patterns of Jewish Conversion in England, 1801–1859," *Jewish Social Studies* 43 (1981): 275–90.

2 *Selections from the Letters of Robert Southey*, ed. John Wood Warter, 4 vols. (London: Longman, Brown, Green, and Longmans, 1856), 4:177.

3 *Sophia de Lissau; or, A Portraiture of the Jews of the Nineteenth Century; Being an Outline of their Religious and Domestic Habits With Explanatory Notes*, 2nd ed. (London: T. Gardiner and Son, 1828), p. 3.

4 See *Sadoc and Miriam: A Jewish Tale*, 2nd London ed. (Boston: James B. Dow, 1834), pp. 8ff., for the first example of the way in which the narrative abruptly ceases in order to record in dialogue fashion the names of the characters in the left-hand margin, beside which we read what they say (without any narrative interventions). On the dialogues written by the Church fathers, see Arthur Lukyn Williams, *Adversus Judaeos: A Bird's-Eye View of Christian Apologiae Until the Renaissance* (Cambridge: Cambridge University Press, 1935), and Marcel Simon, *Verus Israel: A Study of the Relations Between Christians and Jews in the Roman Empire (135–425)*, trans. H. McKeating (New York: Oxford University Press, 1986), chaps. 5 and 6.

5 For example, Gidney, *The History of the London Society*, refers to a speaker at the annual 1889 meeting of the Society who quoted, and then revised, *Daniel Deronda:* " 'The gain of Israel is the gain of the world.' At present the world does not know it; and we might vary that sentence, and say, 'the gain of Israel is the gain of the Church' " (pp. 410–11). Gidney quotes Scott's *Ivanhoe* on the persecution of the Jews during the Middle Ages (p. 22).

6 Gidney, *The History of the London Society:* "His father, Isaac Disraeli, left the Synagogue for the Church, and his son Benjamin was baptized in infancy" (p. 408). Benjamin was not baptized until well after infancy.

7 *The Genius of Judaism*, pub. anon. (London, 1833), pp. 207–8.

8 *Selections from the Letters of Robert Southey*, 4.178.

9 It is important to recognize that conversionists, in response to the many attacks on the London Society, frequently chose (like Norris) to remain true to the cause (if not to the Society itself), or (like Simeon) to remain true to the Society (while trying to improve it). See, for example, Simeon's description of his meetings in 1814 with Way and Wilberforce to try to correct the "sad mismanagement" of the London Society, and his belief after certain changes had been made that "the whole society is placed on a firmer

basis than ever." Also see Simeon's explanation of how his extended tour through Great Britain in 1817 "has removed to a great extent the (*too just*) prejudices which had arisen in the public mind against the society; and we hope the society will flourish, and be made a blessing to the whole Jewish people." *Memoirs of the Life of the Rev. Charles Simeon,* ed. Rev. William Carus (New York, 1847), pp. 231, 274.

10   H. H. Norris, *The Origin, Progress, and Existing Circumstances, of the London Society for Promoting Christianity Amongst the Jews* (London, 1825), pp. 54, 146, 4, 502.

11   Norris, *Origin,* p. 494.

12   "On the London Society for Converting the Jews," pp. 21–35, *British Critic* (Jan. 1819): 25, 22, 22, 22, 22, 23.

13   See, for example, Joseph Wolff, *Missionary Journal and Memoir,* ed. John Bayford, 2nd ed. (London, 1827), p. 68, where Wolff records: "Began Crool's Objections to Christianity with Scott's Answer." See [Charlotte Anley,] *Miriam; or, the Power of Truth,* 9th ed. (London, 1849), p. 146, where the note acknowledges: "The author is indebted for much of the argument in this chapter to the Rev. J. Scott's admirable refutation of Rabbi Crool's 'Restoration of Israel.'" Also see *The Converted Jewess: A Memoir of Maria* —, 4th London ed. (New York: Lane and Tippett, 1847), p. 14, where the young proselyte studies the work of Rabbi Crool.

14   R. Joseph Crool, *The Restoration of Israel* (n.p., n.d.), declaration signed 1812, Cambridge, pp. 4, 3, 4.

15   A Daughter of Israel, *Letter to Mr. Frey, of the Soi-Disant Jews' Chapel, Spitalfields; Occasioned by the Questions Now in Debate at the London Forum, Cateaton-Street* (London, 1810), pp. 3, 4, 4, 7, 5, 8, 7–8.

16   M. Samuel, *Conversion of the Jews: An Address from an Israelite to the Missionary Preachers Assembled at Liverpool to Promote Christianity amongst the Jews* (Liverpool: W. Wales, n.d.), pp. 11, 5–6, 15, 5.

17   *The Inquisition and Judaism. A Sermon Addressed to Jewish Martyrs, On the Occasion of an Auto Da Fe at Lisbon, 1705, By the Archbishop of Cranganor; Also A Reply to the Sermon, by Carlos Vero,* trans. Moses Mocatta (Philadelphia: Barnard and Jones, 5620 [1860]), pp. vi, xi, xi.

18   Hartwig Hundt, "The Mirror of the Jews" (Nov. 1819), quoted by Heinrich Graetz, *History of the Jews,* 6 vols. (Philadelphia: Jewish Publication Society of America, 1891–98), 5.532.

19   For Inglis's characterization of the Jews "as strangers and sojourners in the land," and his reference to Crool, see *Hansard's Parliamentary Debates,* 3rd ser. (London: T. C. Hansard, 1833), 18 (May 22, 1833), 49–50. For Arnold's view that the Jews are "voluntary strangers here, and have no claim to become citizens, but by conforming to our moral law, which is the Gospel," see Arthur Penrhyn Stanley, *The Life and Correspondence of Thomas Arnold, D. D.,* 2 vols. in 1 (New York: Charles Scribner's Sons, 1910), 2.41. On the role of Arnold's ideas in the parliamentary debates, see M. C. N. Salbstein, *The Emancipation of the Jews in Britain: The Question of the Admission of the Jews to Parliament, 1828–1860* (East Brunswick, N.J.: Associated University Presses, 1982), pp. 73–75.

Notes to Chapter 1   307

20 William Cobbett, *Good Friday; or, The Murder of Jesus Christ by the Jews* (London, 1830), pp. 12–13.

21 Paul Van Hemert, *State of the Jews in the Beginning of the Nineteenth Century*, trans. Lewis Jackson (London, 1825), pp. 39, vi.

22 Hemert, *State of the Jews*, p. v.

23 Anthony Trollope, "The Zulu in London," in *Clergymen of the Church of England* (Leicester: University of Leicester Press, 1974), pp. 51, 52, 51, 54, 54, 53.

24 P. P. Pasquin, *Jewish Conversion. A Christianical Farce, Got Up With Great Effect Under the Direction of a Society For Making Bad Jews Worse Christians* (London: T. J. Wooler, 1814), pp. 4, 4, 7, 2.

25 Maria Edgeworth, *Castle Rackrent* and *The Absentee* (London: Dent, 1964), p. 16; Anthony Trollope, *The Prime Minister* (Oxford: Oxford University Press, 1987), 1.146; William Makepeace Thackeray, *Vanity Fair: A Novel Without a Hero* (Oxford: Oxford University Press, 1991), p. 7.

26 Robert Knox, M.D., *The Races of Men: A Philosophical Enquiry into the Influence of Race over the Destinies of Nations*, 2nd ed. (London: Henry Renshaw, 1862), pp. 194, 205, 206, 197, 198, 206.

27 Gidney, *History of the London Society*, p. 73.

28 Hannah Adams, *The History of the Jews, from the Destruction of Jerusalem to the Present Time* (London: London Society, 1818), pp. iii, 73–74, 555. Adams is also the author of *A Concise Account of the London Society for Promoting Christianity Among the Jews* (Boston: John Eliot, 1816), in which she records: "Deeply impressed with the importance of this great object, a number of ladies met on the fifth of June, 1816, and after supplicating the throne of grace for direction and a blessing, formed themselves into an association to be called, the Female Society of Boston and the vicinity, for promoting Christianity amongst the Jews" (p. 16).

29 James Huie, *The History of the Jews, From the Taking of Jerusalem by Titus to The Present Time; Containing a Narrative of their Wanderings, Persecutions, Commercial Enterprises, and Literary Exertions; With an Account of the Various Efforts Made for Their Conversion*, 2nd ed., rev. and enlarged (Edinburgh, 1841), pp. 6, 303.

30 Rev. M. Margoliouth, *Vestiges of the Historic Anglo-Hebrews in East Anglia* (London: Longmans, Green, Reader, and Dyer, 1870), pp. 98–99.

31 Rev. Moses Margoliouth, *The History of the Jews in Great Britain*, 3 vols. (London: Richard Bentley, 1851), 1.85–86, 2.229, 1.iv.

32 Huie, *History of the Jews*, pp. 265–66.

33 Samuel, *Conversion of the Jews*, p. 6.

34 *Conversion of Dr. Capadose* (New York: American Tract Society, n.d.), pp. 2, 11, 3–4. For another example of the Jewish convert's critique of both French Enlightenment philosophy and Roman Catholicism, see Rev. Joseph Wolff, *Missionary Journal and Memoir of the Rev. Joseph Wolff, Missionary to the Jews*, ed. John Bayford, 2nd ed. (London: James Duncan and L. B. Seeley, 1827): "I detest the spirit of Voltaire, Diderot, and Rousseau, because they have blasphemed Christ, who is God over all, blessed for ever; yet must I agree with them, in what they have written against many

who are called ministers of Christ, especially with what they have said against jesuits and monks" (p. 60).

35   See, for example, *The Converted Jew, or, An Account of the Conversion to Christianity, of Mr. Lapidoth and Family, and of the Baptism of Himself, His Wife and Thirteen Children* (Hartford, Conn.: Lincoln and Gleason, 1807): "he succeeded, with much trouble, in providing himself, secretly, with a New Testament. . . . Having, by stealth, continued these researches . . ." (p. 4).

36   *Conversion of Dr. Capadose*, p. 9.

37   Huie, *History of the Jews*, p. 270.

38   Read as an anticipation of Christ, this passage has been called "perhaps the most controversially treated of all chapters in the Hebrew Bible." See *The Fifty-Third Chapter of Isaiah According to the Jewish Interpreters* (1877; rpt. New York: Ktav Publishing House, 1969), 2.1, for the form the controversy took in Victorian England.

39   *Conversion of Dr. Capadose*, p. 10.

40   Huie, *History of the Jews*, p. 270.

41   *Conversion of Dr. Capadose*, p. 10.

42   Isaac Levinsohn, *The Russo-Polish Jew: A Narrative of the Conversion from the Darkness of Judaism, to the Light and Liberty of the Gospel of Christ* (London: Robert Banks, n.d.), p. 104.

43   *Conversion of Mr. and Mrs. Levi* (New York: Burroughs' Steam Presses, 1852), p. 19. Joseph Samuel C. F. Frey, *Narrative of the Reverend Joseph Samuel C. F. Frey, Minister of the Gospel to the Jews* (London: Gale and Curtis, 1809), p. ix; along similar lines, see Wolff, *Missionary Journal and Memoir:* "if you would read without prejudice your own prophets, you would be convinced" (p. 3). *Conversion of Mr. and Mrs. Levi*, p. 19.

44   Daniel Defoe, *Adventures of Robinson Crusoe*, in *The Novels and Selected Writings of Daniel Defoe*, Shakespeare Head ed., 14 vols. (New York and Boston: Basil Blackwell, Oxford University Press, and Houghton Mifflin, 1927–28), 8.7.

45   Defoe, *Adventures of Robinson Crusoe*, in *Novels and Selected Writings*, 8.2.

46   Wolff, *Missionary Journal and Memoir*, p. 42.

47   Gidney, *History of the London Society*, pp. 71, 57.

48   *Conversion of Mr. and Mrs. Levi*, p. 15. Rev. John Dunlop, *Memories of Gospel Triumphs Among the Jews During the Victorian Era* (London: S. W. Partridge, 1894), pp. 205–6. *Seventeenth Report* (1825) of the London Society; quoted in Gidney, *The History of the London Society*, p. 72.

49   Jonas Abraham Davis, *Judaism Excelled: Or the Tale of a Conversion from Judaism to Christianity*, 2nd ed. (Philadelphia, n.d. [1869]), pp. 141, 141, 142, 142, 141, 164, 203, 204–5. The scene of reading in which Hebrew Scripture and the New Testament are placed side by side occurs in many conversionist memoirs. See, for example, *Conversion of Mr. and Mrs. Levi:* "comparing Scripture with Scripture, I found that the predictions concerning the Messiah written in the Old Testament, had been literally fulfilled in the New" (p. 21). Also see *The Messiah Revealed to a Jewess; or, the Merciful Dealings of God with Hannah Nonmus, Who was Born at Frankfort, in Germany, and*

Converted to the Christian Faith in England (Isle of Wight, 1809), in which the Jewish convert to Christianity recommends to her former co-religionists, "read the New Testament, and compare it with the Old, and you will find the most harmonious agreement between them" (p. 32).

50 William, Lord Bishop of St. Asaph, *The Conversion and Persecutions of Eve Cohan, Now called Elizabeth Verboon* (London: Printed by J. D. for Richard Chiswell, 1680), preface; Davis, *Judaism Excelled,* p. 205; *The Narrative of John Henry Marks, a Jew; Now a Follower of the Lord Jesus Christ, Written by Himself,* 3rd ed. (London, 1842), pp. 42, 60; Levinsohn, *The Russo-Polish Jew,* p. 152.

51 Marks, *The Narrative of John Henry Marks,* p. 8; Dunlop, *Gospel Triumphs,* p. 420.

52 Osborn W. Trenery Heighway, *Leila Ada, The Jewish Convert: An Authentic Memoir* (Philadelphia: Presbyterian Board of Publication, n.d. [1853]), p. vii. This novel was issued in at least nine editions between 1852 and 1885.

53 *The Converted Jewess: A Memoir of Maria ——,* 4th London ed. (New York, 1847), p. 8.

54 Heighway, *Leila Ada,* p. 203. Also see "Lydia" in *Children of Abraham or Sketches of Jewish Converts, Being in part a Sequel to "Leila Ada"* (Philadelphia, n.d. [1857]), p. 78, in which Leila Ada's peaceful death, demonstrated in the previous "Sketch," teaches the following moral: "In painful contrast with the preceding death-bed scene, is the following account of the dying exercises of a lovely and intelligent young Jewess, an aunt of Leila Ada, who had no knowledge of salvation by Jesus Christ."

55 Heighway, *Leila Ada,* pp. 204, 206, 203.

56 *The Converted Jewess,* pp. 15, 30–31.

57 Heighway, *Leila Ada,* p. 26.

58 *The Converted Jewess,* pp. 89, 25.

59 John Mills, *The British Jews* (London, 1853), p. 49. Gidney, *History of the London Society,* p. 217. [Charlotte Anley,] *Miriam; or, the Power of Truth: A Jewish Tale,* 9th ed. (London, 1849), p. 6. This novel was issued in many editions in the 1820s, 1830s, and 1840s. [Amelia Bristow,] *Emma de Lissau: A Narrative of Striking Vicissitudes and Peculiar Trials; With Notes, Illustrative of the Manners and Customs of the Jews,* 3rd ed., 2 vols. (London, 1830), 1.25. This novel was issued in several editions between 1828 and 1855. Marks, *Narrative of Henry John Marks,* p. 50.

60 *Miriam; or, the Power of Truth,* pp. 26, 90, 109.

61 *Emma de Lissau,* 1.79, 31, 97.

62 *Miriam; or, the Power of Truth,* pp. 150, 305–6.

63 *Emma de Lissau,* 1.133.

64 *Miriam; or, the Power of Truth,* p. 373.

65 [Annie Peploe,] *Julamerk; or, The Converted Jewess* (London: Ward, Lock, and Tyler, n.d.), pp. 50, 18, 393, 274, 237, 108. This novel was issued in several editions between 1849 and 1878, under such titles as *Jewess of Julamerk* and *Julamerk; Tale of the Nestorians.*

66 *Julamerk,* pp. 287, 295, 294, 424.

67 *Julamerk,* pp. 482–83, 484, 222.

68 *Julamerk*, pp. 485–86.

69 Ford K. Brown, *Fathers of the Victorians: The Age of Wilberforce* (Cambridge: Cambridge University Press, 1961), p. 390.

70 Charlotte Elizabeth, *Judah's Lion* (New York: Dodd, Mead, n.d.), p. 27.

71 Charlotte Elizabeth, *Judah's Lion*, p. 53.

72 Charlotte Elizabeth, *Judah's Lion*, pp. 5, 291. *Emma de Lissau*, 2.75. Levinsohn, *The Russo-Polish Jew*, p. 167. *Miriam; or, the Power of Truth*, p. 7. Charlotte Elizabeth, *Judah's Lion*, p. 315.

73 *The Converted Jewess*, p. 12. Wolff, *Missionary Journal and Memoir*, p. 5. *Mr. and Mrs. Levi*, p. 21. Charlotte Elizabeth, *Judah's Lion*, p. 71. Dunlop, *Gospel Triumphs*, p. 206. Mills, *British Jews*, p. 342.

74 Charlotte Elizabeth, *Judah's Lion*, pp. 27, 36, 42, 55, 87, 384, 404.

75 Charlotte Elizabeth, *Judah's Lion*, p. 72.

76 Charlotte Elizabeth, *Personal Recollections* (New York: American Tract Society, n.d.), p. 187.

77 Charlotte Elizabeth, *Judah's Lion*, pp. 97, 67, 78, 95, 95, 65, 132, 22, 97.

78 "For the Young: An Address on the Jews," in Dunlop, *Gospel Triumphs*, p. 350. In its advice to children, this literature illustrates the way in which the toleration of the Jews became a formula for converting them: "Treat them tenderly and affectionately, and you have done much towards gaining a hearing for the truth" (p. 350). Also see "A Parable for the Young," pp. 307–9.

79 Charlotte Elizabeth, *Judah's Lion*, p. 35.

80 Charlotte Elizabeth, *Judah's Lion*, pp. 403, 35, 404–5, 405.

81 Dunlop, *Gospel Triumphs*, p. iii.

82 Charlotte Elizabeth, *Judah's Lion*, pp. 22 and 25.

83 *The Converted Jewess*, p. 38.

84 "On the London Society for Converting the Jews," *British Critic* (Jan. 1819): 28–29.

85 H. H. Norris, *The Origin, Progress, and Existing Circumstances, of the London Society* (London, 1825), appendix 7, pp. xliii, lii–liii.

86 Emma Jane Worboise, *The House of Bondage* (London: James Clarke, 1885), pp. 337–38, 348, 344.

87 M. Lissack, *Jewish Perseverance, or The Jew, at Home and Abroad: An Autobiography*, 2nd ed. (London: Hamilton, Adams, 1851), p. 191.

88 Huie, *History of the Jews*, p. 302.

89 M. Lissack, *Jewish Perseverance*, pp. 113, 119.

2. Writing English Comedy

1 See *The Education of the Heart: The Correspondence of Rachel Mordecai Lazarus and Maria Edgeworth*, ed. Edgar E. MacDonald (Chapel Hill: University of North Carolina Press, 1977), p. 8, where Edgeworth uses the terms "atonement" and "reparation" to describe the functions of the novel she is writing in response to Rachel Mordecai's letter.

2 Such historic landmarks have been catalogued by Montagu Frank Modder, *The Jew in*

the Literature of England: To the End of the 19th Century (1939; rpt. New York and Philadelphia: Meridian Books and Jewish Publication Society of America, 1960), and Edgar Rosenberg, *From Shylock to Svengali: Jewish Stereotypes in English Fiction* (Stanford, Calif.: Stanford University Press, 1960).

3   The criticism written about the Jew in English literature has had an unusually self-contained and uneventful history because it has been dominated by the single idea of the Jew as stereotype. See Rosenberg's *From Shylock to Svengali* and a study like Anne Aresty Naman's *The Jew in the Victorian Novel: Some Relationships Between Prejudice and Art* (New York: AMS Press, 1980), which approaches the topic essentially from Rosenberg's vantage point (that is, from the perspective of character-types). Instead of criticizing this literary tradition on mimetic grounds (that is, for its failure to produce "realistic" portraits), I will claim that *Harrington* and its literary descendants invent and inspect Jewish portraits through the self-conscious lens of metarepresentation.

4   Maria Edgeworth, *Harrington*, vol. 9 of *Tales and Novels* (New York: AMS Press, 1967); hereafter cited by page number in the text.

5   The novelistic tradition I am describing, from Edgeworth through Joyce, can be called "English" only with some qualification. The novels are written in English, and their authors learned the conventions of representing Jewish identity through the English tongue, primarily through Shakespeare. Nonetheless, this tradition passes from Edgeworth (descended from a long line of Anglo-Irish ancestors) and Scott (the Scot), both writing about England in English, to the Irish Joyce writing of Ireland in English. In fact, I would argue that the origins of this novelistic tradition developed out of the creation and development of the regional novel, in which Edgeworth (in her Irish tales) and Scott (in his Scottish novels) portrayed the Irish and the Scottish people. In other words, when Scott praised Edgeworth for making "the British Empire acquainted with the peculiar and interesting character of a people too long neglected and too severely oppressed," he meant the Irish—but when Edgeworth wrote *Harrington* (1817) and Scott wrote *Ivanhoe* (1819), each undertook to represent the Jews as a people "too severely oppressed" (*The Letters of Sir Walter Scott*, ed. H. J. C. Grierson, 12 vols. [1932–37; New York: AMS Press, 1971], 5.142).

6   *Harrington* describes the way in which "A play altered from Shakespeare's, and called 'The Jew of Venice,' had been for some time in vogue," while Macklin, "in the revived Merchant of Venice, [proposed] to play the part in a serious style" (41) and scored a brilliant success. Macklin's importance in the play's performance history was documented in several contemporary memoirs of the actor's life, such as William Cooke's *Memoirs of Charles Macklin, Comedian, with the Dramatic Characters, Manners, Anecdotes, etc., of the Age in which He Lived* (1804; New York: Benjamin Blom, 1972).

7   See George Eliot, *Daniel Deronda* (Harmondsworth, Eng.: Penguin, 1986); hereafter abbreviated *DD.*

8   Maria Edgeworth, *Castle Rackrent* and *The Absentee* (London: Dent, 1964), p. 134.

9   For this important variant on the story of the bond, Edgeworth sends us to the *Life of Sixtus V,* which can be found quoted in *A New Variorum Edition of Shakespeare,* ed. Horace Howard Furness, 14 vols. (New York: Dover, 1963–66), 7.295–97.

10 James Joyce, *Ulysses,* ed. Hans Gabler (New York: Random House, 1986), p. 168.

11 *Oxford English Dictionary,* s.v. "patron."

12 See Ernest Jones, *The Life and Work of Sigmund Freud,* 3 vols. (New York: Basic Books, 1957), 3.207.

13 For a contemporary example of Mrs. Harrington's doctrine of sympathies and antipathies, see Charles Lamb's characterization of himself as "the veriest thrall to sympathies, apathies, antipathies," by way of which he explains that "A Hebrew is nowhere congenial to me." Charles Lamb, "Imperfect Sympathies," *The Essays of Elia* (London: J. M. Dent and Sons, 1926), pp. 116 and 121.

14 William Shakespeare, *The Merchant of Venice* 2.7.9; hereafter abbreviated *MV.*

15 Sigmund Freud, *Moses and Monotheism, The Standard Edition of the Complete Psychological Works of Sigmund Freud,* trans. and ed. James Strachey, 24 vols. (London: Hogarth Press, 1964), 23.132; hereafter abbreviated *MM.*

16 This disclosure occurs when Mr. Montenero explains that Berenice's dead "mother was a Christian; and according to my promise to Mrs. Montenero, Berenice has been bred in her faith—a Christian—a Protestant" (203).

17 Northrop Frye, *Anatomy of Criticism: Four Essays* (New York: Atheneum, 1966), p. 170; hereafter abbreviated *AC.*

18 On the history of the alternative between conversion and death, see Léon Poliakov, *The History of Anti-Semitism,* 3 vols. (New York: Vanguard, 1973–76), 1.160–62, and Solomon Grayzel, "The Confession of a Medieval Jewish Convert," *Historia Judaica* 17 (Oct. 1955): 89–103. Both of these authors also make clear the relation between the forced conversion of the Jews and Christian theology (see, e.g., Poliakov on St. Paul and St. Augustine).

19 See *The Education of the Heart,* p. 16: "in one event I was disappointed. Berenice was not a Jewess."

20 *The Letters of Sir Walter Scott,* 4.478.

21 My discussion of the means by which this act of displacement was engineered is indebted to James Parkes, *The Conflict of the Church and the Synagogue: A Study in the Origins of Antisemitism* (London: Soncino, 1934), and Marcel Simon, *Verus Israel: A Study of the Relations Between Christians and Jews in the Roman Empire (135–425),* trans. H. McKeating (New York: Oxford University Press, 1986). For a useful guide to the literature that this act of displacement produced, see A. Lukyn Williams, *Adversus Judaeos: A Bird's-Eye View of Christian Apologiae Until the Renaissance* (Cambridge: Cambridge University Press, 1935). For the ways in which this act of displacement is refueled and revised during the later Middle Ages (where the Talmud often replaces Hebrew Scripture as the battleground), see Jeremy Cohen, *The Friars and the Jews: The Evolution of Medieval Anti-Judaism* (Ithaca, N.Y.: Cornell University Press, 1982).

22 While the formulation of the idea of "figurative conversion" is my own, I am indebted to discussions in Parkes, *The Conflict of the Church and the Synagogue,* pp. 160–62, and Simon, *Verus Israel,* pp. 82–85, of the ways in which Eusebius reworks the names "Jew," "Hebrew," and "Christian."

23 For the Latin phrase, see Ambrosiaster, *Commentaria in Epistolam ad Romanos,* 11.28,

in J.-P. Migne, *Patrologia, Series Latina,* vol. 17: "Quamvis graviter peccaverint Judaei reprobando domum Dei et digni sint morte, tamen . . . *regressi ad fidem* suscipientur cum laetitia" (my emphasis).

24 See Ambrosiaster, *Comm. in Ep. ad Rom.,* 9.17, 9.27, in Migne, *Patrologia, Series Latina,* vol. 17. The English translation may be found in Simon, *Verus Israel,* p. 509.

25 For example, I would argue that one can find Eusebius's strategy reinvented, and turned on its head, in Marx's "On the Jewish Question," *The Marx-Engels Reader,* ed. Robert C. Tucker, 2nd ed. (New York and London: W. W. Norton, 1978), pp. 26–52. Whereas Jews are Christians for Eusebius, Christians are Jews for Marx. Both alternatives I read as figurative but nonetheless highly political (anti-Semitic) acts of conversion. Moreover, my emphasis on the act of renaming as the key to conversionist discourse is a way of arguing that the plot of conversion, from Eusebius to Edgeworth through Marx and Freud, is in fact what I have elsewhere called a "naming plot." *Acts of Naming: The Family Plot in Fiction* (New York: Oxford University Press, 1986).

26 The "historic" debates I have in mind are best represented by the famous public disputations between Christians and Jews that occurred during the Middle Ages. For an excellent guide to these, see *Judaism on Trial: Jewish-Christian Disputations in the Middle Ages,* ed. and trans. Hyam Maccoby (East Brunswick, N.J.: Associated University Presses, 1982). The "fictitious" debates I have in mind are those literary dialogues, so central to the *adversus judaeos* literature produced from the second century through the Middle Ages, in which a dialogue between a Jew and a Christian often ended with the conversion of the Jew. It has been difficult in every case to discover whether such literary dialogues were based on debates that in fact occurred.

27 *The Letters of Thomas Babington Macaulay,* ed. Thomas Pinney, 6 vols. (London: Cambridge University Press, 1974), 1.218–19.

3. Writing English History

1 The London *Times* reported these persecutions on June 2, September 22, September 28, and October 13, 1819. On the role of Christian medievalism and the "Christian-German (or Teutsch)" ideology during the rise of German nationalism, see Heinrich Graetz, *History of the Jews,* 6 vols. (Philadelphia: Jewish Publication Society of America, 1891–98), 5.515–21. On anti-French feeling in Germany and the subsequent reaction against the Jews as another foreign influence the Germans wanted to expel, see Léon Poliakov, *The History of Anti-Semitism,* 3 vols. (New York: Vanguard, 1973–76), 3.242–44. Also see Poliakov on the meaning of "Hep! Hep!," namely, " '*Hierosolyma Est Perdita,*' thought to be the cry of the Crusaders in 1096" (3.302).

2 For a discussion of the voluminous millenarian literature that flourished in the 1790s and the opening decades of the nineteenth century, see Mayir Vrete, "The Restoration of the Jews in English Protestant Thought 1790–1840," *Middle Eastern Studies* 8 (1972): 3–50.

3 For example, James Bicheno, *The Restoration of the Jews, The Crisis of all Nations,* 2nd ed. (London, 1807), reviews the elaborate literature on this question and performs his

own evaluation of the qualifications of the French and the English for restoring the Jews (pp. 156–66). See Poliakov, *The History of Anti-Semitism,* on the representation of Napoleon as the Jewish Messiah (3.278–79).

4 Edgar Johnson, *Sir Walter Scott: The Great Unknown,* 2 vols. (New York: Macmillan, 1970), 1.202; Reginald Heber, *The Poetical Works* (Boston: Little, Brown, 1853), p. 16.

5 Page numbers for *Ivanhoe* refer to vol. 9 of the Dryburgh edition of *The Waverley Novels,* 25 vols. (London: Adam and Charles Black, 1893), and hereafter will be cited parenthetically in the text.

6 See John Milton, *Complete Poems and Major Prose,* ed. Merritt Y. Hughes (New York: Odyssey, 1957), *Paradise Regained,* 3.381–82, 3.392, 3.434–35.

7 A review article entitled "On the London Society for Converting the Jews," *British Critic,* Jan. 1819, pp. 22–35, so scathingly attacked a recent pamphlet by Way that he responded with *Reviewers reviewed* (London, 1819). On Lewis Way, see James Parkes, "Lewis Way and His Times," *Transactions of the Jewish Historical Society of England* 20 (1959–61): 189–201.

8 See H. H. Norris, *The Origin, Progress, and Existing Circumstances of the London Society for Promoting Christianity Amongst the Jews: An Historical Inquiry* (London, 1825), pp. 502 and 507.

9 Sharon Turner, *The History of the Anglo-Saxons,* 4 vols. (London: Luke Hansard, 1802), 2.xii.

10 See William Flavelle Monypenny and George Earle Buckle, *The Life of Benjamin Disraeli, Earl of Beaconsfield,* 6 vols. (New York: Macmillan, 1910–20), 1.23.

11 Thomas Preston Peardon's *The Transition in English Historical Writing, 1760–1830* (New York: Columbia University Press, 1933) remains the best survey of such changes in English historiography.

12 Sharon Turner, *The History of the Anglo-Saxons,* 2nd ed., 2 vols. (London: Longman, Hurst, Rees, and Orme, 1807), 1.27–28.

13 Sharon Turner, *The History of the Anglo-Saxons,* 7th ed., 3 vols. (London: Longman, Brown, Green, and Longmans, 1852), 1.viii.

14 *The Romantics Reviewed: Contemporary Reviews of British Romantic Writers,* ed. Donald H. Reiman, 3 vols. (New York and London: Garland, 1972), part B, 1.257.

15 See Thomas L. Ashton, *Byron's Hebrew Melodies* (Austin: University of Texas Press, 1972), pp. 10 and 52.

16 *The Poetical Works of Sir Walter Scott, Bart.,* 12 vols. (Edinburgh: Robert Cadell, 1848), 1.238.

17 See, for example, Bicheno, *Restoration of the Jews,* p. 2, for his use of the phrase. For the use of the phrase in nineteenth-century German discourse, see Jacob Katz, *From Prejudice to Destruction: Anti-Semitism, 1700–1933* (Cambridge, Mass.: Harvard University Press, 1980), p. 81.

18 See Thomas Arnold's letter to the Archbishop of Dublin, May 4, 1836, in Arthur Penrhyn Stanley, *The Life and Correspondence of Thomas Arnold,* 2 vols. in 1 (New York: Charles Scribner's Sons, 1910), 2.41.

19 "Oh! Weep for Those," *The Poetical Works of Lord Byron* (London: Oxford University Press, 1966), p. 79.

20 *The Letters of Sir Walter Scott,* ed. H. J. C. Grierson, 12 vols. (1932–37; New York, 1971), 5.142.

21 On the association between name and face as indicators of familial identity, see Michael Ragussis, *Acts of Naming: The Family Plot in Fiction* (Oxford: Oxford University Press, 1986).

22 See Christopher Hill, "The Norman Yoke," in *Puritanism and Revolution: Studies in Interpretation of the English Revolution of the 17th Century* (London: Secker and Warburg, 1958), on the "propagandist" uses (p. 91) to which the theory of the Norman yoke was put, whether by "seventeenth-century antiquarians, eighteenth-century radicals, or even nineteenth-century Whig historians" (p. 115). See J. G. A. Pocock, *The Ancient Constitution and the Feudal Law: A Study of English Historical Thought in the Seventeenth Century* (1957; Cambridge: Cambridge University Press, 1987), who argues that the Norman Conquest became the ideological pivot in the struggle between king and Parliament in the seventeenth century and that "English historiography has oriented itself about that conquest ever since" (p. 64). On the ideological use of the names "Saxon" and "Norman" as a way of designating "English" national identity in Victorian culture, see Asa Briggs, "Saxons, Normans and Victorians," in *The Collected Essays of Asa Briggs,* 2 vols. (Urbana: University of Illinois, 1985), esp. 2.216 on the "popular pro-Saxon prejudice."

23 See Gilbert K. Chesterton, *Orthodoxy* (New York and London: John Lane, 1908), pp. 127–28.

24 Edward A. Freeman, *The History of the Norman Conquest of England,* 5 vols. (New York: Macmillan, 1873–76), hereafter abbreviated *NC; The Growth of the English Constitution from the Earliest Times* (London: Macmillan, 1872), hereafter abbreviated *EC.*

25 On the European (as opposed to specifically English) quality of Hume's thinking and the lack of patriotic pride that characterizes Hume's *History,* see Duncan Forbes's introduction in David Hume, *The History of Great Britain: The Reigns of James I and Charles I* (Harmondsworth, Eng.: Penguin, 1970), and Forbes's major study, *Hume's Philosophical Politics* (Cambridge: Cambridge University Press, 1975), esp. sec. 3, "Philosophical History." On Millar's "comparative" approach to Saxon institutions, see Duncan Forbes, " 'Scientific' Whiggism: Adam Smith and John Millar," *The Cambridge Journal* 7 (Aug. 1954): 643–70.

26 It is perhaps no accident that the most famous example of mass Jewish suicide in English history occurred soon after the coronation of Richard I in 1189—that is, during the period that Scott describes in *Ivanhoe.* It is a scene that is described time and again by English writers, but I am especially interested in the uses that such millenarian writers as James Bicheno and Thomas Witherby make of the scene in their attempt to establish the basis of English national guilt. Bicheno describes the famous scene at York when "baptism or death was the only alternative": "Each man took a sharp knife, and first cutting the throats of their wives and children, they then cut their own." *Restoration of the Jews,* pp. 24–25. Witherby marks the scene at York as "the first remarkable

persecution of the Jews which I am aware of in this land." *An Attempt to Remove Prejudices concerning the Jewish Nation. By Way of Dialogue* (London, 1804), pp. 6–8.

27   "The closer the Normans and the Anglo-Saxons intermingled to develop the characteristics of a single nation, the more pronounced did the Jews' 'foreignness' become" (Salo Wittmayer Baron, *A Social and Religious History of the Jews,* 2nd ed., 18 vols., New York: Columbia University Press; Philadelphia: Jewish Publication Society of America, 1952–60, 11.203). In fact, the king under whom the new English nation is founded is also the king who expels the Jews. Also see Baron on how the failure of the policy of absorbing the Jews by conversion led to the decision to expel them (11.204–5).

28   Bicheno, *Restoration of the Jews,* p. 65.

29   On the history of this conversionist literature, see James Parkes, *The Conflict of the Church and the Synagogue: A Study in the Origins of Antisemitism* (London: Soncino Press, 1934), esp. pp. 280–93, and Marcel Simon, *Verus Israel: A Study of the Relations Between Christians and Jews in the Roman Empire (135–425),* trans. H. McKeating (New York: Oxford University Press, 1986), pp. 135–221.

30   Thomas Witherby, *An Attempt to Remove Prejudices concerning the Jewish Nation. By Way of Dialogue* (London, 1804), p. 2. References to Witherby's text will hereafter be included parenthetically in the text and abbreviated *ARP.*

31   Edmund Burke, *Reflections on the Revolution in France,* ed. J. G. A. Pocock (Indianapolis, Ind.: Hackett, 1987), p. 10; hereafter abbreviated *R.*

32   On Hugh Peter, see David Katz, *Philo-Semitism and the Readmission of the Jews to England, 1603–1655* (Oxford: Clarendon Press, 1982), pp. 103–4, 179–80, 209–11. For information on the engraving, see Alfred Rubens, *A Jewish Iconography* (London: Jewish Museum, 1954), p. 36. On the allegation that the Jews wanted to buy St. Paul's, see Cecil Roth, *A History of the Jews in England,* 3rd ed. (Oxford: Clarendon Press, 1964), p. 162.

33   The Fifth Monarchists took their name from their belief that, following the rise and destruction of the four world empires described in Daniel, there would emerge a kingdom that would endure forever (Dan. 7)—one of the key ideas of millenarians like Bicheno and Witherby, who, in the period following the French Revolution, returned to the interpretation of Hebrew prophecy that characterized seventeenth-century millenarianism. On the Fifth Monarchists and Hugh Peter's association with them, see B. S. Capp, *The Fifth Monarchy Men: A Study in Seventeenth-Century English Millenarianism* (Totowa, N.J.: Rowman and Littlefield, 1972).

34   The association between Jews and stockjobbers was common at the time. See [Robert Southey] Don Manuel Alvarez Espriella, "Jews in England," *Letters from England,* 3 vols. (London: Longman, Hurst, Rees, and Orme, 1807). "Hence they are great stockjobbers, and the business of stock-broking is very much in their hands" (1.183).

35   On the history of Judaizing in seventeenth-century England, particularly among the Traskites (who, for instance, kept the Saturday Sabbath), see Katz, *Philo-Semitism,* chap. 1 ("Jews and Judaizers"). On Gordon, see Israel Solomons, *Lord George Gordon's Conversion to Judaism* (London: Luzac, 5674 [1914]).

4. Writing Spanish History

1   William H. Prescott, preface to 1st ed., *History of the Reign of Ferdinand and Isabella, the Catholic, of Spain,* 3 vols. (1837; London: Richard Bentley, 1850), 1.vii.

2   William H. Prescott, *Biographical and Critical Miscellanies* (Philadelphia: J. B. Lippincott, 1867), p. 279.

3   See William S. Maltby, *The Black Legend in England: The Development of Anti-Spanish Sentiment, 1558–1660* (Durham, N.C.: Duke University Press, 1971), who explores this idea at the critical moment when the concept of the modern nation-state was beginning to develop in Europe.

4   See, for example, W. T. Gidney, *Missions to Jews: A Handbook of Reasons, Facts, and Figures,* 10th rev. ed. (London, 1912). Gidney quotes Southey under the subtitle "Spain" (p. 54) in "Brief Historical Notes"; in this same section we find the "Hep! Hep!" riots recorded under "Germany" (p. 54) and a passage from *Ivanhoe* on the English abuses of the Jews quoted under "England" (pp. 51–52).

5   Robert Southey, *Letters Written During a Short Residence in Spain and Portugal,* 2nd ed. (London, 1799), p. 273; *Letters from England,* by Don Manuel Alvarez Espriella, 3 vols. (London, 1807), 3.184.

6   See M. C. N. Salbstein, *The Emancipation of the Jews in Britain: The Question of the Admission of the Jews to Parliament, 1828–1860* (London and Toronto: Associated University Presses, 1982), who explains that there were "no less than fourteen attempts to remove parliamentary disabilities. One bill was presented in each of the years 1830, 1833, 1834, 1836, 1847–48, 1849, 1851, 1854 and 1856 and four further measures were considered in 1857 and 1858" (p. 57).

7   J. J. Stockdale, *The History of the Inquisitions; Including the Secret Transactions of Those Horrific Tribunals* (London, 1810); hereafter abbreviated *HI.*

8   For a typical use of the term, see Henry Hart Milman, *The History of the Jews, from the Earliest Period down to Modern Times,* 3 vols. in 1 (1829; New York: A. C. Armstrong and Son, 1881), 3.314. The Edict of Expulsion against the Jews in Spain charged that "they perverted back to Judaism their brethren who had embraced Christianity."

9   See Salbstein, *The Emancipation of the Jews in Britain,* pp. 39–42, 57–63.

10   William Godwin, *St. Leon: A Tale of the Sixteenth Century* (New York: Arno Press, 1972), p. 310.

11   Matthew Lewis, *The Monk* (New York and Oxford: Oxford University Press, 1988), pp. 345, 396.

12   Lewis, *The Monk,* p. 170.

13   Sir Walter Scott, *Ivanhoe,* vol. 9 of the Dryburgh edition of *The Waverley Novels,* 25 vols. (London: Adam and Charles Black, 1893), pp. 215 and 277.

14   Edward Bulwer Lytton, *Leila; or, the Siege of Granada* (Boston: Estes and Lauriat, 1892); hereafter abbreviated *L.*

15   Grace Aguilar, *The Vale of Cedars and Other Tales* (London: Dent, and Philadelphia: Jewish Publication Society of America, 1902); hereafter abbreviated *VC.* Aguilar's novel was issued in many editions in every decade of the last half of the nineteenth

century, and it remained in print through the opening decades of the twentieth century.

16 Scott, *Ivanhoe*, p. 385.

17 According to Aguilar, the chief disability that English Jews "complain of is, being subjected to take an oath contrary to their religious feelings, when appointed to certain offices," *Essays and Miscellanies* (Philadelphia: A. Hart, 1853), p. 272; hereafter abbreviated *EM*.

18 Scott, *Ivanhoe*, p. 449.

19 Aguilar's consistent aim as a writer was to expose certain Christian prejudices that distorted and undermined the place of Jewish women in Judaism, making them the easy target of Christian proselytism. In *The Women of Israel* (1845; New York and London: D. Appleton, 1917), for example, Aguilar openly assigns her text the revisionary task of critiquing a series of works by Christian women who argue that " 'Christianity is the sole source of female excellence,' " "that the value and dignity of woman's character would never have been known, but for the religion of Jesus" (p. 2).

20 George Eliot, *Daniel Deronda* (Harmondsworth, Eng.: Penguin, 1986), p. 411.

21 Eliot, *Daniel Deronda*, p. 410.

22 Grace Aguilar, *Records of Israel* (London: John Mortimer, 1844), p. v.

23 Maria Edgeworth, *Harrington*, vol. 9 of *Tales and Novels* (New York: AMS Press, 1967), p. 128.

24 Grace Aguilar, *Home Scenes and Heart Studies* (1853; New York: D. Appleton, 1870), "The Escape," p. 160.

25 Aguilar, *Records of Israel*, pp. v–vi.

26 See *Records of Israel* (pp. viii and x), where Aguilar goes on to explain the revisionary intention of her "Records": "They are offered to the public generally, in the hope that some vulgar errors concerning Jewish feelings, faith, and character may, in some measure, be corrected" (p. x).

27 See Albert M. Hyamson, *The Sephardim of England; A History of the Spanish and Portuguese Jewish Community, 1492–1951* (London: Methuen, 1951).

28 See Beth-Zion Lask Abrahams, "Grace Aguilar: A Centenary Tribute," *Transactions of the Jewish Historical Society of England* 16 (1945–51): 137–48, who explains that while born in England, Aguilar "sprang from a Sephardi family that still retained the oral traditions of Spain and Portugal, the expulsion, the Inquisition, and even the still living Marranoism of the Iberian Peninsula" (p. 137). In an often reprinted "Memoir" prefixed to Aguilar's works, Sarah Aguilar explained that her daughter "was the eldest child, and only daughter of Emmanuel Aguilar, one of those merchants descended from the Jews of Spain, who, almost within the memory of man, fled from persecution in that country, and sought and found an asylum in England." See, for example, the "Memoir" attached to *The Vale of Cedars; or, The Martyr* (New York: D. Appleton, 1851), p. v.

29 Aguilar, *Home Scenes and Heart Studies*, "The Fugitive," p. 113.

30 Aguilar, *The Women of Israel*, p. 5.

31 Aguilar, *Home Scenes and Heart Studies,* "The Fugitive," p. 116, and "The Escape," pp. 164, 178.

32 *The Inquisition and Judaism. A Sermon Addressed to Jewish Martyrs, On the Occasion of an Auto Da Fe at Lisbon, 1705, By the Archbishop of Cranganor; Also A Reply to the Sermon, by Carlos Vero,* trans. Moses Mocatta (Philadelphia: Barnard and Jones, 5620 [1860]), pp. vi and xiii. Lindo, *History of the Jews of Spain and Portugal* (1848; rpt., New York: Burt Franklin, 1970), pp. iii–iv.

33 M. Lissack, *Jewish Perseverance, or The Jew, at Home and Abroad: An Autobiography,* 2nd ed. (London: Hamilton, Adams, 1851), p. 175.

34 See *Hansard's Parliamentary Debates,* 3rd ser. (London: T. C. Hansard, 1833), 18 (May 22, 1833), p. 50.

35 U. R. Q. Henriques, "The Jewish Emancipation Controversy in Nineteenth-Century Britain," *Past and Present* 40 (July 1968): 138. Henriques goes on to explain: "Their opponents said that, on the contrary, Popish ritual was descended from Jewish rabbinism, and the Jews and Papists together were plotting to overthrow pure New Testament Christianity." With the unhistorical, anti-Semitic formulation of "Jew inquisitors" (p. 138), the obfuscation of the history of the persecution of the Jews during the Inquisition reaches its absurd limit in England. For an example of how this coalition between Jews and Protestants (against Catholics) was articulated, see Rev. John Mills, *The British Jews* (London: Houlston and Stoneman, 1853): "Elsewhere the Jew has to endure the hatred and taunts of that cruel and bigoted system Roman Catholicism, a system ever active to persecute the disbeliever in her fooleries, always thirsty for Protestant and Jewish blood" (p. 342).

36 Aguilar, *Home Scenes and Heart Studies,* "The Fugitive," p. 113, and "The Edict," p. 122.

37 See *George Eliot's Life as related in her Letters and Journals,* ed. J. W. Cross, 3 vols. (New York: Harper and Bros., 1885), 3.30–31.

38 See George Eliot, *The Spanish Gypsy,* vol. 18 of *The Writings of George Eliot,* 25 vols. (Boston: Houghton Mifflin, 1909); hereafter abbreviated as *SP;* citations refer to book and page numbers.

39 Cross, *George Eliot's Life,* 3.33–34.

40 Cross, *George Eliot's Life,* 3.31.

41 See, for example, Eliot's understanding of the way in which Heine's *Almansor* used this Spanish setting: "The tragic collision lies in the conflict between natural affection and the deadly hatred of religion and of race—in the sacrifice of youthful lovers to the strife between Moor and Spaniard, Moslem and Christian." It is interesting to note that in this essay on "German Wit: Heinrich Heine" (1856) Eliot uses the idea of race as her own point of departure. She wonders over the fact that "among the five great races concerned in modern civilization, the German race" has contributed so little to the tradition of wit and humor. She goes on to characterize Heine: "this unique German wit is half a Hebrew." *Essays of George Eliot,* ed. Thomas Pinney (London: Routledge and Kegan Paul, 1963), pp. 229, 222–23.

42   See "Three Novels," *Essays of George Eliot,* ed. Pinney, p. 326.

43   See William Baker, *George Eliot and Judaism* (Salzburg: University of Salzburg, 1975), pp. 152–55, on Eliot's reading of Graetz.

44   Heinrich Graetz, *History of the Jews,* 6 vols. (Philadelphia: Jewish Publication Society of America, 1891–98), 4.215, 205. For an excellent account of the way in which Graetz's antipathy to the Jewish Reform movement (and its strategies to win Jewish Emancipation) shaped the particular view of Jewish history that he presents, see Ismar Schorsch's "Editor's Introduction—Ideology and History," in Heinrich Graetz, *The Structure of Jewish History and Other Essays* (New York: Jewish Theological Seminary of America, 1975).

45   See Salo Wittmayer Baron, *A Social and Religious History of the Jews,* 2nd ed., 18 vols. (New York: Columbia University Press; Philadelphia: Jewish Publication Society of America, 1952–60), 13.84–100.

46   See Stephen Haliczer, "The First Holocaust: The Inquisition and the Converted Jews of Spain and Portugal," p. 10, in *Inquisition and Society in Early Modern Europe,* ed. and trans. Stephen Haliczer (London: Croom Helm, 1987).

47   See Washington Irving, *Chronicle of the Conquest of Granada, from the Mss. of Fray Antonio Agapida* (Philadelphia: David McKay, 1894); hereafter abbreviated *CG.* Also see Prescott, *History of the Reign of Ferdinand and Isabella;* hereafter abbreviated *FI.*

48   See Aguilar's quotation of Irving's text in *The Vale of Cedars,* p. 135. See Cross, *George Eliot's Life,* 3.15, for Eliot's reading of Prescott while working on *The Spanish Gypsy.*

49   See Edgar Johnson, *Sir Walter Scott: The Great Unknown,* 2 vols. (New York: Macmillan, 1970): "Without Scott to have shown the way, Carlyle, Macaulay, Parkman, Motley, Prescott . . . could hardly have achieved their triumphs" (2.1260). Also see David Levin, *History as Romantic Art: Bancroft, Prescott, Motley, and Parkman* (Stanford, Calif.: Stanford University Press, 1959): "they admired no historian more than they admired Sir Walter Scott" (p. 11).

50   See Stanley T. Williams, *The Life of Washington Irving,* 2 vols. (New York: Octagon, 1971), 1.330, 162. On the origins and power of Scott's influence on Irving, see 1.155–62, esp. Williams's remark: "All American pilgrims sought him out, but Irving's worship was more special" (1.159). Scholars have conjectured that Irving, in his turn, made a contribution to Scott—namely, Rebecca in *Ivanhoe* may be modeled on Irving's friend, Rebecca Gratz (1.92). Scott's "The Vision of Don Roderick," with its fierce attack on both the Inquisition and the conquest of the New World, influenced not only Irving; the poem is cited by both Prescott in *Ferdinand and Isabella* (1.331) and Aguilar in *The Vale of Cedars* (p. 58).

51   See Johnson, *Sir Walter Scott: The Great Unknown,* 1.368, on "the destroyed poem of his youth, *The Conquest of Granada.*"

52   Irving consistently defended his text's historical authenticity. See, for example, his 1850 note to the revised edition, where he documents the ways in which serious historians (including Prescott) have relied on his text. Also see Williams, who quotes Irving's fine distinction, after the manner of Scott, that the *Conquest* was "an attempt, not at an historical romance, but at romantic history." *The Life of Washington Irving,* 1.344.

53 Prescott, "Irving's Conquest of Granada," *Biographical and Critical Miscellanies,* p. 95.

54 See Levin, *History as Romantic Art,* chap. 6 ("The Infidel: Vanishing Races"), on the role of the doomed nation or race in nineteenth-century American historians.

55 See C. Harvey Gardiner, *William Hickling Prescott* (Austin: University of Texas Press, 1969), pp. 141–42: "In Britain no other first book by a nineteenth-century American author had received as much unstinted acclaim." Gardiner goes on to say that Prescott's history has been published approximately 150 times and has remained, even in the twentieth century, an authoritative work (p. 144).

56 See George Ticknor, *Life of William Hickling Prescott* (1863; rpt., Philadelphia: J. B. Lippincott, 1904), p. 111, who records Prescott's reading of Turner in preparation for writing *Ferdinand and Isabella.* Also see Prescott's note to Turner, *History of Ferdinand and Isabella,* 2.133.

57 I have in mind a text like Francis Parkman's well-known *Jesuits in North America in the Seventeenth Century* (1867; Boston: Little, Brown, 1874), in which the following justification of the extinction of the Indians relies on the kind of evolutionary history so popular in the nineteenth century: "The Indians melted away, not because civilization destroyed them, but because their own ferocity and intractable indolence made it impossible that they should exist in its presence. Either the plastic energies of a higher race or the servile pliancy of a lower one would, each in its way, have preserved them: as it was, their extinction was a foregone conclusion" (p. 320).

58 William H. Prescott, *History of the Conquest of Mexico* and *History of the Conquest of Peru* (New York: Random House, 1936); hereafter abbreviated *CM* and *CP.*

59 See Parkman's *Jesuits in North America in the Seventeenth Century* for a similar argument: "As for the religion which the Jesuits taught them, however Protestants may carp at it, it was the only form of Christianity likely to take root in their crude and barbarous nature" (p. 320).

60 Prescott, *Biographical and Critical Miscellanies,* p. 286.

61 Milman, *History of the Jews,* 3.328.

62 Milman, *History of the Jews,* 3.326.

63 James Bicheno, *The Restoration of the Jews, The Crisis of All Nations,* 2nd ed. (London, 1807), p. 228.

64 James Joyce, *Ulysses,* ed. Hans Walter Gabler (New York: Random House, 1986), p. 526.

65 See Aguilar, *Records of Israel:* "the land [Spain] which sent her [Israel] forth, from that hour may date her political decline . . . till in its present awful state of anarchy and misery, bloodshed and rebellion, we may justly trace the workings of Him who has so emphatically pronounced a curse upon all those nations or individuals who persecute His people, and a blessing on all who seek their good" (pp. viii–ix). Also see Graetz, *History of the Jews,* 4.559–561. The text that Graetz summarizes, Samuel Usque's *Consolation for the Tribulations of Israel,* circulated among Portuguese crypto-Jews in England in the mid-1550s.

66 See Yitzhak Baer, *A History of the Jews in Christian Spain,* trans. Louis Schoffman, 2 vols. (Philadelphia: Jewish Publication Society of America, 1983), 2.288–89.

67 Bicheno, Introduction to the second half of *The Restoration of the Jews*, p. 79.
68 See Wilberforce's letter to his son (Sept. 13, 1814) in *Private Papers of William Wilberforce*, ed. A. M. Wilberforce (1897; New York: Burt Franklin, 1968), p. 177: "Above all, my dearest Samuel, I am anxious to see decisive marks of your having begun to undergo the *great change*."
69 Prescott, *Biographical and Critical Miscellanies*, p. 283.
70 *The Correspondence of William Hickling Prescott, 1833–1847*, ed. Roger Wolcott (1925; New York: Da Capo, 1970), p. 659.
71 Prescott, *Biographical and Critical Miscellanies*, p. 663.

5. Israel in England

1 Matthew Arnold, *On the Study of Celtic Literature*, in *Complete Prose Works*, ed. R. H. Super, 11 vols. (Ann Arbor: University of Michigan Press, 1960–77), 3.335.
2 Benjamin Disraeli, "Memoir," p. viii, in Isaac D'Israeli, *Curiosities of Literature* (London: G. Routledge, 1858). The accuracy of Disraeli's "Memoir" has been challenged, and it remains uncertain how many, if any, of his ancestors could in fact claim the heritage of the Iberian Jews: "Disraeli, fully aware that his forebears belonged to the so-called Spanish and Portuguese Synagogue in London; knowing that the origins of that community and of its earliest members were bound up with the dramatic history of the Marranos and their extraordinary resistance to Inquisitorial persecution; believing in the spirit of the age that the 'Sephardi' Jews belonged in fact to a more aristocratic branch of their people than their 'Ashkenazi' or Germano-Polish coreligionists, or even the Italian branch; identified himself and his forebears with what he considered to be the best-born, proudest, most romantic and perhaps one might add most flamboyant element of the Jewish people." Cecil Roth, *Benjamin Disraeli* (New York: Philosophical Library, 1952), p. 13.
3 Disraeli, "Memoir," p. viii.
4 Isaac D'Israeli, *Curiosities of Literature, and The Literary Character Illustrated* (New York, 1890), p. 45.
5 *The Genius of Judaism*, pub. anon. (London, 1833); hereafter abbreviated *GJ*.
6 See Isaac D'Israeli, *Vaurien; Or Sketches of the Times*, 2 vols. (London, 1797) 2.239–40, where the same idea is expressed: "The state of the modern Jews is not less severe than that of the ancient. They groaned in ages of persecution, and in ages of toleration they are degraded. In England it is doubtful whether the Jews be citizens; they are merely tolerated inhabitants; even this expression is too gentle. . . . This British land, which when the slave touches he becomes free, retains the child of Jacob in abject degradation."
7 D'Israeli, *Vaurien*, 2.220.
8 See, for example, D'Blossiers Tovey's *Anglia Judaica; or, the history and antiquities of the Jews in England* (1738), to which D'Israeli refers in *Vaurien*, 2.130–31. Tovey's work, it will be remembered, is mentioned in Maria Edgeworth's *Harrington* as one of the standard works on the Jews in England.

9   See Lucien Wolf, "Jews in Tudor England" in *Essays in Jewish History,* ed. Cecil Roth (London: Jewish Historical Society of England, 1934), pp. 73–90, and "Jews in Elizabethan England," *Transactions of the Jewish Historical Society of England* 11 (1928): 1–91. To supplement Wolf's research, see Cecil Roth, *A History of the Jews in England,* 3rd ed. (Oxford: Oxford University Press, 1964).

10   William Makepeace Thackeray, *Codlingsby,* in *Burlesques* in *Complete Works,* 20 vols. (New York: P. F. Collier, 1902), 19:25, 19:17, 19:15.

11   *The Complete Works of Walter Savage Landor,* ed. Stephen Wheeler, 16 vols. (New York: Barnes and Noble; London: Methuen, 1969), 13.358.

12   Quoted by James Ogden, *Isaac D'Israeli* (Oxford: Oxford University Press, 1969), p. 77.

13   D'Israeli, *Vaurien,* 2.222–23.

14   *New Letters of Robert Southey,* ed. Kenneth Curry, 2 vols. (New York: Columbia University Press, 1965), 1.269–70.

15   See Beth-Zion Lask Abrahams, "Grace Aguilar: A Centenary Tribute," *Transactions of the Jewish Historical Society of England* 16 (1945–51): 138: "As a very young child she had been brought up to think of Judaism as a faith triumphant over persecution and to contrast it with that brand of Christianity which was identified in her mind with the Inquisition and the expulsion from Spain and Portugal."

16   On Disraeli's trip, see Donald Sultana, *Benjamin Disraeli in Spain, Malta, and Albania, 1830–32* (London: Tamesis Books, 1976).

17   Lord Beaconsfield, *Home Letters* (London: Cassell, 1928), pp. 27–28.

18   See Washington Irving, *Chronicle of the Conquest of Granada, from the Mss. of Fray Antonio Agapida* (Philadelphia: David McKay, 1894), p. 358.

19   Benjamin Disraeli, *Coningsby, or the New Generation* (Harmondsworth, Eng.: Penguin, 1983); hereafter abbreviated *C.*

20   Benjamin Disraeli, General Preface, *Lothair* (Westport, Conn.: Greenwood Press, 1970), p. xiv.

21   D'Israeli, *Vaurien,* 2.249.

22   Disraeli, "Memoir," p. xxxvii.

23   Sidonia remarks that England has depended on Jewish money "to maintain its credit" (*C,* 270); see, for example, Roth, *A History of the Jews in England,* p. 240, on the role of Nathan Meyer Rothschild in England during the last stages of the Napoleonic Wars.

24   Benjamin Disraeli, *Tancred; or the New Crusade* (St. Clair Shores, Mich.: Scholarly Press, 1970), p. 265; hereafter abbreviated *T.*

25   See Asa Briggs, "Saxons, Normans and Victorians," in *The Collected Essays of Asa Briggs,* 2 vols. (Urbana: University of Illinois Press, 1985), 2.215–35. Briggs explains that this discourse was used both by serious academic historians (John Kemble, Edward A. Freeman, Richard Green, J. W. Stubbs) and by Radical politicians.

26   Benjamin Disraeli, *Sybil, or the Two Nations* (Oxford and New York: Oxford University Press, 1988); hereafter abbreviated *S.*

27   M. Augustin Thierry, *The Historical Essays* (Philadelphia: Carey and Hart, 1845), originally published as *Dix Ans d'Études historiques* (1835); hereafter abbreviated *HE.*

28 Lord Beaconsfield, *Home Letters,* p. 252.

29 See Augustin Thierry, *History of the Conquest of England by the Normans,* trans. William Hazlitt, 2 vols. (London: Bohn, 1861); hereafter abbreviated *HC.* The first English translation of Thierry's influential work was published in England in 1825, within two months of the first French edition.

30 See C. Harvey Gardiner, *William Hickling Prescott: A Biography* (Austin: University of Texas Press, 1969), p. 99. On Prescott's profound identification with Thierry because of their shared misfortune of blindness, and on the correspondence between the two historians, see George Ticknor, *Life of William Hickling Prescott* (Philadelphia: J. B. Lippincott, 1904), pp. 126, 166 n., 234, 354.

31 In his comments on *Ivanhoe,* Thierry transforms Rebecca into a universal figure of oppression: "Rebecca is the type of that moral grandeur, which develops itself in the soul of the weak and oppressed in this world, when they feel themselves superior to their fortune, superior to the prosperous who triumph over them" (*HE,* 55).

32 Sir Walter Scott, *Ivanhoe,* vol. 9 of the Dryburgh edition of *The Waverley Novels,* 25 vols. (London: Adam and Charles Black, 1893), p. 277.

33 Earl of Beaconsfield, "Preface to the Fifth Edition," *Coningsby or the New Generation* (London: Longmans, Green, 1923), p. ix.

34 William Flavelle Monypenny and George Earle Buckle, *The Life of Benjamin Disraeli, Earl of Beaconsfield,* 6 vols. (New York: Macmillan, 1910–20), 4.350.

35 Monypenny and Buckle, *The Life of Benjamin Disraeli,* 3.69–70.

36 For this account of the Eastern crisis, I am indebted to Robert Blake, *Disraeli* (New York: St. Martin's Press, 1967), pp. 570–628.

37 For this account of the position of the Anglo-Jewish community during the Eastern crisis, I am indebted to R. T. Shannon, *Gladstone and the Bulgarian Agitation 1876* (London: Thomas Nelson and Sons, 1963), pp. 198–201.

38 T. P. O'Connor, *Lord Beaconsfield: A Biography* (London: T. Fisher Unwin, 1905); hereafter abbreviated *LB.* O'Connor's work began to appear in 1877 in the form of pamphlets later collected as a book, which went into more than eight editions through the beginning of the twentieth century.

39 "The Political Chameleon" (June 5, 1852); "The Farmer's Will-o'-The-Wisp" (Mar. 31, 1849); "The Game of Speculation" (Mar. 6, 1852); "The Political Leotard" (June 13, 1868); "The 'Extinguisher' Act" (Feb. 19, 1876); "The Great 'Trick Act' " (July 4, 1874); "Dressing for a Masquerade" (Mar. 1, 1851); "Dressing for an Oxford Bal Masque" (Dec. 10, 1864); "Rival Stars" (Mar. 14, 1868).

40 George Henry Lewes, Article V, *Coningsby; or, the New Generation,* 5th ed. (London, 1849), *British Quarterly Review* 10 (1849): 118–38; quotations are taken from pp. 119–20 and 138.

41 Monypenny and Buckle, *The Life of Benjamin Disraeli,* 4.559.

42 Monypenny and Buckle, *The Life of Benjamin Disraeli,* 4.558.

43 Lewes, Article V, *British Quarterly Review,* p. 120.

44 Monypenny and Buckle, *The Life of Benjamin Disraeli,* 4.559.

45 R. W. Seton-Watson, *Disraeli, Gladstone and the Eastern Question: A Study in Diplomacy and Party Politics* (London: Frank Cass, 1971), p. 281.

46 Edward A. Freeman, *The Ottoman Power in Europe: Its Nature, Its Growth, and Its Decline* (London: Macmillan, 1877), p. xix; hereafter abbreviated *OP.*

47 These remarks are best documented in Seton-Watson, *Disraeli, Gladstone and the Eastern Question,* p. 113 ("the Jew in his drunken insolence"), p. 281 (the queen "going ostentatiously to eat with Disraeli in his ghetto"), and p. 437 (doubting whether "the Jew's Hebrew was first-rate or whether he knows any tongue beside the dialect of his own novels").

48 Monypenny and Buckle, *The Life of Benjamin Disraeli,* 4.559.

49 John Morley, *The Life of William Ewart Gladstone,* 3 vols. (New York: Macmillan, 1904), 2.551.

50 Blake, *Disraeli,* p. 601.

51 See Monypenny and Buckle, *The Life of Benjamin Disraeli,* 6.58–59, and Blake, *Disraeli,* pp. 604–8.

52 Morley, *The Life of William Ewart Gladstone,* pp. 551–52.

53 Captain Richard F. Burton, *Lord Beaconsfield: A Sketch* (n.p.: n.p., n.d.), pp. 4 and 5.

54 For a history of this development, see Reginald Horsman, "Origins of Racial Anglo-Saxonism in Great Britain Before 1850," *Journal of the History of Ideas* 37, no. 3 (July–Sept. 1976): 387–410. For an analysis of the development of a specifically "scientific" discourse about race during this period, see Nancy Stepan, *The Idea of Race in Science: Great Britain, 1800–1960* (Hamden, Conn.: Archon Books, 1982), chaps. 1 and 2.

55 Matthew Arnold, *On the Study of Celtic Literature,* in *Complete Prose Works,* ed. Super, 3.299; hereafter abbreviated *CP.*

56 See Robert Knox, M.D., *The Races of Men: A Philosophical Enquiry into the Influence of Race over the Destinies of Nations,* 2nd ed. (London: Henry Renshaw, 1862), pp. 193, 208. On the "pivotal" importance of Knox's work in nineteenth-century racialism in England, see Stepan, *The Idea of Race in Science,* pp. 41–45. On Knox's influence on the founder and president of the Anthropological Society of London, James Hunt, who spoke of having "imbibed [my views] from the late Dr. Knox," see Ronald Rainger, "Race, Politics, and Science: The Anthropological Society of London in the 1860s," *Victorian Studies* 22 (Autumn 1978): 51–70, esp. 55–64.

57 See Henry Lonsdale, *A Sketch of the Life and Writings of Robert Knox* (London: Macmillan, 1870), p. 380.

58 See Monypenny and Buckle, *The Life of Benjamin Disraeli,* 1.375, on the cries of "Old clothes!" and "Shylock" that met Disraeli for nearly an hour when he electioneered in 1837.

59 Knox, *The Races of Men,* p. 206. Henry Lonsdale, Knox's biographer, who styles himself Knox's "Pupil and Colleague," takes a swipe—in the manner of his mentor—at Disraeli's conversion in particular, and at Jewish conversions in general, in *A Sketch of the Life and Writings of Robert Knox,* p. 249n.

60 See Joseph Carroll, *The Cultural Theory of Matthew Arnold* (Berkeley: University of

California Press, 1982), pp. 231–56, for the most comprehensive view of Arnold's debt to Heine; no mention is made, however, of Arnold's debt to Disraeli. Noting that Arnold was "steeped in the novels of Disraeli," Park Honan nonetheless does not explore the way in which Disraeli's novels influenced Arnold. *Matthew Arnold: A Life* (New York: McGraw-Hill, 1981), p. 130. Ruth apRoberts tentatively begins to suggest the effect of Arnold's reading of Disraeli. *Arnold and God* (Berkeley: University of California Press, 1983), pp. 171–75.

61 Thomas Arnold, "Inaugural Lecture" (delivered at Oxford in 1841) in *Introductory Lectures on Modern History* (New York: D. Appleton, 1845), p. 44.

62 See Thomas Arnold, "Inaugural Lecture," p. 42. On Freeman's presence at Thomas Arnold's inaugural lecture and reverence for him as "that great teacher of historic truth," see W. R. W. Stephens, *The Life and Letters of Edward A. Freeman,* 2 vols. (London and New York: Macmillan, 1895), 1.66. Matthew Arnold's conflict with the Anglo-Saxonism and Teutonism of the middle decades of the nineteenth century (and with Freeman in particular) is discussed by Frederic E. Faverty, *Matthew Arnold the Ethnologist* (1951; New York: AMS Press, 1968), chap. 2.

63 See Faverty, *Matthew Arnold the Ethnologist,* pp. 4–7, on the history of the charge of antipatriotism against Arnold.

64 See L. P. Curtis, Jr., *Anglo-Saxons and Celts: A Study of Anti-Irish Prejudice in Victorian England* (Bridgeport, Conn.: University of Bridgeport Press, 1968).

65 See Rainger, "Race, Politics, and Science: The Anthropological Society of London in the 1860s": "In two articles published in 1868, Hunt outlined Knoxian theory on the Saxon and the Celt, insisting that the majority of Irish were Celtic and thus any question relative to their government must be settled in terms of race ('Knox on the Celtic Race')," p. 64.

66 D'Israeli, *Vaurien,* 2.219; *The Genius of Judaism,* p. 14.

67 *Letters of Matthew Arnold, 1848–1888,* ed. George W. E. Russell, 2 vols. (New York and London: Macmillan, 1895), 1.434.

68 *Letters of Matthew Arnold, 1848–1888,* 1.442.

69 See Honan, *Matthew Arnold,* p. 318.

70 *Letters of Matthew Arnold, 1848–1888,* 1.234.

71 *Letters of Matthew Arnold, 1848–1888,* 2.1.

72 *Letters of Matthew Arnold, 1848–1888,* 2.218–19.

73 *Matthew Arnold, Prose Writings: The Critical Heritage,* ed. Carl Dawson and John Pfordresher (London and Boston: Routledge and Kegan Paul, 1970), p. 246 (unsigned review of *Culture and Anarchy, Spectator,* Mar. 6, 1869).

74 *Letters of Matthew Arnold, 1848–1888,* 1.240.

75 See Arnold, *Complete Prose,* ed. Super, 5.638.

76 Benjamin Disraeli, *Lord George Bentinck: A Political Biography* (1852; London: Longmans, Green, 1872), p. 354.

77 Benjamin Disraeli, *Lothair* (London: Oxford University Press, 1975), p. 315.

78 See Sidney M. B. Coulling, "The Evolution of CULTURE AND ANARCHY," *Studies in*

Philology 60 (Oct. 1963): 637–68, who explains the way in which Arnold in response to his critics adds the category of intelligence to his definition of culture as beauty in the second article of *Culture and Anarchy* (pp. 650–51).

79 Disraeli, *Lothair*, p. 108.

80 Disraeli, *Lothair*, p. 316.

81 On Chamberlain's race theories, see Frank H. Hankins, *The Racial Basis of Civilization: A Critique of the Nordic Doctrine* (New York: Alfred A. Knopf, 1931), pp. 86–88.

82 Emile Burnouf, *The Science of Religions*, trans. Julie Liebe (London: Swan Sonnenschein, Lowrey, 1888), p. 196. On the influence of both Renan and Burnouf on Arnold, see Faverty, *Matthew Arnold the Ethnologist*, pp. 178–81.

83 Burnouf, *The Science of Religions*, p. 190.

84 Benjamin Disraeli, General Preface, p. xvi, in *Lothair* (Westport, Conn.: Greenwood Press, 1970).

85 Monypenny and Buckle, *The Life of Benjamin Disraeli*, 4.350.

86 Disraeli, General Preface, pp. xv–xvi.

87 *Letters of Matthew Arnold, 1848–1888*, 2.55–56.

88 Disraeli, *Lord George Bentinck*, p. 365.

89 Disraeli, *Lord George Bentinck*, p. 365.

90 Arthur Penrhyn Stanley, *The Life and Correspondence of Thomas Arnold, D.D.*, 2 vols. in 1 (New York: Charles Scribner's Sons, 1910), 2.328.

91 See chap. 3 for a discussion of the way in which such historians as Sharon Turner and Edward Augustus Freeman formulate the bond between the modern Englishman and his Anglo-Saxon ancestors. See Thomas Arnold's claim that "the land of our Saxon and Teutonic forefathers" was "the birthplace of the most moral races of men that the world has yet seen" (Stanley, *The Life and Correspondence of Thomas Arnold*, 2.328), as opposed to the claim of Disraeli and Matthew Arnold that Israel was the center of the moral universe.

6. Moses in Egypt

1 Robert Blake, *Disraeli* (New York: St. Martin's Press, 1967), p. 542.

2 See *The George Eliot Letters*, ed. Gordon S. Haight, 9 vols. (New Haven, Conn.: Yale University Press, 1975–78), 6.75n; hereafter abbreviated *GEL*.

3 Anthony Trollope, *An Autobiography*, ed. Michael Sadleir and Frederick Page (New York and Oxford: Oxford University Press, 1980), pp. 258–60.

4 See, for example, the review of *Phineas Finn* in *Saturday Review*, Mar. 27, 1869: "On those who read to be startled, his [Trollope's] performances will fall rather flat after those of the older novelist [Disraeli]. . . . [H]e is not versatile and he is not brilliant, at least with the brilliancy and versatility of Mr. Disraeli." *Anthony Trollope: The Critical Heritage*, ed. Donald Smalley (London: Routledge and Kegan Paul, 1969), p. 314. For the modern debate, see Morris Edmund Speare, *The Political Novel: Its Development in England and in America* (New York: Oxford University Press, 1924), pp. 202, 210;

A. O. J. Cockshut, *Anthony Trollope* (London: Collins, 1955), pp. 108–10; Blake, *Disraeli*, p. 217; John Halperin, *Trollope and Politics: A Study of the Pallisers and Others* (New York: Harper and Row, 1977), pp. 5, 27, and 203–4.

5   Blake, *Disraeli*, p. 191.

6   For his praise of *Codlingsby*, see Anthony Trollope, *Thackeray* (New York: Harper and Bros., 1879), p. 77.

7   Anthony Trollope, *Barchester Towers* (Oxford: Oxford University Press, 1991); hereafter abbreviated *BT*.

8   See Halperin, *Trollope and Politics*, p. 168, who gives an informed account of the way in which Disraeli enters Trollope's fiction, focusing on Trollope's envy of Disraeli's successful parliamentary career. Halperin does not discuss the idea of "the secret race," and Disraeli's role in such an ideological construction, in Trollope's fiction.

9   See *The Works of Lancelot Andrewes*, 11 vols. (New York: AMS Press, 1967), 11.91. On Traske and the Traskites, see David S. Katz, *Philo-Semitism and the Readmission of the Jews to England, 1603–1655* (Oxford: Oxford University Press, 1982), esp. pp. 18–42.

10   *The Eustace Diamonds* (Oxford: Oxford University Press, 1983), hereafter abbreviated *ED; Phineas Finn: The Irish Member* (Oxford: Oxford University Press, 1987), hereafter abbreviated *PF; Phineas Redux* (Oxford: Oxford University Press, 1988), hereafter abbreviated *PR; The Way We Live Now* (Oxford: Oxford University Press, 1984), hereafter abbreviated *WWLN; The Prime Minister* (Oxford: Oxford University Press, 1987), hereafter abbreviated *PM*.

11   Anthony Trollope, *Is He Popenjoy?* 2 vols. (London: Oxford University Press, 1965), 2.165.

12   Trollope, *An Autobiography*, p. 296.

13   Halperin, *Trollope and Politics*, p. 116.

14   See, for example, Robert Tracy, *Trollope's Later Novels* (Berkeley: University of California Press, 1978), p. 55.

15   Cecil Roth, *A History of the Jews in England*, 3rd ed. (Oxford: Oxford University Press, 1964), pp. 140–44.

16   Cockshut, *Anthony Trollope*, p. 248.

17   Trollope, *An Autobiography*, p. 180.

18   T. P. O'Connor, *Lord Beaconsfield: A Biography* (London: T. Fisher Unwin, 1905), p. 613.

19   See Duncan Forbes, *The Liberal Anglican Idea of History* (Cambridge: Cambridge University Press, 1952), pp. 51, 65, and 67–70, on the idea of race in the work of Thomas Arnold and A. P. Stanley.

20   Henry Hart Milman, "Preface to the Third Volume of the First Edition," *The History of the Jews, From the Earliest Period Down to Modern Times*, 3 vols. in 1 (New York: A. C. Armstrong and Son, 1881), 1.42. See Gordon S. Haight, *George Eliot: A Biography* (New York and Oxford: Oxford University Press, 1968), p. 472, on Eliot's reading of Milman's *History*.

21   Matthew Arnold, *Letters of Matthew Arnold, 1848–1888*, ed. George W. E. Russell, 2 vols. (New York and London: Macmillan, 1895), 1.433–34.

22 Emanuel Deutsch, "The Talmud," *Literary Remains of the Late Emanuel Deutsch* (London: John Murray, 1874), p. 8.

23 Quoted from a pamphlet by Stanislaus Hoga in *The Jews of the Nineteenth Century: A Collection of Essays, Reviews, and Historical Notices, Originally Published in the "Jewish Intelligence,"* ed. Rev. W. Ayerst (London: 1848), p. 292.

24 Rev. M. Margoliouth, *Vestiges of the Historic Anglo-Hebrews in East Anglia* (London: Longmans, Green, Reader, and Dyer, 1870), p. 98.

25 Deutsch, "The Talmud," *Literary Remains*, pp. 26–27.

26 George Eliot, *Daniel Deronda* (Harmondsworth, Eng.: Penguin, 1986); hereafter abbreviated *DD*.

27 Deutsch, "The Talmud," *Literary Remains*, p. 27.

28 George Eliot, "The Modern Hep! Hep! Hep!," *Impressions of Theophrastus Such, The Writings of George Eliot*, 25 vols. (Boston: Houghton Mifflin, 1909), 20.245; hereafter abbreviated *ITS*.

29 William Flavelle Monypenny and George Earle Buckle, *The Life of Benjamin Disraeli, Earl of Beaconsfield*, 6 vols. (New York: Macmillan, 1910–20), 3.69.

30 George Eliot, *Essays of George Eliot*, ed. Thomas Pinney (London: Routledge and Kegan Paul, 1963), p. 326.

31 Eliot, *Essays of George Eliot*, p. 327.

32 Harriet Beecher Stowe, *Uncle Tom's Cabin or Life among the Lowly* (New York: Penguin, 1986), p. 608.

33 Eliot, *Essays of George Eliot*, p. 326.

34 Eliot, "Silly Novels by Lady Novelists," *Essays of George Eliot*, p. 321.

35 Sir Walter Scott, *Old Mortality* (Harmondsworth, Eng.: Penguin, 1987), pp. 187, 187, 186, 231, 261.

36 The role of Judaic culture in *Daniel Deronda* is significantly different from Arnold's Hebraism, where Judaism is always essentially repressed, alive in the ancient past but sublimated in the present as Protestantism or Puritanism, never functioning purely as itself, a living system of belief. On the similarity between Arnold's and Eliot's ideas, see U. C. Knoepflmacher, *Religious Humanism and the Victorian Novel: George Eliot, Walter Pater, and Samuel Butler* (Princeton, N.J.: Princeton University Press, 1965), pp. 60–71. For an example of the way in which the modern Jew was set against a heroic picture of the ancient Jew, see Coleridge's remark: "The two images farthest removed from each other which can be comprehended under one term, are, I think, Isaiah—'Give ear O Earth' &c and Levi of Holywell Street—'Old Clothes!'—both of them *Jews!*" Samuel Taylor Coleridge, *Table Talk*, ed. Carl Woodring, *The Collected Works of Samuel Taylor Coleridge*, 16 vols. (Princeton, N.J.: Princeton University Press, 1971–90), 14:1:417 (Aug. 14, 1833).

37 Haight, *George Eliot*, documents Eliot's reading of Prescott (p. 378), Milman (p. 472), and Graetz (p. 472).

38 See William H. Prescott, *History of the Reign of Ferdinand and Isabella, the Catholic, of Spain*, 3 vols. (London: Richard Bentley, 1850), 2.128–29. Also see Henry Hart Milman, *History of the Jews, From the Earliest Period Down to Modern Times*, 3rd ed., 3 vols.

(London: John Murray, 1863), 3.311–12. "A Genoese, an eye-witness, describes their landing and their sufferings . . . : 'It was wretched to witness their sufferings; they were wasted away with hunger, especially sucklings and infants; mothers half alive carried their children famishing with hunger in their arms, and died holding them. . . . So many died that the air was infected; ulcers broke out, and the plague which visited Genoa the next year was ascribed to that infection.'" This description entered Milman's *History* in the 3rd ed. ("Thoroughly Revised and Extended"), with a note acknowledging Prescott's *History*. Another version of this historical tableau occurs in Heinrich Graetz, *History of the Jews*, 6 vols. (Philadelphia: Jewish Publication Society of America, 1891–98), 4.363.

39   Eliot, *Romola* (London: Penguin, 1980), p. 642. See Milman on the way in which "some [of the Jewish exiles] were thrown into the sea by the cupidity of the sailors" (*History of the Jews*, 3.318), and Prescott, "on the cruelty and the avarice which they frequently experienced from the masters of the ships which transported them from Spain. Some were murdered to gratify their cupidity, others forced to sell their children for the expenses of the passage" (*History of the Reign of Ferdinand and Isabella*, 2.128–29).

40   Eliot, *Romola*, pp. 649, 649.

41   Haight, *George Eliot*, p. 491n. 3.

42   Benjamin Disraeli, "Memoir," p. x, in Isaac D'Israeli, *Curiosities of Literature* (London: G. Routledge, 1858).

43   For a fine discussion of the relationship between Jewish self-hatred and conversion in the German Jewish community, see Sander L. Gilman, *Jewish Self-Hatred: Anti-Semitism and the Hidden Language of the Jews* (Baltimore: Johns Hopkins University Press, 1986), pp. 22–67. On the phenomenon of conversion in the Anglo-Jewish community, see Todd M. Endelman, *Radical Assimilation in English Jewish History, 1656–1945* (Bloomington: Indiana University Press, 1990), and Benjamin Braude, "The Heine-Disraeli Syndrome among the Palgraves of Victorian England," *Jewish Apostasy in the Modern World*, ed. Todd M. Endelman (New York and London: Holmes and Meier, 1987), pp. 108–41.

44   See Yosef Hayim Yerushalmi, *From Spanish Court to Italian Ghetto: Isaac Cardoso: A Study in Seventeenth-Century Marranism and Jewish Apologetics* (New York: Columbia University Press, 1971), pp. 46–50, on the ways in which the Marranos, denied access to Jewish books and Jewish communities, were reeducated in traditional Judaism after their emigration from Spain and Portugal.

Epilogue

1   George Eliot, "The Modern Hep! Hep! Hep!," *Impressions of Theophrastus Such*, in *The Writings of George Eliot*, 25 vols. (Boston: Houghton Mifflin, 1909), 20.252.

2   *The George Eliot Letters*, ed. Gordon S. Haight, 9 vols. (New Haven, Conn.: Yale University Press, 1975–78), 6.438; hereafter abbreviated *GEL*.

3 *The Letters of Sir Walter Scott,* ed. H. J. C. Grierson, 12 vols. (1932–37; New York: AMS Press, 1971), 5:142.

4 William Flavelle Monypenny and George Earle Buckle, *The Life of Benjamin Disraeli, Earl of Beaconsfield,* 6 vols. (New York: Macmillan, 1910–20), 3.69.

5 "Mordecai: A Protest Against the Critics," signed "A Jew," *Macmillan's Magazine* 36 (June 1877), p. 107.

6 James Picciotto, "Deronda the Jew," rpt. in *George Eliot: The Critical Heritage,* ed. David Carroll (New York: Barnes and Noble, 1971), p. 408.

7 Picciotto, "Deronda the Jew," p. 408. David Kaufmann, in *George Eliot and Judaism: An Attempt to Appreciate 'Daniel Deronda,'* trans. J. W. Ferrier (Edinburgh and London: William Blackwood and Sons, 1877), p. 83, devotes one footnote to the few "mistakes" in *Daniel Deronda.*

8 See *The George Eliot Letters:* "a letter which has certainly gratified me more than anything else of the sort I ever received. It is from Dr. Hermann Adler, the Chief Rabbi here, expressing his 'warm appreciation of the fidelity with which some of the best traits of the Jewish character have been depicted' " (6.275); "I have had some delightful communications from Jews and Jewesses both at home and abroad. Part of the club scene in D. D. is flying about in the Hebrew tongue through the various Hebrew newspapers" (6.321); Lewes remarks on "the testimonies she receives from Jews and Jewesses in Germany, France, America and England" (6.322).

9 Kaufmann, *George Eliot and Judaism,* p. 90.

10 Maria Edgeworth, *Harrington,* vol. 9 of *Tales and Novels* (New York: AMS Press, 1967), p. 66.

11 Picciotto, "Deronda the Jew," p. 408.

12 Picciotto, "Deronda the Jew," pp. 406–7.

13 Picciotto, "Deronda the Jew," p. 413.

14 William Baker, *Some George Eliot Notebooks: An Edition of the Carl H. Pforzheimer Library's George Eliot Holograph Notebooks, Mss 707, 708, 709, 710, 711,* 4 vols. (Salzburg: University of Salzburg, 1976–85), 3.31.

15 James Picciotto, *Sketches of Anglo-Jewish History,* ed. Israel Finestein (London: Soncino Press, 1956), p. xiv.

16 "The Jews in England," *Times,* Apr. 22, 1876.

17 Picciotto, *Sketches of Anglo-Jewish History,* p. xiv.

18 Picciotto, *Sketches of Anglo-Jewish History,* pp. 193, 188, 186, 193, 186.

19 *The Correspondence of an English Lady on Judaism and Semitism,* in Heinrich Graetz, *The Structure of Jewish History and Other Essays,* trans. and ed. Ismar Schorsch (New York: Jewish Theological Seminary of America, 1975), pp. 192, 205–6.

20 "Mordecai: A Protest Against the Critics," p. 107.

21 Graetz, *Correspondence,* pp. 206, 228.

22 Graetz, *Correspondence,* pp. 257, 258.

23 Amy Levy, *Reuben Sachs: A Sketch* (London and New York: Macmillan, 1888), p. 115.

24 Eliot, "The Modern Hep! Hep! Hep!," *Impressions of Theophrastus Such, The Writings of George Eliot,* 20.255.

25 Lucy S. Dawidowicz, *The War Against the Jews, 1933–1945* (New York: Bantam Books, 1986), p. xxxvi.

26 Raul Hilberg, *The Destruction of the European Jews* (Chicago: Quadrangle Books, 1967), p. 4.

Index

Jews: and blacks, 22, 25–26, 208, 251–52, 282–83 (*see also* Africa); civil and political disabilities, 8, 16, 30, 44, 143–45, 151, 188, 197, 292; emancipation, 12, 16, 22–23, 90, 92, 97, 112, 121, 127, 130, 133, 135, 151–52, 174–75, 178, 190, 292; exile, 76–79, 111, 114, 147–48; expulsion, 12, 22, 42, 90, 94, 114, 127–29, 136, 147, 167, 169–70, 176, 255–56, 281–83, 285, 299; as fathers and daughters, 37–41, 70, 114–15, 137–39, 143, 246–47, 284–87; as gentlemen, 205, 251, 255–56; as God's ancient people, 5, 7, 28, 47–49, 190, 217, 278; as "a nation within a nation," 97, 152; persecution, 6–7, 12–13, 29, 35–36, 89–93, 116–19, 125–37, 144, 148–50, 159, 168–70, 174–186, 200, 206, 266, 281–82, 286, 294; restoration to Palestine, 4, 49, 51–52, 90–91, 112, 119, 121, 125, 130, 171, 264, 282, 290 (*see also* Palestine); as "the secret race," 13, 149–50, 174, 176, 180–82, 198, 205, 236, 243, 246, 248, 258, 260, 289, 292, 294 (*see also* Judaism: crypto-Judaism; Marranos); self-hatred, 284–87
Joyce, James: *Ulysses*, 9–10, 58, 62, 64, 169
Judaism, 16, 33, 39, 115, 133, 146–47, 151, 158–59, 175, 179, 194, 224, 239, 284–87, 297; alleged continuity with Christianity, 13, 32, 46–47, 119, 196–98, 208, 218–21, 261–66; crypto-Judaism, 36, 127, 133, 137, 143–44, 148–49, 156–58, 168, 174–77, 180–83, 194, 203, 210, 236, 249, 260, 289 (*see also* Jews: as "the secret race"; Marranos); versus Christianity, 16, 40, 81–82, 260–61
Judaization, 86–87, 96, 121–22, 133, 198, 240–41, 253, 283, 290
Justin Martyr: *Dialogue with Trypho the Jew*, 31

Katz, David S., 302 n.8, 316 n.32
Katz, Jacob, 314 n.17

Kaufmann, David: *George Eliot and Judaism*, 292–93
Kent, duke of, 15, 50
Kingsley, Charles, 12
Knoepflmacher, U. C., 329 n.36
Knox, Robert, 216, 228; *The Races of Men*, 26, 211–14

Lamb, Charles, 312 n.13
Landor, Walter Savage, 180–81
Levinsohn, Isaac: *Russo-Polish Jew, The*, 45, 309 n.50
Levy, Amy: *Reuben Sachs*, 298
Lewes, George Henry, 203, 205, 234–35, 265, 293
Lewis, Matthew: *The Monk*, 135–36
Lindo, Elias Haim: *History of the Jews of Spain and Portugal*, 148, 151
Lissack, M.: *Jewish Perseverance*, 56
London Society for Promoting Christianity amongst the Jews, 4–5, 9–10, 15–23, 26–30, 33–34, 50, 56, 87, 92, 96, 119, 177, 244, 248, 262, 267–68, 296, 299
Lopez, Roderigo, 252, 259

Macaulay, Thomas, 87
Macklin, Charles, 59–60, 63–64, 72
Margoliouth, Moses, 29–30, 262; *History of the Jews in Great Britain*, 295
Marks, John Henry: *Narrative of John Henry Marks, a Jew*, 309 n.50, 309 n.51, 309 n.59
Marlowe, Christopher: *The Jew of Malta*, 38, 141
Marranos, 157–59, 240, 252, 287. *See also* Jews: as "the secret race"; Judaism: crypto-Judaism
Marx, Karl, 313 n.25
Messiah Revealed to a Jewess, The, 308 n.49
Millar, John: *An Historical View of the English Government, etc.*, 111
Millenarianism, 4–8, 49, 52, 90–92, 116–17, 125–26, 168–70, 198, 264, 282, 290

Michael Ragussis is Professor of English at
Georgetown University. He is the author of *Acts of Naming:
The Family Plot in Fiction.*

Library of Congress Cataloging-in-Publication Data
Ragussis, Michael.
Figures of conversion : "the Jewish Question" and English
national identity / by Michael Ragussis.
  p.   cm. — (Post-contemporary interventions)
Includes index.
ISBN 0-8223-1559-9 (cloth). — ISBN 0-8223-1570-X (paper)
  1. English fiction—19th century—History and criticism.
  2. Jews—Great Britain—Conversion to Christianity—
History—19th century. 3. National characteristics, English, in
literature. 5. Group identity in literature. 6. Jews in literature.
I. Title. II. Series.
PR868.J4R34 1995
305.892'4041'09034—dc20   94-38191CIP